Individual Adventure Psychotherapy

Individual Adventure Psychotherapy provides a clinical model for utilizing adventure therapy in individual therapy sessions, exploring key foundations, theories, and ethics of the practice approach.

Structured by summarizing the conceptual foundations for each chapter, followed by a greater emphasis on the practical application of adventure therapy by individual psychotherapists, this book helps readers increase their critical thinking and clinical skills to select, customize, and adapt activities in practice. Chapters focus on how to actively assess participant functioning, select appropriate activities, shape an effective treatment environment, and help participants process and evaluate their experiences as they move toward their clinical goals. Also covered is how to attend to diversity, equity, and inclusion considerations as well as provide trauma-informed adventure therapy.

This text is critical for providing students and clinical practitioners with a strong foundation for ethical, intentional, and effective experiential practice.

Gary Stauffer, LMSW, spent over 40 years working with children, youth, and families in both mental health and school settings. He is co-author of three previous books on adventure therapy.

D. Maurie Lung, PhD, LMHC, LMFT, CCAT, has provided adventure/nature-based counseling, teaching, training, and consulting internationally for over 30 years, focusing on experiential practices for healing and restoration of dignity.

Tony G. Alvarez, LMSW, has spent 50 years providing social work services to youth and families while sharing his passion for experiential and adventure practices through teaching, publishing, and consulting.

Kim Sacksteder, MSW, CCAT, has practiced adventure therapy for 26 years and teaches, trains, and consults through Prescott College and Adventure Therapist, LLC. Kim volunteers with AEE's TAPG and Accreditation Program.

Anita R. Tucker, PhD, LICSW, CCAT, has spent 20 years at the University of New Hampshire engaging in teaching and research focused on supporting the implementation of adventure therapy nationwide.

Bobbi Beale, PsyD, has used adventure therapy for over 30 years due to its natural alignment with trauma-informed care and anti-oppressive practices to bring awareness and change to providers.

"*Individual Adventure Psychotherapy* is a groundbreaking and much-needed resource for practitioners seeking to integrate experiential, justice-centered practices into their one-on-one work with participants. Rooted in the principles of social justice and guided by the innovative Facilitated Wave Model, this book offers both a thoughtful framework and adaptable activities. An essential guide for any therapist looking to bring the healing power of adventure into individual therapy".

Christine L. Norton, *PhD, LCSW, professor, School of Social Work, Texas State University, co-collaborator of the Outdoor Research Collaborative for Health, Wellbeing and Experiential Engagement and editor/author of* Innovative Interventions in Child and Adolescent Mental Health *and* Adventure Therapy Around the Globe: International Perspectives and Diverse Approaches

"*Individual Adventure Psychotherapy* illuminates that healing happens through embodied experience and in conscious relationship with self, other, and place. Rooted in trauma-informed care, social justice, and anti-oppressive practice — it provides both practical guidance and theoretical depth for clinicians committed to whole-person work, integrating body, mind, and spirit. This book will surely uplevel your work with clients".

Katie Asmus, *MA, LPC, BMP, Somatic Adventure Therapy Practitioner and founder of the Somatic Nature Therapy Institute, USA*

"*Individual Adventure Psychotherapy* is a must-have resource for the shelf of any practitioner who brings experiential adventure into their clinical work. It provides the reader with a step-by-step guide through the adventure therapy process, starting with assessment and carrying them through effective evaluation. Additionally, it provides the strongest theoretical overview of the individual adventure therapy process to date. The authors are practitioner and scholars who have distilled their years of knowledge and experience into an approachable text that makes the adventure therapy accessible to all".

Daniel L. Cavanaugh, *PhD, LCSW, CCAT, Associate Clinical Professor and Bachelor of Social Work Director at Oregon State University; Wild Hearts Program Director at Parker Bounds Johnson Foundation, Oregon, USA*

"This book is an invaluable resource for individual adventure therapy practitioners. Balancing research and practical application, the authors deliver an engaging and powerful presentation of this methodology. As someone who has worked in and supervised individual adventure therapy for many years, I'll refer to this book often and readily recommend it to others".

Lynette Spencer, *LCSW, CCAT, Executive Director and Founder of Adventure Works of DeKalb County, IL, and Fractional Executive Director at the Parker Bounds Johnson Foundation in Portland, OR, USA*

"*Individual Adventure Psychotherapy* is practical, engaging and rooted in lived experience. Centering the human and holistic experience, it honours individuals through radical welcoming and ethical practice. A valuable resource and an Honor to learn from – this will be a go-to for many practitioners".

Lise Brown, *MSW, RSW, Co-founder of Momenta Inc. Winnipeg, Manitoba, Canada*

Individual Adventure Psychotherapy

An Experiential Approach to One-on-One Treatment

Gary Stauffer, D. Maurie Lung,
Tony G. Alvarez, Kim Sacksteder,
Anita R. Tucker, and Bobbi Beale

Routledge
Taylor & Francis Group
NEW YORK AND LONDON

Designed cover image: Cover image supplied courtesy of the authors

First published 2026
by Routledge
605 Third Avenue, New York, NY 10158

and by Routledge
4 Park Square, Milton Park, Abingdon, Oxon, OX14 4RN

Routledge is an imprint of the Taylor & Francis Group, an informa business

ISBN: 978-1-032-60169-4 (hbk)
ISBN: 978-1-032-60168-7 (pbk)
ISBN: 978-1-003-45789-3 (ebk)

DOI: 10.4324/9781003457893

Typeset in Times New Roman
by SPi Technologies India Pvt Ltd (Straive)

Contents

Acknowledgments

As authors, we want to acknowledge our gratitude for the Association for Experiential Education's Therapeutic Adventure Professional Group and these individuals' ongoing professional commitment to the growth and evolution of the field of adventure therapy. With their support, care, and critical reflection, we are inspired to continue in this work despite the challenges we face as individuals, practitioners and members of the larger community. We have similar gratitude for the Outdoor Research Collaborative for Health, Wellness, and Experiential Engagement and their financial support which enabled us to meet face to face throughout the writing of this book. This time together in person added to the authenticity and depth of this book due to the community we could build together as authors. In addition, there are individuals who supported our process whom we want to acknowledge. We are immensely grateful for Jason Angione who supported us during our writing retreats and saved us hours of time by feeding our souls and bodies. We want to give a HUGE thank you to Rachel Fox for her commitment to creating professional visuals throughout the book to capture and communicate our ideas and concepts. We also want to thank Jennifer Thompson and Diana Gonzalez, graduate students at the University of New Hampshire, for their careful editing of the book, including attention to the nuances of APA formatting, grammar, and overall comprehension. Their work was invaluable to this process. We also thank Christina Blanchard, Lise Brown, Patrick McMillion, Lynette Spencer, Phillip Stallard, and Julia Stifler for sharing case studies that beautifully illustrate this work. Finally, we want to thank our families for being patient with our process, including time away both physically and mentally focusing on the writing of this book. We feel privileged to have the time and capacity to commit to this project and recognize how lucky we are for this collaboration team.

Figure 0.1 Our author team: Back (L to R), Tony Alvarez, Anita R. Tucker, D. Maurie Lung; Front (L to R), Bobbie Beale, Gary Stauffer, Kim Sacksteder.

Chapter 1

Introduction to Adventure Therapy

The authors would like to invite the reader to do something before they totally settle in with this book. After reading this paragraph, the authors would like the reader to close the book and balance it on three fingers of one hand. Now, the reader should think of at least three things they are hoping to gain from the time and effort spent reading the text that follows. Finally, the reader is invited to find an object to represent each thing they are wishing for and complete the following three tasks:

1 Add all the objects to the top of the book while it remains perched on your three fingers.
2 Move toward a table or other surface, keeping the objects balanced.
3 Deposit the book onto the surface without the use of their empty hand, keeping all the wishes balanced on top. If one or more of the objects falls off, do the work necessary to place them back on top of the book and choose a new surface to deposit the book.

The authors now invite the reader to think about what just happened during this experiential exercise. Consider exactly the actions and the steps taken to achieve the task, and what choices were made along the way. Next, the authors invite the reader to think about ***how*** the task was completed. What thoughts supported the actions and which ones weighed the reader down, for example? What feelings emerged throughout the process? What does the reader make of how they engaged in this action? What does the last answer portend for whether this book fulfills the expectations the reader has for the book?

The authors also invite the readers who sloughed off the activity or skimmed past it to save time to think about the factors affecting that and how common those same responses are with participants who are not fully engaged in adventure therapy practice. If the reader embraced the task and was fully immersed in the action, imagine how they can create similar experiences for participants and how powerful they can be in helping them reach their goals!

Social Justice as a Guiding Force

This book is a collaborative effort of six individuals with vastly diverse lived experiences and a variety of strengths and skills brought into their project. The authors strongly believe that this diversity adds depth and vision to the work of creating this book. While the authors may have different experiences, what does not differ is the collective belief in the power of adventure therapy due to its alignment with both trauma-informed care and anti-oppressive practices. Now more than ever, the need to work diligently as change agents for the participants with whom practitioners work as well as for the larger systems of oppression which impact

DOI: 10.4324/9781003457893-1

the well-being of participants is clear. Hence, contributing toward creating a more just and compassionate world is central to the work and guides the authors throughout the entire book. Since considerations of social justice are essential for effective treatment, the authors challenge the reader to engage in increasing their understanding and **critical consciousness** of the real and accurate impact of the systems of oppression operating in the context in which they work. Then, guided by that knowledge, the reader is challenged to embark in **ongoing reflection** on how their own responses and actions sustain and/or dismantle these oppressive systems.

Finally, the authors challenge the readers to commit to the **actions** they can take to disrupt and dismantle those systems. (See Todić and Christensen's (2022) discussion around anti-oppressive practice in learning). Hence, this book is a collection of the authors' learning, reflection and action. Put simply, this book is an active effort to provide a resource for practitioners that supports the learning of new empowering ways to intervene with participants, as well as a tool for the reader to guide them in the never-ending work of being an anti-oppressive practitioner.

As strongly as the authors are driven by a commitment to anti-oppressive practices, this work is also guided by the firm belief in the **power of experience** and adventure therapy. It might be the authors' collective proclivity toward social justice that drew the authors to this practice; regardless, what is evident is how adventure therapy as a modality naturally aligns with trauma-informed and anti-oppressive practice. This is due to its collaborative and participant guided approach, attention to environmental contexts and their impacts, and holistic engagement providing opportunities for participants to actively participate in treatment guided by their own choices and needs. Hence, the authors invite the reader to be open to the power of experience, be willing to engage in self-reflection, and ready to engage in a treatment method with participants that is not treatment as usual. This is adventure therapy.

What Is Adventure Therapy?

Adventure therapy is a psychotherapy practice approach that can be informed by an assortment of theoretical perspectives, making it adaptable for use by a wide range of practitioners in a variety of settings and levels of care. In recent years, some researchers have identified that the most significant independent variables responsible for participant change are the instillation of hope, provision of a therapeutic rationale, strategies for achieving change, and quality of the therapeutic relationship (Miller et al., 2013; Wampold, 2015). Based on this, **adventure therapy practitioners need to be skilled in talking with participants about what adventure therapy is, why it can work for them, and how it works to achieve positive outcomes**.

Individuals seeking therapy typically desire support in addressing challenges in their lives, as well as relief from suffering, and validation. Being intentional in this work means focusing on the issues that participants identify as pressing as well as supporting them in recognizing how their unique strengths can contribute to the process. Individual adventure psychotherapy provides an especially powerful vehicle to support participants in this process.

This book assumes that the reader wants to engage in individual adventure psychotherapy and that they have foundational clinical knowledge, skills, and scope of practice obtained through formal education and experience in the mental health care field. The hope is that practitioners are able to effectively integrate the adventure therapy modality into their practice when providing psychotherapy with individual participants. The authors of this book believe that the model presented in the following chapters can be used by a variety of practitioners with the aim to collaboratively work with participants toward growth and change. Whether practitioners are providing individual adventure psychotherapy or conducting therapeutic work that is more focused on skill development, the Facilitated Wave Model offers relevance and utility.

Adventure Therapy: A Practice Approach for Psychotherapy

Each practitioner conceptualizes their clinical work from interwoven theoretical perspectives, which inform their understanding of how issues develop and how change occurs. Often, practitioners are trained in multiple practice approaches that inform how they conceptualize, scaffold, and conduct treatment activities. Each practice approach has identified techniques that support its implementation. Figure 1.1 illustrates this conceptualization.

A **theoretical lens/perspective** informs a practitioner's understanding of why certain behaviors or problems exist, as well as how change happens. It is important to note that the language used here is intentional: participants show up seeking support with problems they are facing. This does not assume that the problems are created by participants or that the participants are the problem. Theories provide practitioners with frameworks to make sense of the many factors that contribute to the issues being experienced. A practitioner's theoretical foundations are developed through education and life experience, and inform clinical assessment and intervention choices. It is critical for practitioners to be aware of which theories and beliefs inform their practice. Practitioners have beliefs about how certain behaviors or issues emerge, how a participant's responses to issues are impacting them, and how change happens. These theoretical frameworks inform a practitioner's application of practice models in therapy. When assessing participants, theoretical frameworks influence the clinical lens practitioners employ to understand why particular issues or challenges are occurring in the participant's life. Additionally, when deciding how to intervene to achieve change, a practitioner's beliefs about how change happens will come into play based on these theoretical constructs.

For example, a practitioner working from a behavioral theoretical perspective may understand a child's tantrum to be a result of a parent inadvertently reinforcing this undesired behavior with attention. Alternatively, a practitioner whose theoretical perspective is grounded in neurodevelopmental trauma may understand this behavior to be a trauma response to something occurring in their environment. This example highlights the different ways that a behavior may be understood when viewing it from different theoretical perspectives. This, in turn, influences the way that a practitioner understands what can be done to address these issues or promote change. In the first example, the practitioner may encourage the parent to increase the amount of positive attention provided to the child in calm moments and augment the way they respond to negative behaviors when they emerge. In the second example, the practitioner may encourage the parent to respond in ways that support the child in regulating their nervous system before reaching tantrum states.

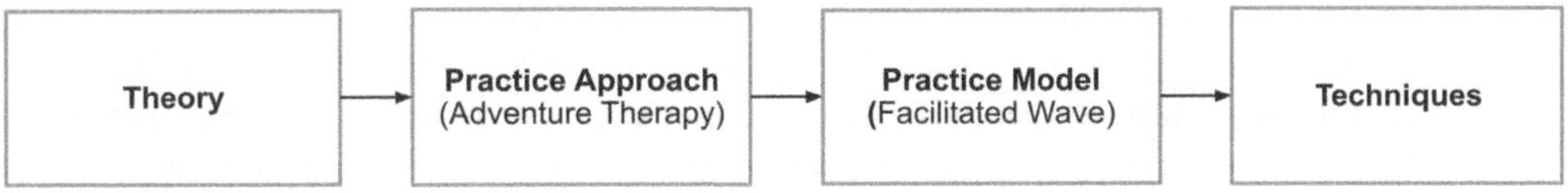

Figure 1.1 Progression from theory to techniques.

A **practice approach** provides practitioners with a structure for how they will work with a participant to achieve their goals, utilizing their theoretical perspectives to foster change. The authors present adventure therapy as a practice approach that includes a number of core elements described in this chapter. This practice approach offers great flexibility in its use, making it ideal for pairing with other accepted mental health practice approaches (Alvarez et al., 2021; Dobud & Natynczuk, 2022; Gass et al., 2020; Gillen, 2003). It also allows practitioners to use tools and techniques from other evidence-based practice models, including techniques used in Cognitive Behavior Therapy (Gillen, 2003; Jelalian et al., 2006), Solution-Focused Therapy (Dobud & Natynczuk, 2022), and the ARC Model for Trauma Treatment (Blaustein & Kinniburgh, 2017), to name a few.

Practice approaches may have a variety of **practice models** for application. Practice models provide structure for implementation of the practice approach. Adventure therapy has a number of models for practice (Gass et al., 2020; Itin, 2003; Schoel & Maizell, 2002). In this book, the Facilitated Wave Model is presented as an adventure therapy practice model applied in individual adventure psychotherapy.

Practice approaches and practice models include specific **techniques** that practitioners may employ in the treatment process. These techniques typically reflect the practice approaches underlying theoretical assumptions. For example, a theoretical foundation of Solution-Focused Therapy (a practice approach) is that participants are often applying solutions to their problems in ways that can be amplified for better results (Dobud & Natynczuk, 2022). *Exception-finding* is one technique of this approach that asks participants to examine times when the problem is less significant and identify what they are doing during those times that may be working to address the problem. Similarly, as will be explored soon, adventure therapy relies on the theory of experiential learning, which posits that people's learning is enhanced by actively engaging with the content to be learned. To that end, adventure therapy techniques rely on active and experiential interventions.

Defining Adventure Therapy

Adventure therapy has a unique origin story; it has evolved in many contexts over time across the globe, with no one founder with the authority to define it. **Many different approaches to experiential healing work evolved independently from one another, resulting in a myriad of unique conceptualizations for how to practice adventure therapy**. As global connections and communications developed, practitioners began connecting more formally through conferences, with the first International Adventure Therapy Conference occurring in 1997 (Itin, 1998). Publications appeared in the mid to late 1980s, beginning to establish adventure therapy as a practice approach for mental health treatment (Gass, 1993; Schoel et al., 1988) and research has grown steadily since (Norton et al., 2014). Through these avenues, adventure therapy has gained much greater presence and acceptance in the mainstream mental health literature over the last few decades, with numerous publications appearing in peer-reviewed journals (Christian et al., 2017; Norton et al., 2019; Tucker et al., 2024; VanKanegan et al., 2019; see ORCollab.org for more information on publications on AT); as well as textbooks describing the approach (Alvarez et al., 2021; Gass et al., 2020; Schoel & Maizell, 2002).

It is critically important to recognize that healers have been using the power of experience for healing since the beginning of humankind. Adventure therapy's origins predate publications and professional conference gatherings. Indigenous cultures and pre-colonial healing practices are under-represented in formal forums yet are integral to understanding this work (Boyd et al., 2023). Across the globe, people have been using the power of relationship and experience as healing agents in different ways, reflective of the varying cultural contexts in which they emerged. Research supports the idea that human neurobiology is wired to heal through relationship and experience (Cozolino, 2010); thus, it makes sense that experiential approaches to therapy arose organically in diverse ways throughout human cultural evolution.

Currently, adventure therapy as a healing practice is conceptualized and applied in diverse ways, with some collective agreement among international practitioners about components that make up the approach. This diversity lends strength and flexibility to the work, but it also contributes to challenges defining and clarifying terms in the literature. Numerous definitions and names have been applied to this work, including adventure therapy, outdoor therapy, wilderness therapy, activity-based therapy, nature-based therapy and more (Dobud & Natynczuk, 2022; Gass et al., 2020). Although the origins of adventure therapy make it difficult to define, definitions help people operationalize the language being used in order to establish a mutual understanding of the content being explored.

Therefore, the authors intend to provide their perspective on this approach while acknowledging and validating the worth of the diverse practices and perspectives that exist internationally. **Adventure therapy practice merges the disciplines of mental health treatment, adventure education, and outdoor education into a flexible and diverse practice approach that utilizes the strengths of each discipline** (see Figure 1.2).

Some adventure therapy practices will rely more on outdoor environments, while some will take place indoors. Some will utilize more challenging activities, while others will lean more into restorative or reflective practice. Some will focus on primary psychotherapy work, while others will be more adjunctive in nature. Rather than attempt to draw clear lines between what *is* and *is not* adventure therapy, the authors will discuss areas of intersection found in various definitions, perspectives, and publications, all in hopes of describing the key components of adventure therapy practice.

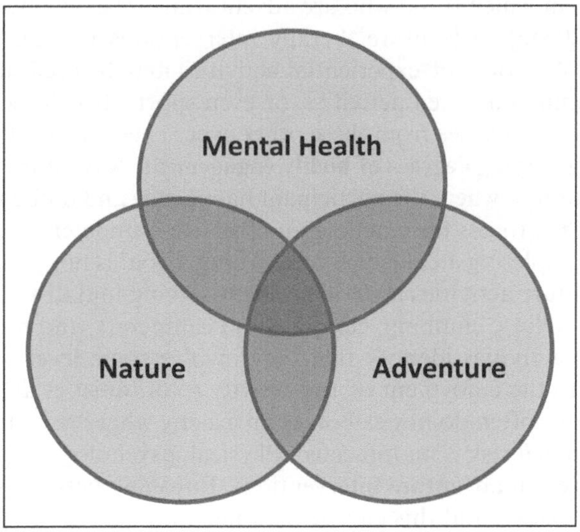

Figure 1.2 Mental health, adventure, and nature overlap in adventure therapy practice.

Components of the Adventure Therapy Practice Approach

Although there are many different definitions of adventure therapy in the literature, there is a high level of agreement on key components of adventure therapy practice. In this section, these key components are outlined, including the intentional use of experience as a change agent, a focus on adventure activities, holistic and in vivo engagement, the active role of the practitioner, the importance of place and physical setting, and clinical work with elements of challenge and risk.

Intentional Use of Experience as a Change Agent

A central feature of adventure therapy practice is the intentional use of adventure and experiential activities to engage participants in **action as the primary agent of change**. Although processing and reflection are part of adventure therapy, this practice is not simply doing talk therapy outside. The experience itself promotes change, whether that change is increased self-awareness, developing a new skill, or addressing unhelpful responses or belief systems.

Adventure therapy is considered a form of experiential learning with roots in experiential education practices (Alvarez et al., 2021; Gass et al., 2020; Warren et al., 2008). From an experiential education perspective, it is through the experience of the adventure activity and the reflections about a participant's responses to the activity that guide learning and growth (Dewey, 2001; Kolb, 1984). Human neurobiology is wired to learn, change, and grow from experiences (Cozolino, 2010; Perry, 2009). Neurons that are fired together grow stronger connections with each use. Brain areas need activation in order to change. These principles are central to understanding how adventure therapy interventions support change and they are explored in more detail in Chapter 2.

Adventure Activities

Definitions of adventure abound and include references to an "exciting undertaking" with an "uncertain outcome" in which those who are adventuring are engaging with the "unknown". (Merriam-Webster, 2025a). Adventure therapy interventions rely on the use of adventure activities in practice. A variety of experiential activities may be used in practice approaches, such as music, art, animal-assisted activities, or even sports. It is important to discuss what differentiates adventure activities from these other experiences. Typically, adventure activities are **activities involving varying degrees of bodily engagement**. Adventure activities tend to activate a sense of exploration, where the participant has agency and influence in the direction the activity goes, where the process for reaching an objective is undetermined and uncertain, and where "success" in completing a challenge or reaching a goal is not guaranteed.

Examples of adventure activities include problem-solving initiatives, games, hiking, water-sports, snow sports, cycling, climbing, camping and campcraft, and many others. Most definitions of adventure activities identify that they involve some level of risk, which is often considered inherent to the enjoyment of the activity (Nordquist et al., 2023; Priest & Gass, 2017). These definitions often do not elaborate on exactly what "risk" they are referring to. It is critical to recognize that risk is multifaceted: Physical, psychological, emotional, social, and other risks are involved in adventure interventions. Engaging with these risks is an inherent part of adventure activities, and this engagement includes the potential for both benefit and harm. Managing risks to an acceptable level for treatment purposes is a primary role of an adventure therapy practitioner.

In Vivo Experience

Like other experiential approaches to psychotherapy, such as Gestalt, Cognitive Behavioral Therapy, or Yalom's Interpersonal Group Therapy, adventure therapy relies on using a participant's present moment responses as a central component of the therapy process (Kendall, 2017; Yalom & Leszcz, 2020). When a participant engages in activity, it allows that participant to show up as their authentic self and provides the practitioner with an opportunity to **observe and experience with the participant in real time**, how their choices impact the experience. Put simply, the activity provides opportunities for the participant to see the immediate results of their choices and learn about themselves (Tucker, 2009). Activities are intentionally chosen to provide opportunities for participants to gain awareness of patterns, recognize both adaptive and maladaptive responses, and practice the skills relevant to treatment goals, or otherwise intentionally address clinical dynamics relevant to the therapeutic work. The practitioner has the opportunity to provide point-of-performance feedback and coaching to support effective skill development and implementation of new behaviors in the present moment of the session. Because human brains are designed to learn through practice, which activates neural pathways and areas of the brain that are targeted for change (Cozolino, 2010; Perry, 2009), the in vivo nature of adventure therapy sessions provides a great learning environment.

Holistic Engagement

Engagement in adventure therapy, like experiential education, is kinesthetic in nature and focuses on the **holistic participation of a learner's physical, affective, somatic, and cognitive** self through activity and experience (Dewey, 2001; Kolb, 1984; Schoel & Maizell, 2002). An experience that engages the whole person results in thoughts, feelings, somatic responses, and behaviors reflective of those that brought participants to therapy in the first place. Rather than just talking about these responses, they are evoked in the course of the session, providing opportunities for rich reflection on patterns or the practice of skills in real time. Research on neurobiology indicates that achieving a moderate level of neuro-arousal is optimal for learning and that learning is best retained when it is learned in a similar state in which it is to be used later (Cozolino, 2010). Hence, adventure activities offer participants the opportunity for holistic engagement in the treatment process.

Active Role of the Practitioner

In individual adventure psychotherapy, **practitioners are an active part of the experience**, often engaging with participants in the action. The practitioner's direct engagement in the experience allows them to work collaboratively with participants, model desired skills, or align more strongly with participants, as the experience is a shared one (Figure 1.3).

Research in the broader mental health field has established that the relationship between the practitioner and the participant in psychotherapy is one of the best predictors of positive outcomes (Horvath et al., 2011; Stubbe, 2018). **The shared experience that occurs in adventure therapy practice has great potential to enhance treatment relationships**. In fact, research has demonstrated that adventure therapy positively impacts treatment alliance (Koperski et al., 2015). A practitioner hiking with a participant, helping them to solve an initiative problem, or facilitating a paddling experience may be seen differently by participants, perhaps as more human and real than the practitioner sitting on a couch scribbling notes (Alvarez et al., 2021; Gass et al., 2020). These concepts will be explored in more depth in Chapter 7.

Figure 1.3 In individual adventure psychotherapy the practitioner and the participant walk together on the treatment journey.

Clinical Use of Challenge and Risk

The use of challenge and risk have long been associated with adventure therapy. Adventure activities, as described earlier, typically include references to "challenge" and "risk" in their definitions. Additionally, the literature is full of articles and book chapters debating the utility and ethics around using these dynamics in therapy, some promoting challenge and risk as necessary components of adventure therapy work and others challenging this narrative and citing examples of ways in which challenge and risk have been applied in unethical and oppressive ways (Gass et al., 2020; Mitten & Whittingham, 2009). The authors propose that when used appropriately and ethically, both challenge and risk are often effective and powerful components in the treatment process. Adventure therapy practice incorporates these components with **clinical intention** to address the assessed needs and goals of participants.

It is important to explore these concepts in more depth, as they are quite complex. For example, **challenge and risk are often thought of as the same thing, but they are not**. An intervention can be challenging but not risky or can be risky but not challenging. Add to this that people tend to default to thinking about physical challenge and risk, when, in fact, they can be physical, psychological, emotional, or social. Consider this scenario: a person is walking along a cliff edge on flat terrain. This activity is likely not physically challenging but high risk.

It could also be psychologically or emotionally challenging. A deeper understanding of these nuances is critical to effective clinical assessment and application of adventure interventions.

Challenge refers to the relative difficulty of a task. In therapy, practitioners may employ clinically relevant challenges that support participants in addressing symptoms or maladaptive responses to stress such as giving up easily or not knowing when to give up. Intervening through offering challenges helps practitioners and participants to see how participants respond when faced with difficulty or stress or to practice more adaptive responses, which is often a central part of the work of therapy.

It is vitally important when using challenges in clinical practice that the work includes **agreement from participants**. Practitioners may inaccurately assess the level of challenge, or dosage of stress, that participants are experiencing, making the participant's voice in the process even more critical. If these dynamics are poorly managed, practitioners risk exposing participants to harm or further trauma. Engaging participants at the optimal level of challenge requires constant assessment, feedback, and collaboration with them.

Risk is often defined as exposure to danger or the likelihood of loss, injury, or harm (Merriam-Webster, 2025b). Facilitating adventure activities requires practitioners to be skilled in managing the actual risks inherent to the activity to an acceptable degree. Additionally, **participants have a right to be informed about the risks and consent to those they will or will not take on**. This is complicated by the fact that there are perceived risks and actual risks, emotional and psychological risks, and medical and physical risks involved. A practitioner's ability to accurately assess these risks relies on communication and collaboration with participants. A participant may perceive adventure activities as physically risky when, in reality, the physical risk of injury is low. However, this perception impacts the psychological and emotional risk encountered when participants are frightened about engaging in the activity. Practitioners have an ethical responsibility to attend to these feelings in a manner that is supportive of the participants choices and that reinforces trust and transparency (informed consent).

Although risk is often thought of as a negative, adventure therapy recognizes the potential benefit of engaging with risk, often referred to as positive or healthy risk-taking (Duell & Steinberg, 2019; Smith, 2021). An example of this is seen in research findings that unstructured risky play helps children learn how to make better decisions, navigate risk, and manage their emotions (Pellegrini, 2009; Smith, 2005). The intentional clinical use of risk in treatment is often incorporated to support participants in addressing treatment goals such as coping with anxiety that inhibits healthy risk-taking, symptomatology that includes negative risk-taking, or other aspects of decision-making and emotional management around engaging with risk. Navigating risk is a life skill that can be meaningfully incorporated into the treatment process. Adventure therapy is well-suited to develop and support this skill and often incorporates risk into the clinical work.

Role of Place and Physical Setting

Physical space has a strong impact in adventure therapy, and the role of "place" is recognized as an important component of the practice approach. Adventure therapy is facilitated in a wide variety of settings, including offices, schools, city parks, participant homes, remote wilderness settings, oceans, and even jails or hospitals. Great value is placed on the environment and its influence in this work.

Nature-based therapy is a related practice approach that relies on relationship and connection with nature as a change agent (Harper et al., 2019; Naor & Mayseless, 2021). Adventure therapy is different from nature-based therapy in that it **intentionally uses experience as a change agent**, yet it is often done in outdoor settings. Integrating these two approaches creates a powerful formula for improving well-being due to the healing impact that nature and the outdoors can have on participants (Beringer & Martin, 2003; Bettmann et al., 2024). In many nature-based therapy approaches, nature is considered a co-therapist in the process, elevating the environment to more than a "space to be used".

In adventure therapy, place is given a special regard. Practitioners consider not only the impacts of the spaces in which they work but also how to intentionally engage with the environment as a dynamic and integral part of the process. **Practitioners in adventure therapy actively work to attend to and shape an environment for treatment** that supports and hopefully optimizes the potential for growth and health for participants. This will be discussed more fully in Chapter 7.

Any discussion of place should address the increased role of **telehealth**. Dismissing the potential for experiential practices in telehealth would be a mistake given the prominence of telehealth practice. Although access to telehealth may be limited for some participants, there are also many for whom telehealth improves their access to therapy. Adventure therapy practitioners have developed a number of ways to bring experiential work to virtual sessions (Cummings, 2020). These techniques may include using the immediate environment of the participant, relying on technical features of virtual platforms, or even doing sessions experientially "on-the-go". What is important to recognize is that practitioners who utilize telehealth and experiential activities will engage in the same intentional processes as those who work face to face with participants, the environment is just different, which influences how they choose and facilitate those activities. It is important for practitioners to follow best practices for telehealth, which have their own type of ethical and technical considerations (US Health Resources and Service Administration, n.d.).

Conclusion

Diverse perspectives exist in the global collective conscious about what adventure therapy is and how it may be practiced. The authors believe these varied perspectives can coexist effectively when the focus is on areas of intersection and connection. This chapter's intent is to support the reader in engaging with the content of this book with a clearer idea of the authors' perspective on adventure therapy and framework for practice. In the next chapter, the foundations of adventure therapy practice are explored in depth to lay the groundwork for the reader to understand the model.

References

Alvarez, T. G., Stauffer, G., Lung, D. M., Sacksteder, K., Beale, B., & Tucker, A. R. (2021). *Adventure group psychotherapy: An experiential approach to treatment*. Routledge.

Beringer, A., & Martin, P. (2003). On adventure therapy and the natural worlds: Respecting nature's healing. *Journal of Adventure Education & Outdoor Learning*, *3*(1), 29–39. https://doi.org/10.1080/14729670385200221

Bettmann, J. E., Speelman, E., Blumenthal, E., Couch, S., & Schmalz, D. L. (2024). Nature exposure, even as little as 10 minutes, is likely to yield short-term benefits for adults with mental illness. A meta analysis. *Ecopsychology*, *16*(3), 174–190. https://doi.org/10.1089/eco.2023.0063

Blaustein, M. E., & Kinniburgh, K. M. (2017). Attachment, self-regulation, and competency (ARC). In M. A. Landolt, M. Cloitre, & U. Schnyder (Eds.), *Evidence-based treatments for trauma related disorders in children and adolescents* (pp. 299–319). Springer International Publishing.

Boyd, F., Allen, C., Robinson, J. M., & Redvers, N. (2023). The past, present, and future of nature and place-based interventions for human health. *Landscape Research*, *49*(1), 129–145. https://doi.org/10.1080/01426397.2023.2244430

Christian, D. D., Perryman, K. L., & Portrie-Bethke, T. L. (2017). Improving the parent/adolescent relationship with adventure-based counseling: An Adlerian perspective. *Journal of Child and Adolescent Counseling*, *3*(1), 44–58. https://doi.org/10.1080/23727810.2017.1281693

Cozolino, L. (2010). *The neuroscience of psychotherapy: Healing the social brain* (2nd ed.). W. W. Norton & Co.

Cummings, M. (2020). *Virtual team building activities*. https://training-wheels.com/wp-content/uploads/2021/03/Virtual-Team-Building-Activities-by-Michelle-Cummings.pdf

Dewey, J. (2001). *Democracy and education*. The Pennsylvania State University.

Dobud, W. W., & Natynczuk, S. (2022). *Solution-focused practice in outdoor therapy: Co-adventuring for change*. Taylor & Francis Group.

Duell, N., & Steinberg, L. (2019). Positive risk taking in adolescence. *Child Development Perspectives*, *13*(1), 48–52. https://doi.org/10.1111/cdep.12310

Gass, M. A. (1993). *Adventure therapy: Therapeutic applications of adventure programming*. Association for Experiential Education.

Gass, M. A., Gillis, H. L., & Russell, K. C., (2020) *Adventure therapy: Theory, research, and practice* (2nd ed.). Routledge.

Gillen, M. C. (2003). Pathway to efficacy: Recognizing cognitive behavioral therapy as an underlying theory for adventure therapy. *Journal of Adventure Education and Outdoor Learning*, *3*(1), 93–102. https://doi.org/10.1080/14729670385200271

Harper, N. J., Rose, K., & Segal, D. (2019). *Nature-based therapy: A practitioner's guide to working outdoors with children, youth and families*. New Society Publishers.

Horvath, A. O., Del Re, A. C., Flückiger, C., & Symonds, D. (2011). Alliance in individual psychotherapy. *Psychotherapy*, *48*(1), 9–16. https://doi.org/10.1037/a0022186

Itin, C. M. (1998). *Exploring the boundaries of adventure therapy: International perspectives. Proceedings of the International Adventure Therapy Conference*. Association for Experiential Education. https://eric.ed.gov/?id=ED424050

Itin, C. M. (2003). The double diamond model of experiential education as a framework for adventure therapy. In K. Richards & B. Smith (Eds.), *The therapy within adventure: Proceedings of the Second International Adventure Therapy Conference* (pp. 111–125). Zeil Verlag.

Jelalian, E., Mehlenbeck, R., Lloyd-Richardson, E. E., Birmaher, V., & Wing, R. R. (2006). 'Adventure therapy' combined with cognitive-behavioral treatment for overweight adolescents. *International Journal of Obesity*, *30*(1), 31–39. https://doi.org/10.1038/sj.ijo.0803069

Kendall, P. C. (Ed.) (2017). *Cognitive therapy with children and adolescents* (3rd ed). Perlego.

Kolb, D. A. (1984). *Experiential Learning: Experience as the source of learning and development*. Prentice Hall.

Koperski, H., Tucker, A. R., Lung, D. M., & Gass, M. A. (2015). The impact of community based adventure therapy on stress and coping skills in adults. The *Practitioner Scholar: Journal of Counseling and Professional Psychology*, *4*(1), 1–16.

Merriam-Webster Dictionary. (2025a). *Adventure*. https://www.merriam-webster.com/dictionary/adventure

Merriam-Webster Dictionary. (2025b). *Risk*. https://www.merriam-webster.com/dictionary/risk

Miller, S. D., Hubble, M. A., Chow, D. L., & Seidel, J. A. (2013). The outcome of psychotherapy: Yesterday, today, and tomorrow. *Psychotherapy*, *50*(1), 88–97. https://doi.org/10.1037/a0031097

Mitten, D., & Whittingham, M. (2009). Be safe out there: Critically thinking risk in adventure education. in B. Stremba & C. Bisson (Eds.) *Teaching adventure education theory best practices* (pp. 251–266). Human Kinetics.

Naor, L., & Mayseless, O. (2021). Therapeutic factors in nature-based therapies: Unraveling the therapeutic benefits of integrating nature in psychotherapy. *Psychotherapy, 58*(4), 576–590. https://doi.org/10.1037/pst0000396

Nordquist, J. et al. (2023). *Manual of accreditation standards for outdoor behavioral healthcare* (3rd ed.). The Association for Experiential Education.

Norton, C. L., Tucker, A. R., Farnham, M., Borroel, F., & Pelletier, A. (2019). Family enrichment adventure therapy: A mixed methods study examining the impact of trauma-informed adventure therapy on children and families affected by abuse. *Journal of Child and Adolescent Trauma, 12*(1), 85–95.

Norton, C. L., Tucker, A. R., Russell, K., Bettmann, J., Gass, M., Gillis, H. L. & Behrens, E. (2014). Adventure therapy with youth. *Journal of Experiential Education, 37*(1), 46–59. https://doi.org/10.1177/1053825913518895

Pellegrini, A. (2009). *The role of play in human development*. Oxford Academic.

Perry, B.D. (2009). Examining child maltreatment through a neurodevelopmental lens: Clinical application of the Neurosequential Model of Therapeutics. *Journal of Loss and Trauma, 14*, 240–255. https://doi.org/10.1080/15325020903004350

Priest, S. & Gass, M. (2017). *Effective leadership in adventure programming* (3rd ed.). Human Kinetics.

Schoel, J., & Maizell, R. (2002). *Exploring islands of healing: New perspectives on adventure based counseling*. Kendall Hunt.

Schoel, J., Prouty, D., & Radcliffe, P. (1988). *Islands of healing: A guide to adventure based counseling*. Project Adventure.

Smith P. K. (2005). Play: Types and functions in human development. In B. J. Ellis, & D. F. Bjorklund (Eds.), *Origins of the social mind: Evolutionary psychology and child development* (pp. 271–291). Guilford Press.

Smith, S. (Ed.) (2021). *Beneficial risks: The evolution of risk management for outdoor and experiential education programs*. Sagamore-Venture Publishing.

Stubbe, D. E. (2018). The therapeutic alliance: The fundamental element of psychotherapy. *Focus, 16*(4), 402–403. https://doi.org/10.1176/appi.focus.20180022

Todić, J., & Christensen, M. C. (2022). Integrating critical, engaged, and abolitionist pedagogies to advance antiracist social work education. *Advances in Social Work, 22*(2), 389–415. https://doi.org/10.18060/24972

Tucker, A. R. (2009). Adventure-based group therapy to promote social skills in adolescents. *Social Work with Groups, 32*, 315–329. https://doi.org/10.1080/01609510902874594

Tucker, A. R., Beale, B., Norton, C. L., Walsh, H., Keefe K., Holmes, L., & Wermer-Colan, R. (2024). The Ohio Adventure Therapy Coalition: A statewide trauma informed group work initiative to meet the needs of CPS youth. *The Journal of Creativity in Mental Health. 20*(3), 376–390. https://doi.org/10.1080/15401383.2024.2386163

US Health Resources and Service Administration. (n.d.). *Best practices guide*. https://telehealth.hhs.gov/providers/best-practice-guides

VanKanegan, C., Tucker, A. R., McMillion, P., & Gass, M. (2019). Adventure therapy and its impact on the functioning of youth in a community setting. *Social Work with Groups, 42*(2), 127–141. https://doi.org/10.1080/01609513.2018.1478761

Wampold, B.E. (2015). How important are the common factors in psychotherapy? An update. *World Psychiatry, 14*, 270–277. https://doi.org/10.1002/wps.20238

Warren, K. J., Mitten, D., & Loeffler, T. A. (Eds.). (2008). *Theory & practice of experiential education: A collection of articles addressing the historical, educational, philosophical, psychological, ethical, spiritual, and social justice foundations of experiential education* (4th ed.). Association for Experiential Education.

Yalom, I. D., & Leszcz, M. (2020). *The theory and practice of group psychotherapy* (6th ed.). Basic Books.

Chapter 2

Foundations of Adventure Therapy

Understanding the foundations of adventure therapy practice is vitally important to intentional, effective, and ethical practice. This chapter summarizes key components that underpin this practice approach, including how one's clinical mindset toward individual psychotherapy informs the practice. Diverse components are discussed as they relate to adventure therapy including theoretical foundations, delivering anti-oppressive and trauma-informed adventure therapy, and attending to the unique ethical considerations encountered in this practice. Utilizing adventure therapy involves considerations related to ethics, participant welfare, participant rights, informed consent processes, and how to discuss this approach with participants.

Rooted in Experiential Education

Adventure therapy has roots in the theory of experiential education, which is based on the understanding that learning is maximized when individuals learn through doing and reflect on that process (Gass et al., 2020). John Dewey's work was foundational in the development of experiential education and has been evolved since its establishment (Quay & Seaman, 2013). While Dewey has been noted as one of the founders of experiential learning and theory, the work of Maria Montessori should be also recognized as foundational. Similar to the writings of Dewey, Montessori understood the importance of learning through activity and engaging students in real life and hands-on experiences both inside and beyond the classroom (American Montessori Academy, 2024a). She believed that children learn by doing and should have agency over their learning with a focus on social justice and equity (American Montessori Academy, 2024b). Her early work was criticized by a student of Dewey, and after an initial establishment of her work, this method faded for 30 years until its resurgence in the 1950s. Today, in the United States (US) alone, there are 5,000 Montessori schools with over one million students (American Montessori Academy, 2024a). Hence, both the work of Dewey and Montessori are important to recognize equally for their influence on the establishment and acceptance of the experiential education process.

From these roots, experiential education grew into a wide-ranging field with practitioners applying these theories from school rooms (NYC Outward Bound Schools, 2025) to nature classrooms (Mann et al., 2022), college campuses (Townley et al., 2024), outdoor programs, and beyond. Adventure therapy is an application of experiential learning theory where the adventure experience, a central vehicle of change, is intentionally planned and processed by practitioners. Kolb's experiential learning cycle is a commonly used tool that helps to guide practitioners in how to process the experience (bring in reflection) with participants. This is

DOI: 10.4324/9781003457893-2

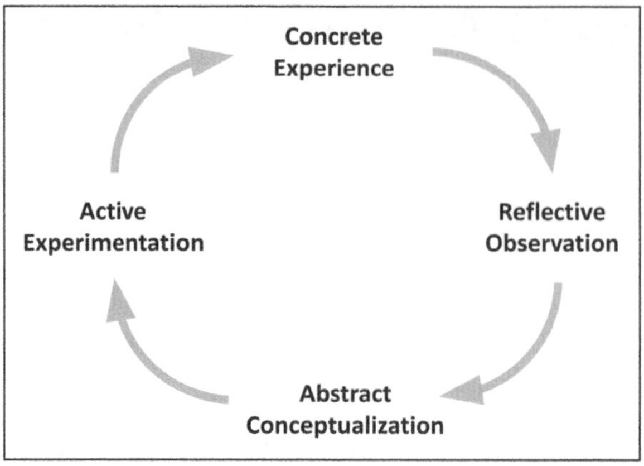

Figure 2.1 Kolb's Experiential Learning Cycle.

applicable to any type of psychotherapy work, whether it is individual, family, or group. Kolb's experiential learning cycle model (1984) includes four components: Concrete Experience, Reflective Observation, Abstract Conceptualization, and Active Experimentation (see Figure 2.1).

In this model, there is an active experience in which participants engage and respond (Concrete Experience), followed by an acknowledgment and reflection on participant responses (Reflective Observation). Next, facilitators and participants explore the meaning behind those responses, the impact of both adaptive and nonadaptive responses, and possible ways of responding in the future based on that learning (Abstract Conceptualization). Finally, that new learning is put into action by participants (Active Experimentation), which often includes the transfer of learning to environments outside those in which the learning took place (Kolb, 1984). As with many models, in actual implementation, these steps are often concurrently happening and not linear or even circular as the process would seem; however, these processes are ongoing and essential to the learning process.

Ecological Perspective

Adventure practitioners understand and acknowledge the importance of the environment of our participants and the intersection and impact of those contexts. One way to frame and understand these dynamics is outlined by Bronfenbrenner's ecological perspective (1979). From this perspective, there are five unique systems that impact individual development and functioning either directly or indirectly. While a developmental theory, it can be applied to all participants, regardless of age, as a way of recognizing and assessing the systems that impact participants. First is a participant's **microsystem**, which includes things that interact and have an immediate influence on a participant such as their identity, health, family, work and school, religion, and peer/social relationships. Microsystems can be both physical and virtual, as in our modern age, the impact of our virtual relationships are important to include for their impact on individuals (Cherry, 2023). The second level is the **mesosystem**, which is the interaction between microsystems like between a participant and their work/school, or family/friends, or their neighborhood, etc. The third system is the **exosystem**, which includes systems that a participant may not be immediately active within, but which has an impact on the participant such as media, local policies, school policies, local social services, extended family, and distant friends. The fourth system is the **macrosystem**, which includes the broader culture in which a participant lives that impacts their functioning, including political systems, cultural norms, the economy, and the values and attitudes associated with larger cultural settings. The final system within Bronfenbrenner's ecological perspective is the **chronosystem**, which focuses on the role of time and how that influences individual development and functioning. This includes things that happen over the course of one's life that impact individuals like family transitions, technological shifts, and historical events (Cherry, 2023). All these systems interact and influence each other in a bidirectional way; hence, understanding the participants within these systems is important when holistically engaging in therapy.

More recently, Bronfenbrenner's Model has been adapted and evolved into **the Social Ecological Model** for health and prevention (Golden & Earp, 2012; Wilkins et al., 2014). In this adapted model, there are four levels/systems for consideration in what impacts and drives behavior, as well as areas to focus interventions (Cramer & Kapusta, 2017; Wilkins et al., 2014)

1 Individual
2 Relationships
3 Community
4 Societal

Based on this, adventure therapy practitioners look at participants in the context of the interconnected relationships with themselves, their families, the community, and the larger society. This evolution of the model aligns with an updated understanding of trauma-informed care, which is the bedrock of ethical and effective adventure psychotherapy and centered on creating safe, caring, and collaborative relationships with participants with an aim to help build resilience within these different contexts (SAMHSA, 2014).

Trauma

Any discussion about doing individual psychotherapy must give attention to the role of trauma, traumatic stress, and the impact on the participants with whom practitioner's work. This is especially true post-COVID-19 pandemic. Research has consistently shown that individuals who seek mental health treatment have a high rate of trauma. **Substance Abuse and Mental Health Services Administration's (SAMHSA, 2014) definition of trauma includes three stages, dubbed the 3 E's: Events, Experience, and Effects**. Trauma results from an event, series of events, or a set of circumstances an individual experiences as physically or emotionally harmful or threatening, which may have lasting adverse effects on the individual's functioning and mental, physical, social, emotional, or spiritual well-being. Traumatic events may be experienced by an individual, a generation, or an entire community or culture. This framework for understanding trauma was developed by a working group of researchers, practitioners, trauma survivors, and family members convened by SAMHSA (2014). It is important because it creates a framework for understanding the complex nature of trauma.

Mental Health America found in their survey of close to 85,000 help seeking individuals that 93.80% screened positive for Post-Traumatic Stress Disorder (Reinert & Nguyen, 2021).

Rates of mental health diagnoses are increasing post-pandemic with research finding a 25.6% increase in anxiety and 27.6% increase in depression globally (Santomauro et al., 2021), as well as a 28% increase in depression for adolescents (Barendse et al., 2023). Practitioners should enter the clinical relationship guided by the understanding that practitioners have a responsibility for providing care that is trauma informed.

An Expanded View of Trauma: The Three ACEs

It is hard to make it through any graduate program or any discussion of trauma and its impact on individuals without being exposed to the findings of the "ACE study" (Felitti et al., 1998). This seminal study, which is now over 30 years old, found that the more categories of adverse childhood experiences one has, the larger the negative impact on one's health and wellness in adulthood, and in certain instances early death (Brown et al., 2009). There were three areas in the study looked at: Abuse (emotional, sexual, physical); Family factors (incarcerated relative, violence against mothers, mental illness, divorce, substance abuse); and Neglect (physical, emotional; Felitti et al., 1998). While this study was seminal in how practitioners should look at the impact of trauma, the original list of events in this study left out several important aspects that can be considered trauma. Ellis and Dietz (2017) critique the original study and introduce the concept of the **"Pair of ACEs"**.

In their model that includes the original list of adverse childhood experiences (ACEs) around the household or family, they stress the need to include **"Adverse Community Environments"**, which act together to create toxic stress and childhood adversity. Adverse community environmental factors include discrimination, historical trauma, substandard schools, lack of jobs, decreased access to healthcare, violence, lack of social capital and mobility, structural racism, food scarcity, substandard wages, poverty, lack of clean water and air, poor housing quality and affordability (Ellis & Dietz, 2017). These Pair of ACEs "produce complex trauma felt at the individual, family, and population levels" (Ellis et al., 2022, p. S19). Research has shown that in the US, Black, Indigenous, and People of Color (BIPOC) have a higher prevalence of household ACEs, live in areas with increased risk of violence, poor schools and a lack of services (Liu et al., 2020), and are more likely to be pulled into both the child welfare (Dettlaff & Boyd, 2020; Waller et al., 2024) and justice systems (Development Services Group, 2022; National Conference of State Legislatures, 2022).

More recently, the ACEs have been expanded to include the impact of the **environment** and **climate** crisis on toxic stress as the 3rd layer of ACEs (PACEs Connection, 2022). Things that impact our participants at the individual, community and societal levels in the environment include tornadoes and hurricanes, volcano eruptions and tsunamis, earthquakes, and pandemics. Climate crisis factors include record heat and droughts, wildfires and smoke, record storms, flooding and mudslides and rising sea levels.

As practitioners, it is our responsibility to understand and explore with participants how these complex systems are at play in our participants lives at the individual, community, and societal levels. For most marginalized individuals, living in a society in which they face constant discrimination is a considerable source of daily and ongoing stress (Bartlett et al., 2022).

Hence, while practitioners are encouraged to shift from blaming the individual by asking "what is wrong with you" to include their circumstances and history by asking "what happened to you", **attention must also include larger systems at play** that both indirectly and directly create chronic and toxic stress for our participants (Bartlett et al., 2022; Sweeney et al., 2018). "It is clear that vulnerable and systematically overlooked communities bear the brunt of each new crisis – from COVID-19 to climate change – and that these communities deserve a much more effective set of buffering systems and supports" (ACES AWARE, 2023. Para 1).

The Trauma Response

With this updated understanding of trauma, it is also important to recognize how trauma impacts our participants and how the world reacts to them. Trauma responses are likely to show up when any stressful situation exceeds a person's ability to respond appropriately with rational thinking. Without access to rational thinking in the prefrontal cortex area of our brain, individuals enter a survival mode referred to as "fight" or "flight". While this is an appropriate reaction to a traumatic event, when individuals are exposed to chronic and toxic stress, their brains continue to be in a constant state of dysregulation leaving the lower levels of their brain in charge (LeWine, 2024). This **constant state of survival leads to emotional and behavioral dysregulation**, which show up as impulsivity, aggression, self-centeredness, disengagement, relationship conflicts, and/or isolation; as well as common health risk behaviors which include sedentary lifestyles, use of tobacco, alcohol and other drugs (Felitti et al., 1998). These responses can distract them from or dampen the impact of the trauma symptoms providing a sort of relief (Felitti et al., 1998).

What is problematic is that **these responses by participants often get misdiagnosed or pathologized differently, when in fact they are a trauma response**. And the way these responses are often addressed is different depending upon a participant's identity. Some individuals are seen as "sick" or as "bad" (Bloom & Yanosy Sreedhar, 2008) and are treated differently in our social systems. BIPOC folks are often punished for trauma responses. This punishment paradigm appears in public school systems in the US (Office for Civil Rights, 2023). In a survey of over 50,000 US public school students, research found that both male and female Black students were two times more likely than White boys or girls to receive out of school suspension or expulsion (Office for Civil Rights, 2023) for similar offenses. This continues into adulthood. In the US, Hispanic and Black individuals represent 56% of incarcerated individuals but make up only 28% of the population (Gramlich, 2020).

Hence, as practitioners enter relationships with their adventure therapy participants, following a trauma-informed approach requires that they acknowledge this disparity and **change the narrative that blames and punishes participants for having trauma responses**. It is easy for practitioners to think that they don't blame or punish trauma responses, when in fact, the mental health treatment system encourages labeling these responses as problems or symptoms to be handled (i.e., overreaction, aggression, withdrawal); hence, practitioners may spend time on trying to decrease or extinguish these responses versus getting to the underlying reason for the behavior, which is a trauma response. Adolescents with a history of being physically abused may struggle with managing their own aggressive responses due to perceiving the behavior of others as hostile, even when that is not the intent of their behavior (Verhoef et al., 2019). For example, an adolescent in a day treatment program who has experienced domestic violence and bullying may exhibit reactive aggression when being mildly teased by peers. Often, this is because the adolescent perceives this behavior as a significant threat, and their alarm system kicks off, resulting in a fight response. The program's response to this behavior is likely to be some sort of punishment or consequence when, in fact, the participant was likely responding automatically to the threat rather than thoughtfully responding. Understanding of the impact of trauma, as well as how our brains and bodies react and change in responses to trauma, are integral to understanding how the holistic engagement of participants in adventure therapy is aligned with trauma-informed care.

Neuroscience and Adventure Therapy

The principles of neuroscience greatly inform an understanding of how adventure therapy works to support change and growth for participants. Table 2.1 provides an overview of some of the important neuroscience points that have been adapted from the author's original discussion in their book, *Adventure Group Psychotherapy* (pp. 7–8). Understanding the way most human brains are wired for growth through experience and relationship is foundational to developing effective adventure therapy interventions for any participant, regardless of their trauma history.

With this neuroscience understanding, adventure therapy's holistic engagement of participants in carefully planned activities is meant to create an optimal learning environment of neurological arousal. The aim is to engage participants in challenges and activities that do not over or underwhelm them. Based on the understanding that when participants are dysregulated, they can no longer access their prefrontal cortex, it is important to focus on regulation for participants to learn new skills (Porges, 2011). The holistic and kinesthetic nature of the adventure activities are not only impactful to dysregulated individuals; but these regulating activities can improve the focus and affect of participants as well. Through repetition and rehearsal, the utilization of adventure experiences can build on a participant's ability to

Table 2.1 Neuroscience and Adventure Therapy

Understanding the Neuroscience
The **impact of neuroscience and trauma** are integral considerations when facilitating adventure therapy. As research has emerged related to neurodevelopment and its interplay with the therapy process, it has become apparent that many of the foundations of adventure therapy are supported by this research. For example, engaging in multisensory or holistic experiences can work to both regulate the brain, as well as increase engagement in learning (Allan et al., 2012; Mackenzie et al., 2014). Hence, experiential practice that engages the whole person provides opportunities for participants to integrate their somatic responses, feelings, behaviors, and beliefs (Hoogendoorn, 2015; Schoel & Maizell, 2002).
Activating Neural Networks
When trying to impact thoughts, feelings, and behaviors as is done in adventure therapy, research suggests that these changes will not occur unless the neural system to be changed is activated (Hoogendoorn, 2015). A common phrase to illustrate this in neuroscience is "neurons that fire together, wire together" (Hebb, 1949). Research on neurobiology indicates that learning is best retained when it is learned in a similar state in which it is to be used later (Cozolino, 2010; Radulovic et al., 2017), a concept referred to as "state-dependent learning". Specifically, to alter emotional/behavioral pathways, these pathways must be **activated** throughout the therapeutic process, and with repeated activation and intentional changes in response, the neural pathways related to those emotions/behaviors to create **new long-term responses can be rewired** (Cozolino, 2010).
Adventure therapy interventions activate areas of the brain where change is desired (such as managing responses to stress), firing neural pathways that can benefit from reinforcement (such as practicing skills for managing stress in sessions), and engaging in state-dependent learning (such as managing responses to stress while under stress).

(*Continued*)

Table 2.1 (Continued)

Optimal Learning States

A foundational concept in neuroscience is the importance of **optimal learning states or optimal neural arousal informs** the focus put on the active engagement of participants (Cozolino, 2010). Participants who are underaroused (bored, disengaged) or overaroused (hypervigilant, dysregulated) are unable to attend to the experience and gain learning from it, as they are preoccupied with their arousal state (Cozolino, 2010). Practitioners aim to create engaging experiences that arouse participants to their optimal learning state, allowing them to effectively activate somatic, cognitive, emotional, and behavioral pathways.

As adventure therapy engages the participant in multisensorial work, it directly influences their level of arousal. Bruce Perry, a leading researcher in child trauma, highlights that rhythmic, repetitive activity is key to helping people regulate themselves (Gaskill and Perry, 2014; Perry & Dobson, 2013). Leading a participant in a problem-solving initiative activity can be an ideal way to help a participant feel more regulated, both emotionally and physically, while attempting a challenge that engages them in a moderate level of stress. It is critical to understand that one great way to help someone emotionally regulate is to help them physically regulate (i.e. get them moving) (Shafir et al., 2016). Applying these principles in adventure therapy practice can help practitioners engage participants to achieve an optimal learning state, moderating the level of stress or nervous system arousal through supporting regulation when needed and utilizing a level of challenge that keeps the work interesting.

Relationships

From a neuroscience perspective, connecting with others triggers chemical responses in the body in many ways. The middle part of the brain engages in threat appraisal in interactions with other people, dedicating part of its energy to figuring out the social cues of others and determining if there is any danger. Additionally, **having safe relational connections to others reduces stress and increases feelings of safety** (Cozolino, 2014). Much of this interpretation happens outside of conscious awareness. The field of psychotherapy has long relied on the importance of supporting participants in developing trusting relationships in order to address the issues that bring them to therapy (Cozolino, 2014). Now it is understood that this approach to healing is neurologically supported by the biology of the brain. Due to the interactional nature of adventure therapy, participants are supported in developing the ability to form healthy relationships and to more realistically assess threats in a social context. This is well aligned with the Social Ecological Model for health that centers relationships within the healing process (Wilkins et al., 2014).

Adapted from *Adventure Group Psychotherapy* pages 7–8.

tolerate and manage the stress of things that may have previously triggered dysregulation. Hence understanding how the brain works helps practitioners to see how adventure therapy can be a natural fit for engaging both the mind and body of participants, further highlighting the holistic nature of this intervention.

Trauma-Informed and Anti-Oppressive Practice in Adventure Therapy

As discussed in the trauma section, when a person is having a trauma response, it is hard to think. Punishment for those trauma responses is seen as another threat, which then perpetuates an individual's symptoms and dysregulation (Anda et al., 2006). Hence, interventions are needed that align with trauma-informed models.

A trauma-informed approach to treatment is also an **anti-oppressive approach** to treatment (Sunderland et al., 2023; Trevino, 2022). In practice, it is important to recognize the practitioner's role in oppression, however unintentional, as well as the participant's historical experience of oppression in the intersection of their identities. It is beyond the scope of this book to discuss all the different frameworks and theories about social justice (i.e., anti-racism, anti-oppression, anti-colonialism, etc.). However, the authors believe it is of the utmost importance that practitioners in any clinical practice setting engage in their own critical reflection and practice to truly meet the participant where they are (Todić & Christensen, 2022). As a practitioner, understanding, learning about, addressing and being an active participant in the work to recognize and manage personal trauma responses is essential. Giving ongoing attention to practitioner's biases, assumptions, and possible participation in perpetuating oppression is equally important. Finally, it is the practitioner's responsibility to not only learn and reflect about oppression, but to engage actively in ways that disrupt or dismantle these systems of oppression (Todić & Christensen, 2022).

US SAMHSA (2014) highlights key principles of a trauma-informed approach which closely align with anti-oppressive practice. **SAMHSA's Guiding Principles include safety, choice, collaboration, trustworthiness, empowerment, and understanding cultural and historical trauma**, which are intertwined with each other. Ensuring that the physical and emotional safety of an individual is addressed is the first important step to providing trauma-informed care; if they don't feel safe, they won't be able to relax and access their frontal cortex. Next, the practitioner needs to demonstrate that they are trustworthy. Trustworthiness can be shown through establishing and honoring appropriate boundaries and providing clarity around what is expected in regard to participation. Next, the more choice and input that they have during their treatment experience, through a collaborative effort with their practitioner, the more likely the individual will participate in services and the more effective the services may be. Identifying and focusing on the participant's strengths and empowering them to utilize those strengths while developing new skills provides a healthy foundation for individuals to fall back upon when they complete or stop receiving services. Finally, being willing and able to discuss the broader topic of cultural and/or historical trauma conveys the message that the practitioner understands that it's not the participants fault and allows the participant to release feelings of self-blame and shame.

Each of the six SAMHSA trauma-informed principles are discussed next to highlight ongoing considerations that are foundational to practitioner's work in individual adventure psychotherapy, which is well-structured to incorporate these principles effectively. In addition, the natural alignment of these principles with anti-oppressive practice is outlined.

Safety

It is a practitioner's responsibility to be educated about and recognize that some participants may never feel "safe" in the spaces in which they move due to real threats of racism, sexism, homophobia and other oppressive systems still actively at play in their environments (Waller et al., 2024). So, in anti-oppressive practice, adventure therapy practitioners are charged with working collaboratively with participants in building a safe enough space for participants to engage in the process. Practitioners must be welcoming. Practitioners invite participants to share and keep their privacy as part of developing safety and trust, while also respecting them for not sharing or being hesitant. Safety is multilayered, and when the practitioner also engages in the other forms of trauma-informed practice, the likelihood of feeling a sense of felt safety increases.

Remember, it is a practitioner's job **to resist retraumatizing** participants (SAMHSA, 2014). Keep in mind that trauma occurs from both systemic oppression and more acute traumatic experiences. The more competent practitioners are in understanding safety and risk management, the greater influence they have on the comfort of participants. For example, if practitioners do not think in advance about having harnesses the right size for participants, or do not pay attention to gear like boots that may give participants blisters, or do not know the trail systems as well as required while hiking with a participant, this all impacts a participant's experience of felt safety. Similarly, when practitioners respond to in-session expressions of a participant's trauma response, such as oppositional or avoidant behaviors, by increasing the level of challenge and expecting that participant to "push through the resistance", the treatment environment will become less safe, and the participant will become further entrenched in their protective response to their trauma. This understanding of safety is related to scope of practice and training, which is discussed later in the chapter under ethics.

Trustworthiness and Transparency

From an anti-oppressive lens, **acknowledging a practitioner's power** in relation to participants helps create transparency (Burke & Harrison, 2002). As the professional in the room with a participant, there is inherent power in the practitioner's role as the so-called expert for which the practitioner is usually being paid for that expertise. This inherently creates hierarchy that shows up in relationships with participants. In addition, there are personal, political, economic, and spiritual/religious roles that influence the relationship (Burke & Harrison, 2002). Ignoring this, or waiting until this comes up in practice, does not necessarily build up trust. Exploring it with participants from their own perspectives allows a practitioner to name what showed up in the room. Remember to consider the expanded three ACE categories (household, community, and environmental trauma), and practice centering the participants' lived experience into the ongoing work to acknowledge and validate their experiences. Additionally, being clear with participants on what they can expect, their rights, and what is expected of them can build this level of transparency (Avasthi et al., 2022).

In AT, the idea of **ongoing informed consent** is key to building trust and transparency with participants. For example, a practitioner and a participant may be engaging in an activity that can use the loss of sight. At the beginning of the session, the practitioner may ask if the participant is interested in engaging in a trust activity with them, to which they respond yes. Then, the practitioner clearly explains the activity, including inviting the participant to put on an eye covering or simply to close their eyes and rely on the practitioner to bring them on a walk in which they guide them physically by the elbow and with their words through a maze. After explaining with depth, the practitioner should ask again, "Now that you know more about the activity, does it seem ok to proceed?" It is this ongoing sharing of information and checking in that allows for authentic trust building between the participant and the practitioner.

Peer Support

Individual psychotherapy work affords fewer opportunities for peer support than other models of treatment, such as group therapy. However, **the participatory nature of adventure experiences helps the practitioner to show up more as a collaborator rather than an expert with the participant** (Tucker, 2009). Practitioners are, in fact, a participant's peer per se in the therapy setting. Practitioners become active members in the process of interpersonal learning as they engage collaboratively with participants in experiential interventions. The experience is shared and there are continual opportunities to redefine help as a co-learning process. The practitioner can engage in the exploration of commonalities and connections that exist between them. Mead (2003) an expert on intentional peer support stresses how trauma-informed peer support practices include building on shared experiences, sharing in the receiving and giving of support, and promoting relationships that look at experiences not as pathological but as symptoms of trauma experiences. This mutual involvement is also a key part of anti-oppressive practice as it provides opportunities for the practitioner and participant to explore how power, values and social difference affect their interactions (Burke & Harrison, 2002). Hence, practitioners have a unique role in adventure therapy to engage in some ways as a peer when sharing active experiences, while intentionally decreasing the power differential and providing support.

Collaboration, Mutuality, Empowerment, Voice, & Choice

These five concepts are closely aligned with each other. When practitioners are truly working in partnership with participants, a natural mutuality is developed. Sharing of power in collaborative goal setting, and choice of activity build a mutual relationship and empower participants as active and vocal participants in their treatment. **The practice of centering the participant's lived experience means that practitioners listen to and believe what participants share about their experiences**; because, if the practitioner's experience does not reflect that of participants, it is easy to minimize and gaslight them unconsciously. Getting participant feedback on how they are experiencing the process is key; however, it is not the participant's responsibility to educate the practitioner (Osborn & Karandikar, 2022) about historical and cultural oppressions.

One of the authors recalls beginning individual treatment with a 12-year-old African American participant. During an initial assessment session with the participant's mother, the practitioner (a White male) noted a guarded or distant approach to how she engaged in the process. Rather than address her behavior directly, the practitioner chose to open a discussion of the way White men have been at the forefront of oppressing other minority groups in order to maintain their power. The practitioner acknowledged that they had a very different experience growing up than her son and pledged to examine how those differences might impact her son's treatment. They also pledged to listen to and value the mother's voice in expressing her thoughts and feelings on how the treatment was going.

Incorporating participants' voices and respecting their choices in treatment are two of the most foundational considerations when thinking of trauma-informed and anti-oppressive practices. The importance of asking for ongoing continual consent supports a participant's choice and honors their voice in raising concerns if practitioners authentically ask for feedback. In a truly collaborative treatment experience, participants have agency over what they do and how they do it. Respecting voice and choice reinforces a participant's position of power in the relationship, reducing the likelihood of being oppressive. For example, a practitioner can talk in advance about the plan for the session (or the next session) by providing a rationale for possible options for activities and asking participants for feedback in choosing their next activity together. This first provides participants with a transparent rationale for the activities and then gives them agency over which activity they would like to do. Practitioners must then respect their choices, even if they may not be aligned with the practitioner's own ideas about the activity choice, except of course if there are real emotional and physical safety concerns. Ideally, a practitioner's role is to support a participant's sense of empowerment in gaining control and resilience after trauma and while living amidst oppressive environments.

Decision-making and problem-solving skills are then practiced and reinforced in the process of including the participants whole heartedly in their treatment process.

Cultural, Historical, and Gender Issues

As previously discussed, it is important to have a broad understanding of the three categories of ACEs in the lives of participants and their impact on them at the individual, family, community, and societal levels. While it is beyond the scope of this book to cover all the current and historical foundations of issues around difference in environments based on culture and gender; it is important that practitioners are aware of some specific issues they may encounter in adventure therapy.

While not all adventure therapy work occurs outdoors, nor does it have to happen outdoors, there are many practitioners who choose to work with participants outdoors. While research shows that access to the outdoors and time spent in nature have positive impacts on mental health (Bettmann et al., 2024), **not all participants may be comfortable outdoors**. While yes, managing bugs and mud can make one "uncomfortable", this discomfort is more about historical relationships some communities have with the outdoors that are negative and/or even traumatic. In the US, until the passing of the Civil Rights Act of 1964, Black people were not legally allowed at national and state parks, beaches, camp groups, and other outdoor spaces (Humphry, 2020). In addition, the common practice of lynching of Black men and women was often done in the forest or wooded areas, making them unsafe spaces for Black folks in the US (Equal Justice Initiative, 2017). Violence against non-White individuals in outdoor spaces continues today in the US, furthering the fear of harassment when accessing the outdoors for people of color (Heiser, 2021). Redlining and economic marginalization have also created heavily populated areas that often have little to no green spaces compared to more economically thriving communities that have larger White populations that are often closer to parks and recreation areas (Nardone et al., 2021). Most outdoor organizations and spaces also lack representation of diverse staff and leaders, furthering the idea that the outdoors are White spaces (Heiser, 2021). In addition, students in outdoor education have historically been White students with economic privilege with educational systems often centering Whiteness in their curriculum (Rose & Paisley, 2012). Hence, practitioners may lack education and understanding around these areas and must increase their social justice literacy and competency (Breunig, 2019).

It is also important to note that the **role of nature for healing is not a novel concept**. In fact, Indigenous populations have understood the healing and curative nature of the outdoors for centuries (Mullan, 2023); however, modern clinical therapy has often erased their history, and "their knowledges have and continue to be marginalized, with little overt recognition or protection" (Boyd et al., 2023, p. 132) or programs have integrated indigenous rituals through cultural appropriation without fully providing education and context around these practices (Skidmore, 2017). Many Indigenous communities believe there is no separation between humans and the land, and our protection of the land is our fundamental responsibility (Boyd et al., 2023). This whitewashing of the outdoors has been a theme, especially in the US when White men like John Muir and others have been praised for the founding of the national parks and environmental protectionism, which only needed protection due to the continued exploitation of natural spaces by White people during the founding and ongoing industrialization of the US (Riley, 2020; Robinson, 2020).

In addition to race and culture, it is important to understand the role of **gender** and how lived experiences show up and influence participants, as well as how patriarchy has influenced the field of adventure therapy. Historically, experiential education was rooted in Western, patriarchal ideology of rugged individualism. Males are often referred to as stronger leaders due to their physical prowess which is more valued than social and emotional skills women bring to leadership; however, true leaders must have a balance of both, and neither should be inherently associated with one's gender (Warren, 2019). This false narrative about capabilities of women and men especially in the outdoors is perpetuated through media, textbooks and training, and lack of representation of female leaders in positions of power in outdoor organizations, similar to Black, Hispanic, Asian, and Indigenous leaders. Hence, participants may have their own internalized assumptions of how they should show up in the activities in which they may engage in the treatment setting. So, it is important as practitioners to be trained both in the technical requirements of the activities as well as building clinical skills. **Practitioners have the opportunity to defy gender norms and be role models** for participants regardless of their identified gender. Of course, this discussion must also be grounded in an understanding that the gender binary is limited and for both practitioners and participants gender can be better understood more as a continuum than as a dichotomy. This further supports the perspective that skills should not be based on gender assumptions or expectations which society has imposed.

Finally, it is important to directly discuss the impact of a culture of **ableism** on accessibility to adventure programming. There are assumptions about physical capabilities needed for participation that can unfairly exclude certain people from participation, while at the same time, it is important to adapt our programming to the true abilities of individual participants. Warren et al. (2014) note that if programs aim to support inclusion, this naturally supports different abilities in all participants regardless of body size and/or physical limitations. Dillenschneider (2007) highlights that to create inclusive environments, practitioners need to provide appropriate accommodations where participants with limitations must be fully involved in making choices in their treatment including opportunities for competence and independence and an expanded range of supports from which to choose. Their impairment or disability is only a part of who shows up; hence, it should be just another consideration for how participants are different (Dillenschneider, 2007). Therefore, practitioners as part of their toolkit of skills need to seek education around accommodations and adaptations available to support inclusive practices and disability awareness (Dillenschneider, 2007; Warren et al., 2014; for more information, see https://www.inclusiveoutdoors.org/ for resources and toolkits; Figure 2.2).

While this is not an exhaustive list of some of the considerations practitioners need to address when engaging in adventure therapy with participants, understanding both a participant's cultural relationship with nature and the outdoors, as well as curiosity around that relationship, is key for practitioners and should not be ignored. However, limiting the exploration of social justice to the participants' experience and perspective is only part of the task. **Practitioners also need to explore and challenge their own experience and perspective around social justice issues**, including both their privilege and oppression, often seen as the harder task. Breunig (2019) adopts an intersectional approach to review relevant literature to offer insights into the concept of social justice literacy, providing opportunities for educators and other outdoor practitioners to better understand their own privilege and to develop new understandings and actionable behaviors. Practitioners are invited to consider the varied and complicated concepts with a curious and growth-oriented mindset, starting with the idea that identities like race, class, sexuality, and gender do not exist independently. They are interconnected and cannot be examined as discrete items on a checklist, just as practitioners are connected relationally with participants and must be simultaneously aware of the complexities of their own social identities as well as theirs.

Figure 2.2 Being in a natural setting enhances treatment.

Ongoing Practitioner Reflection

As previously discussed, as part of a practitioner's ongoing growth in being an anti-oppressive practitioner, **they must continuously engage in reflection both around their own trauma responses as well as addressing internal biases that can show up in the treatment setting** (Todić & Christensen, 2022). Alvarez et al. (2021) discuss practitioner's trauma responses and the impact of secondary traumatic stress:

> As facilitators, practitioners and humans that are impacted by their own experiences as well as their participants, it is important to pay attention to both primary and secondary trauma exposure. The regular use of a formal screening tool, like the ProQOL (Professional Quality of Life measure) can be extremely helpful in monitoring ongoing exposure and impact (Stamm, 2016). Regular monitoring can provide early feedback, so that prevention strategies can be implemented before the onset of STS symptoms. The symptoms of STS are identical to the symptoms of PTSD, and as such, they should be taken seriously. If left unaddressed, those symptoms may contribute to issues including being less effective as a practitioner and decisions to leave the field entirely.
>
> (p. 14)

In addition, ongoing critical reflection as practitioners is essential to truly engage in anti-oppressive practice. Ortega and Garvin (2019), scholars in socially just practices, note,

> The thoughts, feelings, and actions (facilitators) develop reflect their positionalities, that is their standpoints or positions in which they view and experience their reality. Becoming aware of and building on positionalities and standpoints is especially important at the level in which communication and interactions take place. The patterns that emerge are illustrative of how dimensions of power, privilege, oppression, and differences associated with positionalities influence the perceptions, decisions, and actions of (participants) and ourselves.
>
> (p. 8)

Hence, critically paying attention to how biases and positionalities play a role in how practitioners interpret, interact and evaluate their work with participants should be given ongoing attention for all practitioners. The role of **consultation and supervision can be key** to helping to look at practitioner's biases and narratives, something that is not always made central in the supervisory process. In fact, social justice is central to anti-oppressive practice; hence, it should be explored in supervision. Norris (2022) highlights, "Resisting dominant culture narratives that perpetuate marginalization and stigma, examining biases and privilege through critical reflection, and identifying and confronting systemic oppression within our own approaches are all practice behaviors that begin in supervision and expand to therapy" (¶6).

Ultimately, if practitioners are really present with participants, paying close attention to what is happening, listening for understanding, asking questions from curiosity, and engaging in personal ongoing critical reflection, they are on the path to anti-oppressive individual practice.

Ethical Considerations

Adventure therapy practitioners are bound by the ethical codes of their profession, whether that is social work, counseling, marriage and family therapy, psychology or any other mental health profession. In this section, ethical considerations unique to adventure therapy practice are explored. Additionally, the Therapeutic Adventure Professional Group (TAPG) of the Association for Experiential Education (AEE) has established ethical guidelines that adventure psychotherapy practitioners should adopt (TAPG, n.d.). While it might be obvious, it is important to highlight how **ethics are intertwined with good practice that is both trauma-informed and anti-oppressive in nature**. The overlaps are clear; however, this section further explores special considerations in AT practice related to participant welfare, participant rights, clinical relationships, competence, scope of practice, and environmental stewardship.

Participant Welfare

The experiential interventions of adventure therapy invite participants to engage their whole self - physically, emotionally, somatically, and psychologically, in sessions. As a result of this, practitioners are attending to the holistic needs of the participant. In adventure therapy sessions, considerations such as food and water require attention. If operating in outdoor environments, additional attention must be paid to the weather and other aspects of the physical space. Mental health practitioners are ethically and legally concerned with participant well-being and have a professional duty of care to maintain that includes assessing and attending to these additional variables.

To accomplish this, **practitioners identify risks, develop plans to manage these risks, and have an emergency response plan in place in order to respond when issues arise**. Additionally, practitioners inform participants about the risks, providing education about the risks, how to manage them, and what is expected from the participant (Gass et al., 2020; Smith, 2021). This is all part of ongoing informed consent discussed previously. For example, if a practitioner is engaging in an outdoor hike with a participant, that practitioner is expected to work with the participant to make sure they have access to drinkable water, appropriate clothing for the environment, and are aware of any precautions to manage aspects of the environment, such as the weather.

Clinical training supports a practitioner's ability to work with participants experiencing difficult psychological or emotional situations. In adventure therapy, additional techniques may be needed to support participants' psychological and emotional needs, such as knowing how to build participants' comfort level with the varying skill sets needed to engage in adventure activities. This may include starting with the basics, anticipating which aspects of activities may provoke distress, and attending to participants' readiness to engage with the activities. This **intentional scaffolding of expectations and skills** can help to protect participant's overall welfare.

Practitioners are also expected to have appropriate levels of training to facilitate each adventure activity they offer. Each activity and environment utilized, whether it is hiking outdoors or climbing in a climbing gym, has its own unique practices to manage the associated risks. There are many publications available that explore risk management in adventure programs, including the AEE's *Manual of Accreditation Standards for Outdoor Behavioral Healthcare Programs* (Nordquist et al., 2023), which provide guidance on best practices in engaging in AT practice. Hence, it is the practitioner's responsibility to educate themselves to be prepared for the activities in which they are asking participants to engage.

In addition to these aspects of participant welfare, **it is imperative that adventure therapy practitioners weigh the cost of services against the potential clinical benefit**. First, the level of risk engaged in needs to be justified by the potential clinical benefit of the services provided. If the practitioner wants to engage a participant in a wilderness experience where access to emergency services may be limited, delayed, or costly, they should consider if a similar clinical benefit might be achieved through an outdoor experience with better access to emergency services. Additionally, immersive wilderness experiences require more infrastructure, staffing support, and time, and thus are more costly to the participant.

Participant Rights

Practitioners need to be aware of and attend to the rights of participants when providing services. These rights are well-outlined by professional associations, licensing boards, and legal codes. However, in adventure therapy practice, there are unique considerations to highlight in the areas of transparency, consent, autonomy, and confidentiality.

Adventure therapy experiences are often novel for participants, thus engaging in informed consent involves some additional considerations. As it is impossible to eliminate all risk, it is important to be upfront with participants about the actual risks involved and the possibility of harm. As discussed earlier, it is also important that participants understand what to expect, as well as what is expected of them (Smith, 2021). **Adventure therapy interventions need to be described in a way that makes sense to participants, who may be unfamiliar with the activities being utilized**. Therefore, it is helpful to sequence experiences in a way that progressively introduces participants to activities so they may attain a more real understanding for informed consent.

Once participants are informed of what to expect, the risks involved, and the potential benefits, then practitioners are positioned to work collaboratively with them around consent. As practitioners are in a position of power, they may unduly influence or pressure participants to engage in adventure interventions despite their best effort to maintain a practice of ongoing consent. Doing so effectively requires the practitioner's constant attention to engaging collaboratively with participants and assessing consent. Ultimately, participants have the right to consent to or decline treatment.

Consent is more nuanced than a simple "yes" or "no" implies. A participant's consent may ebb and flow throughout the course of treatment or even a single intervention. They may consent to a certain level of physical or emotional engagement and refuse other aspects of the intervention. They may agree to engage in activities that involve problem-solving tabletop exercises and decline activities that involve closing their eyes. It is also important to differentiate consent from comfortability. A participant may consent to try something that is uncomfortable. Alternatively, they may try something that is uncomfortable and then change their mind and withdraw their consent. Because of the complexity of these processes, adventure therapy practitioners conduct ongoing assessment of consent and strive to be highly collaborative in the treatment process.

Engaging in some adventure activities narrows a participant's ability to withdraw consent. For example, if the practitioner and participant are going on a 3-mile hike, there is a point at which the participant cannot reasonably withdraw their consent. If they no longer want to continue walking, there is really no alternative than to walk back or continue forward. Practitioners are expected to inform participants regarding these situations before the choices narrow (i.e., at the start of the hike not in the middle of it). At times, the participant may not really understand what they are consenting to because they lack experience with the activity. For example, they may consent to a 2-mile canoe trip if they've never been in a canoe, only to discover that being in a canoe is terrifying (i.e. too stressful) a quarter mile downriver when it is difficult to turn back. As discussed earlier, practitioners should consider these impacts and build up a participant's experiences so they can actually make informed decisions. And, when the interventions planned include times when there is "no going back" or exit strategies are limited, participants are informed about this ahead of time.

Issues of consent are especially pointed with mandated populations, such as those in an involuntary residential level of care, jail or probation, or with minors (Hachtel et al., 2019). In these settings, participants have often not consented to being placed in the care setting. Their willingness to engage in treatment within these settings is often hindered by the fact that they are forced to be there. In these settings, the importance of respecting participant choices and engaging their input in the process is even more heightened than in voluntary settings to mitigate the potential limitations of the effectiveness of treatment in involuntary settings (Hachtel et al., 2019). While it may be true that participants do not have a choice about the setting in which they are in, adventure therapy practitioners can still provide them with choices within the experience to empower them to have influence over their experience.

Additional challenges to consent exist where there is an assessed developmental or psychological issue related to the participant's capacity for decision-making, such as with children or participants experiencing cognitive impairment, psychosis, or dementia (Dunn et al., 2024). These participants may require more structure and direction from the practitioner, who must balance this need with a healthy respect for autonomy and participant consent.

Ethical, trauma-informed, and anti-oppressive adventure therapy practitioners are expected to navigate these complex issues, responsibly informing participants about risks and gaining their ongoing informed consent, respecting participant autonomy, and ensuring the participant's voice and choice are integrated within the treatment process.

Finally, privacy and confidentiality can be a concern related to adventure therapy sessions that take place in public places (James et al., 2021). **Individual adventure psychotherapy practitioners should discuss potential issues around privacy and confidentiality in public spaces** openly with participants and develop agreed-upon expectations for managing these issues. Practitioners should consider the aspects of the spaces chosen for sessions and how they might impact participant responses. This consideration goes beyond the potential for others overhearing the content of sessions. Public spaces can impact a participant's emotional responses or evoke feelings of shame or self-consciousness when engaging in activities. Who might see the participant? What if they are learning a new skill or being vulnerable? Are they ok with engaging in such activities in public? Practitioners should thoughtfully select locations for sessions that attend to these potential dynamics.

Clinical Relationship

Adventure therapy like all therapy is built upon the relationship between a participant and the practitioner. Hence, there are many considerations detailed in existing professional ethical codes and textbooks regarding aspects of the clinical relationship that practitioners should understand and be aware of. In addition, the unique nature of adventure therapy interventions creates situations that are outside of the bounds of what is typically encountered in other settings (Newes & Bandoroff, 2004).

The first consideration relates to the concept of **dual relationships**. Participants can become unclear about the professional role as a result of the high level of engagement of the practitioner in activities with them (Gass et al., 2020; Newes & Bandoroff, 2004). Interventions often include physical components and participants may experience this engagement as more like that of an older sibling, camp counselor, or peer. Practitioners can help address this through paying special attention to clarifying their role and remaining focused on therapeutic goals in the content of their sessions.

Another consideration is the increased likelihood of **physical touch** when using certain activities in the treatment process. Whether it is checking the fit of a climbing harness or engaging in a trust lean, this type of contact is often atypical of other therapy settings and requires additional attention to explanation and consent. It is advised to include narrative about these aspects of adventure therapy work in your informed consent documents at the outset of treatment, as well as to engage the participant in conversation about what to expect and what they are okay with prior to using interventions that involve physical touch.

The holistic engagement of thoughts, feelings, and the physical body that occurs during adventure interventions is often very useful in the process of therapy, providing windows into our participants' experiences that are difficult to achieve without this holistic engagement. However, these experiences also have the **potential to trigger reactions** that are not helpful to participants if the dosage of stress is not managed appropriately. Unmanageable or overwhelming stress can be harmful to participants, who often arrive with high levels of preexisting stress. As Mitten (2021) discusses, adventure education historically has focused on the benefit of "getting outside of one's comfort zone" assuming that one is in a comfort zone. This can put unnecessary stress on participants who may constantly be out of their comfort zones. So while adventure therapy practitioners often intentionally incorporate aspects of challenge into their work so that participants can gain awareness of how their internal responses to stress are expressed externally or practice coping skills they are learning, it is critical for practitioners to continually assess, inform participants about the intention or focus of these interventions, and gain consent and collaboration about how these situations are to be managed.

Adventure therapy practitioners view their own authentic engagement in the process as an important part of the treatment work, attending to their own reactions to inform the therapy process. Practitioner **"use of self"** is central to many theoretical perspectives and practice approaches (Aponte, 2022). In adventure therapy interventions, a practitioner's engagement *with* participants is believed to support the development of therapeutic rapport. For example, the practitioner can demonstrate their trustworthiness through their actions, behaviors, and other responses while engaged in activities alongside participants. This allows participants to see practitioners "walk their talk", reinforcing that they will be trustworthy. In terms of an ethical consideration, practitioners must monitor their own well-being to show up authentically in a way that centers the participants' needs and the purpose of the treatment work. This further highlights the importance of a practitioner's ongoing self-reflection, as discussed earlier.

Competence and Scope of Practice

It is a practitioner's responsibility to be properly trained in the treatment modality in which they practice. In adventure therapy this involves both **the clinical training and technical training** needed for engaging in activities (Alvarez et al., 2021; Gass et al., 2020). The formal education expected for practitioners doing individual adventure psychotherapy, as well as those doing individual therapeutic work, is the first component of training important to highlight. Individual adventure therapy practitioners generally have a master's degree, or above, in psychology, social work, counseling, marriage and family therapy, recreation therapy, or related field of clinical study. Depending on the setting and the nature of the adventure-based program, a bachelor's degree is often the prerequisite for doing therapeutic work.

In addition to one's foundational education, there is no substitute for mastery of the **basic clinical skills** if one hopes to be a competent and effective individual adventure therapy practitioner. Exploring participant content, using empathic listening and curiosity, and a plethora of other specific interviewing skills directing the participant toward achievement of their clinical goals are examples of techniques that are as needed in an adventure therapy context as they are in any other form of individual psychotherapy.

The final piece of required training relates to **specialized knowledge and skill in facilitation** of the experiential interventions practitioners employ (Alvarez et al., 2021; Gass et al., 2020). In addition to the issue of facilitating these activities in a clinical manner, training is needed to understand the full array of adventure tools available to assist participants' journey toward their goals, the standards for safe application of the adventure tools you will use, risk management policies and procedures, and the ethics of experiential practice (Gass et al., 2020). Whether the activity is a high adventure type such as paddling, rock climbing, and high ropes courses, or activities a practitioner can do in the clinical office space, training is required to ensure they are presenting the activities in a safe manner and paying attention to all potential hazards.

The authors' earlier text, *Adventure Group Psychotherapy*, (2021) summarizes the need for all adventure therapy practitioners, whether working with groups, families, couples, or individuals to receive specialized training to do adventure therapy. The list of training needs identified includes facilitation skills, knowledge of adventure activities and how to adapt them, as well as safety and risk management. It includes the important task of recognizing issues encountered in the process of therapy and responding in a manner that seizes upon the opportunity for learning that is presented. Specialized technical skills and emergency medical training may also be required depending on the type of activity.

Finally, it is a practitioner's ethical responsibility to practice within their **scope of practice**. Being comfortable rock climbing for recreation is not the same thing as knowing how to safely set a climb and facilitate a participant through it. Outdoor rock climbing is a possibly dangerous activity with required safety equipment and a facilitator who is properly trained as a top rope instructor, having a risk and safety plan and preparing the participant for the experience is different than a practitioner who simply likes to climb.

Due to the understanding of the importance of this training for adventure therapy practitioners, the AEE's TAPG has implemented the **Certified Clinical Adventure Therapist** (CCAT) credentialing. To earn their CCAT, practitioners need to show competence in adventure therapy technical skills, facilitation and processing, organizational and administrative processes, conceptual knowledge, therapeutic alliance building, assessment, understanding of intervention techniques, therapeutic monitoring, documentation, professionalism, and the socio-cultural/environmental considerations in adventure therapy (TAPG, 2024c). In addition, practitioners are required to have 75 hours of instruction on adventure therapy, 2000 hours of supervised mental health experience (300 of which is directly using AT), as well as 50 hours of supervision on the use of adventure therapy (TAPG, 2024a). In addition, the Certified Therapeutic Adventure Specialist (CTAS) was also established in 2023. This certification requires an associate's degree with specialization in adventure therapy or a bachelor's degree. It is intended to provide standardization of training and qualifications for individuals doing therapeutic work with clinical and nonclinical populations (TAPG, 2024b).

These requirements highlight the importance of **training and supervision**. The central role of supervision for practitioners cannot be understated. Supervision is not a new concept and plays a significant role in any clinical training but is central to adventure therapy practice (Alvarez et al., 2021; Gass et al., 2020). Choosing a supervisor who has experience in engaging in adventure therapy practice is ideal. At a minimum, a supervisor must understand a practitioner's work in adventure therapy practice and hold a clinical license in their field. While it might seem overwhelming to find a match, unlike in personal supervision required in most states toward licensure, a practitioner's clinical supervision for the CCAT can be both in person and online, as long as the supervisor meets the requirements for supervision. Hence, there are opportunities for support from other CCAT professionals (see https://www.aee.org/certified-clinical-adventure-therapists). Also, seasoned practitioners understand the importance of the parallel process, in which practitioners engage in the experiences they ask of their participants and should be versed in both trauma-informed and anti-oppressive practices. For this reason, experiential supervision that utilizes activities for exploration of supervisory issues and concepts can be a powerful learning tool (Gass & Gillis, 2010). The aim of the authors is not to scare practitioners and dissuade them from trying adventure therapy techniques with their participants, but to stress the importance of learning new skills in a scaffolded manner, in which to build experience and competence. Ultimately, this protects the practitioner and the participant from harm.

Environmental Stewardship

Adventure therapy often takes place in outdoor environments. It is critical for practitioners to be familiar with the ecology of the places in which they work and to engage with these places in a way that promotes their well-being. Adventure therapy practitioners working in the outdoors should strive to go beyond "avoiding harm" in these spaces and act as stewards that work for the benefit of the natural environment. Ethical adventure therapy practitioners treat nature as a collaborator in the treatment process and promote the well-being of nature as they would any participant in the process of therapy (Harper et al., 2019). This often means educating participants as they engage with natural spaces, building relationships with wildlife, and gaining understanding of the impact of their presence. Hence, in adventure therapy with individuals, the practitioner's role is multi-tiered. **Sustainability efforts and environmental stewardship is enhanced when practitioners educate and role model how to be stewards as well as mentor participants in these areas** (Prince, 2016). Hence, practitioners who engage in nature with participants are responsible for educating participants about the environment in which they are doing the work, as well as role modeling how to show up in those spaces. This can also include an understanding of efforts needed to protect those spaces. Leave No Trace is an educational organization that provides excellent resources and education for practitioners seeking additional information about how to be effective stewards (Leave No Trace, 2025). In addition, organizations like the Sierra Club (https://www.sierraclub.org/) and the Nature Conservancy (https://www.nature.org/en-us/), to name a few, can help practitioners understand current issues on climate and conservation and ways to get involved if interested.

Play, Fun, and Laughter

Finally, when discussing the foundations of adventure therapy practice, it is important to discuss the role of play, fun and laughter in the process. While it is true, if asked to think of words associated with therapy, people would not naturally say it is fun; however, adventure therapy incorporates aspects of play and fun that can bring joy and laughter to the treatment setting (Harper et al., 2019). The activities in which practitioners engage can be playful, practitioners may at times be silly and can invite participants to do the same (Alvarez et al., 2021). Adventure therapy practitioners often hear that what they do is different for multiple reasons, including that therapy can be fun. In fact, laughter reduces stress and the stress hormone, cortisol; increases serotonin and dopamine; and when integrated into therapy, it can be an effective treatment for depression and other mental health challenges (Yim, 2016). Play is also a central need for humans, it is one of the seven basic primary emotional systems of our brain and key to our social and emotional learning (National Institute for Play, 2025). Most importantly, play is not only for children but also important throughout the lifespan (National Institute for Play, 2025); hence **practitioners can role model and normalize the importance of play and fun for participants as a healthy part of one's life**.

Conclusion

The concepts discussed in this chapter are provided as a framework to guide how practitioners approach, think about, and implement the work of adventure therapy. The key to adventure therapy is the intention that is put behind all decisions made by practitioners. Based on this review, there are multiple interacting and complex factors that come into play. This further supports the importance of practitioners seeking out the necessary training and supervision essential to providing ethical and effective care for participants. In Chapter 3, we will unpack the six components of the Facilitated Wave Model (Alvarez et al., 2021).

References

ACEs Aware. (2023). *Health equity*. https://www.acesaware.org/ace-fundamentals/health-equity/

Allan, J. F., McKenna, J., & Hind, K. (2012). Brain resilience: Shedding light into the black box of adventure processes. *Australian Journal of Outdoor Education*, *16*(1), 3–14. https://doi.org/10.1007/BF03400934

Alvarez, T. G., Stauffer, G., Lung, D. M., Sacksteder, K., Beale, B., & Tucker, A. R. (2021). *Adventure group psychotherapy. An experiential approach to treatment*. Routledge.

American Montessori Academy. (2024a). *History of Montessori*. https://amshq.org/About-Montessori/History-of-Montessori

American Montessori Academy. (2024b). *Peace and social justice*. https://amshq.org/Educators/Community/Peace

Anda, R. F., Felitti, V. J., Bremner, J. D., Waler, J. D., Whitfield, C., Perry, B., Dube, S. R., & Giles, W. H. (2006). The enduring effects of abuse and related adverse experiences in childhood. *European Archives of Psychiatry and Clinical Neuroscience*, *256*, 174–186. https://doi.org/10.1007/s00406-005-0624-4

Aponte, H. J. (2022). The soul of therapy: The therapist's use of self in the therapeutic relationship. *Contemporary Family Therapy*, *44*, 136–143. https://doi.org/10.1007/s10591-021-09614-5

Avasthi, A., Grover, S., & Nischal, A. (2022). Ethical and legal issues in psychotherapy. *Indian Journal of Psychiatry*, *64*(Suppl 1), S47–S61. https://doi.org/10.4103/indianjpsychiatry.indianjpsychiatry_50_21

Barendse, M. E. A., Flannery, J., Cavanagh, C., Aristizabal, M., Becker, S. P., Berger, E., Breaux, R., Campione-Barr, N., Church, J. A. et al. (2023). Longitudinal change in adolescent depression and anxiety symptoms from before to during the COVID-19 pandemic. *Journal of Research on Adolescence*, *33*(1), 74–91. https://doi.org/10.1111/jora.12781

Bartlett, A., Faber, S., Williams, M., & Saxberg, K. (2022). Getting to the root of the problem: Supporting clients with lived-experiences of systemic discrimination. *Chronic Stress*, *6*, 24705470221139205. https://doi.org/10.1177/24705470221139205

Bettmann, J. E., Speelman, E., Blumenthal, E., Couch, S., & Schmalz, D. L. (2024). Nature exposure, even as little as 10 minutes, is likely to yield short-term benefits for adults with mental illness. A meta analysis. *Ecopsychology*, *16*(3), 174–190. https://doi.org/10.1089/eco.2023.0063

Bloom, S. L., & Yanosy Sreedhar, S. (2008). The Sanctuary Model of trauma-informed organizational change. *Reclaiming Children and Youth*, *17*(3), 48–53. https://uscart.org/wp-content/uploads/2019/02/17_3_Bloom.pdf

Boyd, F., Allen, C., Robinson, J. M., & Redvers, N. (2023). The past, present, and future of nature and place-based interventions for human health. *Landscape Research*, *49*(1), 129–145. https://doi.org/10.1080/01426397.2023.2244430

Breunig, M. (2019). Beings who are becoming: Enhancing social justice literacy. *Journal of Experiential Education*, *42*(1), 7–21. https://doi.org/10.1177/1053825918820694

Bronfenbrenner, U. (1979). *The ecology of human development*. Harvard University Press.

Brown, D. W., Anda, R. F., Tiemeier, H., Felitti, V. J., Edwards, V. J., Croft, J. B., & Giles, W. H. (2009). Adverse childhood experiences and the risk of premature mortality. *American Journal of Preventive Medicine*, *37*(5), 389–396. https://doi.org/10.1016/j.amepre.2009.06.021

Burke, B. & Harrison, P. (2002). Anti-oppressive practice. In R. Adams, L. Dominelli & M. Payne (Eds), *Anti-oppressive practice* (pp. 227–236). Palgrave MacMillan.

Cherry, K. (2023). *A comprehensive guide to the Bronfenbrenner Ecological Model*. https://www.verywellmind.com/bronfenbrenner-ecological-model-7643403

Cozolino, L. (2010). *The neuroscience of psychotherapy: Healing the social brain* (2nd ed.). W. W. Norton & Co.

Cozolino, L. (2014). *The neuroscience of human relationships: Attachment and the developing social brain* (2nd ed.). W. W. Norton & Co.

Cramer, R. J., & Kapusta, N. D. (2017). A social-ecological framework of theory, assessment, and prevention of suicide. *Frontiers in Psychology*, *8*, 1756. https://doi.org/10.3389/fpsyg.2017.01756

Dettlaff, A. J., & Boyd, R. (2020). Racial disproportionality and disparities in the child welfare system: Why do they exist, and what can be done to address them? *The ANNALS of the American Academy of Political and Social Science*, *692*(1), 253–274. https://doi.org/10.1177/0002716220980329

Development Services Group, Inc. (2022). *Racial and ethnic disparity (R/ED) in juvenile justice processing. Literature review*. Office of Juvenile Justice and Delinquency Prevention. https://ojjdp.ojp.gov/model-programs-guide/literature-reviews/racial-and-ethnic-disparity

Dillenschneider, C. (2007). Integrating persons with impairments and disabilities into standard outdoor adventure education programs. *Journal of Experiential Education*, *30*(1), 70–83. https://doi.org/10.1177/105382590703000106

Dunn, M., Strnadová, I., Scully, J. L., Hansen, J., Loblinzk, J., Sarfaraz, S., Molnar, C., & Palmer, E. E. (2024). Equitable and accessible informed healthcare consent process for people with intellectual disability: A systematic literature review. *BMJ Quality & Safety*, *33*(5), 328–339. https://doi.org/10.1136/bmjqs-2023-016113

Ellis, W. R., & Dietz, W. H. (2017). A new framework for addressing adverse childhood and community experiences. The Building Community Resilience Model. *Academic Pediatrics*, *17*(7), S86–S93. https://doi.org/10.1016/j.acap.2016.12.011

Ellis, W. R., Dietz, W. H., & Chen, K. D. (2022). Community resilience: A dynamic model for public health 3.0. *Journal of Public Health Management and Practice*, *28* (Supplement 1), S18–S26. https://doi.org/10.1097/PHH.0000000000001413

Equal Justice Initiative. (2017). *Lynching in Ameria. Confronting the legacy of racial terror* (3rd ed.). https://lynchinginamerica.eji.org/report/

Felitti, V. J., Anda, R. F., Nordenberg, D., Williamson, D. F., Spitz, A. M., Edwards, V., Koss, M. P., & Marks, J. S. (1998). Relationship of childhood abuse and household dysfunction to many of the leading causes of death in adults: The Adverse Childhood Experience (ACE) study. *American Journal of Preventive Medicine*, *14*(4), 245–258. https://doi.org/10.1016/s0749-3797(98)00017-8

Gaskill, R. L., & Perry, B. D. (2014). The neurobiological power of play. In C. A. Malchiodi & D. A. Crenshaw (Eds.), *Creative arts and play therapy for attachment problems* (pp. 178–194). Guilford Press.

Gass, M. A., & Gillis, H. L. (2010). Clinical supervision in adventure therapy: Enhancing the field through an active experiential model. *Journal of Experiential Education*, *33*(1), 72–89. https://doi.org/10.1177/105382591003300106

Gass, M. A., Gillis, H. L., & Russell, K. C., (2020) *Adventure therapy: Theory, research, and practice* (2nd ed.). Routledge.

Golden, S. D., Earp, J. A. L. (2012). Social ecological approaches to individuals and their contexts: Twenty years of health education & behavior health promotion interventions. *Health Education & Behavior*, *39*(3), 364–372. https://doi.org/10.1177/1090198111418634

Gramlich, J. (2020). *Black imprisonment rate in the U.S. has fallen by a third since 2006*. Pew Research Center. https://www.pewresearch.org/short-reads/2020/05/06/share-of-black-white-hispanic-americans-in-prison-2018-vs-2006/

Hachtel, H., Vogel, T., & Huber, C. G. (2019). Mandated treatment and its impact on therapeutic process and outcome factors. *Frontiers in Psychiatry*, *10*, 219. https://doi.org/10.3389/fpsyt.2019.00219

Harper, N., Rose, K., & Segal, D. (2019). *Nature-based therapy: A practitioner's guide to working outdoors with children, youth and families*. New Society Publishers.

Hebb, D. O. (1949). *The organization of behavior: A neuropsychological theory*. Wiley.

Heiser, M. E. (2021). *The white space of the American outdoors: Race, representation, and public lands*. [Honor's Thesis, University of North Dakota]. https://nchcureca.com/wp-content/uploads/2021/11/The-White-Space-of-the-American-Outdoors_-Race-Representation-and-Public-Lands.docx.pdf

Hoogendoorn, C. (2015, October 15). *The neuroscience of active learning*. https://openlab.citytech.cuny.edu/writingacrossthecurriculum/2015/10/15/the-neuroscience-of-active-learning/
Humphry, N. (2020). *Breaking down the lack of diversity in outdoor spaces*. National Health Foundation. https://nationalhealthfoundation.org/breaking-down-lack-diversity-outdoor-spaces/
James, G., Kidd, K., Cooley, S. J., & Fenton, K. (2021). The feasibility of outdoor psychology sessions in an adult mental health inpatient rehabilitation unit: Service user and psychologist perspectives. *Frontiers in Psychology*, *12*, 769590. https://doi.org/10.3389/fpsyg.2021.769590
Kolb, D. A. (1984). *Experiential Learning: Experience as the source of learning and development*. Prentice Hall.
Leave No Trace. (2025). https://lnt.org/
LeWine, H. E. (2024). *Understanding the stress response: Chronic activation of this survival mechanism impairs health*. https://www.health.harvard.edu/staying-healthy/understanding-the-stress-response#
Liu, S. R., Kia-Keating, M., Nylund-Gibson, K., & Barnett, M. L. (2020). Co-occurring youth profiles of adverse childhood experiences and protective factors: Associations with health, resilience, and racial disparities. *American Journal of Community Psychology*, *65*(1–2), 173–186. https://doi.org/10.1002/ajcp.12387
Mackenzie, S. H., Son, J. S., & Hollenhorst, S. (2014). Unifying psychology and experiential education: Toward an integrated understanding of why it works. *Journal of Experiential Education*, *37*(1), 75–88. https://doi.org/10.1177/1053825913518894
Mann, J., Gray T., Truong, S., Brymer, E., Passy, R., Ho, S., Sahlberg, P., Ward, K., Bentsen, P., Curry, C., & Cowper, R. (2022). Getting out of the classroom and into nature: A systematic review of nature-specific outdoor learning on school children's learning and development. *Frontiers in Public Health*, *10*, 877058. https://doi.org/10.3389/fpubh.2022.877058
Mead, S. (2003). *Defining peer support*. https://mhepinc.org/defining-peer-support/#%20
Mitten, D. (2021). Critical perspectives on outdoor therapy practices. In N. J. Harper & W. W. Dobud (Eds.). *Outdoor therapies: An introduction to practices, possibilities, and critical perspectives* (pp. 175–187). Routledge.
Mullan, J. (2023). *Decolonizing therapy: Oppression, historical trauma, and politicizing your practice*. W. W. Norton & Company.
Nardone, A., Rudolph, K. E., Morello-Frosch, R, & Casey, J. A. (2021). Redlines and greenspace: The Relationship between historical redlining and 2010 greenspace across the United States. *Environmental Health Perspectives*, *129*(1), 017006. https://doi.org/10.1289/EHP7495
National Conference of State Legislatures. (2022). *Racial and ethnic disparities in the justice system*. https://documents.ncsl.org/wwwncsl/Criminal-Justice/Racial-and-Ethnic-Disparities-in-the-Justice-System_v03.pdf
National Institute for Play. (2025). *Scientific disciplines researching play*. https://nifplay.org/play-science/scientific-disciplines-researching-play/
Newes, S., & Bandoroff, S. (2004). What is adventure therapy? In S. Bandoroff & S. Newes (Eds.), *Coming of age: The evolving field of adventure therapy* (pp. 1–30). Association for Experiential Education.
Nordquist, J., BeVard, K., Funnell, A., Pace, S., Sacksteder, K., & Wolf, P. (2023). *Manual of accreditation standards for outdoor behavioral healthcare* (3rd ed.). The Association for Experiential Education.
Norris, P. (2022, August). What does social justice have to do with therapy? Critical conversations in clinical supervision can help reclaim social work's mission. *The New Social Worker*. https://www.socialworker.com/feature-articles/practice/what-about-social-justice-confronting-race-based-trauma/
NYC Outward Bound Schools. (2025). *What is the EL educational* model? https://www.nycoutwardbound.org/el-education/
Office for Civil Rights. US Department of Education. (2023). *Student discipline and school climate in U.S. public schools*. https://www.ed.gov/media/document/crdc-discipline-school-climate-reportpdf-21409.pdf

Ortega, R. M., & Garvin, C. D. (2019). *Socially just practice in groups: A social work perspective*. Sage Publications.

Osborn, P. R., & Karandikar, S. (2022). Practice-based knowledge perspectives of cultural competence in social work. *Journal of Ethnic & Cultural Diversity in Social Work*, *32*(6), 285–297. https://doi.org/10.1080/15313204.2022.2046228

PACEs Connection. (2022). *3 realms of ACEs*. https://www.pacesconnection.com/ws/Handouts_3RealmsACEs_EN.pdf

Perry, B. D. & Dobson, C. (2013) The Neurosequential Model (NMT) in maltreated children. In J. Ford & C. Courtois (Eds.), *Treating complex traumatic stress disorders in children and adolescents* (pp 249–260). Guilford Press.

Porges, S. W. (2011). *The polyvagal theory: Neurophysiological foundations of emotions, attachment, communication, and self-regulation*. W. W. Norton & Co.

Prince, H. E. (2016). Outdoor experiences and sustainability. *Journal of Adventure Education and Outdoor Learning*, *17*(2), 161–171. https://doi.org/10.1080/14729679.2016.1244645

Quay, J., & Seaman, J. (2013). *John Dewey and education outdoors: Making sense of the 'educational situation' through more than a century of progressive reforms*. Sense Publishers.

Radulovic, J., Jovasevic, V., & Meyer, M. A. (2017). Neurobiological mechanisms of state-dependent learning. *Current Opinion in Neurobiology*, *45*, 92–98. https://doi.org/10.1016/j.conb.2017.05.013

Reinert, M. & Nguyen, T. (2021). *Trauma and COVID-19: Communities in need across the U.S.* Mental Health America. https://mhanational.org/sites/default/files/Trauma%20and%20COVID-19.pdf

Riley, K. (2020). Posthumanist and postcolonial possibilities for outdoor experiential education. *The Journal of Experiential Education*, *43*(1) 88–101. https://doi.org/10.1177/1053825919881784

Robinson, J. (2020). John Muir, national parks and civil rights? An interview with Shelton Johnson. *The Statesider*. https://statesider.us/shelton-johnson-john-muir-civil-rights/

Rose, J., & Paisley, K. (2012). White privilege in experiential education: A critical reflection. *Leisure Sciences*, *34*(2), 136–154. https://doi.org/10.1080/01490400.2012.652505

Santomauro, D. F., Mantilla Herrera, A. M., Shadid, J., Zheng, P., Ashbaugh, C., Pigott, D. M., Abbafati, C., Adolph, C., Amlag, J. O., et al. (2021). Global prevalence and burden of depressive and anxiety disorders in 204 countries and territories in 2020 due to the COVID-19 pandemic. *The Lancet*, *308*, 1700–1712. https://doi.org/10.1016/S0140-6736(21)02143-7

Schoel, J., & Maizell, R. S. (2002). *Exploring islands of healing: New perspectives on adventure based counseling*. Project Adventure, Inc.

Shafir, T., Tsachor, R. P., & Welch, K. B. (2016). Emotion regulation through movement: Unique sets of movement characteristics are associated with and enhance basic emotions. *Frontiers in Psychology*, *6*, 2030. https://doi.org/10.3389/fpsyg.2015.02030

Skidmore, K. (2017). *Stealing wisdom: Cultural appropriation and misrepresentation within adventure therapy and outdoor education*. https://www.outdoored.com/articles/stealing-wisdom-cultural-appropriation-and-misrepresentation-within-adventure-therapy-and/

Smith, S. (Ed.). (2021). *Beneficial risks: The evolution of risk management for outdoor and experiential education programs*. Sagamore-Venture Publishing.

Stamm, B.H. (2016). *The secondary effects of helping others: A comprehensive bibliography of 2,017 scholarly publications using the terms compassion fatigue, compassion satisfaction, secondary traumatic stress, vicarious traumatization, vicarious transformation and ProQOL*. https://proqol.org/uploads/CF-CS-VT-ProQOL_Term_References_Posted_1-16-2016.pdf

Substance Abuse and Mental Health Services Administration (SAMHSA. 2014). *SAMHSA's concept of trauma and guidance for a Trauma-Informed Approach*. HHS Publication No. (SMA) 14-4884. Author.

Sunderland, N., Stevens, F., Knudsen, K., Cooper, R., & Wobcke, M. (2023). Trauma aware and anti-oppressive arts-health and community arts practice: Guiding principles for facilitating healing, Health and wellbeing. *Trauma, Violence, & Abuse*, *24*(4), 2429–2447. https://doi.org/10.1177/15248380221097442

Sweeney, A., Filson, B., Kennedy, A., Collinson, L., & Gillard, S. (2018). A paradigm shift: Relationships in trauma-informed mental health services. *BJPsych Advances*, *24*(5), 319–333. https://doi.org/10.1192/bja.2018.29

Therapeutic Adventure Professional Group. Association for Experiential Education. (2024a). *Certified Clinical Adventure Therapist (CCAT) credentialing application overview*. https://assets.noviams.com/novi-file-uploads/aee/pdfs-and-documents/Certifications/Certified_Clinical_Adventure_Therapist__CCAT__Credentialing_Criterial-4bea4bd1.pdf

Therapeutic Adventure Professional Group. Association for Experiential Education. (2024b). *Certified Therapeutic Adventure Specialist credentialing (CTAS) manual*. https://assets.noviams.com/novi-file-uploads/aee/pdfs-and-documents/Certifications/CTAS/AEE_CTAS_Certification_Credentialing_Manual_revised_8-23.pdf

Therapeutic Adventure Professional Group. Association for Experiential Education. (2024c). *Core elements of adventure therapy training*. https://assets.noviams.com/novi-file-uploads/aee/pdfs-and-documents/Certifications/Core_Elements_of_Adventure_Therapy_Training_List.pdf

Therapeutic Adventure Professional Group. Association for Experiential Education. (n.d.). *Best practices: Ethical guidelines for the therapeutic adventure professional*. https://assets.noviams.com/novi-file-uploads/aee/TAPG_Adventure_Therapy_Best_Practices__1_-3905b298.pdf

Todić, J., & Christensen, M. C. (2022). Integrating critical, engaged, and abolitionist pedagogies to advance antiracist social work education. *Advances in Social Work*, *22*(2), 389–415. https://doi.org/10.18060/24972

Townley, C. T., Martinez, M. E., & Clark, B. A. (2024). Outdoor learning at U.S. higher education institutions: A systematic review of research—1996 to 2020. *Sage Open*, *14*(4). https://doi.org/10.1177/21582440241296784

Trevino, A. (2022). Anti-oppressive work is trauma-work: A call for a new perspective when teaching multiculturalism in classrooms. *Psychotherapy Bulletin*, *57*(2), 36–40.

Tucker, A. R. (2009). Adventure-based group therapy to promote social skills in adolescents. *Social Work with Groups*, *32*, 315–329. https://doi.org/10.1080/01609510902874594

Verhoef, R. E. J., Alsem, S. C., Verhulp, E. E., & De Castro, B. O. (2019). Hostile intent attribution and aggressive behavior in children revisited: A meta-analysis. *Child Development*, *90*(5), e525–e547. https://doi.org/10.1111/cdev.13255

Waller, B. Y., Giusto, A., Tepper, M., Legros, N. C., Sweetland, A. C., Taffy, A., & Wainberg, M. L. (2024). Should we trust you? Strategies to improve access to mental healthcare to BIPOC communities during the COVID-19 Pandemic. *Community Mental Health Journal*, *60*(1), 82–86. https://doi.org/10.1007/s10597-023-01124-y

Warren, K. (2019). Reflections on social justice in experiential education: Expanding the dialogue. *Journal of Experiential Education*, *42*(1), 3–6. https://doi.org/10.1177/1053825918823680

Warren, K., Roberts, N. S., Breunig, M., & Alvarez, M. A. (2014). Social justice in outdoor experiential education: A state of knowledge review. *Journal of Experiential Education*, *37*(1), 89–103. https://doi.org/10.1177/1053825913518898

Wilkins, N., Tsao, B., Hertz, M., Davis, R., Klevens, J. (2014). *Connecting the dots: An overview of the links among multiple forms of violence*. National Center for Injury Prevention and Control, Centers for Disease Control and Prevention, Prevention Institute. https://www.cdc.gov/violence-prevention/about/connecting_the_dots-a.pdf

Yim, J. (2016). Therapeutic benefits of laughter in mental health: A theoretical review. *The Tohoku Journal of Experimental Medicine*, *239*(3), 243–249. https://doi.org/10.1620/tjem.239.243

Chapter 3

Overview of the Facilitated Wave Model

Talk about wild experiences! Two of the authors, Tony and Gary, landed a gig at the University of Hawai'i' teaching a class and doing some training on the use of the adventure therapy model of Social Work practice. It was quite literally a dream come true.

The two authors could not have had more different backgrounds. Tony grew up in the Philippines, routinely swimming in the ocean, and was accustomed to both the tropics and island living. He felt at home in Hawai'i. Gary grew up on a farm in the Midwest of the United States and had never even seen the ocean until his mid-20s. He had swum in the calm waters and collected seashells on the Florida side of the Gulf of Mexico, but that was the sum total of his ocean-water experience.

The sun was shining, and it was 82 degrees on Oahu on the day after the training. In addition to the beautiful weather, word on the island was that the waves were high on the north shore. The two authors joined what seemed like half of the island's population and made the journey. Traffic was backed up on the road parallel to the shore, prompting them to stop short of their destination at a cove known as Wai'le'e Beach Park. The waves fascinated as they crashed into shore. Tony waded in up to his ankles and soaked it in. Gary entered the water and discovered that he was more than able to brace himself and easily withstand the force of the ocean waves.

Familiar with the power of the ocean, Tony sounded alarms: "Be careful, Gary"; "don't go too far, Gary"; "Gary, I'm getting worried!" The Midwesterner slowed his pace and stopped, about waist deep, but clearly did not understand the gravity of Tony's concern.

"I'm fine, Tony. I just brace myself before the wave comes". Gary knew to brace for the waves as they came in but had no experience with the fact that these waves traveled forcefully in both directions!

After successfully absorbing the hit from a large wave that crashed into the shore, Gary was taken down as it forcefully traveled back out toward the horizon. He tumbled over the first set of rocks and scraped his body on the second as the sea had its way with him. Gary was fortunate that Tony had slowed his progress and was able to scramble up between waves and hurry over the rocks to the safety of the beach and the welcoming aura of his Filipino friend. Bloody knees and a scratched torso were the souvenirs of that experience, along with some memorable life lessons.

What were those lessons, beyond that the ocean is more powerful than he thought? The first was that the very same event – an afternoon at Wai'le'e Beach Park – was not the same experience for Gary as it was for Tony. The differences in their previous life experiences gave them different perceptions, thoughts, attitudes, and expectations about waves. These different starting points, or **Point A's**, turned the same event into a different experience for each of them.

DOI: 10.4324/9781003457893-3

The second lesson was a confirmation that an experience is an entire process. To define this experience as simply a stop at the beach would be completely inadequate. It would not only leave out the disparity in Point A's but also gloss over the environmental factors at play. The experience wasn't just a stop at the beach. It was a stop at the beach when the beauty of the weather seduced them into the water, when the power of the waves filled their ears and minds, when the camaraderie of two life-long friends palpably filled the air. In that environment, Gary believed that only good things could happen. Tony was equally seduced by the magic of the environment. Fortunately, his response also included a greater appreciation for the power of the natural forces.

As the pair left Wai'le'e Beach Park behind, they reflected on what had just happened. Gary dwelled on his shock about waves "being able to get you on the way out", to which Tony repeatedly replied, "Really?" incredulous to Gary's naivete. The two tried to learn as much as possible about what increasingly felt like a life-threatening experience.

Even after leaving Hawai'i, the two authors would continue to reflect on this moment, working to understand how one's life experiences might integrate into the clinical work they were doing, both for themselves as practitioners and for their participants. Their first understanding of the components of life experience are shown in Figure 3.1.

The authors knew that understanding the process of normal life experiences could lead to harnessing that power in clinical sessions. They had learned that everyone enters an experience with their unique **Point A**. These internal factors make every experience distinctive to the individual. That part was made abundantly clear at Wai'e'le Beach!

Equally significant is the **environment** that surrounds the experience. What can be accomplished through every experience is greatly influenced by external factors, such as the things Tony and Gary learned while on that beach. The relationships with others present, the norms and expectations in the setting, and the physical setting were all powerful actors in that drama. It is only after considering the impact of all these environmental factors that what is actually happening during the experience, the event, is taken into account. And finally, the individual's **response** to the experience is significant to understanding the nature of each experience.

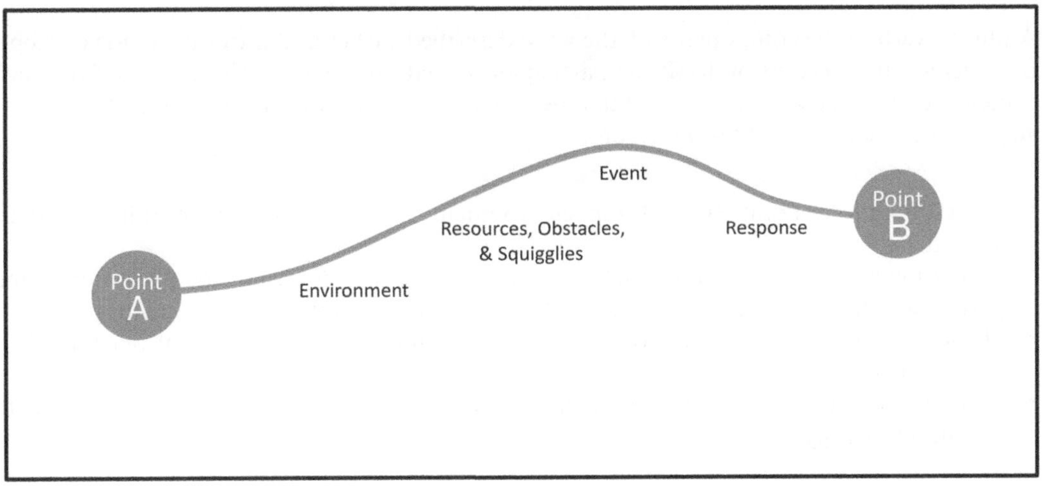

Figure 3.1 The experiential wave.

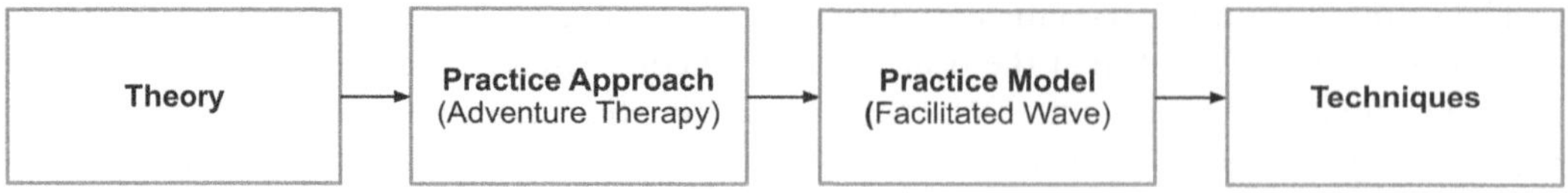

Figure 3.2 Progression from theory to techniques.

The authors propose that all life experiences occur according to the process described earlier. With that perspective, the logical response for anyone seeking to engage in an experiential form of therapy is to ask, "How can practitioners duplicate that process to make interventions as true to life as possible?" What model for practice can provide a clear vision for how to offer experience as a means of change?

The remainder of this book is dedicated to describing how this practice model, the Facilitated Wave, applies to doing individual psychotherapy using the adventure therapy practice approach. As elaborated in Chapter 1, individual adventure practitioners approach their work with a variety of theoretical foundations (cognitive behavioral, narrative, solution focused, psychodynamic, etc.) that offer a basic understanding of the nature of the clinical problems and what is required for the process of change. All these theories are compatible with the Facilitated Wave Model for practice described in this book. This model provides a clear vision of the entire treatment process and a structure for how the practitioner can effectively assist participants.

The concept for how one's theoretical foundation and approach to practice relate to one another is illustrated in the chart in Figure 3.2. **While this book does not teach practitioners about clinical theories, it does focus on outlining the last three steps in this process**. The authors assume that practitioners will have already been educated on clinical practice and the theories that guide them (see Figure 3.2).

What Is the Facilitated Wave Model?

Adding a verb to the components of the wave described earlier and introducing the concepts of *matching* an intervention to fit the participant's needs and *guiding* the learning from each experience turns the wave into a tool that describes the process of adventure facilitation. The steps in the model of facilitation become:

- **Assess** Point A, Point B, and the environment, that is, complete a full diagnostic assessment.
- **Match** the assessment with a timely and appropriate plan for what the practitioner and participant do during each session, which includes application of the treatment plan.
- **Shape** a treatment environment that gives the participant the best chance of reaching their treatment goals (Point B).
- **Facilitate** the intervention(s), using clinical interviewing skills, as well as skills specific to adventure therapy.

- **Guide** the participant's learning in ways that help participants reflect on the meaning of experiences in the therapy session and move forward in the process of change.
- **Evaluate** the clinical process.

Figure 3.3 illustrates the six components of the Facilitated Wave Model (Alvarez et al., 2021). This model will be used throughout the book to describe the process of Individual Adventure Psychotherapy.

To summarize the previous diagram, individual practitioners are called upon to **Assess the participant's Point A**. That is, to pull together all the relevant information about the participant's past experiences, cultural and ancestral backgrounds, occupational or school status, social identities, current family, friend, and work relationships – everything internal to the participant that they bring with them into the therapy experience.

It is equally important to assess the impact and/or the potential impact of the environment on the participant's Point A, as well as the clarity about what they hope to gain from involvement in the therapy, that is, their **Point B** for seeking assistance.

The diagnostic assessment directs the practitioner in the process of **Matching Interventions** that fit the participant's needs. Practitioners match interventions to shape the treatment environment that will be the most conducive for the participant to reach their treatment goals, as well as what primary interventions are the best suited to move the treatment process forward. This process includes what is commonly thought of as treatment planning.

Adventure therapy is distinctive in the emphasis placed on **Shaping the Treatment Environment**. The entire culture of the therapeutic experience, including the development of the therapeutic relationship, the impact of the physical setting, the level of participant engagement in the process, and the acceptance of the necessary beliefs as norms for how the work will be accomplished are all attended to and acted upon by the practitioner.

During the **Facilitate the Experience** phase of the Facilitated Wave, practitioners engage in the process of introducing the intervention, leading it, and guiding or processing the participant's responses. To add somewhat to the complexity, the process of **Guiding the Learning** is ongoing

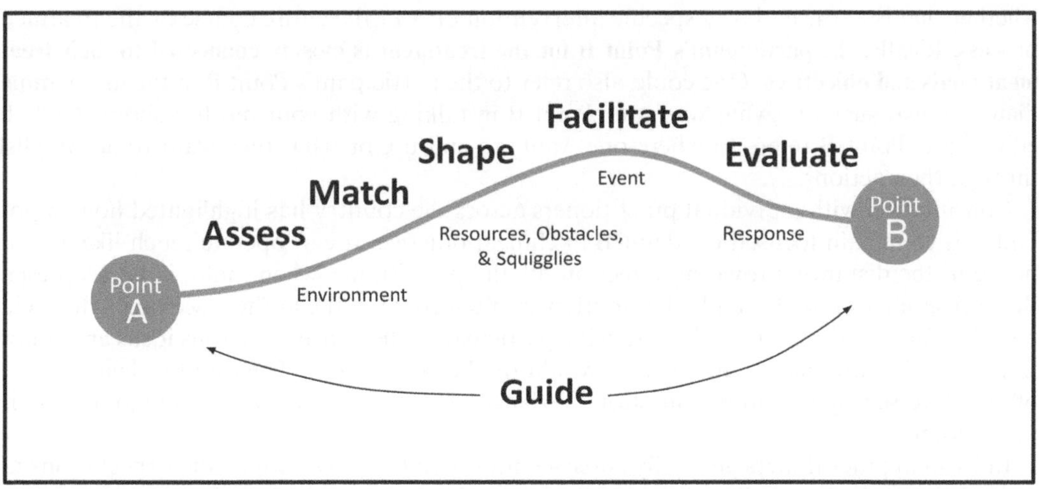

Figure 3.3 The facilitated wave overview.

throughout the entire experience. Practitioners guide participants in various ways of reflecting on the whole process from beginning to end, in many cases as the experience is happening.

Finally, effective clinical practice, as well as practitioner reflection and self-care, requires practitioners to **Evaluate the Process** that occurs during every session. Most often, this is an organic, informal practice of reflection that touches on the major points of the Facilitated Wave after each session. This will both improve the likelihood of intended Point B for the participant and improve the practitioner's skill and resilience in the long run. That practice starts by evaluating whether the assessment of Point A and the environment was effective. It continues by asking if efforts to shape the treatment environment were sufficient and whether the choices made to match the interventions used in the session were optimal. This process includes considering how well the activities were facilitated and if every opportunity to guide the participant in making meaning of their experiences was seized and pursued. Working through this sort of personal evaluation of what happened during each session is an invaluable habit for practitioners to develop. Other evaluation approaches include routinely engaging participants in a discussion of how they think the therapy is progressing. More formal evaluation can include surveys, interviews, or focus groups to gather information that can be used both in the moment for treatment but also for program evaluation, grants, or other more formal program reporting needs.

Understanding Point A and Point B

It is often helpful for participants to take a broad view of where they are in the treatment process. This perspective-taking opportunity includes both a review of where they were at the start of therapy, their Point A, as well as what they hope to accomplish in treatment, their Point B. Having this broad view is helpful to developing and adapting a treatment plan with the participant.

Depending on context, Point A could be referring to the participant's functioning in the immediate moment or to how they were functioning months ago when the treatment started. Similarly, Point B refers to where the participant and/or the practitioner want to end up, whether that is at the end of a specific intervention or over the entire course of the treatment process. Ideally, **the participant's Point B for the treatment is closely connected to their treatment goals and objectives**. One could also refer to the participant's Point B in the more immediate context, such as "what was your Point B in talking with your mother about that?" In either case, Point B refers to where one wants to end up, or what they want to accomplish through their actions.

Consultation with individual practitioners across the country has highlighted how important it is to remain focused on Point B in clinical practice. It can operate much like a lighthouse in the distance, providing direction for the practitioner when multiple issues present themselves all at once. Individual practitioners often come to the authors seeking help deciding what intervention to use with a specific participant. They have numerous ideas about how to proceed but are unsure about what would be the best option. Their ambivalence is most often addressed by the simple question, "What is your Point B, or desired outcome, for the next session?"

Individual practitioners generally enter sessions with their own hopes and expectations for what their participants will gain, including the influence of ethical guidelines in their practice. This concept, referred to as the practitioner's "**Universal Point B's**", is strongly influenced by the writing of Richard Schultz who defines similar concepts as one's true "Self" (Schultz, 2021).

The Universal Point B's that practitioners have for their participants and bring into the treatment environment include the following:

- Compassion
- Hope
- Meta-perspective
- Authenticity
- Anti-oppression

Change is often made possible by the impact of a response by the practitioner that highlights one of these principles. For example, one of the authors recalls working with an adult participant who was furious with her mother for not intervening and stopping the aggressive behavior of her father. During the middle phase of treatment, a version of an **Unsighted Walk** through an area of obstacles was set up in the clinical office (see Appendix 1). When it was the practitioner's turn to be unsighted and follow the participant's directions toward safety on the other side of the obstacles, the participant inadvertently led the practitioner into the obstacles multiple times. Agreed upon consequences for this result required the practitioner to return to the starting point and begin again, only to be led into another one of the obstacles. The participant was profusely apologetic after every failed attempt. As the practitioner explored her responses of getting increasingly anxious and agitated with every round, she stated that she thought the practitioner must be getting so irritated by her blunders.

This participant's response and corresponding intervention was remarkable. "I'm fine with how this is going. My biggest concern is how hard this is for you", was the practitioner's expression of compassion and understanding. The remarkable part is that the participant burst into tears and expressions of gratitude to the practitioner for "being so kind". In the exploration that followed, "being kind" was defined as an expression of **compassion** for the participant. It didn't excuse her responsibility for leading the practitioner "into trouble"; it merely recognized that circumstances were mounting up and making each successive attempt more difficult for her.

As she described how feeling overwhelmed led her to miss "obvious things" that could have helped, a parallel process was uncovered between her responses in the experiential intervention and what she imagined her mother may have experienced. Experiencing the practitioner's compassion for her was the catalyst for the participant making expressions of compassion toward her mother, who was now seen in a parallel process of being overwhelmed and perhaps being unable to respond to "obvious things". The participant was able to see that having compassion for the difficulty of her mother's situation did not reduce her mother's responsibility for not being more protective. At the same time, having compassion for her mother's situation was a first step in releasing the participant from the perpetual anger and blame that she previously experienced.

A second clinical example clarifies how the practitioner's desire for the participant to develop a **meta-perspective** influences practice. This goal refers to the practitioner's desire for the participant to develop the ability to see the big picture of their problems and the world as opposed to being stuck in the limiting perspective of their current life problems or circumstances. As participants achieve mastery related to their presenting problems, those problems have less and less control over their everyday experience. This process naturally results in the participant "seeing things differently" and being able to respond to stimuli in their environment differently. The example is provided next:

> A participant, Jane, came to treatment due to burnout from her profession as a hospital nurse, difficulty dealing with her 13-year-old daughter as a single parent, and a general sense of being overwhelmed with her life. In the middle phase of treatment (session 6), the practitioner introduced a version of **Junk in the Middle** (see Appendix 1). This intervention involved the practitioner tossing a bucket full of objects in the air (approximately 30 stuffed animals) and tasking the participant with catching as many of the objects as possible. The following process recording illustrates how this experience helped the participant look at things with a meta-perspective:

P: *(practitioner)*: On the count of three, I am going to toss this entire bucket full of objects over your head. Your task is to catch as many as you possibly can. Are you ready?
J: I guess as ready as I'll ever be.
The practitioner threw the objects. J screamed and literally jumped up and down, dropping several objects and ended up just standing in the circle looking at her empty hands.
P: Ahh, you came up empty-handed. What do you make of that?
J: I can be such a spaz! I had a couple of them but let them go to catch others, that was stupid.
P: So, you think you were the problem. Is that what you are saying?
J: Well, the fact that there are so many things to focus on was a problem too.
P: So, what do you think is the main problem: you "being a spaz" or this system of throwing too many things at you at once?
J: It's how I feel at work too. There are so many things to do all at once that I get rattled and don't do anything well.
P: And the friends you have talked about. Are they able to catch everything that is thrown at them at work?
J: Well no. We all talk about being frustrated and annoyed that we don't have time to spend on individual patients.
P: Interesting. And I wonder if how you responded here with negative self-talk that blamed yourself for not catching more objects is similar to how you respond at work when the same thing happens.
J: I think it is. I feel horrible and think I need to work harder, but that always comes up short, and I feel even worse.
P: So, no matter how hard you work, you end up feeling terrible.
J: Yes, like I am going to get into trouble or disciplined for not doing more.
P: And, you aren't the only one who feels that way, right?
J: No, I am not. That makes me wonder if this problem isn't really about how good I am at the job. Maybe there is something wrong with the job!

The other four Universal Point Bs are equally important to practice. Valuing the installation of hope and incorporating a sense of peace related to one's capacity to deal with the issues they bring to therapy are also things practitioners want for their participants. In Chapter 4, the need for anti-oppressive practice as well as the importance for authenticity will be further explored.

There is one extremely important caveat to this concept of the practitioner bringing their own goals for participants into the treatment setting. Their presence must be thoroughly understood by the practitioner. **Without self-awareness, there is a high probability that the practitioner will at some point blur the distinction between their wishes and those of the participant.** When this happens, the practitioner's connection with the participant is damaged, and the potential for missteps by the practitioner is greatly increased. This further highlights the importance of ongoing critical self-reflection and supervision for practitioners to minimize these risks.

Assess Point A, Point B, and the Conditions in the Treatment Environment

The Facilitated Wave Model consistently refers to what the participant brings into the session as their Point A. It includes all the things internal to the participant that impact how they interact with the world, including mood, attitude, thoughts, previous life experiences, and their intersectionality. Best practices in individual psychotherapy all begin with the practitioner assessing these factors.

Part of the assessment task for individual practitioners is to integrate all of the external information related to the participant (previous intake assessments, psychological reports, social histories, school and/or job performance reports, court records, just to name a few) with how the participant presents in the here and now. A thorough diagnostic assessment integrates these two bodies of information.

How the participant responds in the moment, or in the here and now, is referred to as their **current experiential functioning (CEF)**. One's assessment takes on a fresh dynamic when informed by seeing first-hand how the participant functions in the here and now of experiential interventions. This rich opportunity to add observation of the participant's CEF to the diagnostic understanding is a powerful aspect of the adventure therapy practice approach.

An additional component of assessment in the practice of adventure therapy involves attention to the treatment environment. Vigilant and continual assessment of the conditions currently operating within the treatment setting is required to choose appropriate interventions and to fully understand what can be accomplished through mutual efforts with participants.

The final outcome of assessment in adventure therapy is the creation of **a case conceptualization** that includes identification of the primary issues to be addressed in treatment, an understanding or rationale for what is contributing or has contributed to those issues, and a plan for how to achieve the desired outcomes (Point B's).

Match Interventions

An essential task for the individual practitioner is linking assessment to intervention in a manner intended to move participants forward in meeting their clinical goals. It results in a planful and intentional process in which the diagnostic assessment of the participant and of the current environmental conditions are taken into consideration in designing interventions to address the clinical needs and goals of the participant. **Essentially, the practitioner chooses interventions that are a good fit to the participant's clinical needs**. Matching is where the participant's treatment plan comes to life as assessment and intervention meet.

The steps the individual practitioner uses in daily practice to choose interventions that are a good fit with the participant's clinical needs, as described in the case conceptualization, includes applying the following concepts (described in detail in Chapter 6):

- Sequencing the intervention
- Scaffolding the intervention
- Selecting the intervention
- Customizing the intervention

Shape the Treatment Environment

Shaping the physical, social, cultural and emotional treatment environment to allow for change and growth in the participant is arguably the most important step in the process of treatment. Regardless of one's theoretical approach or skill level in facilitating participant change, **what can be accomplished in any treatment setting is defined by the environment that exists**. If a participant does not feel safe or has negative feelings toward the practitioner, for example, what can be accomplished is limited. On the other hand, when participants feel a sense of safety and belonging in the session and experience a generally positive regard for the practitioner, optimal progress toward clinical goals is possible.

Efforts to establish a desired treatment environment always relate to four factors:

- Establishing a **therapeutic relationship** with the participant that includes both a positive regard between the participant and practitioner and an agreement regarding what they will work on together, also known as the treatment alliance.
- Supporting an **authentic engagement** of the participant in the treatment goals.
- Monitoring the **physical setting** to ensure it is supportive of positive movement toward the treatment goals.
- Developing a set of **beliefs** as both the culture of the treatment sessions and the guide for appropriate behavior. Cultivating these beliefs within the treatment setting establishes the optimum conditions for growth to occur.

In the Facilitated Wave Model, the authors define **seven adventure beliefs** that support the development of the optimal conditions for growth and change for participants. They are listed next. Naming environmental conditions necessary for change is not unique to adventure therapy (see Glasser, 1999; Brendtro et al., 2009: Yalom & Leszcz, 2020). However, the way in which adventure practitioners attend to these beliefs as they seek to shape the treatment environment with their words, actions, and interventions is a distinguishing feature. More discussion of the relevance of the beliefs to the practice of individual adventure therapy can be found in Chapter 7.

- Safety
- Trust
- Belonging
- Freedom
- Challenge
- Effective Communication
- Enjoyment or Fun

The authors' experiences leading individual adventure therapy interventions suggest that while less time and effort goes into establishing and maintaining the adventure beliefs in individual treatment than other practice methods, they are no less central to effective practice.

The environmental factor that seems to require the most time and attention in individual work is the treatment relationship. Maintaining positive regard between participant and practitioner, while maintaining appropriate boundaries, is an ongoing task. Equally salient to successful treatment is the collaboration required to establish a clear treatment alliance, sometimes referred to as a treatment contract, identifying what the participant and practitioner will focus on accomplishing during the sessions.

Maintaining the participant's **authentic engagement** in working toward the clinical goals and monitoring the **physical setting** to ensure it supports the participant's work to achieve their goals are the final two components of establishing an effective treatment environment. Failure to attend to either of these factors can have a negative impact on treatment outcomes.

These seven beliefs are foundational for developing an effective treatment environment. Working collaboratively with participants to establish a treatment environment is an integral part of the adventure therapy practice approach. These are the conditions that define the culture of the treatment environment and the norms for practitioner-participant interaction. As such, efforts made to share and establish the beliefs go a long way toward shaping a treatment environment that will give the participant the best chance of reaching their goals.

These conditions for growth are similar to Yalom's curative factors (Yalom & Leszcz, 2020) as well as the five basic needs that are central to Glasser's choice theory (Glasser, 1999). Significantly, they also align closely with SAMHSA's Trauma-Informed Care (TIC) principles (SAMHSA, 2014). This alignment highlights how the practice of adventure therapy is naturally suited for work with survivors of trauma (see Table 3.1).

The nature of clinical practice is that the adventure beliefs, as well as the TIC principles, build upon one another and are not realized in a strictly linear fashion. For example, as conditions of safety are developed, gains will also be made in establishing trust.

Since there are no peers to offer support in individual treatment, the role of the practitioner engaging in shared experiences becomes especially important. For example, it is through sharing experiences with the participant that adventure practitioners work to establish collaboration and mutuality, as well as a sense of belonging and freedom within the treatment environment that values the voice and choice of each participant.

Table 3.1 Alignment of Seven Adventure Beliefs and TIC

The Adventure Beliefs	*SAMHSA TIC Principles Model*
• Safety • Challenge • Trust • Freedom • Belonging • Communication • Enjoyment	• Safety • Trustworthiness and Transparency • Collaboration and Mutuality • Empowerment, Voice, and Choice • Peer Support • Considerations for Cultural, Historical, and Gender Issues

Facilitate the Experience

This phase of the Facilitated Wave Model refers to what the practitioner does in the moment to move the clinical process forward. Chapter 8 is dedicated to this phase of the Facilitated Wave and describes the following issues:

- The typical session structure employed by adventure practitioners
- The common clinical skills for doing adventure, such as how to introduce or brief interventions, to lead experiences with the participant, and to process the material that is presented by the participant during activities
- A variety of skills needed to manage clinical issues, such as resistance, relationship ruptures, and the use of metaphorical interventions

Guide the Learning

Guiding the Learning refers to actions the practitioner takes within every phase of the wave to help participants make meaning from their responses in the clinical session. These actions vary greatly, depending on one's assessment of the participant and the environment that exists for their treatment sessions. The tool chosen for this purpose might be asking the participant to take an action, such as to move to a space that most clearly describes how they are feeling, to make a different non-verbal expression through art or written communication, to engage in a mindfulness activity, or to respond verbally to interventions intended to assist the participant in talking about what happened and how it is significant to them, just to name a few of the options.

To fully understand this phase of the Facilitated Wave, practitioners need to consider the following issues related to successfully facilitating attempts to guide the learning of participants:

- training and supervision
- practitioner resources
- clinical mindset

Practitioner resources and clinical mindset of an adventure practitioner are fully discussed in Chapter 4, while training and supervision are discussed throughout this book.

Evaluate the Process

The two primary roles of the practitioner in this phase of the Facilitated Wave are **to evaluate participant progress toward clinical goals (Point B's) and to review the effectiveness of their own facilitation.** It is important for practitioners to invite participants to participate in this process by offering the opportunity for them to share their perspective on both the progress they are making toward the clinical goals and the effectiveness of the facilitation (Figure 3.4).

A Word About Squigglies

In the vernacular of the Facilitated Wave, a squiggly is something that shifts the focus of the participant from working toward the intended clinical goal to attending to something else currently in the here and now environment. Many practitioners who do sessions in the

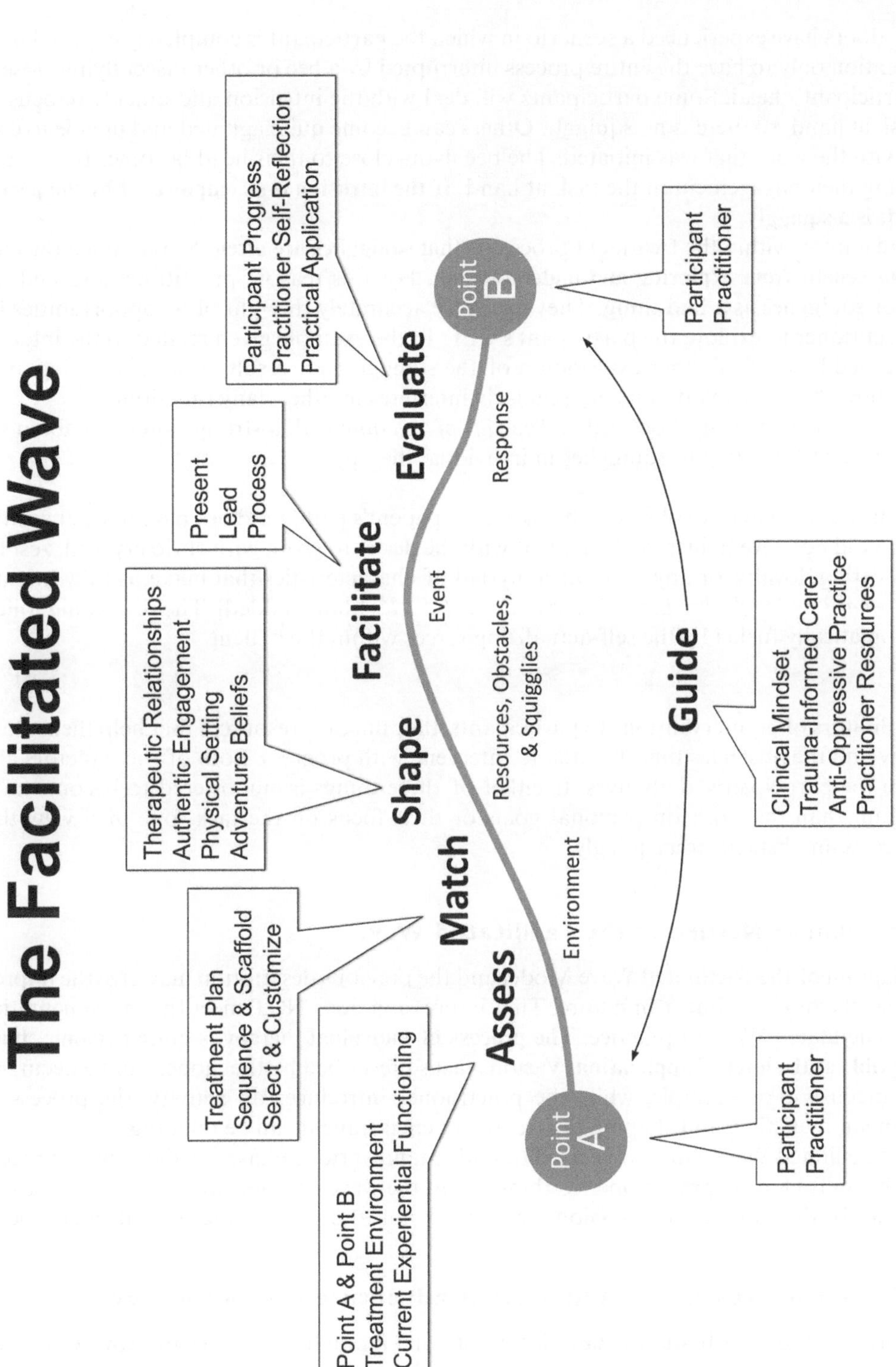

Figure 3.4 The faciliated wave model in depth.

out-of-doors have experienced a scenario in which the participant is completely engaged in an intervention only to have the entire process interrupted by a bee or other insect flying close to the participant's head. Some participants will deal with the intrusion and quickly refocus on the task at hand, so there is no squiggly. Others can become quite agitated and unable to continue with the work that was initiated. The bee flying close to their head becomes their focus, replacing their engagement in the task at hand. **If the intrusion is so empowered by the participant, it is a squiggly**.

A great irony within the treatment process is that **squigglies are often the very thing the therapy can benefit from exploring and understanding**. For this reason, practitioners should not think of squigglies as a bad thing. They are more accurately thought of as opportunities for the practitioner to explore the participant's CEF. In the example given related to the interference caused by a bee, further exploration of the squiggly may result in understanding more clearly how the participant's anxiety regularly interferes in other daily functioning.

Yalom (2017) opens his book titled *The Gift of Therapy* with a strong statement about the importance of attending to squigglies in individual therapy:

> My task was to remove obstacles blocking my patient's path. I did not have to do the entire job; I did not have to inspire the patient with the desire to grow, with curiosity, will, zest for life, caring, loyalty, or any other of a myriad of characteristics that make us fully human. *No, what I had to do was identify and remove obstacles* [italics added]. The rest would follow automatically fueled by the self-actualizing forces within the patient.
>
> (p. 1)

As facilitators offer interventions to participants, they uncover resources that help them along the way and the obstacles that threaten to intervene with progress. Both of these factors also arise in the participants' daily lives. If either of these things is empowered to become more important than the work on personal goals or their focus on the task, one may view that resource as an obstacle or a squiggly.

The Nonlinear Nature of the Facilitated Wave

The diagram of the Facilitated Wave Model and the previous description may give the impression that the model is linear in nature. That impression does NOT meet the implementation of the Facilitated Wave in practice. **The process of individual therapy is quite dynamic, fluid, and flexible at the level of application**. Various tasks prescribed by the model can be occurring simultaneously. For example, while the practitioner introduces an activity, the process of assessment, matching, and shaping the treatment environment can be ongoing.

The Facilitated Wave can also be used to understand various phases of the clinical process. It can be useful for the practitioner to think about the wave components for a single activity, as well as for the entire clinical session, or for the whole duration of the clinical engagement.

The Phases of Treatment in Individual Adventure Psychotherapy

In several parts of this book, the description of what a practitioner does to provide effective adventure therapy is broken into three stages of the treatment: the beginning, middle, and end, illustrated in Figure 3.5.

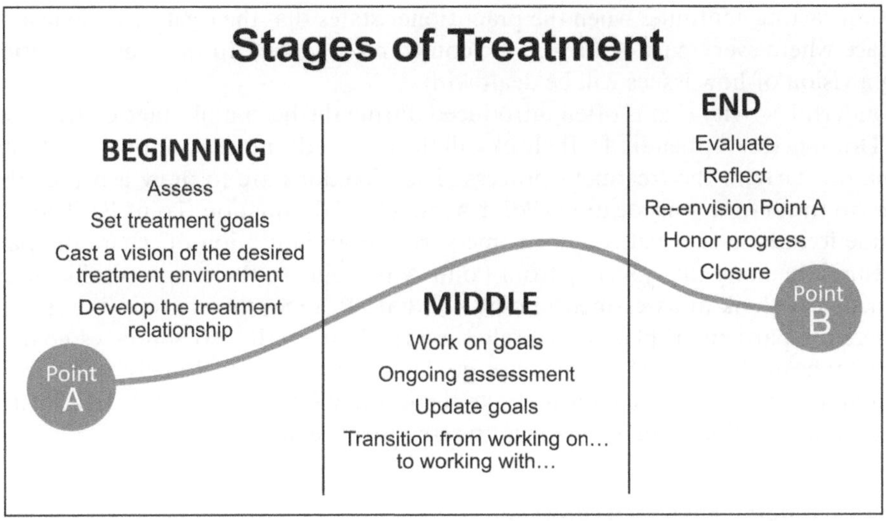

Figure 3.5 Actions across the stages of treatment.

During the Beginning Phase of Treatment

In general, there are four things that practitioners focus on in the beginning phase of treatment:

- Assessing
- Developing clear treatment goals
- Casting a vision of the desired treatment environment
- Developing the treatment environment

It is not coincidental that attending to these factors has benefits in developing the core elements of a treatment environment, as well. The process of assessment, developing clear treatment goals, and casting a vision requires the practitioner to listen attentively, share their understanding of what the participant has brought into the session, and engage mutually with the participant in the activities. This interaction with the participant models what is required to build the four core elements of the treatment environment.

The task of clarifying the treatment goals is not as straightforward as it appears. What participants share as their presenting problem over the phone or through an email is often different from what gets expressed as they engage in experiences with the practitioner. It is possible, for example, for a participant who sought therapy due to dissatisfaction in their primary relationship in life to refine their goal from changes in their primary relationship to a more general desire of "being heard and valued in relationships" after engaging actively in experiential interventions with the practitioner.

The task of casting the vision for what type of environment is needed to achieve the treatment goals is a huge part of how the practitioner ascribes meaning to the adventure therapy practice approach. For example, a vision is being cast about how the practitioner plans to operate when they state that the treatment session will be different from the usual social environments, that it will be a safe place where the participant can share freely and openly about themselves.

The vision casting continues when the practitioner states that the treatment environment will be a space where every part of them is welcome and accepted. In this way, practitioners are casting a vision of how issues will be dealt with.

A wonderful activity that is often introduced during the beginning stage of treatment is the **Bridge Drawing** (see Appendix 1). It checks all the boxes adventure therapy practitioners want to check off early in the treatment process. The directions are to draw a bridge that has a pathway to travel from one location (Point A) to a final destination (Point B). The bridge has to include foundations, a pathway of some sort and an indication of where the participant sees themselves along that journey from Point A to Point B. Reflection on this intervention often includes a look at assessment: Point A, what resources they have in life (foundations) and where the participant places themselves on the journey. It also addresses goals: Point B and how far away the participant perceives goal achievement to be. Finally, reflection on what will be required for the participant to make the journey falls directly at the feet of the vision the practitioner is attempting to shape in the treatment sessions.

During the Middle Phase of Treatment

It is extremely important for the practitioner not to take their eyes off the importance of nurturing the treatment environment as the treatment enters the middle phase. Many things were established in the beginning phase: The practitioner's vision for the optimal environmental conditions has been communicated and embraced; treatment goals have been set and become the primary focus of each session; the therapeutic relationship has been established to include a mutual positive regard; and agreement or alliance about working together to achieve the goals that have been established. While all this has become a reality in the treatment sessions, it still needs to be refreshed, adjusted, and in some cases, expanded upon as participants begin to work diligently on what brought them into treatment.

The primary foci of the middle stage of treatment are as follows:

- Work on goals
- Ongoing assessment
- Update goals
- Transition from working on to working with

When the objectives for the beginning stage of treatment have been established "well enough" that the participant is free to begin working directly on their treatment goals, the middle stage of treatment begins. **The shared understanding of the treatment goals and what the next steps are allows practitioners to facilitate a shift from "working on" the treatment environment into "working with" the participant** on the difficult next steps required to achieve the treatment goals. To the extent possible, participants work with the practitioner to co-monitor issues related to the treatment environment and to collaborate on what actions need to be taken to address any part of the treatment environment identified as needing work.

During the End Phase of Treatment

The primary objective in this stage of treatment is to review what occurred in the treatment. Some general tasks that will help accomplish this objective include creating opportunities for feedback on the strengths they demonstrated during the treatment process and reflecting on both the successful and unsuccessful attempts to move toward change.

The end stage of individual treatment is marked by a focus on these issues:

- Evaluation
- Reflection
- Honoring Progress
- Re-envisioning Point A
- Closure

The end phase of treatment provides an opportunity for reflection, closure, re-envisioning Point A and evaluation all while honoring the participant's progress. Intentional efforts to help the participant reflect on each of the environmental components that assisted their progress and consider how those factors can be replicated in their life after treatment are valuable to both closure and evaluation of the treatment.

Looking at what can be expected in the future for the participant can also be a useful topic. Reflection on what they need to continue working on, how they can respond to challenges that may arise, and offering ways to increase the influence of the lessons learned are typical ways the practitioner can help the participant transition out of the treatment.

Case Example: Jane

Jane, who was also featured in the case example earlier in this chapter, requested treatment for help managing her 13-year-old daughter, high work-related stress, and feeling overwhelmed with her life. She was a single parent who identified as a heterosexual, cisgendered female from a family strongly connected to their Dutch heritage. Grandparents on both sides of her family immigrated to the United States from the Netherlands. Her immediate family internalized a value for hard work that was demonstrated in their truck farming business, which Jane participated in on a six-day per week schedule as a child. They also held to rigid religious beliefs and harsh behavioral expectations for all of their four children.

The initial session with Jane was quite remarkable. She spoke rapidly and seemed to be in constant motion. In an initial activity that involved crossing from one side of the room to the other as an expression of her personal preferences (**Continuums**, see Appendix 1), she literally started moving rapidly to her preferred side of the room, even before the practitioner stopped talking. When the practitioner noted the apparent contradiction from how she acted in the activity and what she said previously about being exhausted, she merely smiled and said, "That's my life!"

When asked to talk more about how this contradiction shows up in her life, she reported having high adrenaline during work, coming home and needing a cup of tea to relax and focus on being in her home space. She acknowledged being irritable with her daughter, who made demands of her that Jane knew were reasonable but came at her when she was still trying to recover from her day at work.

As the practitioner prepared for the second session with Jane, the memory of her frenetic, impulsive, and distracted behaviors from the initial session were calling out as issues with the potential to disrupt the therapeutic process. That Point A made choosing the check-in activities for this session seem daunting at first. The thing that helped the most was to start with deciding what the desired Point B was for these initial activities.

After deciding that the purpose of the check-in activities (the Point B) was to help Jane engage fully in the here and now, choosing activities to accomplish that objective had a much sharper focus. First, the practitioner prepared the office to have a relaxing cup of tea available (because Jane mentioned it as helpful to her relaxation process), as well as to present the option of opening each session with a **Mindfulness** activity (see Appendix 1). Specifically, the practitioner thought of introducing a small gong that would produce a sound when struck that very slowly faded away. The intent was for the participant to practice deep breathing until all sound from the gong had slipped away. To complete the check-in, an activity was introduced that asked both the practitioner and Jane to select a physical object they were carrying that could be used to introduce something new about themselves to the other person (**Personal Object Check-In**; see Appendix 1). In addition to accomplishing the Point B, the practitioner hoped this activity would add to the assessment and enhance relationship development. A Facilitated Wave diagram of the check-in process is presented in Figure 3.6.

Jane accepted the idea of opening every session with some sort of mindfulness exercise. The practitioner committed themselves to making their clinical office a haven, of sorts, that offered a quiet space, a cup of tea, and the opportunity for the participant to destress from the rigors of her normal life. Mindfulness would be addressed using the **gong activity** (see Appendix 1) for now with thoughts of expanding by introducing other activities she could use at home and work.

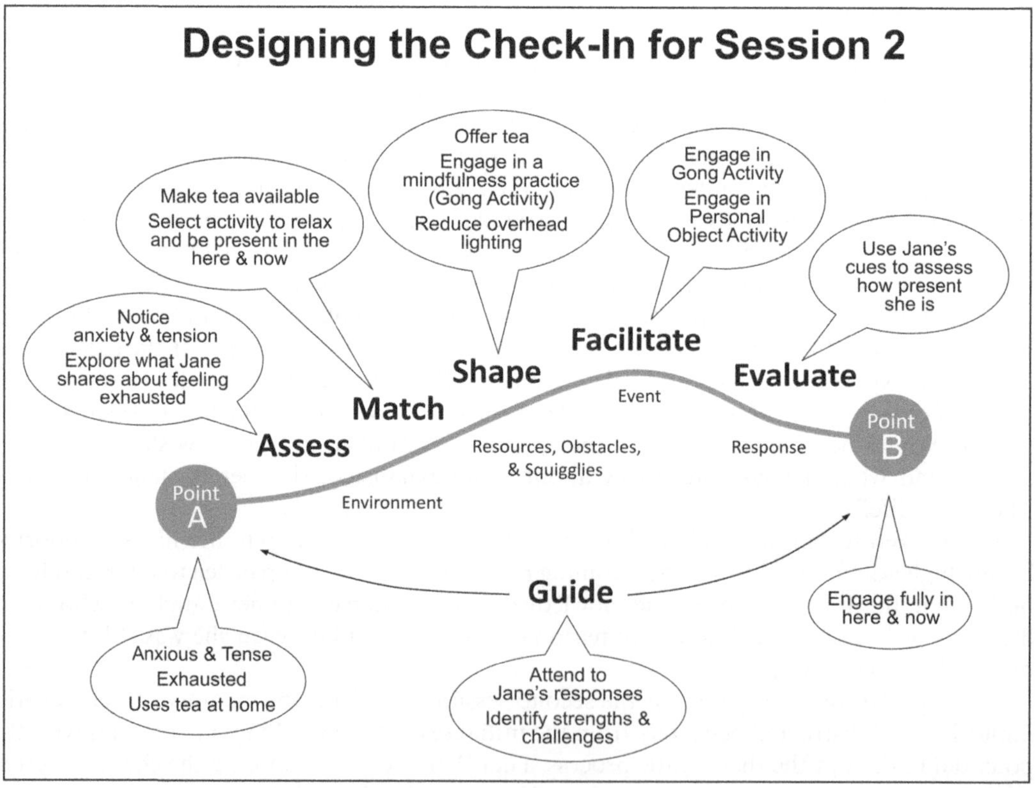

Figure 3.6 Applying the wave model: Designing the check-in for Session 2.

In the first two sessions, so many issues had been presented with little focus given to any one thing that the primary goals of treatment were not clear. As a result, planning for the third session began by identifying the Point B for the session as clarifying treatment goals. Clarity would require an activity that focused on assessment and identification of what was the most important for Jane within all the things that had surfaced in the first two sessions.

The practitioner chose to introduce the **Plate Activity** to assist in moving toward the session Point B (see Appendix 1). This activity is intended to diagram cause and effects of the participant's presenting problems and develop a prioritized list of clinical goals. In this activity, the participant is invited to write one of the presenting problems on a paper plate, designated as a <u>*Cause*</u> plate and place it on the ground/floor. Next, they use as many paper plates as necessary to write down the *Effects* of that problem (called <u>*Effects*</u> plates) and place them on the floor surrounding the *Cause* plate. The only other prop, in addition to the paper plates and a marker, is a stick with one end painted red. The red tips sit on one *Effects* plate with the non-painted end resting on the associated *Cause* plate. The process is repeated for each presenting problem. Once this sculpture is completed, the participant is asked to consider the full picture and remove the one plate that would have the largest positive impact if it ceased to exist. Removing plates is a way to stimulate a collaborative discussion of clinical goals ending in a prioritized list. The completed "plate sculpture" is pictured in Figure 3.7.

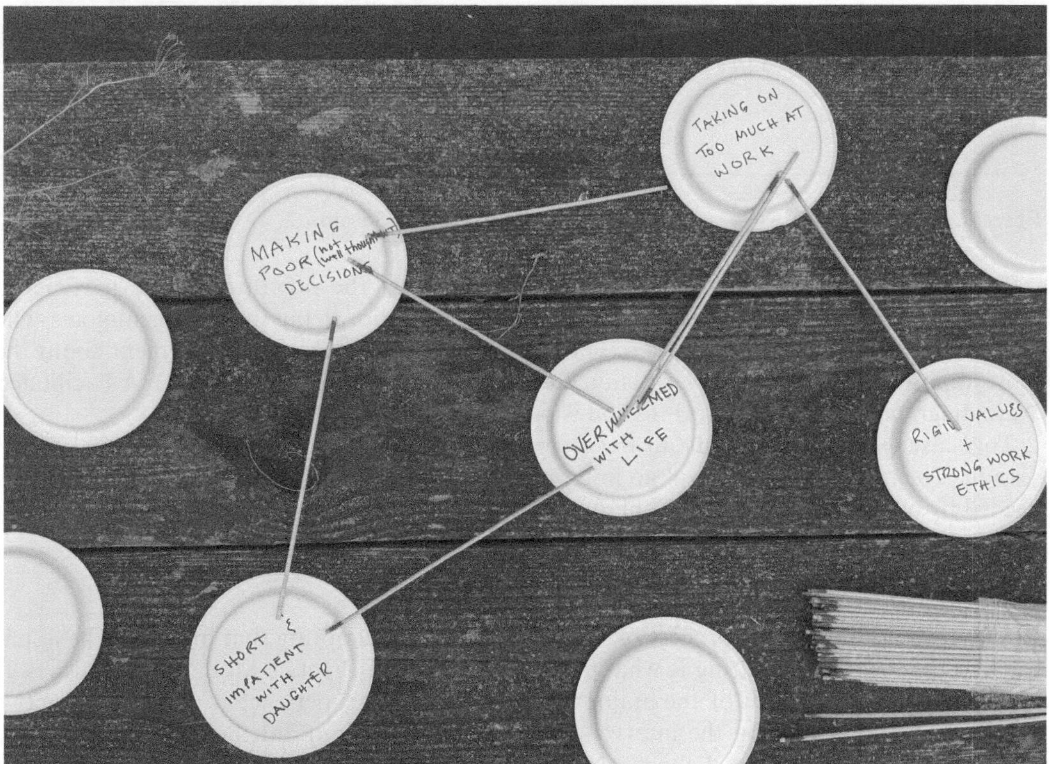

Figure 3.7 The Plate Activity visually highlights the connections between feelings, values and responses.

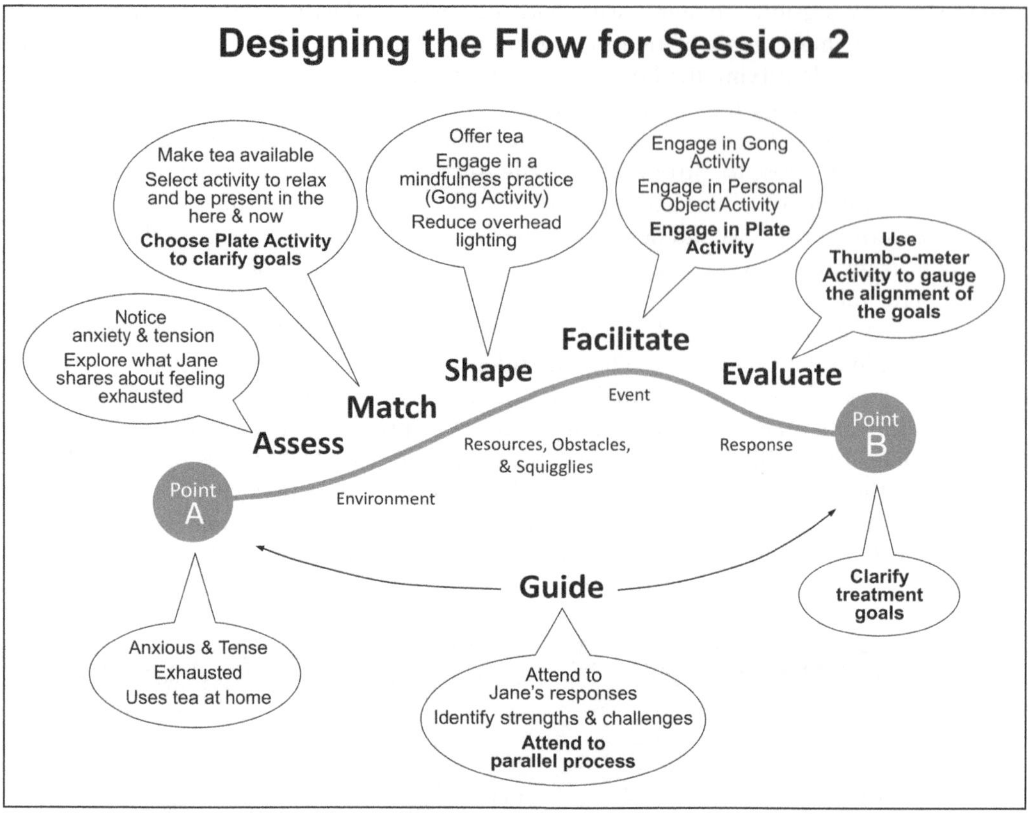

Figure 3.8 Applying the wave model: Designing the flow for Session 2.

This session plan concluded with the expectation that the practitioner and participant would collaborate and come to a mutual decision about prioritizing the treatment goals. The use of a quick **Thumb-O-Meter** exercise to evaluate whether there was agreement about the most important clinical goals was planned to end the session (see Appendix 1). A Facilitated Wave diagram of the entire third session is presented in Figure 3.8.

This case example highlights all the steps of the Facilitated Wave Model in one clinical session. The rest of the book will go in more depth to describe each step and considerations needed by practitioners in each of these steps.

Conclusion

Understanding the normal process of life experiences and adapting that process to be applicable to the therapeutic setting is what the Facilitated Wave Practice Model accomplishes. It simply puts a verb in front of the major components of life experience to identify the active process and adds matching the intervention to the list to round out the adventure practice approach. The components of the model become:

- **Assess** Point A, Point B, and the environment
- **Match** an intervention to the assessed needs

- **Shape** the environment
- **Facilitate** the intervention
- **Guide** the learning
- **Evaluate** the process

Other things generic to the Facilitated Wave Practice Model are the acknowledgment that squigglies can appear in the here and now of therapy sessions that rob the participant of clear focus on their treatment goals, the identification of Universal Point B's that all practitioners bring into the treatment environment, and the recognition that in actual practice the Facilitated Wave does not progress in a truly linear manner.

Reflection

- Do you use a particular practice model in your work? Can you describe how it guides your approach to practice?
- If you imagine yourself using the Facilitated Wave Practice Model in your work,
  - Can you visualize and articulate where you are in the process of treatment using the wave model?
  - How would you use the wave model to plan sessions?
  - Thinking of a current participant, how would you plot their overall progress using the wave model?
- Can you describe how the identification of a squiggly in the treatment environment can be an opportunity that assists the process of treatment?
- How would you use the components of the Facilitated Wave to describe the process of treatment?

Now What?

- Prepare your clinical space for the adventure therapy practice approach by including wall posters or ground spots with the belief words printed on them.
- Integrate fun activities into your practice as important interventions aimed at enhancing the treatment relationship and encouraging authentic engagement in the process.
- Evaluate how the universal Point Bs are operationalized in your practice.

References

Alvarez, T. G., Stauffer, G., Lung, D. M., Sacksteder, K., Beale, B., & Tucker, A. R. (2021). *Adventure group psychotherapy. An experiential approach to treatment*. Routledge.

Brendtro, L, Brokenleg, M., & Van Bockern, S. (2009). *Reclaiming youth at risk: Our hope for the future* (Revised ed.). Solution Tree.

Glasser, W. (1999) *Choice theory: A new psychology of personal freedom*. Harper Collins.

Schultz, R. (2021). *No bad parts*. Sounds True.

Substance Abuse and Mental Health Services Administration (SAMHSA. 2014). *SAMHSA's concept of trauma and guidance for a trauma-informed approach*. HHS Publication No. (SMA) 14-4884. https://library.samhsa.gov/sites/default/files/sma14-4884.pdf

Yalom, I. D. (2017) *The gift of therapy*. Harper Perennial.

Yalom, I. D., & Leszcz, M. (2020). *The theory and practice of group psychotherapy* (6th ed.). Basic Books.

Chapter 4

Preparing to Guide

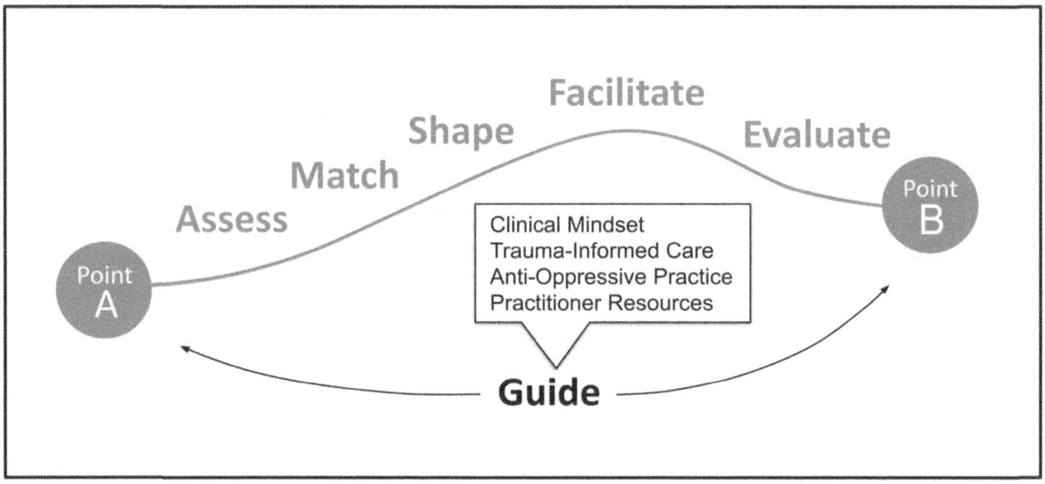

Participants come to practitioners seeking help navigating life circumstances that have confused them or become difficult to manage in some way. When professionals are being asked for help, they are responsible for preparing the best service possible, to guide the participants effectively along their path toward healing. Preparation for the role as an individual adventure therapy facilitator is not limited to skill development. It also includes **nurturing the necessary mindset and beliefs about how to engage participants in the process of change, how to work in an anti-oppressive manner, and how to incorporate trauma-informed care (TIC) principles in the practice of adventure therapy activities**. Preparing to guide happens officially throughout school, training and continuing education, but it also happens each time professionals prepare to guide a participant through an experiential session, no matter how skilled and experienced a guide may be.

The following story is intended to illustrate what the practitioner does to prepare themselves to guide a participant through the unknown territory of personal change and growth:

The practitioner received a call from a middle-aged woman named Alice, who was asking for individual therapy to deal with anxiety. She described getting anxious and freezing up when she needed to respond to people quickly in the moment despite knowing exactly what she wanted to say. She also reported being in individual therapy previously where she dealt

DOI: 10.4324/9781003457893-4

with the experience of sexual and emotional abuse throughout her childhood. The practitioner she saw for that round of therapy was no longer available.

From that brief introduction, the practitioner knew that they would need to be mindful of the importance of consent. This preparation led them to take several actions. The first was to share that the practitioner's adventure therapy approach to practice would mean that they actively engage in experiences together during the session. Her responses to those experiences in the session would become the primary agent of change because they would most likely be the same as the ones she was concerned about at home and work.

The second thing the practitioner did was to assure the caller that the adventure therapy approach was always collaborative, and that mutual consent would be sought before engaging in any intervention. To establish conditions of safety and trust in the therapy sessions, the plans for treatment would begin with low-risk activities and move to other experiences with mutual consent and collaboration. Finally, because the caller identified previous trauma work, the practitioner expressed that they wanted to be sensitive to the principles of TIC, and to continually check in with the participants about their experience.

During the initial session, Alice described her experiences of feeling "frozen" and unable to make simple decisions in her personal and professional life. For example, while standing in the break room of her office with two male superiors, one of the maintenance staff members, who reported directly to her, approached to ask how often the filter in one of their furnaces needed to be changed. One of the men she was talking to spoke for her and gave the wrong answer. Although she knew the correct answer immediately, she was not able to speak and felt "frozen" at that moment. This vignette from her work life was important for two reasons: (1) it clearly described her reasons for seeking treatment, and (2) it was an example of oppressive behavior by a man for which she was, once again, assigning blame to herself. The practitioner noted the significance of this story, realizing that it opened the door for exploration of oppression and social justice issues.

As suggested, Alice experienced the same difficulties during experiential activities that she did at work. When asked to choose one card from a deck of cards with pictures and symbols that represented something about herself (**Processing Tools**, see Appendix 1), for example, she appeared deep in thought and was not able to take a card for several minutes. The practitioner recognized this freezing behavior as a trauma response and waited patiently to give the participant space. As more of these "frozen moments" happened in sessions, a pattern of "getting stuck in her thoughts" was identified and recognized mutually as a trauma response. The adventure practitioner's preparation in trauma-informed practices was instrumental for effective treatment moving forward.

What Is Preparing to Guide?

Preparing to guide is the underpinning of all adventure work. **It includes not only the awareness of self and a practitioner's social identities and ways of being in the world, but it also includes how practitioners interact in the clinical setting**. From this foundational understanding of self, practitioners can then actively participate in their preparation to guide participants through their journey of personal reflection, growth, and change. Building on the foundational knowledge from Chapter 3, the preparation process is influenced by the practitioner's clinical mindset, personal resources, education, and additional training needed to be a competent individual adventure therapy practitioner.

In the previous story, the adventure practitioner demonstrated their preparation to guide the treatment in several ways:

- By believing in the transformative power of experience and describing the rationale for an adventure therapy intervention approach to the participant from the very beginning of treatment
- By working collaboratively with the participant to shape a treatment environment that would give the participant the best chance to reach her treatment goals
- By responding in a manner consistent with the principles of TIC
- By making intentional efforts to respond in an anti-oppressive manner in providing choice and sharing power in decision-making

The hope is that this chapter empowers practitioners to show up as their authentic selves. Practitioners may have seen others lead interventions and thought they may never be able to do the work the way others do. Hopefully, they are right! **The aim is for practitioners to show up as they are and lead that activity in their authentic way**. All the topics touched on in this chapter have this caveat attached: **Everything hinges on practitioners being genuinely present with participants**.

Clinical Mindset of the Adventure Practitioner

"A mindset is an established set of attitudes of a person or group concerning culture, values, philosophy, frame of mind, outlook, and disposition. It may also arise from a person's world-view or beliefs about the meaning of life" (Oxford English Dictionary, 2023). The authors believe the necessary set of attitudes and beliefs that comprise the clinical mindset of an effective individual adventure practitioner is built on the following:

- Believing in the transformative power of experience.
- Understanding the significant influence of the treatment environment.

In addition, the following five tenets are critical beliefs of an effective individual practitioner regardless of their practice approach.

- Showing up as their authentic self.
- Being rooted in trauma-informed, anti-oppressive practices.
- Approaching clinical work with curiosity and compassion.
- Integrating the universal objectives for participants that all practitioners bring into treatment.
- Collaborating with participants to ensure their voice is honored and invited in the treatment process.

Transformative Power of Experience

The individual adventure therapy practitioner is continually thinking about, reflecting upon and putting the tenets described earlier into action as they ask participants to engage in active and holistic experiences. John Dewey (1859–1952), an early writer on experiential education, famously said, "Give the pupils something to do, not something to learn; and if the doing is of such a nature as to demand thinking; learning naturally results" (Dewey, 1916, p. 191). This axiom, as well as other components related to the transformative power of experience discussed in the *Foundations of Adventure Therapy* chapter, is at the very heart of the authors' experiential approach to clinical practice. As practitioners prepare to guide, it is important to explore how they operationalize this belief in practice. The following concepts are central in keeping the transformative power of experience at the core of what practitioners do (Alvarez et al., 2021).

- Valuing the Participant's Response
- Focusing on the Here and Now
- Utilizing a Nondeliberative Approach
- Attending to Process, as well as Outcome

Woven into each of these areas of focus are multiple components of TIC. Adventure therapy's innate, relational focus on collaboration and mutuality, for example, ensures the participant is honored, welcomed and included in the treatment process.

Valuing the Participant's Response

The important work of exploring the participant's responses to the experiential intervention begins by understanding, appreciating and recognizing that participants have whole-body responses (i.e., verbal, behavior, somatic, cognitive, affective, social, existential) during the session. This acknowledgment often leads to the **practitioner making observational comments that simply verbalize what is seen from the participant, using as little judgment or interpretation as possible**. The practitioner strives to honor the participant's response exactly as it shows up, even if it is not what one would expect, or hope for, or even find productive right in that moment.

Valuing the participant's response is an active application of the TIC principle of Empowerment, Voice and Choice (SAMHSA, 2014). **Attending to their response in the moment is one of the primary ways practitioners demonstrate to the participant that they are 100% present and focused on what they bring to each session, including how they engage with and participate in the experiences practitioners offer them**. For example, "I notice you are sharing your resources and ideas with me", or "you are moving quickly without voicing your intended actions; can you help me understand what made you go in this direction?" When it is ignored how the participant responds, or external value is placed on how the participant responds without participant input (e.g., "great job sharing", or "I see some unwanted aggression"), it can limit the benefit of adventure interventions and disregard the participant as a valued person. This value drives the practitioner's adventure practice.

The belief that how participants participate in the adventure interventions directly mirrors how they think, feel, behave, and respond to stimuli in their daily life is central to adventure therapy practices (Yalom & Leszcz, 2020). It is this belief that gives us the confidence to know that exploring the content of the participant's responses to adventure interventions will be relevant to their presenting problems and their quest for something different in their lives. This is guided by the belief in the participant's potential and ability to heal.

This principle of a parallel process between actions in the therapy session and the participant's real life is also central to helping participants who are beginning therapy ascribe meaning to their therapeutic experience (Walkins, 2012). Thus, the adventure therapy practitioner typically explains to participants that they are asking them to respond fully as themselves with no role play or acting "as if" each experience was anything less than a real-life problem to be solved. **The belief that the participant's responses in therapy will be like their responses to other real-life situations becomes a vital part of the treatment alliance**. Hence, the participant is invited to engage in shared experiences with the practitioner that offer opportunities to build a mutual and authentic therapeutic relationship.

Valuing the participant's response has significant ramifications for working through issues related to anti-oppression work in general. **Watching how participants respond to experiential interventions, as well as to the practitioner, helps the practitioner explore the meaning that lies beneath what is being expressed**. One example of the deeper meaning that can arise is a microaggression the participant may experience from the practitioner that needs to be addressed. The actions of the practitioner to recognize the microaggression, affirm the participant's response, and take responsibility without justification can be a healing process for the participant in itself. For example, a practitioner may be working with an individual who identifies as transgender, and during the first meeting, the practitioner may accidentally misgender them. It is imperative to notice, acknowledge honestly, apologize, and move on, remembering not to do it again.

Other examples of the participant's responses in a session carrying deeper meaning include negative self-statements or an apparent shying away from taking action that, upon full exploration, turns out to be an expression of internalized distortions about the participant's self-worth. This practitioner's attention to how these types of participant responses may be connected to their positionality and sense of who they are deepens the therapeutic rapport and supports the development of an emotionally safe treatment environment.

A powerful example of valuing the participant's response happened during the middle phase of treatment with a Black woman in her 50s. The practitioner's session plan was to do an activity that required the participant and the practitioner to exchange places using a rope swing. The participant had been a remarkably engaged and passionate participant in every experiential activity presented to her in previous sessions. During this session, however, she was quiet and withdrawn. When the practitioner commented that she was more quiet than usual during the intervention, she reported how she walked out of the building to the outdoor setting for the intervention and became overwhelmed by the sight of the rope hanging from a tree. She spoke of the historical trauma her family had experienced in the South and her grandmother's lynching. What ensued was a powerful conversation about the impact of that history on her life. Her response to the rope in the moment provided the opportunity for the adventure facilitator to validate and explore the impact that historical and systematic oppression had on her current experiential functioning and how her own sense of safety is relative and guided by this history.

The case vignette underscores that **a practitioner cannot anticipate what may bring about a re-traumatization of the participant**. The tools that are used, the paintings or photos that are in the room, and what is referenced all have the potential to do that! What is important to know is that should this happen, practitioners are prepared to respond by valuing the participant's response and staying open to seek more information about what it means to the participant.

Focusing on the Here and Now

Yalom and Leszcz (2020) describe the here-and-now focus in an interesting manner. They state that it does not mean discarding historical information. Rather, it can include anything that has occurred throughout the treatment relationship or the participant's life that comes up during the session. Simply put, **any experience that comes up or impacts the current moment becomes a valuable means of treatment, change, and healing**. The commitment to engaging with the participant in a shared experience in the moment and being present to help them understand their responses almost guarantees that a practitioner's clinical focus will remain in the here and now.

The focus of adventure therapy activities on here-and-now issues does not limit sessions from addressing past experiences. Observations that some participant responses are out of context or remarkable in some manner while describing historical events can demonstrate how historical events are still impacting the participant's current experiential functioning. The example related to the rope swing illustrates this point (see **Nitro Crossing** in Appendix 1).

Sitting with the participant and talking about things that happened during the past week is not a here-and-now approach. Attending to and commenting on how the participant is reporting the week's events, on the other hand, brings the focus to the here-and-now information. For example, commenting that the participant's jaw was clenched and fists held in tight balls as they talked about the week's events brings the focus of the session to here-and-now functioning rather than a sterile or intellectualized recitation of events.

Another example of staying focused on the here and now comes from a clinical session with a participant around a campfire. The participant began talking about how their favorite uncle loved campfires. During that discussion, the practitioner simply asked them, "What is it like for you to be around this campfire right now?" That question shifted the discussion from an intellectual or factual report to one that involved here-and-now issues of the bodily responses they were experiencing and a more emotion-ladened discussion of what this history with their uncle meant to them.

The clinical mindset of an individual adventure practitioner is also keenly aware that somatic or body-based interventions (somatic interventions) can help people process and heal from current, historical/generational, relational, or systemic trauma (Kuhfuß et al., 2021). Generally speaking, **adventure practitioners choose to use multiple trauma-processing interventions** (Kearney & Lanius, 2022), including those that involve settling the body, paying attention to the sensations that arise, accepting any pain and discomfort, and then safely discharging that tension. The somatic practices of mindfulness or intentional movement are examples of the type of interventions introduced throughout treatment.

Acknowledging participant responses as they are happening in the clinical setting means giving the participant feedback in the moment that is clear, respectful, pragmatic, and directional toward clinical goals. This invites the participant into a partnership with the practitioner to explore how and why the participant is responding behaviorally, verbally, socially, cognitively, emotionally, and somatically, as well as how the participant is interacting with the practitioner. A growing sense of connection and trust with the participant is the result of this here-and-now focus.

Utilizing a Nondeliberative Approach

Tucker et al., (2016) describe the nondeliberative practitioner as presenting "opportunities for growth and learning without prescribing when that growth and learning may occur and allowing the activities themselves to gain admission to un-accessed parts of participants even unknown to themselves" (p. 205). **Actions by the practitioner, such as allowing their participants to engage in experiences without being told the "correct" way to accomplish the task**

and allowing the participant to utilize trial-and-error repetitions are examples of being nondeliberative. In this approach, practitioners can share the power and decision-making with the participant.

Embracing a nondeliberative approach to treatment is particularly valuable for shaping and maintaining the desired treatment environment. One example of this process comes from the engagement of a high school aged participant in the **tennis ball pyramid** activity (see Appendix 1). This participant worked diligently to create a pyramid, three tennis balls high, using all of the 14 tennis balls provided by the practitioner. The participant's struggle came when they were invited to move the pyramid from the floor to a desktop nearby without losing the pyramid shape of the balls. They used the same methods repeatedly, only to watch as the tennis balls collapse. The practitioner, using a nondeliberative facilitation style, remained engaged but did not offer any unsolicited advice or critique of the participant's efforts. Finally, the participant looked up from the problem and told the practitioner that it did not seem possible. It turned out that this scenario was a mirror image of how this participant was approaching his problems getting along with teachers and with their parents. They remained focused on the details of the arguments with these adults and were never able to get out of the trouble the arguments caused (Figure 4.1).

The practitioner made two observations. The first was that the participant worked extremely hard to solve the problem and did not give up easily. These personal strengths were described as important resources for achieving the treatment goals. Second, the practitioner noted that through all the struggles, the participant never once asked for help to move the pyramid.

Figure 4.1 Mutual effort in the activity mirrors the collaborative nature of treatment.

The participant agreed that not asking for help was a common feature in their efforts to get things done. Further, they also agreed that the problems with adults were not likely to change if they kept doing the same things over and over like they did with the tennis balls. It was the practitioner's nondeliberative facilitation of the intervention that allowed the participant to process the parallel process between their current experiential functioning in the session and in their arguments with adults outside of the session. One important result was a strengthening of the treatment alliance, which centered on the participant asking the practitioner for help resolving the relationship problems with adults in their life.

The gains in the treatment described earlier were achieved by the practitioner intentionally presenting the intervention in a nondeliberate manner. **Practitioners need to be prepared to step aside and allow the participant to do with the intervention what they choose.** This nondeliberative approach to interventions means that the outcomes are unknown, allowing the participant to express aspects of themselves in their responses to every experiential intervention presented. Following a nondeliberative approach, practitioners can partner with and share power with participants, giving them choice in how their treatment unfolds.

Another way of understanding the nondeliberative approach is what Tucker et al. (2016) described as being "noncurricular." The practitioner does not have learning objectives with teaching points and conclusions to present to the participant. **Rather, practitioners shape experiences for participants that serve as a springboard for exploring the participant's genuine responses that shed light on how best to achieve their goals.**

Although the needs of a specific participant may lead the practitioner to respond differently than the following suggestions, there are some specific skills necessary for the practitioner to maintain a nondeliberative approach.

- *Tolerate Silence*: The ability to tolerate silence takes on new meaning for individual adventure practitioners. Long silences, which happen more often than in group and family therapy sessions, may leave the individual practitioner wondering whether their presentation of the activity was clear or whether the participant fully understood what resources were available, for example. These considerations often tempt the individual practitioner to interrupt the participant's silence with explanations or suggestions about what needs to be done. While sometimes necessary, these interruptions often interfere with important clinical work. A silent participant may be processing information, calming their anxious thoughts, reflecting on what has happened, or simply demonstrating to the practitioner one part of their typical experiential functioning (Vago & Zeidan, 2016). **The practice of tolerating silence often supports the participant's agency and honors their choice in the process, as well as provides opportunity for the practitioner to learn more about their experiential functioning.**
- *Let the Participants Do the Work*: As participants grapple for a solution to an adventure intervention or simply take their time considering all their options, the practitioner is often tempted to help. As helping professionals, the natural tendency is to make comments that will lead the participant in what the facilitator sees as a positive direction. However, a practitioner's influence or coaching may diminish their sense of accomplishment or, worse, bypass a legitimate barrier they may be struggling with. Maria Montessori (1870–1952) taught practitioners to, "Never help a child with a task at which he [they] feels he [they] can succeed" (Daily Montessori, 2021). In the same way, unless a practitioner's interruptions in the participant's process are specifically matched to a participant's needs, they do not fit with the preferred nondeliberative clinical mindset for facilitating adventure interventions.

The practitioner is called upon to "bite their tongue" and simply narrate how the participant *chooses* to respond to what they are experiencing. In this way, they can show the participant their belief and recognition in their abilities and strengths. **Allowing participants to struggle and persevere may be time-consuming or messy but sweetens the ultimate success.**

A clinical situation in which the practitioner may choose to intervene in a directive manner, rather than remaining nondeliberatively, is when the treatment goals revolve around skill development. For example, developing the skill of regulating emotions with the use of mindfulness activities that the participant can engage in independently is often facilitated by the practitioner coaching the participant in how to utilize the desired skill during a stressful moment. This coaching approach is supported by a neuroscience-development perspective that indicates practicing the skill in a moment of dysregulation is an important part of cementing the ability to use the skill outside of sessions. In vivo practice of the skill is intended to fire the neurons that the therapy is hoping to permanently wire in the participant's brain (Shapiro et al., 2024)

In general, the individual adventure therapy practitioner needs to be prepared to manage healthy doses of challenge or stress with their participants. Ungar (2019) posits that manageable stress is good; toxic stress is bad. **It is the practitioner's job to find the right balance between stress load and resources, so the capacity for future resilience will be enhanced.** While this makes sense, individuals often do exactly the opposite of what is good for them. There is plenty of good science showing that when children get outdoors and get dirty, their physical and mental well-being improves (Paluch et al., 2025). The more germs that are experienced as children, the better one's immune system will handle stress later in life. So does being allowed to wander and explore.

Participants also need the psychological immunity that comes from an environment that occasionally forces them to self-regulate. **To be resilient is not about having one's every need met. It is about being given the right amount of stress and the right resources to overcome manageable challenges, which leads to healthy biological and neurological development** (Denckla et al., 2020).

- *Letting the Process Unfold*: Effective adventure therapy practitioners demonstrate their belief in the transformative power of experience by giving up any sense of control over the outcome of the experiences they invite participants to complete (Tucker et al., 2016). A great deal of cognitive flexibility is required to give up on hoped-for-outcomes developed during the clinical planning phase and simply going where the participant takes you. It requires an attitude of determination and intention, as well as significant skill as a facilitator, to allow the flow of the activity to follow its natural course in the moment. **Letting the process unfold means to embrace and support a participant's resilience, strengths and their ability to heal (Alvarez et al., 2021).**

  Another clinical reality that supports the idea of trusting the process is the belief that if something is clinically significant, it will continue to emerge as a pattern in participant's responses. For example, a practitioner should not be terribly concerned about their failure to bring up how a participant dismissed their own abilities during one session. If that behavior is significant, it will emerge during other interventions, at which point the practitioner has the option of noting that the same response was observed previously and wondering if it might be a pattern.

Before leaving this section, it is important to note that as adventure therapy practitioners who invite participants to act, **there is a deep responsibility to employ practices that manage risks**

(Smith, 2021). While simultaneously working to empower participants, guiding professionals must plan to intervene when safety might be compromised. Practitioners must model for the participant the aim to keep them as safe as possible (Gass et al., 2020). This is integral in building trust and transparency with participants, as well as creating healthy boundaries and expectations.

Attending to the Here-and-Now Process as well as Outcome

Key to adventure therapy is that the practitioner attends to the process of HOW participants engage in adventure therapy interventions, as well as the resulting outcome of their efforts. The relationship between the two is that the participant's engagement in achieving a successful outcome is what provides the practitioner with the opportunity to observe their responses to various stimuli in their everyday life. This process is called their **current experiential functioning**. Uncovering the nuances of their current experiential functioning is central to healing and growth, as well as the achievement of their clinical goals.

Additionally, the achievement of outcomes involves a process for both the participant and the practitioner. Some outcomes are intended, while others are not. For example, a practitioner ignoring rule-breaking behavior during an intervention so the participant can experience a successful outcome may unintentionally reinforce undesirable behaviors that contribute to the presenting problems. Optimal progress can be seen toward the participant's clinical goals when the practitioner is sufficiently available to see what the participant is doing and to guide them toward awareness of how their current experiential functioning is impacting the achievement of their treatment goals.

Another way of thinking about this same issue is that it is important for the practitioner to maintain a distinction between the task of an activity (e.g., the participant stacking 14 tennis balls in a pyramid shape, three layers high, and moving it to a new location without losing the original pyramid shape) **and the goal of using that activity** with the participant (e.g., inviting the participant to engage in an activity that will require collaborative effort between the participant and practitioner). The facilitator is careful to present clear instructions about the task of every activity to provide continual consent and transparency in the process. The task is presented for its importance to participant engagement and the opportunity to observe the process the participant uses to reach a solution. At the same time, the practitioner's focus while the participant is working on the task is almost always on two additional issues: identifying the participant's whole-body responses to the intervention and noticing the process they are using to tackle the task. The tennis ball pyramid intervention, for example, often shines a light on the participant's reluctance or inability to ask for help when presented with a task (i.e., the process they are using to achieve the task). Helping the participant move toward the goal of engaging collaboratively with the practitioner will be addressed by literally identifying this self-reliant process and engaging with them in something different. An example of intervening with the participant's whole-body responses in the moment may be noticing with the participant that they have given two loud sighs while working on the task and asking them to describe what those sighs mean. Just the verbalization of this observed bodily response generally engages the participant in discussion of the process they are engaged in.

Both practitioner interventions described earlier (identifying a process and working with a specific response from the participant) highlight the importance of understanding that **the goal of interventions is distinct from the task for successful completion**. Individual adventure therapy practitioners are generally more interested in helping participants develop awareness of their whole-person responses and the process they are using to accomplish tasks than whether or not the task presented to them is achieved.

Whether the task is accomplished or not, the practitioner's attention will be on moving the participant toward achievement of the clinical goals. Attention to patience and level of frustration, to persistence, to the use of humor and creativity, or to how they honor success are just a few dynamics practitioners might see the participant actually do while engaged in the task. Noticing and acknowledging these strengths and skills help to address the participant's clinical goals. It shows the participants areas of growth or where they might require more support. For example, when the task feels too overwhelming and requires too much from the participant, the practitioner can think about what skills the participant can use to stay on track, such as asking for help or adapting the task for the immediate moment. The practitioner might intervene in the previously described tennis ball intervention by suggesting the following, "I can see that you are working really hard to keep that pyramid together and that it keeps falling apart; so, I wonder what might change things for you." Whatever it is that assists the participant in solving the tennis ball pyramid problem is likely to also help them achieve one of the objectives identified for their clinical goals (e.g., stopping to take a breath and reflecting more on what is happening, asking the practitioner for help, and so on).

The Influence of the Treatment Environment

Maria Montessori (1870–1952) explains that "the environment must be rich in motives that lend interest to activity and invite the child to conduct his [their] own experiences" (Montessori, 1995 p. 84). This quote says a great deal about the treatment environment used to shape individual practices. "Rich in motives" is a phrase that conjures up the importance of instilling a set of beliefs that define the expected behavior and the culture of the treatment setting. Inviting participants to guide their own experiences limits distractions from the external or physical environment that might deprive the participant of their freedom to act intuitively.

Nothing is more important to the individual adventure therapy practitioner's preparation than instilling a belief that the nature of the treatment environment will dictate what can be achieved in the treatment overall. A treatment environment that has been shaped mutually with the participant will influence the planning, delivery, and effectiveness of interventions. It is key to also consider aspects outside of the immediate clinical context. Psychosocial factors, financial considerations, legal and ethical considerations, cultural and linguistic factors, technology, equipment, community and environmental factors, practitioner's influence are all factors that impact the treatment environment.

Since the environment is so important, this book includes a whole chapter on shaping the treatment environment (Chapter 7), which addresses the following factors:

- Awareness of the impact of the **physical space** on what happens in treatment
- Establishing a set of **beliefs** that serve to define how the treatment environment operates
- Attention to the **treatment relationship**, including both the positive rapport with participants and the alliance with them to work on clinical goals
- Vigilant efforts to ensure the participant's **authentic engagement** in the clinical process

Most of the practitioner's efforts to shape the environment center around establishing the treatment relationship and ensuring that the participant is authentically engaged with the treatment goals. While it is just as important that the adventure beliefs are operating in the individual treatment environment as it is in any other form of treatment, the fact that these norms and culture are being established between just two people makes the process more straightforward.

Showing Up as One's Authentic Self

Truly knowing oneself and recognizing that this level of self-awareness is an ongoing process of work is an essential component for effective individual adventure therapy. **Self-awareness includes an understanding of self-identity and positionality**. Self-identity refers to an individual's understanding and perception of themselves internally as a unique and distinct person (Erikson, 1968; Marcia, 1980). It encompasses the beliefs, values, thoughts, feelings, and experiences that shape their sense of who they are. This prerequisite awareness of self includes the impact of an individual's positions in society, including the impact of race, gender identity, sexual orientation, socioeconomic status, religion, various abilities, and cultural background, for example.

The call for mental health practitioners to bring a full and genuine awareness of themselves into sessions with the participants who come to them for help is not a new concept (Williams et al., 2008). **It is imperative that the practitioner, who is guiding others toward greater self-awareness, has done that same work for themselves to avoid superimposing unintentional biases or expectations on participants that are counterproductive or even harmful.**

This call toward self-awareness is universally true, regardless of race, ethnicity, religion, or other social identifiers of the practitioner. Nevertheless, there is a special need for the message to be heard by White practitioners. Practitioners with privilege have a unique responsibility to be aware of the privilege they, and others in the dominant culture of the United States, have been afforded (Bergkamp et al., 2022). Most individual adventure practitioners identify as being straight, cis-gendered, and White, since current statistics show that 88% of therapists in the United States are heterosexual, and 73% of therapists in the United States are White, 11% are Asian, 8% Hispanic/Latino, and 4% are Black (Zippia, 2025). Being fully aware that these socio-emotional and cultural realities have been internalized allows the White practitioner to show up aware of their generational privilege and engage with participants in a genuinely humble and open manner---neither overly ingratiating and patronizing or insensitive to the impact of their cultural heritage on prospective participants. This awareness sears into practice a determination to seek ways to empower one's participant, to engage collaboratively as a means of sharing power, and to allow for participant choice in every aspect of the treatment process.

Self-Identity

Self-identity is a complex and multifaceted concept influenced by various factors (Hammack, 2008; Leary & Price Tangney, 2012), including the following:

- *Personal Characteristics*: This includes the collection of social identities (such as gender, age, ethnicity, race, sexual orientation, ability, and physical appearance). Each of these characteristics can play a significant role in shaping how the individual practitioner perceives themselves. Comfort and clarity within the practitioner around how these issues are presented to participants and the level of transparency that suits the practitioner's position in the world in general is a prerequisite for anyone offering individual therapy to participants.

- *Psychological Factors*: Beliefs, values, personality traits, and self-esteem are essential components of self-identity. For example, someone with a strong sense of altruism may identify themselves as a caring and compassionate person. It is imperative that the individual practitioner understand how these factors influence their interactions with participants.
- *Social and Cultural Influences*: Society and culture can have a profound impact on how individuals perceive themselves. Cultural norms, religion, family values, peer groups, and societal expectations all contribute to a person's self-identity. Understanding the role these influences play in forming an identity allows providers to appreciate the differences in how these factors have influenced participants' self-identity.
- *Life Experiences*: Positive and negative life experiences, such as achievements, failures, trauma, and personal milestones, can shape an individual's self-identity. For example, someone who has overcome adversity may see themselves as resilient and strong. Effective individual practitioners understand that both the privileges that helped them along the way and the obstacles that presented themselves in their specific life story are different and quite often not present in the life stories they will hear from participants.
- *Interactions with Others*: Relationships with family, friends, and romantic partners can influence self-identity. Feedback and validation from others can reinforce or challenge one's self-concept. Any individual practitioner who is not clear about the role that interpersonal interactions with others has had on their self-identity is not likely to consistently understand the influence these factors have on their participants.
- *Developmental Stages*: Self-identity evolves and changes throughout a person's life. It often undergoes significant development during adolescence and may continue to evolve in adulthood. A basic understanding of this principle is imperative for the individual practitioner to create an effective treatment plan with the participants they see.

Table 4.1 provides an example of how a practitioner may think about the application of this topic and their own self assessment of who they are and who shows up to treatment sessions.

A practitioner's self-identity is not static; it evolves and adapts over time in response to various life experiences and personal growth. It is a deeply personal and subjective aspect of human existence. There is a continuum of privilege and oppression for all these characteristics that is extremely nuanced and varied, not as simple as Black/White, gay/straight, and so on.

The degree of self-awareness and sense of purpose and belonging the practitioner develops in their work is ultimately acted upon and expressed in the relationships with participants (Posluns and Gall, 2020). Regardless of one's approach to practice, participants in individual treatment will respond to ways that reflect the issues they are attempting to resolve. Adolescents will respond with defiance, victims of trauma will respond to the practitioner with a variety of fight, flight, and/or flee responses. Individuals who have experienced abandonment or neglect will see the practitioner as doing those very things. In all of these examples, the practitioner relies on having a solid and clear sense of who they are in helping the participant develop the ability to respond in a healthier manner. It is important for practitioners to recognize this growth process in their own lives to recognize it as a parallel process in the work the participant is doing, as well as to clearly differentiate their own experiences from those of participants.

The shared nature of the adventure therapy practice approach requires full, whole-person participation for both the participant and practitioner. The transparency of the practitioner's self-identity that results from these shared experiences makes the practitioner's self-awareness an even more essential part of effective practice (Figure 4.2).

Table 4.1 Self-Identity and Planning Application for the Practitioner

Self-Identity Category	*Personal Considerations*	*Potential Participant Impact*
Personal Characteristics (e.g., cultural identity and physical appearance)	• identified female • 30s • White • western European • queer • larger body size	• ensure that safety equipment fits comfortably and is functional • avoid over emphasizing appearance
Psychological Factors (e.g., beliefs, values, personality traits, self-esteem)	• takes a bit to warm up • sensitive to feedback • belief people are good • belief outdoors is best	• sometimes jokes to connect, and it doesn't land well • participants may not be as comfortable outdoors
Social and Cultural Influences (e.g., norms, religion, family values, peer groups, and societal expectations)	• west coast casual • raised Catholic, not currently practicing • large family • sporty • lower middle class	• be aware of supplies (such as gear or snacks) or additional fees (such as parking) • activity narratives that include fantasy may match a strict religious family
Life Experiences (e.g., positive and negative life experiences, such as achievements, failures, trauma, and personal milestones)	• master's degree • serious boating accident • snake bite	• may overemphasize boating safety • may use academic explanations • startle with snakes – may also spook participants
Interactions with Others (e.g., previous and current relationships with family, friends, and romantic partners influences)	• single and dating • no children • strong peer group • family estranged	• uncomfortable being alone with adult male participants • parents may not trust that care for their child
Developmental Stages (e.g., emerging adulthood, young adulthood, middle adulthood, late adulthood)	• early career adult	• May take risks (or not take risks) because of expectations at this point in the career

Figure 4.2 One's theoretical lens changes one's perspective.

Positionality

Another aspect that influences a practitioner's authenticity is how self-identities show up and impact the external or environmental contexts of individuals' lives, as well as how the external contexts influence or shape actions. A person's beliefs about their position in different social, family, work or community settings influence how they act in those different settings. It is the recognition that how participants and practitioners have internalized their position in society, including their race, gender, religion, ability, socioeconomic status, cultural background, and other factors, influences their worldview and the way they interpret and engage with the world around them.

Lack of awareness of one's self-identity and the impact of one's own positionality, or that of their participant's, on therapeutic interaction has often led practitioners, for example, to assume that participants who look like them share their cultural values and the privileges that are given to them through that position. For example, assuming a participant who "looks" White has a similar level of experiences can be harmful when those participants may be biracial or Hispanic with light skin or even other White participants with histories of chronic poverty. There is always a potential to retraumatize participants with assumptions of how they have experienced their environments.

Here are a few key points to consider related to positionality:

- *Subjectivity*: No one is entirely objective. Practitioners must remain vigilant to the fact that their personal experiences and social identities shape their perspectives and biases. This knowledge will influence their understanding of various issues and interactions with participants.
- *Intersectionality*: As a practitioner who has taken on the responsibility of providing therapy for another individual, it is imperative to understand how the various aspects of identity, such as race, gender, class, sexuality, disability, and other social categories, can intersect and interact with one another (Breunig, 2019). Regardless of good intentions, this intersectionality can create unique and complex experiences of discrimination and privilege (Faissner et al., 2024). It is a practitioner's understanding of these issues that allows them to operate in an anti-oppressive manner in the therapy environment.
- *Cultural Relativism*: What may be true or acceptable in one cultural or social context may not be the same in another or universal across that one culture and no one system should be considered superior to the other (Arat, 2022). Anti-oppressive practitioners need to consider how cultural background, and values affect their judgments and behaviors, as well as those of the participants.
- *Power Dynamics*: The practitioner's awareness of power dynamics and understanding that those in positions of privilege may have different perspectives and experiences than those who are marginalized or oppressed. Being able to apply that knowledge to the daily life and here-and-now experience of the participants is a core aspect of trauma-informed, anti-oppressive practice (Todić & Christensen, 2022).
- *Reflectivity*: Self-reflection and an ongoing examination of one's own biases and assumptions is critical for practitioners as a way of assessing how their position in society may affect their views and actions. Like previously discussed, ongoing supervision is an important part of this ongoing task of a practitioner (Norris, 2022).

Like self-identity, positionality is not static. The feedback received from society and the world offers an opportunity to examine pre-established beliefs and alter or change them. There is a healthy parallel process of practitioners experiencing their own personal growth in recognizing the impact of their positionality to appreciate the same work required of the participants.

An example of how one's self-identity and positionality impact the practice of individual adventure therapy can be seen in a consideration of clinical situations when these two factors conflict with one another. As a practitioner with a personal view of oneself (self-identity) as being kind, compassionate, and sensitive to other people, it can be startling to be confronted about one's own prejudice toward individuals of particular positionality such as race, gender or sexual orientation. The ability to learn from and process this new information in a manner that transforms one's self-identity and changes their interactions with those participants is crucial.

Because individual adventure therapy is practiced in a broad array of settings with diverse participants, practitioners must be aware of how positionality impacts the service delivery. Public school settings, community mental health clinics, private clinical practices, and substance abuse treatment programs are just a small sample of venues that bring participants into the practice of adventure therapy from a cross section of society. In preparation to provide trauma-informed, anti-oppressive treatment to people across the spectrum of positionalities, practitioners need to identify and understand their own privilege (which everyone has in one way or another), as well as pain associated with their positions in life.

The shared nature of the practice of adventure therapy, where all the varied responses to the here-and-now moments are openly apparent to the participant, magnifies the importance of practitioner authenticity. This factor is magnified when considering how to manage the less visible aspects of identity that come with societal judgments. There may be different levels of transparency put into place for the safety of the practitioner or to protect the integrity of the treatment. For example, practitioners who identify as gay or lesbian need to consider the risks to their personal safety when sharing this part of themselves publicly. Similarly, requests from an adolescent to know the practitioner's history of drug use may be best redirected with the intent of exploring their desire to know.

The bottom line in all this is that authenticity is a critical component of being an effective adventure practitioner. **The critical and conscious use of self requires that awareness of self-identity and positionality are clear**. It is this clarity that allows the practitioner to interact effectively with a diversity of participants.

Rooted in Trauma-Informed, Anti-Oppressive Practices

As discussed in Chapter 2, anti-oppressive practice, which is true TIC, must be a central part of clinical work. For example, most people don't consciously engage in racism – but they often perpetuate it, nonetheless. Access to the roots of underlying racism or any other sort of unjust processes is not easily granted by intellectual conversations alone. These deeply ingrained responses become more accessible when experiences that are formed together elicit genuine somatic, physiological, emotional, behavioral, cognitive, and social responses (i.e., whole-body responses).

An understanding of neuroscience and somatic responses helps practitioners to harness the transformative power of experience in ways that heal, instead of (continuing to) harm, the participants. In his book, *My Grandmother's Hands*, Menakem (2017) suggests that racism has failed to end because the focus has been on the mind and not the body. To Menakem, racism operates in the entire body, but most powerfully in the limbic cortex part of the brain, which determines what is dangerous and safe. He explains that racism is always a bodily experience, for both victims and perpetrators and is a trauma caused by the cumulative effect of American history, the country's social and economic systems, and daily injustices. And it is buried deep in the body of every American. Thus, it is imperative to have an intentional focus on attending to the participant's whole-body response, including the somatic reactions connected to an anti-oppressive approach to treatment.

Practitioners understand that it is paramount to recognize one's own positionality, possible trauma histories and how that impacts work. The work that needs to be done falls on the practitioner's shoulders to understand how personal issues impact the multiplicity of factors that blend to define anti-oppressive practice. Otherwise, one might unconsciously maintain an approach that transfers the responsibility for anti-oppressive practice onto the participant and maintains an inappropriate power differential in the treatment relationship. It is not enough for the practitioner to inform the participant that individual cultural differences between the practitioner and the participant often come up during treatment; it is imperative that the practitioner is accountable to recognize and then attend to repairing the impact as it arises. This action normalizes the process and does not put responsibility solely on the participant.

An example of the need for practitioners to be attentive to the impact of their positionality on participants in their individual adventure therapy practice comes from a school social work setting. The practitioner, who was White, noticed a similar pattern of withdrawal and disengagement of Black students referred for services occurring between the third to fifth individual session. Development of the therapeutic relationship seemed to be progressing well when the participants would suddenly stop sharing about themselves and become aloof from the practitioner. During supervision, the pattern was further identified as a response to a session when the experiential intervention elicited content related to family functioning or problems the participant was having related to other family members. The supervisor suggested that although formal parental permission was obtained for the individual sessions to be provided in the school setting, it may not extend beyond working on the problems specifically related to school performance. The supervisor, who identified as a member of the local Black community, suggested that in general, the cultural norms within this community value keeping family business in the family. Her thoughts were that the permission form parents signed at the beginning of treatment did not extend beyond the school doors. Even though a measure of positive regard was developed with the participants, this practitioner was still a White man who may represent authority that was not to be trusted.

This insight from the supervision sessions resulted in two opportunities for the practitioner's work with these participants. First, parental permission to speak about family business in the sessions needed to be given in-person. This may be done by simply inviting the parent to say to their child (the participant) that it is okay to speak freely here. This process was often deeply emotional, and as such, frequently needed to be attended to a second time in the middle of treatment, even if a general permission was granted by the parents at the beginning.

The second opportunity presented to the practitioner was to connect the issue of developing trust in the therapeutic relationship to the practitioner's awareness that White people have abused their power by doing hurtful things to the Black community. The practitioner took responsibility to understand and address the impact of that history on therapy as it was manifested. In addition, the practitioner reiterated the pledge for confidentiality within the therapy, including clarification of the limitations around being harmed or harming others, in a manner that enhanced a sense of safety for the participants.

The approach suggested here for how to practice in an anti-oppressive manner is systemic, involving every aspect of the practitioner's service delivery. What is revealed about the practitioner in public forums, what is shared on one's website about inclusion, how the clinical office is decorated, and what the choice of outdoor locations for treatment communicates are all opportunities to shape an environment that is welcoming and inclusive for all participants. Another way of expressing "good intentions" is to explain to ALL participants that issues related to diversity, equity, and inclusion are most likely to emerge from the actions that are taken together in sessions, and that all of these issues will be explored and discussed as a natural part of the therapy. This approach opens the door to honest reflection on the issues that arise without shifting responsibility to the participant to raise those issues.

Preparing to Provide Trauma-Informed, Anti-Oppressive Therapy

In Chapter 2, anti-oppressive practices were identified as synonymous with TIC and outlined SAMHSA's six trauma-informed guidelines including Safety, Trustworthiness and Transparency, Peer Support, Collaboration and Mutuality, Empowerment, Voice and Choice, and Cultural, Historical, and Gender Issues. Understanding these concepts is the first step, but putting them into action must follow. Outlined next are some broad considerations and **actions** for each area to guide practitioners in their work (for more information see the National Child Traumatic Stress Network at https://www.nctsn.org/).

Safety

- Do no harm.
- Recognize that safety is relative.
- Create a socially and emotionally safe environment.
- Prevent and intervene on secondary traumatic stress.
- Engage the participant in thinking critically about their safety needs as they take action in interventions presented inside the session, as well as what they need in order to be safe outside of the treatment environment.

Trustworthiness and Transparency

- Recognize history of abuse and mistrust by authority.
- Be authentic and genuine.
- Acknowledge limitations.
- Have appropriate boundaries.
- Provide clear and transparent descriptions about the adventure activities to illicit continuous informed consent from participants.
- Be aware that the participant's whole-person responses to adventure interventions will reveal issues related to trusting systems, trusting others, trusting the practitioner, and trusting themselves.

Peer Support

- Foster connection with others.
- Encourage genuine relationships.
- Encourage mutual support.
- Plan activities with participants that support the participant's need to work with the practitioner in building skills and successful resolution of a problem-solving initiative.
- Initiate reflection on whether the participant was able to ask for and utilize the support available from the practitioner during interventions.

Collaboration and Mutuality

- Share power with participants, families, participants in decision-making and sharing information.
- Choose activities that encourage collaboration between participant and practitioner.
- Use a nondeliberative facilitation style, when appropriate, with the intention of joining with the participant in mutually working through the difficulties that arise during interventions.

Empowerment, Voice and Choice

- Recognize and communicate with participants around their own resilience and strengths.
- Build self-advocacy skills.
- Understand that people are capable and able to heal.
- Provide hope.
- Offer ongoing choice through the adventure process. (It is important, however, to recognize that offering choice for how participants engage in interventions also raises the issue of accepting the consequences of those choices. True empowerment involves developing the resiliency and belief in one's capacity to deal with these consequences effectively.)

Cultural, Historical, and Gender Issues

- Practice cultural humility.
- Learn about implicit bias.
- Cultivate cultural connections.
- Attend to participant's multiple identities.
- Recognize a legacy of trauma.
- Offer gender responsive services.
- Be aware that manifestations of these issues, while participating in an intervention, are often nonverbal whole-person responses that the practitioner needs to recognize and deal with during the session.

Approaching the Work with Curiosity and Compassion

The urge an individual feels to know more about something or someone is called curiosity. When acting in a curious manner with a participant, it lets them know that the practitioner has a strong urge to know more about them. This is demonstrated to participants by seeking clarifications, asking questions, and inviting follow-up comments from them about something they have already shared. Secondarily, the state of being curious demonstrates the belief that participants know their life and their life experiences best. Being curious about participants will help facilitators to know them better and know where to guide them best!

Compassion is the feeling that arises when you are confronted with another's suffering and respond with warmth, understanding, and kindness (Brill & Nahmani, 2017). A key value of compassion is that one suspends judgment so that one can appreciate others' perspectives or situations when they are different from one's own.

In the adventure therapy practice approach, curiosity is one of the primary drivers of WHAT is done as the practitioner facilitates the Facilitated Wave Practice Model. It combines with compassion to describe HOW the practitioner interacts with participants. Together, these two qualities are also the basis of cultural humility, which supports a nonjudgmental, compassionate, and collaborative therapeutic environment that can significantly benefit participants. Curiosity helps to build participant rapport, improves the ability to show empathy, explores a variety of perspectives, and encourages openness and continuous learning. In practice, curiosity is used to learn who showed up that day (their Point A) and what factors in the treatment environment are working to move the treatment forward and what factors need attention. Practitioners explore these factors collaboratively and in partnership with participants in a compassionate manner to gain an assessment of the whole therapeutic climate. This assessment, in turn, leads to curiosity about finding an experiential intervention that practitioners can tailor to fit the circumstances, as well as to explore how the participant is responding to the here-and-now stimuli that comes available during the experience.

Just as what is done needs to be fueled by curiosity, how it is done needs to communicate a sense of compassion for the participant and their circumstances. Compassion serves as a cornerstone for effective counseling. It drives the desire to be helpful, helps build trust, supports empathy, decreases shame and stigma, enhances therapeutic alliance, and cultivates positive change. **The fact that individual adventure therapy practitioners partner with their participants and have shared experiences provides the perfect opportunity to fully, authentically, and compassionately engage with participants**. The adventure practitioner does not intentionally position themselves as the expert or in any way superior to the participant. Rather, practitioners should constantly be seeking to understand the participant's response compassionately and to help them reflect on this information in ways that illuminate the path toward achievement of their clinical goals. This intentional position with participants supports the TIC principle that it's not what's wrong with you, it's what happened to you. Practitioners should intentionally assume participants are doing their best with what they've been dealt with, as opposed to blaming them for their symptoms.

Universal Point B's: Hopes and Expectations for Participants

While preparing to guide participants through the experience of individual adventure therapy, it is important for practitioners to recognize that they optimally enter every treatment event with a set of goals, or Point B's, for every participant. These goals describe how the practitioner is committed to interacting with every participant, as well as what they hope every participant will gain from the therapy. In their essence, these practitioner goals pave the way for participants to travel past the problems that brought them into the treatment and into the future they desire for themselves.

These **Universal Point B's**, which are described in more detail in Chapter 3, are another expression of the aforementioned trauma-informed principles for clinical practice. They are included here to emphasize that being an effective adventure practitioner and being trauma-informed in practice are the same thing.

- Compassion
- Hope
- Peace
- Meta-perspective
- Authenticity
- Anti-oppression

Collaboration

Collaboration with participants to ensure their voice is honored and invited in the treatment process is so important and ever-present in the practice of adventure therapy. **It is especially imperative in the practice of adventure therapy activities, where practitioners deliberately take leadership in selecting interventions and choosing how to present those activities, that they remain diligent in their efforts to hear the participant's voice and to collaborate with them throughout the course of treatment**. It is all too easy for adventure practitioners to operate on the choices they have made, thinking their choices are the best for the participant. This pitfall is easily avoided by the regular practice of gathering participants feedback and collaboratively matching interventions for the next session.

Listening to the participant's voice and collaborating with them is important for many reasons, including the following:

- Maintaining high engagement of the participant in working toward achieving treatment goals
- Incorporating the participant's perspective in all interventions
- Choosing how to expect and invite the participant to engage
- Letting the action go to where the participant needs it to go

All these actions demonstrate the importance of the participant's engagement and empowerment in the therapeutic process.

Practitioner Resources

All practitioners show up bearing gifts. Many of these gifts fall into four distinct areas, called "buckets" (Alvarez & Alvarez, 2019), which include:

- session plan,
- self-awareness,
- personal toolkit, and
- contextual awareness.

Regardless of the participant, practitioners are expected to enter every session with some intention about what needs to be done. That intention, which leads to the **session plan**, comes from the application of the Facilitated Wave Practice Model that provides direction for the practitioner. The session plan includes how the practitioner envisions the structure of the session and how any activity will match with the participant's needs and treatment plan. Even if the participant's presentation in the moment dictates abandoning that plan, the practitioner's baseline expectations for the session will provide a valuable frame of reference for adjustments that need to be made in the moment and how one can help the participant bring meaning to their experience during that session.

Just like every other type of individual therapy, practitioners work to be present and authentic in every session. **Self-awareness** is key to effective adventure therapy practice. Consider what a practitioner should say to any new participant when asked to describe their approach to therapy. The practitioner will probably describe joining with them in experiences that will become a primary part of their change process. Perhaps the practitioner would even share how the participant's responses in the therapy session will be a parallel process with their responses outside of the session. No matter how well the practitioner describes the way adventure therapy works, a major component of the needed answer will be missed if they neglect to emphasize the importance of a shared, genuine, and human experience with the participant.

The third resource practitioners bring is a collection of all their skills and knowledge of doing individual adventure psychotherapy. That **personal toolkit** includes their training and theoretical orientation, the list of activities they know and adaptations they have attempted, the props they bring into sessions, the stories they have used to promote learning, and the ability to draw on various facilitation skills and techniques. Practitioners who have been facilitating for years are likely to have more activities in their internal library from which to choose, as well as access to more facilitation skills used to enhance the effectiveness of each session, than less experienced practitioners. That discrepancy is expected and should not be confused with effectiveness, in general. A practitioner's personal tool kit will grow with experience; and they can be a highly effective practitioner during that process.

A final, extremely important, practitioner resource is **contextual awareness**, commonly known as the ability to read the room by observing and determining how the individual participant is showing up for each session and what environmental conditions are impacting the process of therapy. The purpose of this intentional focus on these Point A and environmental issues is to determine whether the plan the practitioner has created has the best chance of helping the participant move toward their Point B. **Contextual awareness enables practitioners to change many aspects of the plan in the moment**, including what activities to present, how those activities are delivered, what facilitation skills to utilize, the timing of things, the topics to cover, and whether to intervene in the participant's process or allow it to play itself out.

Practitioner Use of Self

The general guidelines for self-disclosure by any mental health practitioner also apply to the individual adventure facilitator. The first general guideline is that any self-disclosure by the practitioner is done only for the benefit of the participant. Practitioners do not share about themselves to satisfy their own needs for acceptance or approval, for example. Anytime the choice to use self-disclosure is made, it must be out of the practitioner's assessment of what the participant needs and not coming from a place of personal gratification or need. This axiom is a guiding principle in individual adventure therapy just as in any other form of mental health treatment.

The experiential nature of adventure therapy also provides some unique considerations for the use of self in treatment. The most obvious is that **the practitioner is often cooperatively engaged with the participant in an activity, meaning that the participant can observe how the practitioner is responding in real time**. This dynamic is both an inevitable facet of experiential practice and an invaluable component of what can be accomplished in this method of practice. It is inevitable because the nature of the interventions provided often require the involvement of more than one person to execute properly. The practitioner's participation in interventions results in opportunities for modeling desired behaviors, as well as providing the palette for rapid development of a positive treatment relationship.

The invaluable component of the practitioner being cooperatively involved with the participant is that so much can be learned from the interactions that transpire. Individual adventure practitioners often have visceral responses during an intervention that teaches them, in real time, what it is like to interact with the participant. These insights can be invaluable to the process of treatment. Like all mental health practitioners, they also need to identify any countertransference or other unhelpful responses they may experience.

One of the authors remembers working with a seventh-grade student, referred for counseling due to extremely aggressive acting out and oppositional-defiant behaviors toward adult authority. During the first several sessions, which this seventh grader was forced to attend as a condition for reinstatement in his educational program, he responded very negatively to the suggestion that he engage with the practitioner in physical activities. The author remembers experiencing a strong sense of humiliation when the participant rolled his eyes and made comments about the absurdity of the suggestion. The author's self-awareness that humiliation was not an emotion he typically experienced made it possible for him to remain objective and avoid the temptation to respond punitively, as did most other adults in his family and at school.

The practitioner persevered through these initial challenges to engagement in the treatment process until uncovering an interest the participant had in magic, or as he put it, "tricks based on the ability to cover up what was really going on." With this exchange in magic tricks (a skill left over from the author's college days) and the practitioner being engaged fully with the participant in every experience they had together, a positive therapeutic rapport was forming. As the sessions progressed, the curious, more lighthearted part of the participant emerged. He eagerly awaited the next problem-solving initiative and their time shared together. It turned out he was uncommonly smart and loved thinking outside the box with the practitioner about various ways to solve the problem. It was the power of sharing these experiences together with the practitioner engaging fully and allowing the participant to know things about himself that allowed this relationship to bloom.

As the author was briefing an initiative with this same participant, he recounted his experience of feeling small and humiliated by the participant's responses to this same activity introduced to him several weeks earlier. The participant remembered the scenario and stated that he knew what that felt like. His older stepbrother, who sexually abused him, made him feel just like that in front of his parents – small and humiliated over what the brother had done to him. The road to achievement of this level of self-disclosure from this participant was paved by the practitioner's use of self as they actively engaged in experiential interventions together.

Self-Care and Burnout

Before leaving this section focused on the practitioners specifically, it is important to talk about **self-care and burnout**. As Jennifer Mullan (2023) describes in *Decolonizing Therapy*, it is important to understand that the solution to practitioner burnout is not self-care. Certainly, personal self-care is an important aspect of being fully present and effective in the role as an individual practitioner. However, lack of self-care is not the typical cause of burn out. It is not the practitioner's fault.

The primary issue behind practitioner burnout is systemic in nature (National Academies of Sciences, Engineering, and Medicine, 2019). It is caused by unreasonable demands being placed on the practitioner by their employers to see more people to stay financially profitable. The system these mental health agencies is built upon, including insurance companies and government regulations, do not privilege or value the personal needs of practitioners. The time necessary for the practitioner to "take a breath" or reflect on the clinical work that has been done to effectively match future interventions to the participant's expressed clinical needs is often not valued in existing organizational models.

One logical consequence of this conceptualization around practitioner burnout is to recognize the need for mental health professionals to be politically active in the pursuit of policy and organizational change (Mullan, 2023). Without seeing systemic change, the rate of staff attrition and chronic burnout among mental health practitioners will continue and likely increase along with the growing demands for service.

Conclusion

Some of what is written in this chapter is applicable to every individual practitioner regardless of their practice approach. Every practitioner needs to be aware of who they are and what they value (self-identity). Understanding one's positionality, as well as the power and privilege that has been invested in them simply by their position in society is a central part of preparing for the role of someone's individual practitioner. Being rooted in trauma-informed anti-oppressive practices, approaching the clinical work with compassion and curiosity, and collaborating with participants to ensure their voice is honored and invited into the treatment process are as true for the preparation of individual adventure practitioners as they are for every other practice approach.

Reflections

- What power and privilege is granted to you due to your position in our society?
- Which one of the practitioner resources (buckets) is the most full? Which one is the most empty? What does this say about your practice approach? Your use of resources?
- How do you imagine the belief in the transformative power of experience will be put into practice with your individual therapy participants?

Now What?

- Do an inventory of your toolkit. Gather the props you have for interventions in one place and imagine the primary use you have for each tool, as well as what adaptations are possible to accommodate various participant needs.
- Look at the setting you use for individual sessions from a participant's point of view. Are there any things you need to change as you prepare to welcome all participants?
- Review the six SAMHSA principles of TIC and consider how you implement each of them into action steps for your practice.
- Do your own assessment using the four buckets discussed in this chapter and see where you need building up and/or toning down.

Preparing in Action

A case example from the field was shared with us by Lise Brown. We can see several things about how Lise has prepared herself to provide individual adventure therapy to her target population of children and families. The first is her commitment to decolonial practices and honoring antiracist and equitable service delivery. This commitment begins with her understanding of the context she works within and how that impacts her facilitation. The authors stand with her in asserting that being antiracist, anti-oppressive, and equitable in practice requires intentionality, commitment, and action on the practitioner's part to address these issues proactively.

The second thing we find remarkable is the clarity of how she presents the necessary practitioner resources. The case example shares her understanding of all four buckets the authors' described as necessary practitioner resources.

- Session Plan: Lise presents a detailed session plan that is described as an important piece of structure for her young participants.
- Self-Awareness: Lise comfortably acknowledges her power and privilege and shares how she manages those issues with her participants.
- Personal Toolkit: Lise shares descriptions of all the activities she lists in her session structure. They are available in Appendix 3.1 along with the description of other activities discussed in the book.
- Contextual Awareness: The importance of a felt sense of safety and inclusion is clearly a part of Lise's practice of Individual Adventure Therapy.

Practitioner Information

Lise Brown, facilitator, and owner at Momenta Inc. Lise has a bachelor of recreation management and community development (2002), is a registered social worker with the Manitoba College of Social Work, and completed a master of social work (2007). Lise lives in win-nipi, manitowapow, kanata, also known as Winnipeg, Manitoba, Canada. She is a solo parent and prefers to work and play outside rather than inside. She began her career at camps in Manitoba as an outdoor educator and guide. Lise also completed a certificate in expressive arts therapy in 2012, and the Forest School practitioner training in 2015. Lise combines these practice areas to provide clinical direction, facilitate groups, and counsel individuals in urban and wilderness environments with a focus on physical and emotional safety, successful participation, fun, meaningful activity, and group cohesion.

Lise has been a clinical social worker since 2007 and has worked with individuals, families, groups and communities facilitating and counseling, leading with adventure therapy theory. Prior to graduating with a MSW, Lise facilitated experiential activities to create connections and meet goals and noticed the therapeutic value of time spent outdoors and learning alongside others through activity and adventure.

"Manitoba, much like the rest of Canada, has a long history of separating Indigenous children from their families. Stemming from colonial ideologies, this seeks to assimilate

Indigenous populations and works against Indigenous sovereignty. Beginning with Residential Schools, this has continued through the Sixties Scoop and is upheld to this day with the current Child and Family Services. Not only does this have detrimental impacts on Indigenous populations and communities, this upholds colonial legacies that have and currently dominate Canadian society" (Manitoba Association for Rights and Liberties, 2018, ¶ 1).

Despite being only the seventh-largest city in Canada, Winnipeg has the largest total population of urban and off-reserve Indigenous people in one city (90,995), including the largest total Métis population (47,915) and the largest total First Nations population (40,290; Statistics Canada, 2023).

This is the context that I work within. I am committed to being radically accepting in my practice, to create spaces that feel safer and that build on people's strengths and capacities. I do constant work to address colonialism and racism in my practice. I also acknowledge my power and privilege and the history of harm that the field of social work has caused Indigenous peoples in Canada. I work toward decolonizing my practice and creating spaces of joy, truth and hope alongside individuals and their families.

Participant Description

To maintain anonymity, I have included a common demographic in my practice.

Demographics: Children 5 to 11 years old – a mixture of children with biological, adoptive or foster families

Diagnosis: None or ADHD

Strengths: Creativity, imagination, storytelling, playful, energetic, movement supports growth and learning

Presenting Problem: Behavior challenges, anxious thoughts

Treatment Context

Children are referred to me through my private practice at Momenta Inc. (exprliencemomenta.com). I book a minimum of 6 sessions with a family for the individual child at the beginning of the relationship over the span of 12 weeks. I complete a consultation with the parent, guardian or social worker over the phone prior to the first session. I encourage caregivers to join in the sessions whenever they can to support the child and the process. The sessions I am describing here are indoors, in my office, which is about 20 feet x 14 feet.

Session Description

To maintain anonymity, I have included a one-hour session plan (typically session three or four) that I used as a guide for all my indoor, one-hour sessions with the demographic outlined earlier. Structure is important to maintain consistency and predictability which supports the children to have felt safety and reduce anxiety.

Session Progression	*Activities*	*Notes*
Settle In 5 minutes	1 A cup of water is waiting on the coffee table for the child. 2 Lise shares one thing that happened at the last session that was significant and highlighted a strength. "Do you remember when we reached our goal of 50 playing Moon Ball last time? You were able to set a goal that could be accomplished with support, and we were able to communicate what we needed from each other to succeed". 3 Lise and child story share about something that happened in between sessions: "Sometimes we play **Catch** (description follows) to support regulating and to remind ourselves that we are good storytellers when we are not too focused on the telling of the story – we have important and brave voices and experiences".	
Check In 5 minutes	1 Lise reminds us of the expectations and confidentiality. Lise offers ideas of how to successfully meet expectations if needed. "To be safe today, we have to stay in the counseling room" 2 Lise and the child check in with "mood dudes"* or **Weather Report**.	Expectations: Have fun, take care of each other, be respectful, join in and be safe. *Multicultural mood dudes can be purchased through training-wheels.com
Warm Up 5 to 10 minutes	**Squiggle Drawing** **Don't Pick the Card** OR **Spaghetti and Meatballs**	These are three of my favorite warmups. Activity descriptions follow.
Activity One 5 to 10 minutes	Obstruction Junction **Game of Life** OR Incomplete Bridge	All three of these activities are in Lung et al., 2008 Purpose: Identifying "obstacles", trust, support, decision-making, listening and planning
Activity Two 5 to 10 minutes	**Moon Ball** **Help Me Please** OR **Pressure Points**	Activity descriptions follow. Purpose: Goal Setting, Asking for Help OR Coping Strategies

Session Progression	*Activities*	*Notes*
Story Time 5 to 10 minutes	*What Do You Do with a Problem?* by Kobi Yamada *When Things Aren't Going Right, Go Left* by Marc Colagiovanni *Repeat After Me: Big Things to Say Everyday* by Jazmyn Simon and Dulé Hill	These are three of many examples of story books I share with children based on their reflections and experiences during the session.
Memory Lane 2 minutes	Lise retells the progression of the activities they did that day.	
Reflection 5 to 10 minutes	Lise facilitates a reflection using Climer Cards. "Lots just happened! Did you notice that….? Which card will help us remember why today's adventures are important? What card will help us remember what to do next time?"	climercards.com
Challenge to Go and Communication with the Family 5 minutes	Lise offers the child a challenge in between sessions and supports the child to communicate the challenge to their family at the end of session. For example, "I wonder what it would feel like if you did a weather report with your grandma every day at supper time? Let's go check in with her about that."	

Bolded activities in this session plan can be found in Appendix 1.

Submitted by Lise Brown

Momenta Inc.

Winnipeg, Manitoba

Canada

References

Alvarez, A. G., & Alvarez, J. (2019, November 11). *Continuing our journey towards clarity and intentionality while finding our grounding: Our clear and muddled path. The Association of Experiential Education Therapeutic Professional Group Pre-Conference*, Spokane, WA.

Alvarez, T. G., Stauffer, G., Lung, D. M., Sacksteder, K., Beale, B., & Tucker, A. R. (2021). *Adventure group psychotherapy: An experiential approach to treatment*. Routledge.

Arat, A. (2022). Cultural relativism types and its elements. *Global Journal of Sociology and Anthropology*, *11*(3), 001. https://www.internationalscholarsjournals.com/articles/cultural-relativism-types-and-its-elements-91499.html

Bergkamp, J., Olson, L., & Martin, A. (2022). Before allyship: A model of integrating awareness of a privileged social identity. *Frontiers in Psychology*, *13*, 993610. https://doi.org/10.3389/fpsyg.2022.993610

Breunig, M. (2019). Beings who are becoming: Enhancing social justice literacy. *Journal of Experiential Education*, *42*(1), 7–21. https://doi.org/10.1177/1053825918820694

Brill, M., & Nahmani, N. (2017). The presence of compassion in therapy. *Clinical Social Work Journal*, *45*, 10–21. https://doi.org/10.1007/s10615-016-0582-5

Daily Montessori. (2021). *Maria Montessori theory*. https://www.dailymontessori.com/montessori-theory/

Denckla, C. A., Cicchetti, D., Kubzansky, L. D., Seedat, S., Teicher, M. H., Williams, D. R., & Koenen, K. C. (2020). Psychological resilience: An update on definitions, a critical appraisal, and research recommendations. *European Journal of Psychotraumatology*, *11*(1), 1822064. https://doi.org/10.1080/20008198.2020.1822064

Dewey, J. (1916). *Democracy and education: An introduction to the philosophy of education*. The Free Press.

Erikson, E. (1968). *Identity: Youth, and crisis*. Norton & Co.

Faissner, M., Gaillard, A. S., Juckel, G., Yeboah, A., & Gather, J. (2024). Intersectionality and discriminatory practices within mental health care. *Philosophy, Ethics, and Humanities in Medicine*, *19*(1), 9. https://doi.org/10.1186/s13010-024-00159-7

Gass, M. A., Gillis, H. L., & Russell, K. C., (2020) *Adventure therapy: Theory, research, and practice* (2nd ed.). Routledge.

Hammack, P. L. (2008). Narrative and the cultural psychology of identity. *Personality and Social Psychology Review*, *12*(3), 222–247. https://doi.org/10.1177/1088868308316892

Kearney, B. E., & Lanius, R. A. (2022). The brain-body disconnect: A somatic sensory basis for trauma-related disorders. *Frontiers in Neuroscience*, *16*, https://doi.org/10.3389/fnins.2022.1015749

Kuhfuß, M., Maldei, T., Hetmanek, A., & Baumann, N. (2021). Somatic experiencing - effectiveness and key factors of a body-oriented trauma therapy: A scoping literature review. *European Journal of Psychotraumatology*, *12*(1), 1929023. https://doi.org/10.1080/20008198.2021.1929023

Leary, M. L., & Price Tangney, J. (Eds.). (2012). *Handbook of self and identity* (2nd ed.). Routledge.

Lung, M. D., Stauffer, G., & Alvarez, T. G. (2008). *Power of one: Using adventure and experiential activities within one-on-one counseling sessions*. Wood 'N' Barnes.

Manitoba Association for Rights & Liberties. (2018). *Impacts of colonialism on indigenous children and families in Manitoba*. https://marl.mb.ca/blogs/impacts-of-colonialism-on-indigenous-children-and-families-in-manitoba/

Marcia, J. E. (1980). Identity in adolescence. In J. Adelson (Ed.), *Handbook of adolescent psychology* (pp. 159–187). Wiley.

Menakem, R. (2017). *My grandmother's hands: Racialized trauma and the pathway to mending our hearts and bodies*. Central Recovery Press, LLC.

Montessori, M. (1995). *The absorbent mind: A classic in education and child development for educators and parents*. Henry Holt and Company.

Mullan, J. (2023). *Decolonizing therapy: Oppression, historical trauma, and politicizing your practice*. Norton.

National Academies of Sciences, Engineering, & Medicine. (2019). *Taking action against clinician burnout: A systems approach to professional well-being*. The National Academies Press. https://doi.org/10.17226/25521

Norris, P. (2022, August). What does social justice have to do with therapy? Critical conversations in clinical supervision can help reclaim social work's mission. *The New Social Worker*. https://www.socialworker.com/feature-articles/practice/what-about-social-justice-confronting-race-based-trauma/

Paluch, R., Zayatz, C., Hopko, O., & Gambino, K. (2025). Pre-adolescents' hiking, health, sleep: Relationships between outdoor physical activity, health-related quality of life, and sleep in 8-to-12-year-old children. *Frontiers in Sports and Active Living*, *7*, 1–8. https://doi.org/10.3389/fspor.2025.1516699

Posluns, K., & Gall, T. L. (2020). Dear mental health practitioners, Take care of yourselves: A literature review on self-care. *International Journal for the Advancement of Counseling*, *42*(1), 1–20. https://doi.org/10.1007/s10447-019-09382-w

Shapiro, S. L., Carlson, L. E., & Sawyer, B. A. (2024). *The art & science of mindfulness: Integrating mindfulness into the helping professions* (3rd ed.). American Psychological Association.

Smith, S. (Ed). (2021). *Beneficial risks: The evolution of risk management for outdoor and experiential education programs*. Sagamore-Venture Publishing.

Statistics Canada. (2023). *Census Profile: 2021 Census of Population - Winnipeg, Manitoba*. https://www12.statcan.gc.ca/census-recensement/2021/dp-pd/prof/details/page.cfm?Lang=E&SearchText=Winnipeg&DGUIDlist=2021A00054611040&GENDERlist=1,2,3&STATISTIClist=1&HEADERlist=0

Substance Abuse and Mental Health Services Administration (SAMHSA, 2014). *SAMHSA's concept of trauma and guidance for a trauma-informed approach*. HHS Publication No. (SMA) 14-4884. Author.

Todić, J., & Christensen, M. C. (2022). Integrating critical, engaged, and abolitionist pedagogies to advance antiracist social work education. *Advances in Social Work*, *22*(2), 389–415. https://doi.org/10.18060/24972

Tucker, A.R., Norton, C., Itin, C., Hobson, J., & Alvarez, M.A. (2016). Adventure therapy: Non-deliberative group therapy in action. *Social Work with Groups*, *39*(2–3), 194–207. https://doi.org/10.1080/01609513.2015.1048416

Ungar, M. (2019). Designing resilience research: Using multiple methods to investigate risk exposure, promotive and protective processes, and contextually relevant outcomes for children and youth. *Child Abuse & Neglect*, *96*, 1–7. https://doi.org/10.1016/j.chiabu.2019.104098

Vago, D. R., & Zeidan, F. (2016). The brain on silent: Mind wandering, mindful awareness, and states of mental tranquility. *Annals of the New York Academy of Sciences*, *1373*(1), 96–113. https://doi.org/10.1111/nyas.13171

Watkins, C. E. Jr. (2012). Some thoughts about parallel process and psychotherapy supervision: When is a parallel just a parallel? *Psychotherapy*, *49*(3), 388–400. https://doi.org/10.1037/a0026246

Williams, E. N., Hayes, J. A., & Fauth, J. (2008). Therapist self-awareness: Interdisciplinary connections and future directions. In S. D. Brown & R. W. Lent (eds.), *Handbook of counseling psychology* (4th ed., pp. 303–319). John Wiley & Sons, Inc.

Yalom, I. D., & Leszcz, M. (2020). *The theory and practice of group psychotherapy* (6th ed.). Basic Books.

Zippia. (2025). *Therapist demographics and statistics in the US*. https://www.zippia.com/therapist-jobs/demographics/

Chapter 5

Assessment

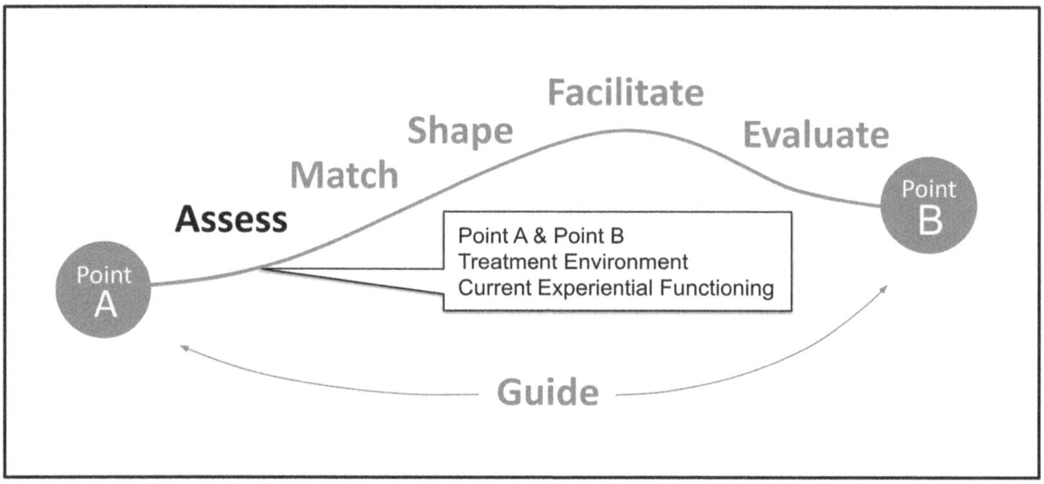

What Is Assessment?

For some, the first thought of assessment is of a validated research-based survey that one is required to complete to be able to bill insurance, or perhaps it is a psychosocial checklist taught in a required course in school. Hopefully, it at least includes the observations made when meeting the participant since often practitioners only think about assessment during their first session. However, no matter the methods or the timing, the process of assessment is what matters more.

In adventure therapy, assessment includes gathering information about the participant, as well as about the treatment environment, the participant's Point Bs, and self-assessment of the practitioner. While the primary goal of assessment is to clarify treatment goals and to develop the treatment plan, it also is about deepening understanding of the **current experiential functioning (CEF)** of the participant and how it intersects with the CEF the practitioner brings into the session to better inform the decision-making about specific interventions, the environment, and the therapeutic relationship. Ultimately, the assessment process is the foundation for building trust and engagement. It helps practitioners figure out the support and guidance a participant might need; differentiate between physical, psychological, developmental and social health; and provides the practitioner with a general overview of participant wellness.

DOI: 10.4324/9781003457893-5

As discussed in Chapter 3, how the participant responds in the moment, or in the here and now, is referred to as their CEF. The practitioner's assessment takes on a fresh dynamic when informed by seeing firsthand how the participant functions in the here and now of experiential interventions. CEF is about the participant in relation to their lived narrative, their bio-physiological makeup, their intersection with the practitioner, and the influence of their positionality in the interpretation of their experience. It includes having meaningful information about the participant's Point A and then comparing that assessment to the ongoing assessment that the practitioner engages in every session. Additionally, part of understanding the participant's CEF includes assessing the influence of the environmental context, both within session and externally, and THEN understanding the intersectionality of all these things as they relate to how the participant shows up in this moment.

Adventure therapy practitioners gather pertinent information from external sources, established assessment tools, conversations with the participant and other supporting or significant individuals (e.g., family members, teachers, probation officers, medical professionals, etc.), and observations of how the participants shows up (what does the practitioner see and hear) during each session. **This is when participants come off the paper and show their assets and strengths in person through their responses to the experiences practitioners share with them, as well as responses that may not be as adaptive or useful as participants would like**.

It is the practitioner's job to then explore with the participant what drives how they show up and what influences their responses. Of course, they may be driven by past experiences of trauma, as well as resiliency and their own health history and psychological makeup (processing speed, neurodiversity, anxiety etc.) which are important to know. In addition, as discussed in Chapter 1, practitioners are guided by their theoretical lens. When assessing participants, theoretical frameworks influence the clinical lens practitioners employ to understand why particular issues or challenges are occurring in the participant's life. However, practitioners, regardless of theoretical orientation, must not assume to know the source of those responses without assessing the environment in which participant responses exist and working collaboratively with the participant to identify from their perspectives what influences their responses to the experience.

What is critical is knowing how much of the current participant behavior is coming from their Point A versus coming from their environment. Hence, **the process of assessment in adventure therapy is ongoing, evolving and active by gathering information through activity** (Gass et al., 2020; Schoel & Maizell, 2002) **and collaboratively making meaning of that information with participants**. The assessment of each experience then guides practitioners in how to choose the next experience with the participant. This includes being flexible within the experience to adapt the activity if the practitioner's assessment of the participant's needs changes within the session experience. Hence, practitioners must understand that **assessment is a process that never ends** within adventure therapy.

Guided by both an understanding of trauma-informed and anti-oppressive practices, this chapter addresses the critical importance and active nature of assessment in adventure therapy. These assessments involve actions by the practitioner before meeting with the participant, as well as during sessions together. Before meeting, practitioners gather information about the participant's stated reasons for seeking therapy, what can be known about their Point A from external sources, and what is known about the nature of the external environment that may influence their functioning. During adventure therapy sessions, practitioners strive to understand the participant's CEF and the impact of the environmental conditions within the therapy sessions. This guides the co-creation and evolution of the participant's

Point B, and informs the choice of experiential interventions, how the interventions are facilitated, and how the participant's responses to these interventions are addressed with during treatment sessions

Anti-Oppressive Assessment

At the time of publishing this book, the understanding of how the social and physical environment impact participants is evolving. This is especially relevant to how practitioners engage in assessment. Ongoing marginalization and oppression are present in the lives of many participants. Practitioners need to be aware of the depth and potential impacts of this dynamic on participants. As discussed in the *Foundations of Adventure Therapy* chapter, trauma and ongoing oppression can impact the participants' ways of thinking and behaving, as well as their affective and somatic responses. In taking an anti-oppressive practice approach, practitioners will be actively engaging in building critical consciousness and awareness of the systems of oppression that exist in the environment, as well as seeking to understand with participants both their family and ancestral history and their roles in their current lives.

As a reminder, trauma-informed practices are closely aligned with anti-oppressive practice, hence practitioner assessments need to focus on understanding if participants have a felt sense of safety, trusted and transparent relationships in their lives, choice and voice in their current situation, as well as how cultural, historical and gender issues impact them. **In addition, practitioners need to engage in ongoing critical reflection to help them minimize biases, assumptions, and decisions made about participants** (Ortega & Garvin, 2019). For example, practitioners need to explore how societal gender norms may show up with participants in adventure practice, recognizing historically how males have been associated with competence more than women in the outdoors (Gray & Mitten, 2018; Warren et al., 2014). These notions can influence a participant's confidence in engaging in activity and outdoor based endeavors. Similarly, there is a history of associating adventure participants with ideals of thinness and certain ways individuals who engage in adventure should look, as well as assumptions of physical ability (Breault-Hood et al., 2017; Warren et al., 2014). This false narrative around body size and ability is important to recognize. Exploring with participants their history and perceptions of adventure and activity is critical for engaging them in the adventure therapy process.

Accurate assessment and exploration with participants allow providers to match activities that can meet participants where they are at, without inadvertently limiting them. This is all an ongoing practice of learning and growing so that dominant culture narratives do not perpetuate the marginalization of participants through experiences with practitioners in treatment.

In assessment, practitioners identify what brought a participant to see them. Often, there is a "presenting problem", or the participant is asked, "What is the problem?" and starts exploring their behaviors or experiences and the responses to their behaviors that have been "problematic". **Only focusing on the individual and individual responsibility ignores the context of the so-called problem, including systems and institutions that are inherently racist, sexist and oppressive**. For people of color and/or those who have marginalized identities, it is important to be aware of the ongoing and deep impacts of systemic oppression on human functioning. It is important to assess the impact of a participant's environment and how it impacts how they show up. Imagine a practitioner who is seeing a 6-year-old, male-identified student due to reports that he is stealing and acting out in class when confronted on his behavior. His behavior, of course, is of concern. Now imagine learning that his mom works two jobs to pay the bills; there is often not enough money for necessities, and this is a subject often discussed at home. This would be enough information to understand this child's behavior in context, and often, participants are experiencing even more systemic stressors than these. For example, they may live in a historically marginalized community with few resources. While this participant's behavior of stealing in the school needs to be addressed, understanding and recognizing the environmental contexts of this young boy are just as important. With a full assessment of his situation, a practitioner can focus on his strengths, including how resourceful this young boy is in trying to help his family by stealing things for them. Focusing only on the problem perpetuates the negative narrative often associated with participants, especially marginalized participants, which lead to often punitive responses and disempowerment. An author of this book, Dr. Bobbi Beale can often be heard saying, **"We need to stop punishing people for having trauma responses"**. As discussed in Chapter 2, trauma responses are often overlooked. People may say that the person/child knows better, so they should be held accountable for the behavior, which often ignores the neuroscience that highlights when an individual is dysregulated, they don't have access to their prefrontal cortex. Meaning, they can't make clear decisions and choices at that moment (Tucker et al., 2024).

This complexity is why supervision is so critical. It is in that space that practitioners can and should engage in ongoing critical reflection of their own biases, assumptions, and responses that can negatively impact participants and the clinical process. It is a practitioner's responsibility to continue to learn and do better in order to actively disrupt and/or dismantle these systems of oppression.

Active Assessment and Observation in Adventure Treatment

Although adventure practitioners will utilize passive sources of information (e.g., teacher reports or survey results), **the primary way adventure practitioners gather assessment information is through the power of observation and exploration applied in experiential sessions**. In assessment, this refers to the ability to accurately notice, interpret, and analyze behaviors, actions, and contextual clues to form a meaningful evaluation or judgment. This skill is crucial, as it allows the observer (practitioner) to gather valuable information about a participant's functioning, abilities, and needs in real-time and natural settings. This process is enhanced when the participant is actively engaged in the process; hence, the practitioner is advised to provide ongoing opportunities for the participant to use their voice to explain what is being observed and noticed.

Observational assessment is flexible, allowing assessors to continuously refine their understanding based on evolving evidence, and it can be tailored to fit the specific context or participant needs. While powerful, observation is subject to personal biases and interpretations, making it important for practitioners to be aware of their own preconceptions and strive for objectivity and engage in exploration with the participants around their assessments. Key aspects of observation in active assessments in adventure therapy include the following:

- **Real-Time Insights**: Observation provides immediate and direct information about how a participant shows up in a real-life environment, which may differ from how they perform in structured tests or artificial scenarios.
- **Nonverbal Cues**: Nonverbal behavior, such as body language, facial expressions, and gestures, as well as tone of voice, volume, and cadence can offer additional insights into the participant's emotional state, engagement level, and social interactions.

- **Contextual Understanding**: Observing participants allows for better understanding of how external factors, like the environment, social dynamics, and available resources, influence their experience and their responses.
- **Holistic Evaluation**: Practitioners can capture the complexity of human behavior, exploring aspects of somatic, cognitive, emotional, social, and physical experience, offering a more comprehensive assessment than one-dimensional testing methods.

Current Experiential Functioning (CEF)

Practitioners in adventure therapy use assessment to create an understanding of the **CEF** of the participant. CEF specifically looks at how participants show up and respond to experiential activities in which they engage with the practitioner. **CEF is rooted in the understanding that people's responses are strongly influenced by their perceptions of the environment, including expectations of behaviors, felt sense of safety, and previous experiences**. For example, a 16-year-old adolescent who "swears like a sailor" will clean up their language while in the company of their beloved grandmother because their grandmother is uncomfortable and incensed by such language. Or, a young Black person might behave differently in a setting of other Black people than when in a setting with all White people. This understanding of how the participant shows up (CEF) is developed and constantly evolves throughout the treatment process. Often, a participant's CEF or responses to their environment have created issues that have brought them into treatment in the first place. Hence, CEF can be adaptive as well as create challenges and negative consequences for participants.

Assessment of CEF involves intentionally thinking about the co-identified main concern and assets, observing and exploring ways those show up organically through activity, and considering resources available to address and move participants toward their goals – all within an environment of shared expectations. As practitioners, engaging participants in experiences helps to identify clinically relevant patterns. How a participant responds to the experience during sessions is often parallel to how they show up outside of the treatment setting. As practitioners, it is important to use curiosity as a driver for assessing CEF. **Practitioners should approach assessment objectively and use processing to extract and explore participants' responses in the moment (what are the thoughts, feelings that accompany the behavior) to start to engage in the analysis part of assessment, which is where meaning is ascribed**. This also allows practitioners an opportunity to role model for participants skills for self-assessment and awareness. Hence, as treatment unfolds, CEF changes and goals for participants evolve.

It is important to note that the practitioner is also continuously self-assessing their own CEF while facilitating the process of assessing the participant's CEF. **CEF assessment most often occurs as the practitioner engages the participant in experiences**. Formalized assessments are generally focused on the past or potential future (not the "here and now"). Furthermore, most formalized assessments are limited and often based on the medical model of symptoms, problems, and diagnostic criteria (Gass et al., 2020).

Factors that influence a participant's CEF include the following:

- *Participant's Point A:* Their lived narrative, bio-physiological makeup, trauma history, social identities, medical history and/or ability levels, current mental status, and previous experiences in treatment and/or the natural world.

- *Participant's Point B:* Their wishes, hopes, and intentions.
- *Environment:* Whether the environmental conditions support their desired actions or not, which includes physical setting and the relationship with the practitioner.

Hence, how one shows up (Point A) interacts with participants' expectations/goals (Point B), the environment, and the experience to expose a participant's CEF.

General Areas to Attend to in Assessment

Regardless of a practitioner's treatment modality or theoretical lens, all use the process of assessment to gather information about a participant's emotional, psychological, physical and behavioral health to help identify concerns as well as assets or strengths, develop treatment plans, and monitor progress. By tailoring assessments to the individual's needs and circumstances, practitioners ensure a comprehensive understanding of their mental health. The assessment tools a practitioner chooses depends on considerations about the participant; hence, no one tool fits all situations. Practitioners could choose observation, formal assessment tools completed by participants and ancillary people, and experiential methods. The following are **common general areas addressed in assessments**:

- *Psychological Well-Being:* Symptoms of distress, self-esteem and self-concept, coping strategies, thought patterns, daily functioning, risk behaviors, habits, treatment motivation.
- *Social, Cultural, and Environmental:* Interpersonal dynamics, support systems, social identities, cultural background, influence of culture, community, society or environmental stressors on mental health (including practitioner positionality), relationship with nature.
- *Cognitive Functioning:* Memory and attention, problem-solving and decision-making, learning assets and challenges.
- *Developmental and Medical:* Childhood development, trauma history, medical conditions and disabilities.
- *Intrapersonal:* Traits, identity formation, self-concept, roles, and sense of purpose, skills, talents, knowledge, abilities, habits, past experiences, suicidal ideation or attempts, self-harm, harm to others.

When analyzing information gathered from **an assessment of auxiliary people**, there are several critical considerations to ensure the evaluation is accurate, comprehensive, and tailored to the individual. Context, relevance, validity, reliability, bias, ethical standards, and practitioner theoretical framework all play a role in the analysis process. Consider the following when making sense of the information gathered:

- Relationship of source to the participant
- Perception of participant by the source
- Accuracy and completeness of information
- Biases (i.e., of sources and/or practitioner)
- Fit for scope of practice (e.g., practitioner skills, setting, individual work)

These are all general actions that most practitioners engage in when developing an assessment. As mentioned earlier, assessment for an adventure practitioner is focused on gathering information about the participant (which includes all of the above and exploration with the participant), the state of the treatment environment (see also Chapter 7), and the self-assessment of the practitioner (see also Chapter 4). **The adventure therapy approach is different in this attention to "who showed up right at this moment"**. While assessment supports the goal of developing the treatment plan, truly understanding the CEF of both the participant and the practitioner is the nuance that differs it from more traditional assessment.

Initial Assessment

The assessment process starts well before meeting the participant for their first session. There are several key aspects to assess to ensure that the first session is productive, respectful, and appropriately tailored to the individual's needs. Collaboration is core to this process, especially as it influences the shared process of adventure therapy. Including individuals in the assessment process makes them feel heard, increasing their commitment to the intervention. Additionally, a thorough assessment demonstrates that interventions are based on a genuine understanding of their circumstances. **This initial assessment sets the stage for effective treatment planning, rapport-building, and understanding the participant's mental health concerns. Plus, this collaboration is an essential component of trauma-informed practice**.

Common Methods of Assessment:

- Written referral (e.g., form, email, note)
- Verbal (e.g., phone, interview, voicemail)
- Observational (e.g., direct/indirect observation in a specific setting, such as a classroom or waiting room)

Common Sources to Gather Information:

- Participant
- Ancillary (e.g., parent, teacher, peers, probation officer, social worker, spouse, boss, adjunctive providers, insurance)
- Practitioner

Common Areas to Assess During Treatment

Ongoing assessment is crucial in matching the interventions to stay on course toward Point B (or to readjust Point B) (continue reading for an expanded discussion of Point B), typically through the assessment of CEF and exploration with participants of their responses and current CEF. Customizing interventions becomes even more important as the level of support changes. Additionally, **the intensity or complexity of the intervention may shift simply due to the participant's in-the-moment experience. Ongoing assessment helps the practitioner to prioritize actions for both resources available, as well as target attention on current needs showing up for participants**. The following are ways to engage in assessment during experiences with participants.

- Mental status exam
- Observation

- Check-in prompts or activities
- Initiative activities
- Experiential activities
- Creative/expressive arts
- Formal assessments (survey, interviews)

Using these various methods, ongoing assessment is continually monitored about a participant's Point A, Point B, and the treatment environment.

Gather Information about Point A

Participant and practitioner's Point A are complex and include how a participant and practitioner show up to the treatment experience. Hence, it includes everything already discussed at the beginning of this chapter in terms of participant history, as well as how participants physically, cognitively, behaviorally, and somatically show up at the practitioner's office or treatment meeting (i.e., their CEF). **The adventure therapy practitioner is especially interested in assessing the way participants enter the space for treatment**. What is critical to understand is where any changes are coming from. Has there been a change in their Point A? Based on this focus, the following are some questions to guide and gather information about a participant's Point A:

- What are the observations of the attitudes being presented during engagement of activities? How is this being expressed (e.g., annoyance, excitement, fear, detachment)?
- How are the participants experiencing the interaction with the setting (i.e., nature, props, spatial limitations)?
- What might be getting in the way of optimal learning?
- What is the participant's general sense of being?
- What is their current energy level?
- What was their day like?
- What do they want the practitioner to know today?
- What patterns of responses show up for participants during activities (i.e., responding in angry or avoidant ways to the practitioner, looking for rewards, seeking clues or guidance, violating rules, or being a helper)?
- Are participants responding in their typical manner regardless of the activity?
- How does the participant's Point A compare to the practitioner's observations of how the participant is showing up in the present?

To help address these questions, practitioners can engage in the following actions:

- Use a gathering activity to help the participant transition and engage in the treatment session.
- Consistently use a check in to provide regular opportunities to reflect upon and share their thoughts, feelings, observations, and concerns, such as the relationship with the practitioner, the facilitated environment, or squigglies that occur during the process.

Gather Information about Participant's Mental Status

Part of the Point A assessment always includes understanding the mental status of how participants show up. Consider that appearance and behavior can help identify problems with substance use, as well as other health problems. To look at mental status, practitioners should seek to assess and address the following questions:

- What affect (i.e., expressions reflected in movements or changes in voice tone, posture, or stance) is occurring? Is both affect and mood aligned?
- Are the participant's thoughts logical or consistent? What thoughts might participants be blocking?
- Are there distressing feelings, such as hopelessness or suicidality, being expressed?
- What is the cognitive functioning demonstrated (e.g., ability to focus or perform simple tasks)?
- How well does a participant solve problems and make informed choices (i.e., judgment)?
- How does the participant understand the challenges that have led them to seek (or be sent) to treatment (i.e., insight)?
- What is the participant's style of dress?
- How is their personal hygiene? What stands out about their behaviors?

Note: A common type of mental health assessment that most practitioners learn is a Mental Status Evaluation (MSE; Voss & Das, 2020).

To help address these questions, practitioners can engage in the following actions:

- Integrate metaphoric check-ins, direct questions, journaling, or observations from the practitioner that invites self-reflection.
- Consider formal psychological testing (often through a referral) for questions about obsessions, phobias, delusions, and suicidal or homicidal thoughts.
- Use journaling or activities that invite self-assessment, such as scaling continuum or selecting a picture or item that represents the answer to this question or topic.
- Observe cognitive functioning through noticing what happens when providing written directions, reading aloud a quote, or offering opportunities to write notes or to journal.
- Facilitate a task that involves some sort of problem-solving, which allows the practitioner to observe skills, such as frustration tolerance or discernment or how a participant might handle making a mistake.
- Use of any problem-solving activity to provide opportunities for observations of behavior that indicate the level of judgment and insight.

Gather Information about Participant's Point B

Like the Point A of participants, goals and expectations also evolve over the course of treatment; hence, it is important to engage in regular assessment of the Point B of treatment. To attend to Point B, practitioners should seek to assess and address the following questions:

- What are the participant's own ideas about their desired outcomes and clinical goals (Point B)? Are they vague and unclear (i.e., "I just want to feel happier", or "I want more people to care…", or "I don't know; ask [fill in the blank – mom, spouse, teacher, etc.]!")?
- Am I (the practitioner) the right person to be in the room with them?
- Is the participant willing to reflect on their responses and ability to connect them to what they are hoping to achieve by being in treatment?

- What shows up about their ability to generalize and integrate new lessons, skills about sharing thoughts or expressing emotions – all in relation to how these impact movement toward the participant's Point B?

To help address these questions, practitioners can engage in the following actions:

- Facilitate any activity that includes opportunities to listen, acknowledge, clarify, and invite reflection.
- Invite the participant to join collaboratively to figure out what it is they really want out of the time together (especially helpful in the beginning stage).
- Use journaling, goal worksheets, or experiential activities, such as **Vision Path** (see Appendix 1), to observe resistance, motivation, and even differing energy levels.

Assessing the Treatment Environment

In addition to Point A and Point B, ongoing assessment includes assessing the environment of the treatment process, including the physical space, the nurtured norms and beliefs, the therapeutic relationship between participant and practitioner, and the authentic engagement to the work. As early as 1946, Maria Montessori (2012) spoke to the importance of adapting to the learning environment. To do this, practitioners must first be aware of such/its presence. In adventure therapy, attention to the setting is critical! Whether the practitioner and participant decide to meet online, indoors or out, on a trail or in a kayak, the determination comes from a thorough assessment of "a highly effective learning environment". To do this, practitioners need to engage in ongoing assessment and attention to the physical space, norms and beliefs, the therapeutic relationship, and authentic engagement.

Gather Information about the Physical Space

To evaluate the physical space, practitioners should seek **to assess and address** the following questions:

- Is there anything in this space that will distract the participant or limit their ability to focus on the Point B of this session? (Is it a crowded outdoor space, are there others in the room with the participant when doing an online session, etc.?)
- Is the outside able to be safely managed?
- Has the participant shared information that will affect an outdoor session?
- What might an outdoor setting do from the perspective of a participant needing an external boundary?
- Does the practitioner have the proper gear for the participant to feel comfortable and functional?

To help address these questions, practitioners can **engage** in the following actions:

- Routinely scan the area and remove anything that may negatively impact safety or the participant's ability to focus on the work toward their goals.
- Inform participants about the appropriate clothing for the outdoors or the activity (and perhaps have back up available).

- Monitor level of comfort (clothing that fit, access to a bathroom, etc.) so that it doesn't activate the stress load of the participant.
- Address fears or concerns (i.e., bees, allergies, animals, etc.)
- Select locations to address distractibility, confidentiality, and focus.
- Discuss in advance with telehealth participants where they plan to log into the session and what may be the best environment to plan for the session.

Gather Information about the Nurtured Norms and Beliefs

To evaluate norms and beliefs, practitioners should seek to **assess and address** the following questions:

- Are any of the seven adventure beliefs missing or not operating optimally?
- Are any being integrated successfully?
- Did something activate a change in the environmental norms such that the participant is now feeling less open to talking?

To help address these questions, practitioners can **engage** in the following actions:

- Select or adapt the activity to highlight the adventure belief or norm desired to be addressed.
- Present opportunities for the participant to physically represent how well the beliefs are operating in the treatment space. For example, ask the participant to physically arrange floor spots (one belief per spot) in a proximity to them that represents the extent to which that belief is present in the experience for them. Closer proximity is associated with a stronger presence of that belief.
- Look for opportunities to bring to the participant's attention the beliefs that support the desired changes. For example, processing an experience or activity with a participant and asking, "which adventure belief do you feel was necessary for completing the activity? Was there something missing or ignored?"
- Look for evidence of applying insights or skills learned in counseling to real-life situations.
- Provide opportunities for self-reflection where participants can bring up realizations or changes in their thinking or behavior outside sessions.
- Align participant actions with previously set counseling goals.

Gather Information about the Therapeutic Relationship

To evaluate the therapeutic relationship, practitioners should seek to **assess and address** the following questions:

- What is the collaboration process like?
- What is the participant's willingness to share personal information and their level of vulnerability?
- What are the indicators of progress toward treatment goals?
- Is a warm, trusting relationship with the practitioner evident?

To help address these questions, practitioners can **engage** in the following actions:

- Facilitate an activity that provides opportunity to observe the participant's body language, eye contact, and engagement during sessions, such as a collaborative tower building activity.
- Evaluate the flow of conversation, interruptions, and responsiveness.
- Notice how well the participant collaborates on treatment goals and tasks.
- Address trust and openness by presenting interventions that require the participant to trust the practitioner (**Human Camera, Trust Leans, Unsighted Walks**, see Appendix 1).
- Continuously reflect on the quality of the therapeutic relationship and how it influences the participant's progress toward their goals.
- Collaborate with participants to actively participate in setting goals and cocreating the counseling process.
- Invite the participant to provide feedback on techniques or interventions.

Gather Information about Authentic Engagement

To evaluate authentic engagement, practitioners should seek to **assess and address** the following questions:

- How has authentic engagement shown up (i.e., a genuine, active, and collaborative involvement between the participant and the practitioner around the treatment process and goals)?
- Does the participant share openly? Is the participant responsive? What is the depth of the conversation?
- Does the participant show curiosity by asking questions about the counseling process, techniques, or their progress?
- Do the participant's actions match what they are saying about their goals for treatment? In other words, are they walking their talk?
- What about the practitioner's toolkit? Is the practitioner walking their talk about how to reach the participant's goals? (e.g., is the practitioner's adventure bag that is needed to engage in experiences with the participant still in the trunk of their car in the parking lot, and does it have the mud boots they and the participant were expecting to use for the planned trek into the swamps?)
- What was learned from last week's session, and is the participant applying it in the intervention today?
- Did the choice of activity move the participant toward their goals? Was the practitioner's sequencing effective?

To help address these questions, practitioners can **engage** in the following actions:

- Provide opportunities to openly discuss thoughts, emotions, and experiences without excessive hesitation or defensiveness.
- Notice if the participant responds thoughtfully to questions and prompts, indicating they are processing the dialogue actively.
- Use follow up questions to guide the participant beyond surface-level discussions and engage with deeper, more personal topics.
- Notice behavioral responses, such as body language (relaxed posture, eye contact, and open gestures indicate comfort and attentiveness), facial expressions (expressive and congruent), ability to stay focused, consistency with participation, and prepared to participate.
- Invite participants to practice skills (i.e., therapeutic homework) in-between sessions.

- Observe emotional indicators, such as vulnerability, insight development, and emotional investment.
- Consider takeaways from prior sessions and determine the session flow/plan depending on how the practitioner as well as the participant are showing up. For example, might the practitioner need to offer a more structured environment to manage the distractibility they (or the participant) are experiencing?
- Explore both the internal experience of the participant and the external aspects impacting the participant experience in relation to the process.
- Identify the patterns that appear and offer that observation up for additional reflection.

Assessment to Inform Treatment

Accessing information prior to treatment is crucial because it allows for a beginning understanding of the participant's needs, strengths, and circumstances. This will link directly to a practitioner's decision around selecting interventions because it ensures that interventions target specific needs rather than generic issues. It also helps to customize interventions to fit the unique characteristics of the individual, identify the initial level of support needed from the practitioner or others, and distinguish the intensity or complexity of the intervention required. Additionally, it helps the practitioner to prioritize actions with resource allocation and to differentiate between urgent issues requiring immediate attention and those that need long-term planning.

Common areas assessed:

- Fit, goals, and previous treatment experience
- Well-being and physical health
- Cultural background and strengths
- Resources and relationships

The following are some examples of connecting the dots between assessment and matching interventions with adventure therapy treatment. Different questions are outlined for a practitioner's consideration during this process.

Fit, Goals, and Previous Treatment Experiences

- Is the adventure setting and approach a good fit for the participant's issue(s)?
- Does the participant have any preferences about theory (e.g., cognitive behavioral therapy, narrative therapy) or communication styles in counseling?
- Does the practitioner have the skill/training to provide the appropriate adventure interventions?
- Do the participant and the referring source agree about the main concern(s)?
- What is the participant's Point B?
- Are there any legal or ethical considerations regarding confidentiality, especially if there are mandatory reporting requirements (e.g., child abuse, harm to self or others) or involvement with the legal system (e.g., court mandates, probation, custody battles)?
- Has the participant been previously diagnosed with a mental health condition or received therapy before? If so, what was helpful or not helpful in past experiences?

- Is the participant currently taking any psychiatric medications, or have they used them in the past?
- Has the participant done any active or experiential therapy (e.g., art therapy, music therapy)?
- Has the participant connected with nature for healing?

Once practitioners have gathered this information across sources (participant, auxiliary, etc.), the following are some actions that can be put into place for participants.

- Refer to a specialist (i.e., physician, behavioral specialist, psychologist, psychiatrist, neurologist, intensive outpatient therapy, residential treatment, etc.) or refer to other types of support (i.e., groups, books, coaching, etc.).
- Conduct additional assessment to identify additional concerns (e.g., developmental assessment, medication assessment, learning assessment).
- Collaborate within care team meetings to create shared goals among involved ancillary people (i.e., family meeting, school meeting, staffing, etc.).
- Provide crisis intervention if the participant is in immediate danger (e.g., experiencing a crisis or severe mental health episode).
- Set clear, realistic goals and align the therapeutic approach with participant needs, which includes connecting previous success or preferences with the current experience, as well as providing opportunities to manage expectations and address concerns through revealing the participant's mindset, including hopes, fears, or skepticism about treatment. The **Rubber-Band Goal Setting** is one type of experiential intervention that could help achieve this objective (see Appendix 1).
- Select activities to enhance motivation and engagement. **Burden-Bearing** is an example of an experiential intervention focused on engagement, for example (see Appendix 1).
- Identify what to avoid based on a participant's report and preference. Notice that novelty can be either engaging or distracting; familiarity can be comforting or boring.
- Use an activity at the beginning of therapy to identify progress markers, also as observational opportunities for change in the moment to be noticed and engaged in treatment. For example, use a **Continuum** exercise (see Appendix 1) for progress around a skill, and have the participant self-identify on the continuum their current progress.
- Think about whether environments that are frequently used or heavily populated may impact confidentiality concerns (e.g., for crowded parks or fields) and select locations based on previous experience and cognitive preference.

Gather Information about Well-Being and Physical Health

- What are the behaviors that are being noticed?
- What emotions are being expressed?
- How is the individual feeling emotionally right now? Are there signs of distress, hopelessness, or heightened anxiety?
- What thoughts are being expressed? Are they experiencing confusion, disorganized thinking, or impaired decision-making?
- How is this impacting the participant and the people around them?
- Does this show up in similar ways in other settings?
- What (if any) strengths are mentioned?

- Does the participant have any medical conditions or physical health concerns that could influence their mental health?
- Are there any current or past use of alcohol, drugs, or other substances that may affect mental health or complicate treatment?
- How does their sleep, diet, and exercise impact their mental health?

Once practitioners have gathered this information across sources (participant, auxiliary, etc.), the following are some actions that can be put into place for participants.

- Select initial activities based on participant's already known interests or skills to develop rapport or increase engagement (for example, adapting the **Maze Journey** to involve moving through various rooms of a video game; see Appendix 1).
- Include both familiar and novel activities to gauge urgency and readiness for this type of counseling.
- Designate a time frame for the activities based on the participant's attention span.
- Address medications that may have adverse reactions outside. Many medications – including antibiotics, antihistamines, non-steroidal anti-inflammatory drugs (NSAIDs), diuretics, antidepressants, acne medications, diabetes medications, chemotherapy drugs, hormones, seizure medications, and sedatives – can increase sensitivity to sunlight, potentially leading to adverse effects such, as sunburn or photodermatitis (Gupta & Bansal, 2013).
- Adapt treatment resources to accommodate differing abilities, for example, use stripes instead of colors for people who are color blind. Select paved trails or accessible trails with easy access to parking and facilities (see https://www.inclusiveoutdoors.org/ for resources and toolkits).
- Clarify clothing function and comfort (e.g., back up shoes, adjustable gear).
- Address assumptions about physical limitations – reinforce that all bodies can engage in adventure activities.

Gather Information about Strengths and Cultural Background

- How does a participant's cultural background, values, or religious beliefs influence their views on mental health and counseling?
- What are any relevant identity factors that may affect their mental health or contribute to stress, including discrimination or identity struggles?
- What are the strengths or coping mechanisms they already use successfully? How can these be leveraged at this time?
- What are their interests or hobbies?
- What are areas that the practitioner and participant have in common (i.e., music, movies, etc.)?
- What are the lived experiences and historical narratives participants have around the outdoors and engaging in leisure and outdoor activities?

Once practitioners have gathered this information across sources (participant, auxiliary, etc.), the following are some actions that can be put into place for participants.

- Consider the participant's relationship and comfort with nature or belief of their role in nature (especially stewardship) when selecting a location or activity. For example, it may be useful to engage in a **Nature Sculpture** as an introductory outdoor experience to assess the participant's comfort level with being outside (see Appendix 1).

- Explore perceived power dynamics around gender, race, skill level, class, or age (e.g., using an activity like **Cultural DNA**; see Appendix 1). This may also show up because of the presence of physical contact (i.e., spotting, checking a life jacket/personal flotation device (PFD), belaying, etc.).
- Identify and reinforce healthy strategies for navigating stress or change. Enhance knowledge and skills that are already present, e.g., movement or mindfulness. Scaffold experiences to reinforce progress and build upon small successes.
- Explore themes with participants that highlight strengths rather than problems or symptoms. Move the focus from the participant as the problem to the participant having the skills with support to grow and change.

Gather Information about Resources and Relationships

- Does the participant have the resources to access treatment (e.g., transportation, finances, time)?
- What resources are available from the provider (e.g., insurance, transportation)?
- Who is in the participant's life to offer support (i.e., family, friends, or community groups)?
- Are there any significant external pressures contributing to their mental health concerns (e.g., job loss, academic difficulties, financial stress, relationship challenges)?
- What is their home environment (e.g., stable or unstable housing)?
- Are there any domestic or family issues that provide context?
- What aspects about their relationships are positive and going well?
- What other resources do participants have that provide stability and support?

Once practitioners have gathered this information across sources (participant, auxiliary, etc.), the following are some actions that can be put into place for participants.

- Select accessible meeting locations (i.e., along a bus route, at a convenient location, at a familiar location, at a novel location, etc.).
- Select locations based on exposure to other people (e.g., sometimes it is helpful to see activities normalized, like hiking; other times, there may be a need for more privacy, such as a botanical garden.)
- Choose between familiar or novel props (e.g., how might a participant's previous experience with mousetraps influence using them in a game?) Identify equipment and supplies needed for the experience (e.g., snacks, extra clothing, water bottles).
- Connect with funding options (i.e., grants, scholarships, insurance, etc.) and to others outside of treatment to help the participant access services and connecting with the community (i.e., local outdoor recreation groups, affiliation groups, online resources).
- Acknowledge the expanded role of the adventure practitioner to address aspects in addition to asking questions or providing reflection (e.g., provide physical safety as a spotter, or exercise proximity by adjusting distance from participant while walking, working, or snacking near each other).

Case Conceptualizations and Ongoing Assessment

In assessment, the case conceptualization is the organized holder of all that the practitioner has learned from time with the participant, starting with the first contact. A **case conceptualization** represents how practitioners approach a case. It includes relevant information about the participant's history; their functioning at home, school, and/or work; community environments; and their CEF. A case conceptualization typically includes the following:

- Conducting an **assessment** in which data is gathered and analyzed through the practitioner's theoretical and clinical lens in collaboration with the participant. The assessment results in identification of the primary issue the participant is coping with and a rationale for the factors contributing to or explaining why the issue exists. The assessment also identifies participant strengths and assets that will support the treatment process.
- Identifying collaboratively with the participant the primary **goals** of treatment, which address the issues highlighted in the assessment and build on participant strengths. In the Facilitated Wave Model, treatment goals are part of "Point B" – the desired end result of the treatment process.
- Developing an **intervention** plan and structure to address the identified treatment plan goals and objectives.

Assessment involves data collection (which is ideally objective) paired with an analysis of that data (filtering the information through theoretical frameworks). For example, perhaps a practitioner is informed by a participant that they "freeze up" in social interactions that are tense and that this has become a problem at work where they supervise people and need to give them difficult feedback. Additionally, the participant reports that they grew up in a household where open conflict was not accepted, and if it did occur, it escalated conflict and crisis followed. The data shared with the practitioner at this stage is objective and factual based on participant reporting.

In the analysis part of assessment, subjective meaning is ascribed based on the clinical lens of the practitioner. If the practitioner's theoretical framework is cognitive behavioral, they are likely to see this freezing behavior as a result of learned behavior and conditioning. If the practitioner's theoretical framework is more neurobiologically based, they may view this a response to stress that activates the nervous system's alarm response. This assessment's findings might look like this:

Cognitive Behavioral Lens: As a result of learned behavior reinforced in childhood, the participant struggles to communicate and manage difficult conversations effectively, resulting in reduced performance at work.

Neurobiology Lens: As a result of trauma and repeated activation of their nervous system's alarm response during childhood, the participant struggles to manage their stress responses, resulting in "freezing" responses to stressful social situations and conflict.

Because of the experiential nature of adventure therapy, assessment processes include the opportunity to collect data that emerges during experiential interventions and incorporate this into the assessment. Participant responses bring to light strengths and challenges, as well as clinically relevant patterns. **For this participant, their in-session responses to adventure activities may yield a lot of information about the nuances of what happens when the participant**

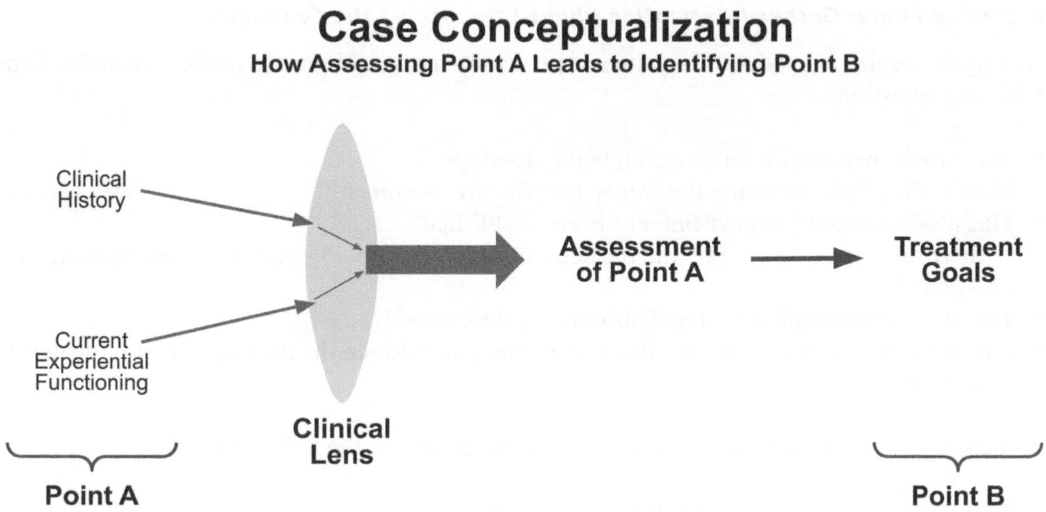

Figure 5.1 Clarity on where you are going requires knowing where you are.

encounters varying challenges with the practitioner. The practitioner may see what the freezing looks like, explore the participant's thoughts and feelings about the situations that led to the participant freezing, or even explore the moments when the participant did not freeze and was successfully able to communicate in a potentially conflictual interaction.

Figure 5.1 highlights this process of how the participant's CEF and their clinical history is then seen through the clinical lens of the practitioner, which helps them to develop an understanding of the reasons for coming to treatment, as well as the strengths and resources of the participants. This leads to an assessment that identifies the primary issues that help to identify the goals for treatment (Point B). For case conceptualization, a more formal document is often created so that at any time during the treatment process, it can be used as a tool to guide the matching of sessions and activities to the participant's needs, strengths, and goals. This is most useful as a dynamic process, meaning that any current information can be referenced, incorporated, or updated easily. Hence, case conceptualizations evolve as the treatment process evolves. This chapter ends with a sample case conceptualization for reference, while the goal, treatment plan, and intervention aspects of case conceptualization are addressed in more depth in Chapter 6.

Assessment Across Phases of Treatment

As discussed already, practitioners are always engaging in assessment; in fact, it never ends. **This ongoing assessment ensures that the treatment process is still going where it needs to be heading**. The initial assessment provides information to select appropriate themes, activities, and locations. Once those are implemented, continuous assessment ensures that interventions can be adapted if they are not meeting goals.

Due to the changing dynamics, foci, needs and skills of participants, practitioner assessment evolves over time throughout the treatment process. The following are considerations and actions practitioners can pay attention to during the beginning, middle, and ending phases of the treatment process, in addition to the areas covered already in this chapter.

Beginning Phase: Gather Information about Establishing the Foundation

During the beginning stages of treatment, practitioners should seek to assess and address the following questions:

- Is a strong therapeutic relationship being developed?
- How is the physical setting the "*stage for effective treatment?*"
- Has a safe, supportive environment been established?
- Is there an understanding of the participant's history and alignment on current concerns, and goals?
- Has the treatment plan been collaboratively developed?
- Are there clear expectations for the roles of the practitioner, the participant, and the nature of therapy?

To help address these questions, practitioners can engage in the following actions:

- Build rapport and trust through shared experience.
- Gather additional information by conducting additional assessments to understand the history, current concerns, and goals.
- Identify goals through observations, exploration, and insight of experiences.
- Clarify participant's (and auxiliary people's) expectations.
- Provide multiple and diverse opportunities to assess strengths and skills being demonstrated in the session (e.g., ability to focus, can they laugh at themselves, what is their effectiveness/modes of communication, frustration tolerance).
- Self-assess the practitioner's ability to be in the room with the participant, to be helpful with what they will need, and their ability to show up as their best self.

For example, during an early session, the practitioner brought out the paper plate that contained all the words normally used to describe weather as the tool for the check in (See Appendix 1, **Weather Report**). After the participant circled the cloud on the paper plate, the practitioner proceeded to offer placating words (oh, so sorry, …) and then proceeded to invite the participant to "put words on their selection of the cloud". The participant proceeded to describe a great week she had had, which puzzled the practitioner, who considered choosing the cloud to mean something else. Inviting the participant's voice through curiosity helps to better define what their actions and choices mean and tells a better story.

Middle Phase: Gather Information about Working on Goals

During the middle stages of treatment, practitioners should seek to assess and address the following questions:

- Are the goals established in the beginning phase still relevant and being worked on?
- Do the matched and chosen strategies and techniques help participants manage symptoms and make desired changes?
- Have underlying patterns, beliefs, and emotions contributing to the presenting problems been uncovered and processed?
- Are positive changes and coping strategies being reinforced?

To help address these questions, one can engage in the following actions:

- Notice progress toward (or clarify) goals while facilitating interventions that increase knowledge, desired behaviors, or process emotions that address identified issues.
- Introduce strategies and techniques through scaffolding and sequencing activities.
- Explore deeper issues through reflection of experiential opportunities via discussion, journal, or expressive arts activities.
- Build resilience by introducing new skills, reinforcing positive changes, and rehearsing healthy coping strategies.

For example, during a session where the **Tennis Ball Pyramid** activity was being used, the practitioner noticed the participant repeatedly creating a pyramid by putting five tennis balls on top of seven tennis balls, all placed in a line (see Appendix 1). This response by the participant surfaced a visual skill deficit in this participant that had never surfaced in other formal assessments. Discovering the presence of this visual disability and learning ways to accommodate for it enhanced the participant's performance in reading and other subjects that were academically difficult.

Ending Phase: Gather Information about Integration, Consolidation, and Termination

During the ending stages of treatment, practitioners should seek to assess and address the following questions:

- How has the participant prepared for independence and ending the therapeutic relationship?
- Have the participant's achievements been reviewed and strategies learned reinforced?
- Has a relapse prevention or maintenance plan been developed?
- Have feelings about ending therapy been addressed?
- Has the participant been empowered to continue progress outside of therapy?

To help address these questions, practitioners can engage in the following actions:

- Consolidate progress by providing an overview of the treatment journey.
- Plan for the future by collaborating around a plan for the next steps.
- Process termination by doing an activity that helps to process the ending of therapy, including grief, gratitude, or anxiety.
- Promote independence by empowering the participant to continue to learn and grow.

Clinical Case Example and Conceptualization: Wendy

The case example of Wendy is used to highlight the important role of active assessment throughout the treatment process. It includes both initial assessment activities using the **Four Corners** exercise (see Appendix 1) and ongoing assessment with the practitioner. Figure 5.2 shows the structure of the Four Corners activity, which can be used with a participant to look at the different environments they live in. It is used to gather information, invites participant voice in its completion, and offers a visual representation for the participant of the systems that both support and stress the participant.

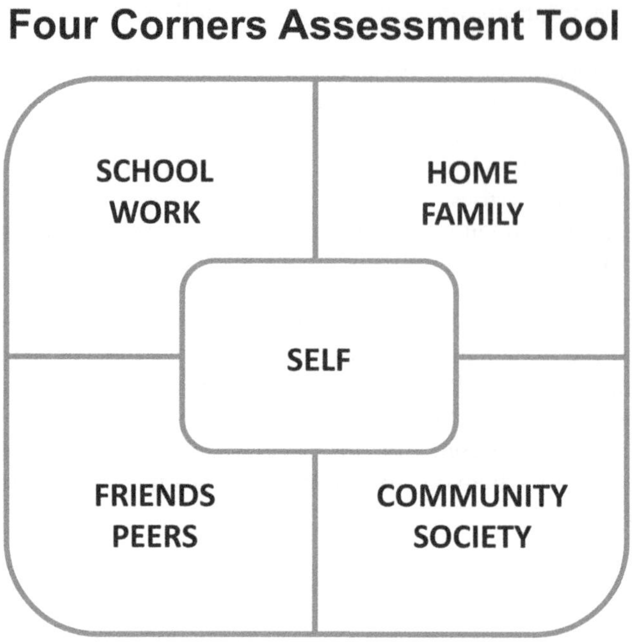

Figure 5.2 Four corners: An ecological perspective.

Overview

Wendy identifies as a White, female, 11-year-old in the sixth grade and was referred to the school social worker by her teacher for her "distractibility, laziness, shyness, and a blasé attitude". The school Wendy attends was designated as a Title I school (more than half the families fell under the poverty line) and was staffed mostly by all-White, female-identifying teachers who live outside of the county line. The racial/ethnic breakdown of the school was 50% White, 35% Black, and 15% Mexican (mostly migrants working in the farms in and around the county). The families of color lived exclusively "across the tracks" from the city proper, while the upper-class White families lived in specific parts of the city and did not send their children to this particular school. The rest of the White families lived in rural areas around the eastern side of the city, as well as in neighborhoods with families of color.

Prior to First Meeting with Participant

Teacher Meeting and Referral

A pre-referral meeting provided an opportunity to see if Wendy's current situation was a good match for counseling in the school setting. The practitioner needed to consider whether individual versus group treatment might best address Wendy's situation. During the meeting, the teacher was concerned about Wendy's "fit" in the classroom, both with others and with the structure of the class. The teacher summed up her thoughts by describing Wendy as "so uncaring about how she presents as a young lady".

During this meeting, as well as due to the previous interactions with this teacher, the practitioner understood that the teacher was invested in this student and selective about referrals. The teacher had already referred her to the school counselor, invited her parents to a meeting (parents were no-shows), and used classroom strategies to manage continued disruptions and negative behaviors in the classroom (a time out corner, sent her to the hallway, and kept her in the classroom during the lunch break). This 20-minute consultation resulted in a written referral request for individual counseling. The teacher's formal referral described behaviors such as "seems to be on another planet", "loves playing like a boy", "spends a lot of time away from others", "loves writing and doodling", and "often is the butt of jokes, especially by the girls". Figure 5.3 shows the Four Corners created by the practitioner after this initial meeting with the teacher.

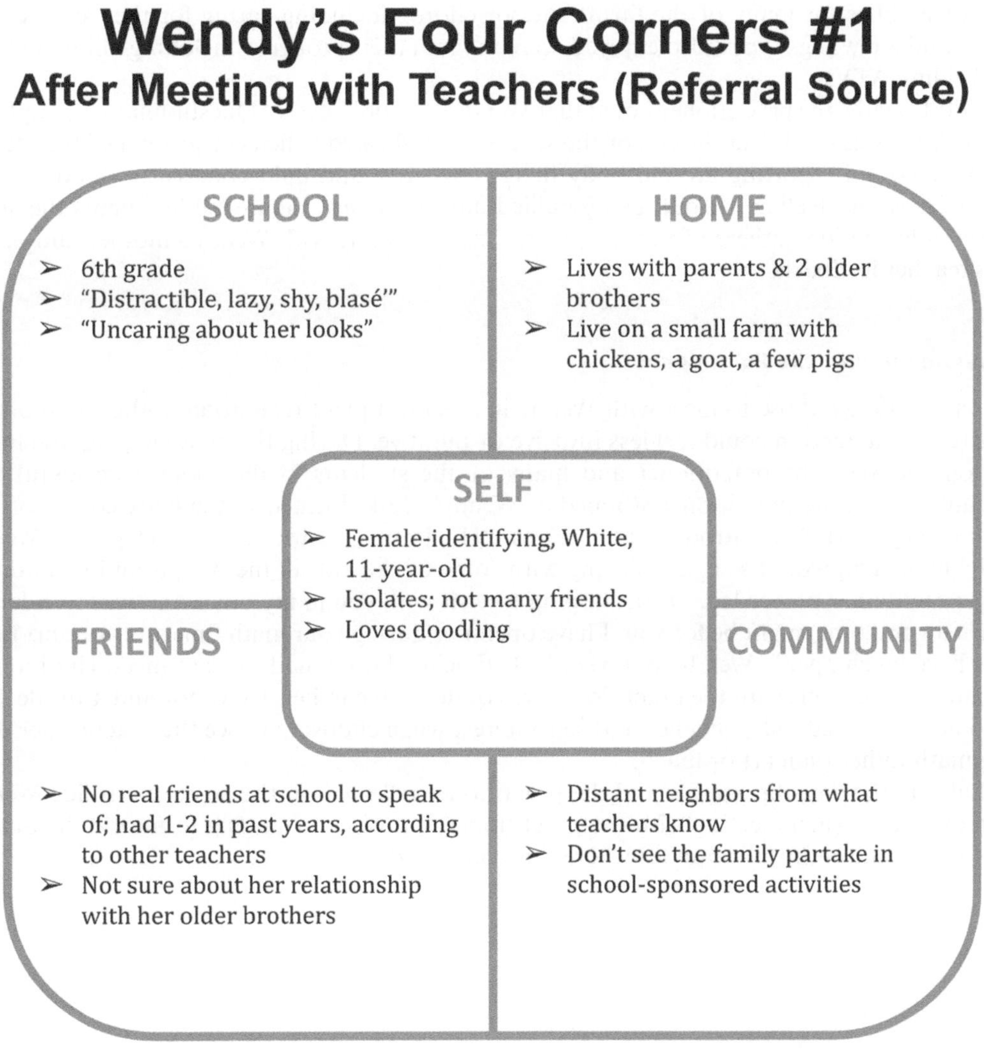

Figure 5.3 Teacher perspective on Wendy's current experiential functioning.

Gathering Information with Auxiliary Individuals

In addition to the formal written referral from the teacher, the practitioner was also interested in gathering information from the family (in this case, her biological mom), and previous teacher reports or assessments. During a call to set up a visit, the mother asked that this interview be done over the phone because of her busy schedule with farm chores during the day.

A phone call provided an opportunity to gather information from Wendy's mother. During this conversation, she offered more insights into life for Wendy at home. She reported that Wendy was the youngest of three, including two older brothers ages 14 and 16. The parents lived on the outskirts of a small city, on a property that had been a small farm, before they bought the property. Wendy's father was a laborer at a business in town, and her mother managed the home and the small farm. According to the mother, her three children had daily responsibilities for many of the farm/outdoor chores, including caring for their chickens, a goat, and a few pigs. They also enjoyed recreating on their property, including climbing trees and riding ATVs.

Additionally, the practitioner noted that Wendy's School Success Questionnaire (completed by the previous teacher at the end of the school year) showed deficits in academic motivation, heightened self-reporting around body image concerns, and mild concerns around anxiety and depression (feeling left out, being bullied, not fitting in). Figure 5.4 highlights the additional information gathered from the practitioner's meeting with Wendy's mother and previous teacher feedback.

Assessment with the Participant

The practitioner chose to meet with Wendy in a neutral place (classroom rather than office) where the interaction could feel less invasive or punitive. During this first meeting, the interactions between the practitioner and many of the students in the room were joyful and friendly. When the practitioner stopped at Wendy's desk, located in the back corner of the room, they started to introduce themselves, "Hi, I am ___; we haven't met yet…" Wendy quickly interrupted, "I saw you playing with some of the kids in the playground yesterday". The practitioner proceeded, "I was hoping to visit with you in my office and was wondering when a good time might be for you. I have openings during your math time and your art time, or I have lunch open". Wendy took very little time to choose math time to meet. Her interest in pursuing sessions with the practitioner was quite visible in her demeanor and attitude. She also demonstrated independence and self-interest when choosing to see the practitioner during math rather than art or lunch.

Later in the day, the teacher and the practitioner reflected on the positive attitude Wendy demonstrated when meeting with the practitioner and when arranging to meet individually. Both felt quite enthusiastic about where this could lead.

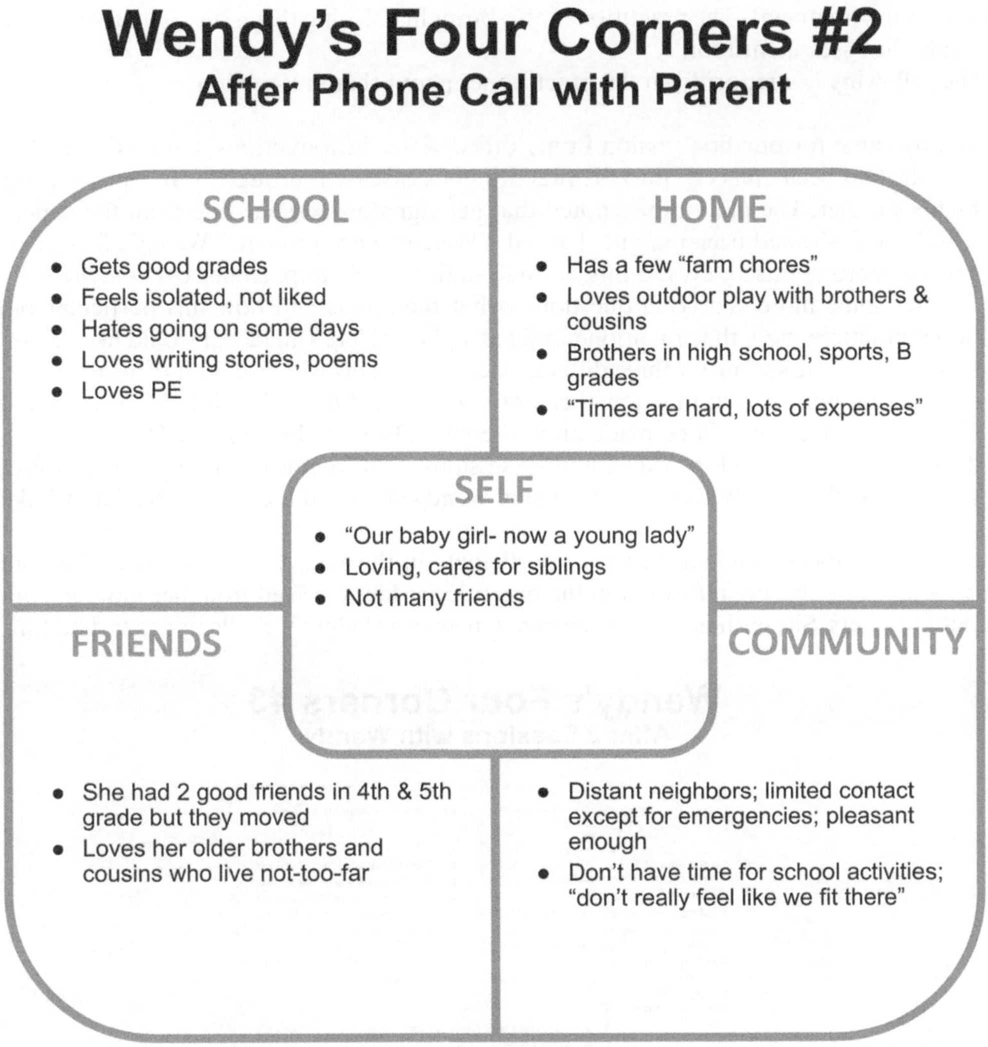

Figure 5.4 Parent perspective adds meaning and depth.

Assessment in the First Sessions with the Participant

Before their first meeting with Wendy, the practitioner took into consideration the following gathered information:

- Teacher indicating Wendy's strengths in writing, doodling, and quiet drawing
- Wendy's noticing of the practitioner joyfully playing outside
- Report from both her mother and the teacher that when pressed, Wendy backs off and isolates
- Wendy's capacity to talk and draw at the same time

Based on this information and their own observations of Wendy, the practitioner chose the paper/pencil activity of the Four Corners for gathering information, as well as engaging

Wendy in the treatment. The practitioner also brought coloring materials so that Wendy could decorate the assessment tool.

The following is a report from the practitioner about that first session:

> Wendy came for our first session in my office. After introductions, I shared with Wendy that she had been "placed" into the practitioner's caseload through an IEP process, signed by her mother. The practitioner noted that her signature was missing from the paper and wondered if she had been present? I asked, "Were you not present?" Wendy's facial expressions (eyebrows raised, eyes rolling, a snide smile) clearly implied not being invited.
>
> After some more clarifying questions (what therapy is and how this particular practitioner practices, etc.), the practitioner offered a plan: "Here's an idea. I would like to ask you to agree to come see me on three different occasions. This will give both of us the opportunity to determine if that time together would prove useful and helpful. After the third session, a joint decision will be made around continuance of the sessions. Depending on the decision, we can move forward with more sessions or move toward ending our sessions. Are you good with this?" Without hardly a gap, Wendy approved the plan with a handshake.

Then the practitioner invited Wendy to participate in the Four Corners activity. The practitioner started by sharing information the practitioner had received from her mother, counselor, and teachers. She enthusiastically engaged in acknowledging, challenging, and adding her

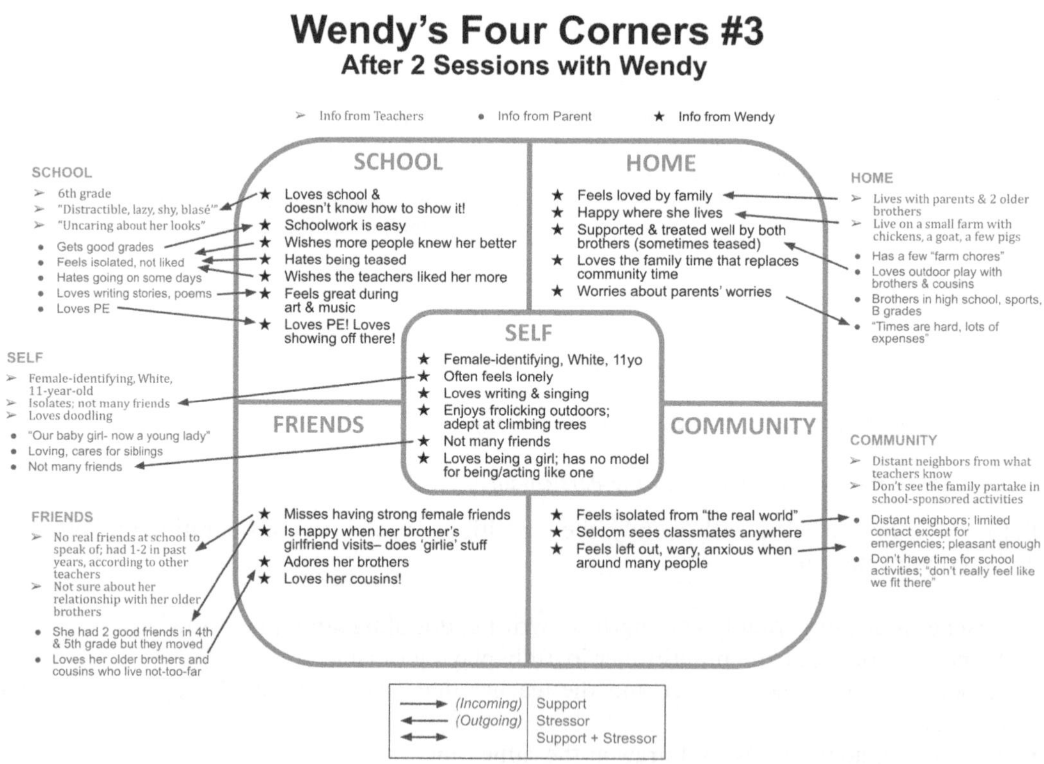

Figure 5.5 Adding Wendy's voice to the assessment is essential.

information as the practitioner put it on paper. Very quickly, she took over with filling in the blanks. During this session, the practitioner and Wendy ran out of time and decided to continue the activity for the next session. At the end of two sessions, the practitioner, with Wendy's help, had a clear understanding of Wendy and her current situation. Wendy's Four Corners can be seen in Figure 5.5.

During these two sessions, the practitioner noticed Wendy's active engagement in exploring parts of her life and her appreciation of being allowed to make decisions about how and what things occurred in sessions. This in fact was consistent with Wendy's ongoing engagement in therapy. Despite the picture provided by her teacher at intake, she showed enthusiasm throughout the treatment process, successfully participated in treatment, and completed treatment in six months.

Initial Case Conceptualization

Based on the information gathered from individuals in Wendy's life, the practitioner, and Wendy, a case conceptualization of Wendy was created by the practitioner as seen in Table 5.1.

Table 5.1 Wendy's Case Conceptualization

Clinical History	• 11 y/o White cisgender-identifying female • Difficulty in school since fourth grade (academically and socially) • Ongoing disruptive behaviors in classes • Teacher reports difficulty engaging Wendy in school and classroom activities • Reported to be sad (maybe depressed?)
Current Experiential Functioning	• Reacts by isolating, shutting down when confronted • Tries to get along with peers but isn't good at it • Has great rapport with nonauthoritative adults • Actively engages in adventure therapy sessions
Assessment	• Struggling with who and what she wants to be • Strong sense of her strengths • Strong sense of her values, to the detriment of peer relationships • Isolated from peers, which caused some sadness (maybe could develop into depression) • Eager to be guided, to be accepted
Treatment Goals	• Build skills in expressing herself, in giving feedback • Build her confidence in who she is/wants to be • Enhance skills in seeking help
Interventions	• Individual adventure psychotherapy sessions • Scaffold activities that provide her opportunities to reinforce her own abilities and skills, including her physical strength especially around more challenging activities • Utilize activities that elicit emotional responses to help her recognize her emotions and express them in ways that support her needs and the environmental expectations • Choose activities that require her to practice skills she has learned to be successful in their completion • Intermittent sessions with Wendy's mother to suggest ways to provide Wendy the support she needs as she approaches adolescence

Assessment of Adventure Beliefs with the Participant

Assessing and attending to the adventure beliefs is an integral part of the individual treatment process. The following highlights one interaction in which the practitioner addressed issues around those beliefs during Wendy's treatment. Wendy came in for her regular session (fifth); she promptly sat down, pulled up her hoodie (which she had stopped doing since session two), and stared at her fingers and nails for a good three minutes. The practitioner had seen this before and responded accordingly by remaining silent. Finally, Wendy hemmed and hawed and quickly stated, "My mom said she talked to you!" The practitioner quickly acknowledged this call did happen and clarified the extent of information shared with her mother. Satisfied that her sessions remained confidential, Wendy relaxed! This assessment of and attention to the adventure beliefs (in this case, confidentiality that serves to enhance trust and safety) is critical throughout the treatment process.

Ongoing Assessment During Treatment

Over the course of treatment, Wendy's case conceptualization evolved. In the sessions with the practitioner, she showed an ability to actively engage in any activity provided by the practitioner. In the activities in which they engaged, Wendy grew in her ability to ask for help from the practitioner when needed. Over the course of the sessions, Wendy began to recognize and embrace her athletic prowess and physical strength as assets that she can bring into activities and sports that she may want to engage in. Globally, Wendy was also preparing for the transition to junior high school, hence the focus of the interventions evolved to discuss and practice skills she would need in a larger peer environment and increased academic expectations. Skills aimed at recognizing if she needed help and how to appropriately ask for help beyond the practitioner were explored. While the practitioner tried to reach out and work with Wendy's mother, it was hard to engage with the family, even though the mother was appreciative that the practitioner was supporting her daughter.

In addition, based on the practitioner's assessment of her increased ability to communicate and collaborate with the practitioner, she was referred to group adventure therapy in order to provide opportunities for her to practice these skills with her peers before the transition to junior high school.

Assessment at the Closing of Treatment

Participation in the adventure group, and the additional opportunities to reflect more deeply into how Wendy saw and understood herself provided the exact support that she needed to negotiate a critical time in her pre-teen life. This change in her sense of self showed up in school, in her social life, and a little bit in her home. She continued to feel isolated and not always understood at home. The last time the practitioner observed Wendy was during the end-of-the-year Field Day activities, when Wendy successfully competed in many activities, including rope climbing and flag football (see Figure 5.6). Her success in these areas were embraced and celebrated by her peers.

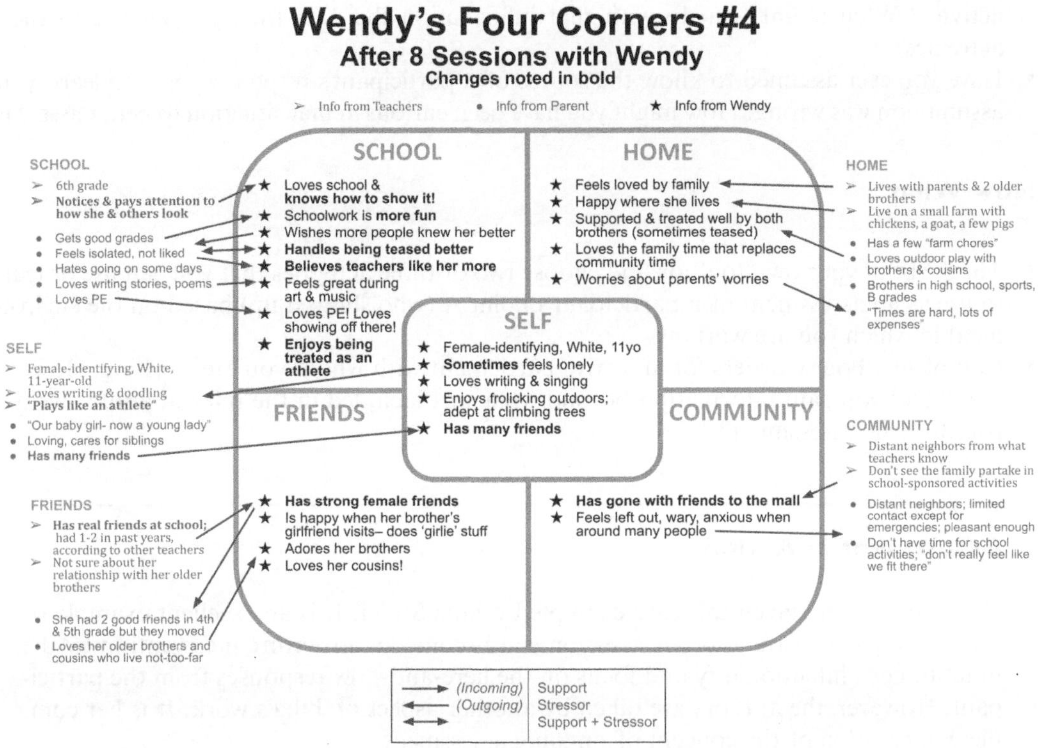

Figure 5.6 Monitoring the four corners throughout treatment provides direction and evaluation.

Conclusion

Assessment is ongoing and never ending. It is the practitioner's responsibility to be paying attention to the messages that participants are providing us through their responses to the activities in which the practitioner invites them to engage. However, it does not end with the practitioner noticing a participant's responses: A practitioner then needs to explore with the participant the meaning and source of those responses to build an accurate and participant-informed understanding of the reasons for seeking treatment. This collaboration then informs what Point B is developed and the plan for how to move toward those goals. Good assessment invites evolution in treatment to meet the changing needs and goals of the participant, which supports participant voice and choice throughout treatment.

Reflections

- How might ongoing active assessment change the way you work with participants versus receiving predetermined information about a participant which could be considered unchanging?
- Consider your own personal experience engaging in activities (games, hikes, camping, climbing, etc.) with family or friends. What did you learn about these relationships through

activity? What might you do with that information the next time you engage in those activities?

- Have you ever assumed to know the source of a participant's responses, only to learn your assumption was wrong? How might you have been curious in that situation to better assess it?

Now What?

- Think about your own toolbox and choose two or three activities that you can use or learn to use as an assessment of a participant's Point A (who showed up) based on the environment in which you are working.
- Complete a Four Corners for an active participant with whom you are working. How did it go? Did you gain information beyond what was included in the referral and/or written psychosocial assessment?

Assessment in Action

The authors were given this case example by Julia Stifler. It is an excellent example of how the typical "walk and talk" session can become an adventure intervention by the practitioner's intentionality and focus on the here-and-now responses from the participant. However, the authors are taken by another aspect of Julia's work. It is her complete integration of the concept of ongoing assessment.

In reading this case example, notice how Julia is making assessments of her participant's Point A, of what physical setting would be best for the Point B of her interventions, of how her participant was presenting in that moment, and of what needs were being expressed. The process of assessment is ongoing throughout the session Julia describes.

Practitioner Information

I have a dual master's degree in social work and outdoor education from the University of New Hampshire. Prior to attending graduate school and formalizing my adventure therapy training, I spent about a decade working in various outdoor and experiential settings, including summer camps, wilderness expedition programs, a wilderness therapy program, an inpatient hospital, and an independent school. I have been practicing adventure therapy more formally since 2015 and currently use it on a regular basis in my private practice. Adventure therapy is appealing to me because it often serves as a catalyst for building stronger relationships with my participants and launching them into more growth and healing than we tend to achieve by sitting and talking. I also love the energy boost I get as a practitioner when I can put on my adventure therapy hat.

Participant Description

My participant is an 18-year-old who lives in rural Vermont with her mother and younger brother. She has experienced symptoms of major depressive disorder for about four years and reports frequent anxiety. Her childhood included a lot of major transitions, such as several moves across state lines and her father's decision to essentially opt out of being her parent. She and I have worked together for about two years, and one of the main issues we have addressed has been her tendency toward perfectionism and the pressure she puts on herself to achieve success at all costs. She attended a local high school that has a reputation for high levels of academic rigor, where she often felt simultaneously overwhelmed by a need to perform and disappointed in herself for not reaching certain standards.

Treatment Context

Early in treatment, I invited my participant to engage in walks in the woods. She very quickly observed that walking felt good and allowed her to experience a sense of having "done something" in her therapy sessions, regardless of the content. We walk most of the time when we meet, and the goals and intentions around the walking activity vary depending on her presentation and expressed needs in each session. In this particular recent session, we focused on her pattern of pushing through high levels of academic stress without being able to find opportunities to rest, recover, or enjoy other activities. She had done some good reflection in the previous session about her problematic perception that rest is bad and that the "right" thing to do is to keep working, no matter the cost to her mental health.

Session Description

My office is located within a block or two of a hiking trail and a small park. We usually walk on the hiking trail, but for this session, I invited her to walk to the park with me because it has a steep hill that I wanted to use. As we walked toward the park, we discussed her goal of getting more comfortable with taking breaks and inviting calm and self-compassion into her experience. I framed the activity by telling her that we were going to intentionally embark on something that would be physically challenging, with the goal of approaching the task with mindful self-compassion. At the bottom of the hill, I facilitated a brief grounding exercise, inviting her to tune into her five senses and notice her current balance of exertion and calm. We briefly discussed the concept of success and the tendency one might have to assume that success means getting to the top of the hill in a reasonable amount of time or even getting to the top without stopping. I invited her to challenge that assumption and to focus on our identified task, which was to practice rest and self-compassion. Together, we walked up the hill, and I suggested that she stop us for a break when she noticed a straining sensation and/or a nice spot to take in the view. She did just that, and we stopped for a few moments to take some breaths, place our hands on our hearts, and tune into an experience of doing something kind for ourselves. We then walked the rest of the way up the hill and used the rest of the session to walk slowly back to the office while my participant reflected on ways to incorporate this experience into her day-to-day life. She observed that it felt somewhat uncomfortable and unnatural to stop and rest, and that she also benefited from the practice and would probably benefit from more rest during this season of high academic pressure. We explored ways that she might practice finding that space on her own outside of the session.

Practitioner Comments Regarding Session

Over the years, I have noticed that this participant often struggles with self-advocacy. She went through a psychological evaluation process in 2021 that resulted in a list of accommodations for school, but she has been resistant to using those accommodations because she doesn't feel that she deserves them. She puts a lot of pressure on herself despite having a level of awareness of her mental health diagnosis and trauma history and the ways they can affect her functioning. Sometimes this pressure serves as a strength in helping her get a lot done and be accepted to several competitive colleges, but often, it also serves to intensify her self-loathing and depression when she inevitably doesn't meet her own standards for herself. We have spent a lot of time discussing and practicing self-compassion through mindfulness exercises and "homework" assignments that involve making subtle changes in her routines. We have also used some principles of CBT to work on challenging some of her cognitive distortions about what hard work should look like. In this session, I also tapped into some concepts of somatic experiencing while we were tuning into sensations related to exertion and rest. My hope was to facilitate an experience that would solidify a felt sense of the importance of taking care of herself to achieve her goals.

Submitted by Julia Stifler, LICSW

Bennington Adventure Therapy, PLC

Bennington, Vermont

References

Breault-Hood, J., Gray, T., Truong, S., & Ullman, J. (2017). Women and girls in outdoor education: Scoping the research literature and exploring prospects for future body image enquiry. *Research in Outdoor Education*, *15*, 21–46. https://doi.org/10.1353/roe.2017.0002

Gass, M. A., Gillis, H. L., & Russell, K. C., (2020) *Adventure therapy: Theory, research, and practice* (2nd ed.). Routledge.

Gray, T., & Mitten, D. (2018). *The Palgrave international handbook of women and outdoor learning*. Palgrave Nature.

Gupta, S., & Bansal, R. (2013). Nanocarriers and nanoparticles for skin care and dermatological treatments. *Indian Dermatology Online Journal*, *4*(4), 267–272. https://doi.org/10.4103/2229-5178.120635

Montessori, M. (2012). *The 1946 London lectures*. Montessori-Pierson Publishing Company.

Ortega, R. M., & Garvin, C. D. (2019). *Socially just practice in groups: A social work perspective*. Sage Publications.

Schoel, J., & Maizell, R. S. (2002). *Exploring Islands of Healing: New perspectives on adventure based counseling*. Project Adventure, Inc.

Tucker, A. R., Beale, B., Norton, C. L., Walsh, H., Keefe K., Holmes, L., & Wermer-Colan, R. (2024). The Ohio Adventure Therapy Coalition: A statewide trauma informed group work initiative to meet the needs of CPS youth. *The Journal of Creativity in Mental Health*, *20*(3), 376–390. https://doi.org/10.1080/15401383.2024.2386163

Voss, R. M., & Das, J. M. (2020). *Mental Status Examination*. StatPearls. https://www.ncbi.nlm.nih.gov/books/NBK546682

Warren, K., Roberts, N. S., Breunig, M., & Alvarez, M. A. (2014). Social justice in outdoor experiential education: A state of knowledge review. *Journal of Experiential Education*, *37*(1), 89–103. https://doi.org/10.1177/1053825913518898

Chapter 6

Matching Interventions

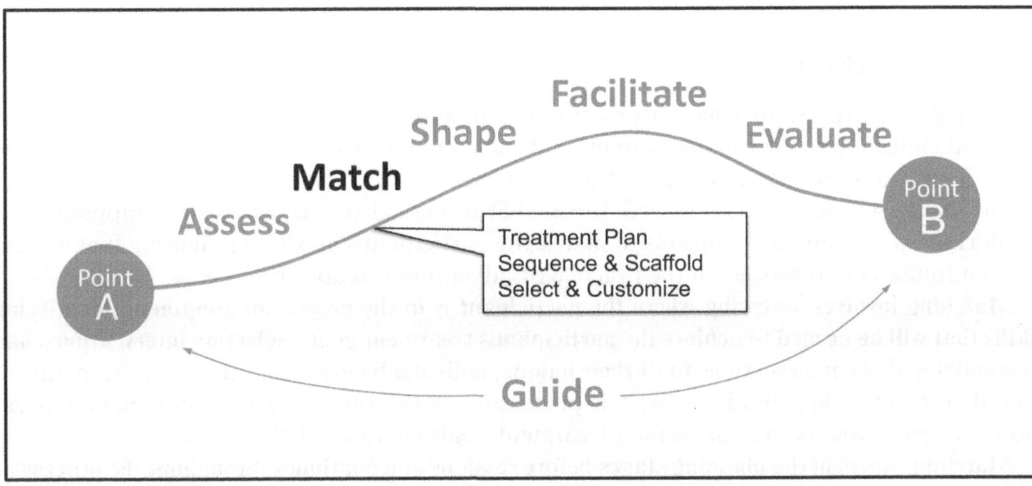

Sitting at Thanksgiving dinner with both family and friends, Brian's wife asked everyone to share what they were thankful for this year, and Brian blurted out that after all these years, he is grateful that he has realized that he is gay, and he no longer wants to be married. The room was silent, and then his wife burst into tears and his father began swearing and stormed out of the room. It immediately took him back to when he was a child, and he was responsible for checking the oil in the car before a family trip. At 10 years old, Brian felt proud that his father gave him this important task. That feeling lasted less than an hour into the trip when Brian's father heard an unusual knocking sound coming from the engine. He pulled into the parking lot of a gas station still closed from the previous evening and found the car dangerously low on oil. Somehow, Brian had misread the oil indicator and failed to add the necessary oil.

After some initial angry sputtering and swearing directed at Brian, his father became silent. The entire family sat in that uncomfortable silence for almost two hours until the station opened and oil could be purchased. Brian learned from this experience that mistakes are not tolerated and that he would have to struggle to be a "real" man. In therapy, he pointed to this moment as one of the foundations for a pattern of hypervigilance (checking and double checking), as well as striving to be who he thinks a "man" should be. These characteristics served him well in his job as a financial advisor where he was responsible for participants'

DOI: 10.4324/9781003457893-6

retirement fund portfolios. However, those same characteristics were quite dysfunctional for intimate relationships and daily living.

Brian sought therapy for problems negotiating issues in his personal relationships. Exploration of those issues quickly revealed difficulties in Brian's friend and work relationships as well. Both his ex-wife, with whom he has a strong relationship, and his new (male) partner were especially concerned about how controlling he was, how unhappy it often left him, and how difficult it was for him to communicate effectively and express his thoughts and feelings in a caring way. These concerns resulted in Brian's decision to seek his own individual therapy to address the impact of his controlling behaviors, hypervigilance, and emotional distance.

Throughout this chapter, examples from Brian's course of individual treatment will be used to describe the skills involved in matching adventure interventions that fit Brian's current clinical situation.

What Is Matching?

Matching is a process in which a practitioner intentionally designs interventions with the assessed clinical needs of the participant and the collaborative vision for achievement of the participant's desired Point B's (goals) in mind. Schoel et al. (1988) introduced the idea of intentionally selecting activities, and Itin (1995) discussed the idea of "gift-wrapping" and "tailoring" adventure interventions to match the participant's needs, highlighting that matching is a fundamental process in the practice of adventure therapy (Itin, 2003).

Matching involves assessing where the participant is in the process of treatment, identifying skills that will be needed to achieve the participant's treatment goals, selecting interventions, and customizing those interventions to fit their unique, individualized needs. Interventions in adventure therapy include activities as well as processing, with practitioners working in collaboration with participants to address their treatment goals (Alvarez et al., 2021).

Matching starts in the planning stages before sessions and continues throughout the process as practitioners respond to what the participant presents in sessions. To connect with the issues the participants present "in the moment" and match the intervention to fit their needs (Lung et al., 2008). In the 1:1 context of individual adventure psychotherapy sessions, practitioners can readily identify dynamics, patterns, or issues in the moment that are harder to recognize in group or family contexts. In addition, they have more flexibility to respond by adjusting activities, plans, or other aspects of their facilitation when only dealing with one participant.

This chapter begins by further developing Brian's case. It continues by thoughtfully considering how to sequence and scaffold therapeutic experiences based on where Brian (the participant) is in his progress toward goal achievement. Considerations are explored for selecting and customizing activities that fit the assessed needs of the participant as a way of individualizing treatment.

Case Example: Brian

The practice of adventure therapy is guided and powered by assessment. The interventions chosen for the participant, as well as decisions about facilitation techniques, are driven by the accumulated and expanding clinical understanding of the individual participant.

These choices are also impacted by the practitioner's theoretical understanding of how people make changes in their lives. As discussed in the chapter, *Assessment*, a participant's presentation and assessment information might yield very different intervention selections based on the practitioners' different theoretical foundations. For example, a practitioner who processes assessment information from a psychodynamic lens may choose different interventions than one who operates from a neurodevelopmental perspective. Next, this process is applied to the case of Brian in order to illustrate how assessment informs matching intervention processes.

Brian's Case Conceptualization – Point A

Brian came to treatment asking for help in improving his relationships at home and work. In the initial session, Brian spoke at the practitioner for most of the session, to the point that it was hard to get a word in during the session. He spent most of the time sharing that if others understood him, they would realize the validity of his intentions and emphasized how good he is at communicating. From his perspective, others do not listen to him.

After this, the practitioner commented, "I am confused. How you think of yourself and how others experience you do not seem to match. How do you make sense of that?"

With that context, the practitioner helped Brian focus on describing himself rather than telling stories about the other people in his life. However, as Brian continued to describe himself, what he does occupationally, and how he interacts within his family, the natural tendency for him was to return to his rigid narrative of being misunderstood. Without the guardrails put up by the practitioner, Brain remained convinced that he *is* helpful to others, and the change required was for others to understand the intent behind his actions.

After the first session, the practitioner had collected the following information about Brian:

- Brian was a 45-year-old White, cisgender gay male who was neurotypical, divorced (from a female), and remarried to his current husband/spouse.
- He was diagnosed as a child with Type 1 diabetes, which requires continual management.
- His wife was the first person he dated during college. Their current relationship is positive and friendly despite the divorce.
- His current spouse has two children, ages 11 and 14. He shares custody with his first wife.
- He works full-time as a financial advisor, where his attention to detail is a strength. He is successful in his job; however, relationships with his colleagues are strained.
- He was the youngest child of four children in his family of origin. His siblings cut off communication with him after he came out as gay in his 30s. He described his father as cold and distant and his mother as focused on how to avoid upsetting his father.
- He grew up in a family that was often financially stretched and worried about how to make ends meet.
- His family was very active in their local church. Ideas of what it means to be a man and how to have appropriate romantic relationships are deeply influenced by these religious expectations.
- He is perfectionistic in everything he does, which often leads to criticism of others and negative repercussions within his environment at home and beyond.
- One of his characteristic features is that he talks a lot about things external to his inner processing. He demonstrates little awareness of his emotional and somatic processes.

Brian and the practitioner agreed that his emotional distance, unrealistic expectations of others, confusion about who he should be, and occasional angry outbursts were problematic. Table 6.1 details the case conceptualization created by the practitioner based on their work with Brian.

Table 6.1 Brian's Case Conceptualization

Clinical History	• Brian was a motivated, successful student in school through college. • Brian reports that he and his spouse have a good relationship; however, according to his spouse, Brian is overly controlling and can take up all of the space in the relationship. • At work, Brian's interactions with others are positive, as he takes initiative and has strong analytical skills. However, Brian reports that his supervisor has described him as argumentative, and his coworkers find him "annoying". • His parents have both been emotionally inaccessible throughout his life. His father is emotionally distant, while his mother is avoidant and always "busy". His father's extremely critical nature was exacerbated by Brian's coming out as gay. • Childhood, Type 1 diabetes developed in his early teenage years. Brian struggled to manage his symptoms independently, creating conflict with his parents. • No history of physical or sexual abuse. There was indication of neglect and emotional abuse. • No history of drug or alcohol abuse. • A serious family car accident when he was 8 years old resulted in his mom being hospitalized for 6 weeks. Brian says he was often left to fend for himself during and after this hospitalization.
Current Experiential Functioning	• Inability to recognize, express, or verbalize affect. • Excessively verbal in most situations, dislikes silence. • Frenetic energy, always active, always busy. • Avoidant of feedback, fear of failure and its reflection on him, hence not as open to novel experiences. • Nonplayful, uncomfortable with silliness and how he might be seen. • Frequent attempts to help others, often unsolicited. • Intellectualizes in most situations. • Very analytical and a good problem-solver, which serves him well in his occupation, but over-reliance on details and intellectualization creates difficulties in life outside of work. • Expresses desire to have an authentic and loving relationship with his spouse.
Assessment	• Brian's trauma from childhood neglect, childhood diabetes and experience of abandonment at age 8 contributed to his constant sense of overt stimulation, hypervigilance, and inability to self-regulate or co-regulate. • Egocentrism and the need to control others results in conflicts in close relationships. These relationship issues strongly impact his well-being. • As a result of his trauma, Brian fears emotions and deflects by intellectualizing and controlling situations. • Brian's self-narrative is filled with anxiety around uncertainty, belonging, and self-worth. He compensates for these perceived faults by overperforming, competitiveness and keeping busy.

In this case conceptualization, the practitioner's theoretical framework reflects aspects of a narrative, relational-cultural theory, and a neurodevelopmental theoretical lens with attention to the stories that influence how Brian experiences his world. **This theoretical perspective informs how interventions are matched with the assessment of the participant**. Narrative theory shows up with the practitioner interested in how the participant understands and creates a story about their current experience. Because of their relational-cultural theoretical lens, the practitioner views human relationships as vital to well-being, thus the impact of strained relationships is highlighted. The practitioner's neurodevelopmental lens incorporates an understanding of how trauma impacts the brain, the ability to manage emotions, and a participant's resulting trauma responses. All three influence the next steps of selecting interventions by connecting story, relationship, and the science of the brain.

It is important to emphasize that in order to select appropriate activities, practitioners must know the Point A of the entire treatment setting, including the participant's clinical history and current experiential functioning, the impact of the physical environment, the resources and obstacles present in the moment, and whatever personal characteristics the practitioner brings into the setting.

Bringing the Treatment Plan to Life

The practitioner works in collaboration with the participant to clarify the assessment of presenting problems and identify treatment goals, including prioritizing which to address first. **These goals are broken down into smaller steps that support participants in reaching their overarching goals, which are called objectives in most treatment plan outlines.**

Cocreating Point B

Cocreating treatment plans with participants is essential in developing insight into their Point A and which treatment approaches may be the most successful. Developing clarity around the participant's desired Point B involves collaboration and significant engagement with the participant. Questions of whether the clinical focus should be developing awareness, adjusting a behavior, changing an attitude or belief, or learning a skill must be answered. **It is this knowledge that guides the individual practitioner in their choices of what interventions to utilize, as well as how to manage the participant's responses to experiential interventions.**

> **Box 6.1 Brian's Case Example: Treatment Goals**
>
> Through the initial assessment process, Brian and the practitioner collaboratively identified the following goals:
>
> - Learn emotional regulation and expression skills to improve emotional communication with others.
> - Improve his relational connections with others.
> - Recognize and reduce symptoms of anxiety in his daily life.

Treatment Planning in Adventure Therapy

Treatment planning is part of the process of matching and therefore an integral bridge between assessment and intervention. Once a case conceptualization is developed, including identifying the desired Point Bs (treatment goals), the practitioner and participant work together to create an action plan for reaching these goals. **Treatment plan documents include**

problem areas, treatment goals, steps for reaching those goals (objectives), and interventions for each objective. The interventions recorded in treatment plans are often vague, such as "individual psychotherapy", with some detail included about the frequency and duration of sessions. This allows for flexibility in changing the treatment approach even after the plan is sent to insurance. Treatment planning, like everything else, is informed by the practitioner's theoretical foundation, clinical focus, and professional experience; however, ideal treatment plans are cocreated by the participant and practitioner together and adapted over time.

Assessment and case conceptualizations inform how a practitioner engages with participants using general counseling skills learned through experience and education. It is this understanding of the clinical issues that guides practitioners about when to support, confront, listen, direct, or explore content further with participants. These choices are all part of the process of matching.

Practitioners make numerous intervention choices related to which activities to use, how to customize these activities specific to participant needs, and how to make meaning of the experience. To be effective, these choices need to have a clear sense of the intent of the intervention. Is the intent to increase awareness of a pattern, adjust a behavior, practice a skill, or change attitudes, beliefs, or opinions that have been unhelpful in their lives, for example?

Once the treatment plan goals (Point B) are established, the process of breaking these goals down into action steps ensues. In treatment planning, these steps are most often referred to as objectives. **The objectives can be thought of as the next step toward Point B from the participant's Point A**. Then, considerations for interventions that support taking that step are incorporated.

Box 6.2 Brian's Case Example: Treatment Plan Objectives & Interventions

To illustrate how goals are broken down into objectives, Brian's first treatment plan goal is addressed next.

Goal #1 (Point B): Learn emotional regulation and expression skills to improve emotional communication with others.

Objectives for Goal #1 (Point B)

The practitioner and Brian established the following objectives:

1 Discern two to three emotions in the moment during a session.
2 Implement emotional regulation skills when experiencing emotional flooding.
3 Integrate emotional experiences with his thoughts and behaviors.

Interventions to Work Toward These Objectives

1 Allow Brian the opportunity to practice the skills required for self-expression during experiential interventions. **Human Camera** (see Appendix 1), which requires the participant to give up control by being unsighted and relying on the practitioner to guide them, is an example of an appropriate intervention.

2 Engage Brian in experiential interventions that will provide the context for discussion of how his anxiety responses impact relationships, including that with the practitioner. **Balloon Rocket Release** (see Appendix 1) is another example of an activity with an unpredictable outcome that can offer the opportunity to address Brian's anxiety.
3 Use a nondeliberative facilitation approach that allows Brian the freedom to make choices and demonstrate his typical patterns of experiential functioning.

As the participant's Point B changes throughout the course of treatment, the focus of interventions must be updated to reflect these developments. **In effective treatment, the internalization of the lessons and insights occurring in real time changes the participant's Point A, which then invites perspective shifts from what their Point B might have originally been**. This dynamic flexibility is key to acknowledge, to embrace, and to manage through shifts in direction of treatment – that is, in the treatment plan. One author recalls working with a participant who came in to address their problematic heterosexual relationship and was seeking help to "fix it". After a few sessions in which the participant expressed his same-sex attraction, it became clear to the participant and the facilitator that being in a heterosexual relationship WAS the problem. This insight required major shifting of the Point B!

Considerations for Sequencing

Sequencing refers to choosing the order of interventions. This is often based on where the participant is in the process of treatment (beginning, middle, or end), as well as how the participant has responded to previous experiential interventions. Sequencing is chronological in nature: Practitioners consider session-by-session what intervention selection makes the most sense to optimize progress in treatment. **Participants who are in the beginning stage of treatment need interventions that are qualitatively different than when they advance to the middle or end phases**. Similarly, the practitioner and participant collaborate about what happened during each of the previous interventions to learn what type of interventions might be effective moving forward (Lung et al., 2008). This collaboration includes decisions about the order in which treatment goals are addressed, as well as what issues might be prioritized in sequencing decisions.

Sequencing is influenced by many factors in adventure psychotherapy sessions, including the following:

- Treatment context – e.g., quantity of sessions allotted – participant engagement, physical setting
- Successes and challenges of previous interventions
- Stage of treatment
- Participant engagement in pursuing therapy goals
- Rapport between participant and practitioner
- Development of the adventure beliefs – e.g., feels safe and has trust in the treatment environment

Individual psychotherapy is presented next in three stages. These stages provide some guidance for sequencing based on common considerations during those stages of treatment.

- In the **beginning** stage of treatment, activities that serve to establish the therapeutic relationship, build the norms for the treatment environment, clarify the purpose of therapy, and assess the participant's Point A take the forefront. For example, the practitioner and participant can be invited to choose an object they carry with them that has special meaning and share this with one another. Experiential interventions will focus on the assessment process and target learning more about the participant and their patterns, as well as defining the nature and purpose of using experiential activities in the treatment, enhancing the participant's engagement in therapy, clarification of goals, and establishing the treatment alliance.
- In the **middle** stage, participants are more prepared to manage the more difficult parts of therapy. The practitioner may present interventions that require confronting more challenging issues, such as dismantling unhealthy belief systems, processing trauma, or practicing new skills. For example, to practice thinking through options before acting, the participant can be invited to engage in the **Egg Drop Challenge** (see Appendix 1), where they work to create a protective structure for an egg that will be dropped from a height. This activity is often isomorphic to (the same as) the participant's need for safety and thoughtfulness in their daily life. Clinical issues such as resistance, relationship ruptures, and the need to practice new skills, such as resiliency or coping strategies, can all be addressed with properly sequenced experiential interventions. These interventions are more likely to focus on change processes, such as developing more healthy thought patterns or enacting new skills in the "here and now" of sessions.
- In the **end** of treatment, activities that celebrate progress made, consolidate treatment gains, and allow for reflection and closure are advised. Interventions will highlight the individual participant's accomplishments and encourage processing related to change and transition. For example, participants can be asked to build a rock cairn and reflect on how each layer reflects their progress. Repeating activities done in the earlier stages of treatment with an eye toward identifying the gains the participant has made can also be useful.

Choosing interventions that fit with the participant's progression through the stages of treatment is vital. When Brian was in the middle stage of treatment and working on his tendency to emotionally distance himself from the people he loved, for example, activities aimed at establishing an initial rapport with the practitioner would have carried little usefulness for attainment of the clinical goals.

Equally important to the process of sequencing is the practitioner's effort to gather information from the participant regarding their response to previous interventions. What the participant has experienced and how they have processed those experiences informs the practitioner's choice of what type of intervention to present, as well as how to present the experience.

Importance of Scaffolding

Much like a physical scaffold provides structured support to build something, **a scaffolded approach to treatment includes creating a supportive session structure, laying a foundation by attending to the needs of the treatment environment, building something new through the choice of intervention and how one processes the learning so that the scaffolding can be taken down and the individual can navigate the world independently**. One can see from this description that scaffolding is a central component to the overall process of therapy.

The concept of scaffolding comes from educational theory on learning (Frank, 2013; Vygotsky, 1978; Wood et al., 1976). In education, scaffolding refers to engaging students in their learning process such that the educator provides help where help is needed and encourages the student to do what they can do independently. This process allows the learner "to solve a problem or achieve a goal that would be beyond his [their] unassisted efforts" (Wood et al., 1976 p. 90). Vygotsky (1978) suggested decades ago that educators assess a student's "zone of proximal development" – that is, the zone between where they are competent and the desired goal, which is not achievable independently. **Treatment should begin with activities that are immediately achievable with support and continue toward the desired level of mastery**. This concept applies to the practice of adventure therapy in that the practitioner's task is to support participants in building skills one step at a time, allowing them the opportunity to develop mastery.

In adventure therapy, the practitioner and participant must jointly assess the participant's current experiential functioning to determine what skills will be required to achieve their clinical goals, and choose interventions suited to the acquisition of those skills. **The heart of scaffolding is providing experiences that help participants progressively gain the skills and/or abilities to bridge the gap between where they are currently and what is needed to accomplish their clinical goals**. Choosing interventions that result in a series of small successes builds a participant's confidence while they slowly gain the skills and knowledge needed to achieve their clinical goals. If participants experience repeated failure and frustration, it will likely result in disengagement; therefore, attending to these incremental steps is an important practitioner focus.

Figure 6.1 illustrates the relationship between sequencing and scaffolding in which interventions are utilized in an order that helps to build skills thoughtfully over time.

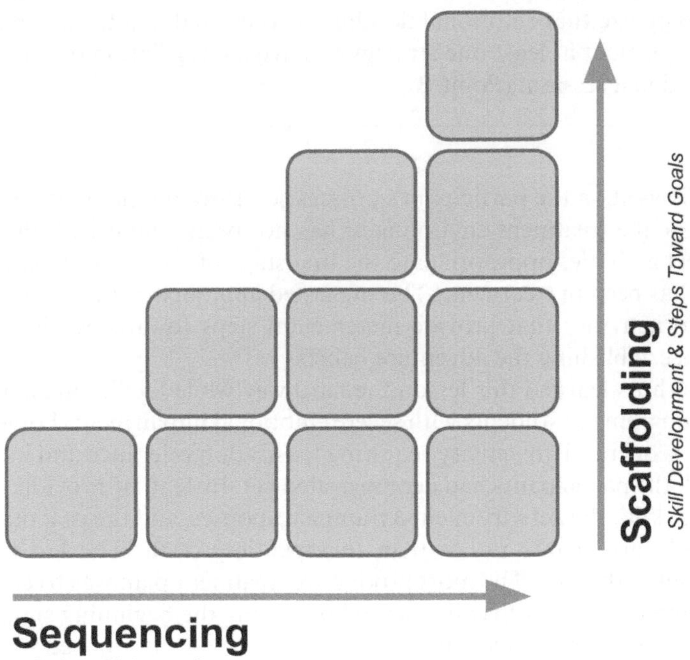

Figure 6.1 The relationship between sequencing and scaffolding.

Box 6.3 Brian's case example: Plans for sequencing and scaffolding

The following highlights how this concept of sequencing and scaffolding intersect for Brian's progress toward his Point B.

Goal #1 (Point B): Improve ability to express emotions in the moment in a regulated way that increases the chances he will feel heard.

Objectives for Goal #1 (Point B)

The practitioner and Brian established the following objectives:

1 Discern two to three emotions in the moment during a session.
2 Implement emotional regulation skills when experiencing emotional flooding.
3 Integrate emotional experiences with his thoughts and behaviors.

Scaffolding of Steps for Goal #1 (See Figure 6.2)

1 Talks excessively and intellectualizes about emotion (Point A)
2 Can identify and name the emotions he experiences
3 Shares about uncomfortable emotions felt outside of session
4 Shares about somatic and emotional responses felt in the moment during an experience in a session
5 Able to verbalize the connection between thoughts, behaviors, and emotions
6 Able to recognize that emotional flooding is connected to a trauma response
7 Able to implement at least one strategy to navigate regulation of an emotion that is experienced in a session. (Point B)

Scaffolding is based on the participant's progression through the stages of treatment. If the basic structure of the treatment environment has not been established, the most productive choice is to select activities appropriate to the first stage of treatment regardless of how long the participant has been in treatment. The suggested approach in this circumstance is to continue to scaffold activities that provide incremental steps toward developing the treatment relationship and establishing the adventure beliefs.

One of the authors learned this lesson the hard way while facilitating a group session at a day treatment program for students with severe emotional impairment. Forgetting to scaffold, the practitioner sequenced an activity requiring frustration tolerance and interpersonal skills, neither of which the participants had demonstrated yet. Instead of providing the opportunity to practice these skills, the activity elicited trauma responses, and the practitioner had to manage dysregulated participants rather than therapeutic growth. The lesson learned applies equally to individual therapy. The most productive treatment plan was to continue to scaffold activities that targeted issues typically focused on during the beginning stage of treatment.

If the practitioner does not recognize that the participant has moved to the middle phase of treatment and continues to sequence activities as if the needs of the participant have not progressed, the participant can also become frustrated. This problem often results from

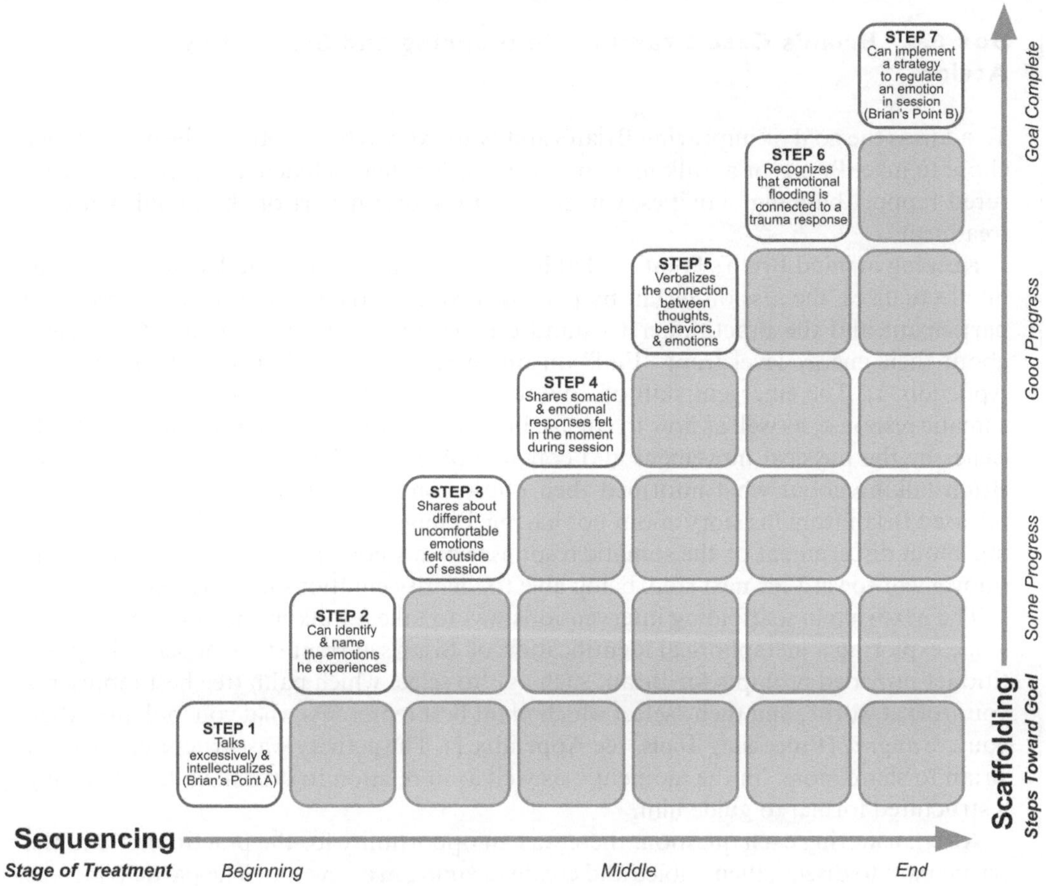

Figure 6.2 Effective sequencing and scaffolding of Brian's treatment from Box 6.3.

practitioners only providing activities in which the participant can be easily successful. **Proper sequencing and scaffolding reflect the participant's positive development and continues to provide opportunities for participants to learn how to manage conflict, confusion, or difficult life situations in progressively challenging situations.**

A balance between participant success and challenge is needed to keep the participant moving toward their goals. This balance comes from the practitioner's understanding of the clinical issues and of the participant's consent to engage with challenges. These decisions require a keen awareness of the Point Bs for the participant (skill development, self-awareness, communication skills, etc.). If the Point B for a specific participant is anger management, for example, it can be useful for the practitioner to observe an angry response from the participant. After an outburst, the practitioner can better understand the anger response, help identify if it is a reaction to other uncomfortable feelings, and fine-tune the participant's specific goals regarding their anger.

Processing is a skill that requires scaffolding as well. Practitioners should sequence efforts to support processing, matching discussions to participants' abilities and readiness for verbal reflection. For some participants, practitioners may need to begin with education, role modeling, and practice to develop the ability of effective self-reflection.

Box 6.4 Brian's Case Example: Sequencing and Scaffolding in Action

To address the goal of improving Brian's ability to express his emotions, the practitioner chose to meet Brian for a walk in a botanical garden that included a sequence of structured rapport building activities, which are an important part of the initial phase of treatment.

Keeping in mind Brian's Point A, that he is at the stage where he talks excessively and intellectualizes, the session began by placing a rope on the grass and asking both the participant and the practitioner to stand on the rope that represented a **Continuum** about their energy level from "Full" on one end to "Empty" on the other end (see Appendix 1). The emergent skill of how to identify and then verbalize his emotional somatic response, as well as how to engage in a shared or mutual conversation was made easier by the physical movement and concrete objective of both the practitioner and Brian talking about what informed their chosen spot on the same rope. This action released Brian from his story about not having feelings, as well as helped to begin learning about discernment of the somatic responses of his body in relation to his emotions (movement toward his next step, being able to identify emotions he experiences)

The next step in scaffolding interventions was to take a walk in the botanical garden while exploring a metaphorical identification of Brian's current story of self. The practitioner provided prompts for Brian, such as, "to select which palm tree best represents your role at work", and then "select which plant best represents what you look like when you are angry" (**Processing Tools**, see Appendix 1). The activity was structured to allow Brian to share more "in the moment", as well as in relation to others while still having a structured format to guide him.

After answering each question, there was an opportunity for the practitioner and the participant to discuss their choice and create meaning in a new way. The participant was able to practice the skills necessary for the achievement of his goal to become more expressive of his feelings, as well as for the practitioner to model the desired skills. The practitioner noted that Brian was moving closer to the step of sharing about somatic and emotional responses felt in the moment.

The regulating movement and the nature of the questions made it possible for Brian to begin talking more freely about his emotional experience, both historically, and in the moment of his treatment session. It was during this activity that the practitioner made a mental note that Brian was starting to shift his story from "I don't have feelings" to "I have trouble identifying what my feelings are; but I remember having feelings" as well as beginning to place a value or preference for some feelings (e.g., pleasure, joy) over other feelings (e.g., uncertainty, isolation). These responses from Brian reflected progress toward the next steps in his journey toward reaching his first clinical goal.

Because of the observation that Brian had made progress toward identifying and sharing about difficult emotions, as well as the general sense that he had become more comfortable in the treatment setting, the practitioner thought he had moved into the middle phase of treatment. That movement meant that the primary focus of interventions could transition from developing rapport and therapeutic alliance to addressing the resources and obstacles to achievement of his clinical goals.

Selecting and Customizing the Intervention

Once there is a clear idea of where the participant is in their treatment process, an understanding of how they have responded to all previous experiential interventions, and what skills the participant still needs to acquire to reach their goals (Lung et al., 2008), the practitioner must select a specific intervention from the array of options available and customize that selection to the participant's specific characteristics. The clinical mindset continues to inform the matching of each part of the adventure therapy process, including planning sessions, selecting activities, "fine-tuning" interventions, and responding to how the participant shows up in the moment during sessions.

Activity Selection

Activity selection refers to the process of choosing the appropriate activity or experience for this particular participant at this particular point in time. Activities used in adventure therapy are incredibly diverse. Each activity has inherent qualities that make the activity more or less likely to support achievement of certain clinical outcomes, and with a little creativity, activities can be applied to support progress on a variety of clinical goals.

The following is a list of some common adventure therapy activities and some associated clinical objectives; however, this list is not exhaustive and there is a lot of room for creativity and adaptation by practitioners. Additionally, the associated clinical goals are meant to illustrate possible applications for each activity grouping. They are not meant to "assign" specific clinical objectives to specific activities. As practitioners evolve their skills, many agree that they can adapt any activity to meet the needs of participants due to the flexibility of experiential interventions.

Nature-Based Activities

Nature-based activities engage participants in connection with nature, whether that is outdoors or indoors. There are mental health benefits simply to being outside in nature (Bettmann et al., 2024) and opportunities for participants to explore real and metaphoric aspects of relationship through nature connection.

- *Examples:* **Walk and Talk Sessions, building Nature Sculptures** (see Appendix 1), and exploring natural areas together, such as a creek or field.
- *Possible clinical applications:* Hiking can be structured so that participants are involved in route-finding to help develop problem-solving skills or it can be more focused on the emotional regulation of walking while discussing difficult topics.

Cooperative Activities and Problem-Solving Initiatives

Cooperative activities and initiatives are manufactured challenges that provide opportunities for problem-solving, collaboration, conflict resolution, and frustration tolerance.

- *Examples:* **The Dump, Infinite Circle, Tower Building (such as Spaghetti-Marshmallow Towers**; see Appendix 1).

- *Possible clinical applications:* In tower building, the participant can work to build the tallest tower they can out of materials provided by the practitioner, working through the steps of problem-solving on their own or completed cooperatively with the practitioner to enhance the collaborative nature of their work. Similarly, a participant who struggles to acknowledge their need for help in solving problems may be invited to engage in an activity that is difficult to complete without asking for help from the practitioner, such as The Dump.

Trust Activities

Any activity that requires the participant to trust or be trusted by others is valuable in both building rapport and exercising the parts of them that are wary of relying on or being relied on by others.

- *Examples:* **Unsighted Walks** or **Trust Leans, Human Camera**, or **Mousetrap Challenges** (see Appendix 1).
- *Possible clinical applications:* Those struggling with anxiety and decision making may benefit from guiding the unsighted practitioner through obstacles. A different participant who has difficulty trusting anyone to know their personal thoughts and feelings, including the practitioner, may benefit from **an activity that elicits vulnerability in the session and encourages participants to trust the practitioner to keep them safe**, such as trust leans and being the one without sight on a walk.

Hiking Activities

A wide variety of experiential interventions can be included in this category. Walking and hiking in nature is useful for emotional and somatic regulation (Song et al., 2015; Sudimac et al., 2022). For many participants, just recognizing what their body feels like when stress and emotions are regulated can be healing.

- *Examples:* **Walk and Talk Sessions** (see Appendix 1), hiking, day-long backpacking, treks through creeks or other natural areas, map and compass skills, route-finding.
- *Possible clinical applications:* It can be invaluable to give participants who experience high anxiety or tension daily a taste of what being regulated and physically calm actually feels like. **Using repetitive motion, such as hiking, a calm and regulated state can be experienced by the participant and used as a model for what they are striving to achieve in their daily life**. Additionally, hiking might involve reaching a specific destination, which incorporates themes of setting and achieving goals.

Climbing Activities

Climbing activities involve climbing on manufactured climbing structures, in the outdoors on rocks, or even on ice! (Figure 6.3). Often, these activities will include technical components, such as use of harnesses, helmets, and belay systems.

- *Examples:* Rock climbing, bouldering, manufactured climbing walls, challenge course elements, indoor climbing walls, rappelling, canyoneering, and technical elements such as learning to tie climbing knots.

Figure 6.3 Climbing enhances trust and mutuality with participants.

- *Possible clinical applications:* Rope-climbing experiences can evoke a variety of emotions that allow participants and practitioners to explore and link physical, emotional, and cognitive responses, such as negative self-talk or the way stress or anxiety shows up in the body. Climbing may also involve the process of setting and working toward goals, navigating barriers and using strengths in the process. **Issues related to implementing coping skills are often part of interventions such as rappelling and outdoor rock climbing**. A participant who struggles with persistence, working through strategies for getting through "stuck spots" on a challenging climbing route can practice working through barriers.

Water Activities

Water activities rely on engagement with bodies of water, in which participants may be in watercraft or simply in the water.

- *Examples:* Paddleboarding, kayaking, canoeing, swimming, surfing, wading, sailing, and pool activities.
- *Possible clinical applications:* Participants can explore metaphors of balance while working on how to stand up on a paddleboard, reflecting on themes of overcorrection, freezing, or grounding. Canoeing provides opportunities to practice working collaboratively. In addition, participants can learn emotional regulation, communication, and coping skills.

Camping and Camp Craft

Camping and camp craft activities typically center around living in an outdoor environment in some capacity. Although this implies an overnight component, these activities can be facilitated in shorter sessions rather than only during overnight experiences.

- *Examples:* Hiking with backpacks, fire making, setting up a camp or shelter building, cooking in the outdoors (all of which can be facilitated in the time of a one-hour community-based session!).
- *Possible clinical applications:* Developing mastery over skills such as fire building or cooking in the outdoors can address struggles with confidence. Alternately, the collaborative nature of planning, cooking and eating a meal together can be a powerful intervention to build rapport and connection.

Individual adventure psychotherapy affords the opportunity to be very flexible in intervention selection. The practitioner has the flexibility to change the structure of a trust activity in the moment, for example, to accommodate an unexpected level of anxiety from the participant. **This factor also creates opportunities to introduce interventions with a developmental progression of skills specific to the individual participant**. One result of this level of specificity is that participants can simultaneously address their own patterns of self-doubt, anxiety, frustration tolerance and other important clinical dynamics.

Box 6.5 Brian's Case Example: Activity Selection

Brian's case can provide a good example of how the practitioner can adapt activity selection in the moment. In this example, information from the beginning phase of each session impacts selection of the intervention to be used in the middle of the session. Say the practitioner had planned to engage Brian in a session of paddleboarding aimed at supporting his efforts to *balance* his emotions, thoughts, and behaviors. However, Brian initiated the session by telling the story of how he had spent months planning a surprise birthday party for his spouse, who Brian stated hated surprises. Despite knowing his spouse's feelings about surprises, Brian reported being upset that his spouse was not more appreciative of all his efforts. To make a meaningful transition from this story into an appropriate intervention in the middle phase of the session, the practitioner chose to change the planned activity in hopes of creating a clearer parallel process. The revised intervention involved making a sandcastle on the beach and moving it to a picnic table nearby. After the sandcastle collapsed during Brian's attempt to transport it, the practitioner offered Brian a spray bottle with a mixture of water and Elmer's glue to coat his second sandcastle. This mixture allowed the castle to "hold together" during the transport to the table. Processing of this activity led to reflections on what is necessary in relationships for things to "hold together" rather than fall apart like his surprise birthday party plans. It was the practitioner's attunement to who showed up for this session and what showed up with them that made the transition to a sandcastle activity in the middle phase of the session feel both fluid and effective.

Session Structure

A general concept that figures into matching decisions is the structure of each individual session. **Think of sessions as being roughly divided into the beginning, middle, and end phases. It is important for the practitioner to consider what is required to transition effectively between these stages.** The beginning phase often focuses primarily on assessing participant Point A for today and clarifying expectations for the session, including the clinical focus. The middle phase of the session is typically dominated by work toward the identified clinical goal or purpose. Moving from the beginning into the middle phase of the session often requires intentional interventions by the practitioner.

The transition into the ending phase of each session is equally important and all too often neglected by the practitioner. This phase involves evaluation of the progress toward treatment goals, summarizing learning from the session and monitoring the participant's perspective on how the treatment is progressing. It is important to plan accordingly and leave time for this essential part of the session and treatment.

Match the Conditions of the Treatment Environment

As will be discussed in Chapter 7, **the treatment environment includes aspects of the physical space, therapeutic relationships, promotion of the adventure beliefs, and authentic engagement with the purpose of the treatment.** Effective matching includes taking the consideration of the current environmental conditions into account. Whether the individual adventure psychotherapy is taking place in an office, in the outdoors, in public spaces, or even in virtual sessions, what can be accomplished is dependent on what sort of treatment environment exists. Practitioners need to consider things like whether the treatment relationship is marked by mutual positive regard, whether the participant is fully engaged, if the physical setting is accommodating the treatment focus, and whether all the adventure beliefs (conditions for optimal growth) are operating effectively within the treatment culture.

Treatment environments offer both limitations and opportunities. Consider features of the environment that the practitioner may be able to incorporate into sessions, such as a park bench along a walking path or a water feature as well as weather for the day. For example, during a session with Brian, an unexpected summer storm showed up, and the session needed to move to a shelter. Brian shared that there were many unexpected "storms" in his family growing up due to his father's temper. When attempts to explore that comment further were unsuccessful, the practitioner introduced a weather report activity. Brian and the practitioner were invited to share about the weather inside their bodies at that moment (**Weather Report**, see Appendix 1). Brian's report was, "I feel stormy inside my head and body". It was the first time Brian had identified and verbalized emotional content in the session.

Choose Activities to Meet Participant Needs and Goals

When choosing activities, it is vital that they are intentionally aligned with what the practitioner knows about the participant. Activities should be appropriate, achievable, and in line with individual clinical goals.

Aligned with Treatment Goals

When selecting activities, it is best to start your search by identifying the clinical focus of the session. If Point B for the session is to build a skill, consider what dynamics of an activity will provide the best opportunity to practice that skill. If Point B for the session is to increase awareness of a particular response, consider what activities possess a structure that can increase awareness of an identified dynamic. For example, if a participant lacks awareness of how their communication lacks specificity, the practitioner may select a **Back-to-Back Drawing** activity. This activity requires use of specific communication and is likely to create a parallel process with the communication problems experienced in other settings (see Appendix 1).

Appropriate

Appropriate activities are ones that effectively engage participants with consideration for who they are and how they are showing up. Intervention choices should consider a participant's strengths, interests, and limitations (Alvarez et al., 2021). They should be developmentally appropriate and accommodate for varying physical and cognitive abilities. For example, if a participant struggles neurodevelopmentally with insight-oriented verbal processing, nonverbal reflection methods may be the most appropriate. Additionally, old notions about stress being "essential" and the idea that everyone needs to get out of their comfort zone to make meaningful change are no longer a part of good practice in adventure therapy (Mitten. 2021). Activities should engage participants at a level that maintains their interest but are not so stressful as to cause harm. Interventions should not overwhelm a participant's ability to cope, and it is a good practice to incorporate continual participant consent into the process.

Achievable

Part of the practitioner's responsibility to the participant is to choose activities that fit within the range of the participant's physical, mental, and emotional capabilities. Ideally, activities are scaffolded to build participant confidence through a series of successes. Participants can also benefit from the struggle of working through challenges or coping with failures encountered on the road to success; however, **ethical practice involves choosing activities that are structured such that participants, in collaboration with the practitioner, are able to achieve some success in the process**. The factors that determine if these challenges are beneficial is whether they lead to growth toward treatment goals and they do not cause harm.

Valuing how the participant responds is one way practitioners can stay within the guidelines described earlier. For example, if the participant responds to an activity by giving up quickly when frustrated, the practitioner may work to identify the positive things about that response, as well as the limitations it poses and any potential connection it may have to achieving the treatment goals. In this manner, the practitioner avoids diminishing the importance of that response to the experience during the session. It also functionally keeps the choice of activities moving forward aligned, appropriate, and achievable.

Gass (2025) discusses designing adventure experiences using isomorphic metaphors. Isomorphic means "same structure". In this application, the practitioner selects activities in which "successful resolution of the adventure experience would assist in or lead to successful resolution of the therapeutic issue" (p. 8). The key is to intentionally select activities that are a good structural match that evoke aspects of the clinical dynamics present in the participant's life that are being addressed in the session. An activity selected with an isomorphic metaphor in mind will set up the intervention in a way that initiates the same responses from the participant in the session as the ones they desire to have outside of the session. For example, any type of tower building activity (**Newspaper Towers, Building Block/Lego Structures, Spaghetti-Marshmallow Tower**, see Appendix 1) with Brian could be structured to include a planning session that requires collaboration with the practitioner to agree on a plan followed by the requirement that the participant and the practitioner take turns placing objects in the building process. This structure is isomorphic to Brian's goal of wanting to increase his connection in his personal relationships.

As participants work through activities isomorphic to their lives, practitioners observe their responses and seek ways to enhance the transfer of learning through facilitation that draws on these comparisons or metaphors. In Brian's case example, the sandcastle activity was presented with an isomorphic frame. The facilitation of the activity instructions and processing were personalized to Brian, and the practitioner made observations to clarify the similarity of what happened during the session to the birthday party scenario that unfolded in his life outside of the therapy.

Although selecting activities with metaphoric alignment can be beneficial, it is not necessary for this to be articulated for change to occur. The experiential nature of adventure practice allows for skill building through behavioral rehearsal or practice, with or without a direct metaphoric connection to the participant's daily life challenges. This rehearsal is a more concrete avenue for change for those skeptical of the power of metaphors and relies on the parallel process of the adventure experience to the participant's life outside of therapy instead of drawing a direct connection.

From a neurodevelopmental perspective, there are also advantages to selecting activities that mirror circumstances, dynamics, or issues like the stormy weather and its relationship to Brian's "stormy family" and his "stormy" internal experiences. Neuroscience indicates that brain areas need to be activated in order to change (Cozolino, 2010). If participants want to learn how to express their emotions with family members; for example, they must have the opportunity to practice identifying and expressing emotions. If they want to learn how to persist through anxiety symptoms, they need to practice coping skills and emotional regulation tools while experiencing anxiety. Choosing activities that support specific skill practice is an important part of effectively matching interventions.

Choose Activities the Practitioner Can Facilitate

Facilitators need to consider which activities and experiences they have the skills to facilitate. Activities range from those as simple as taking a walk or as complex as engaging in a technical climbing experience. A practitioner should only utilize tools that they have developed the expertise, infrastructure, policies, and procedures to facilitate responsibly (Alvarez et al., 2021; Gass et al., 2020; Tucker & Norton, 2013).

Practitioners have a responsibility to address participants' unique needs rather than relying on an intervention merely because it is the one available to them. Even if the practitioner is expected to follow a sequence of activities, each intervention can be tailored by adapting the rules, the props used, the desired end point, the style of framing, or the way in which the practitioner attempts to process or reflect on the participant responses during the intervention.

Alvarez et al. (2021, p. 79) report that when deciding which activities to facilitate, practitioners should choose activities based on the following considerations.

Activities That Are Available to Them

Availability of interventions to use with individual participants may be impacted by program or practitioner resources, accessible local camps or parks, cost, physical setting, or several other factors. If practitioners live in a region with air quality concerns and work with participants who are vulnerable to respiratory issues, their ability to do outdoor activities during air quality alerts will be significantly reduced. Similarly, short hours of daylight and/or temperature extremes need to be considered. For some practices, the expectation may be that all sessions will be inside an agency, school, office, or virtual setting. Understanding the space available and activities that can be facilitated within those spaces is important.

Activities in Which They Have Expertise

Practitioners are ethically bound to operate within their scope of practice, which includes having training from experts and supervised experience in facilitating activities they intend to use in practice (Gass et al., 2020; Tucker & Norton, 2013). If a practitioner lacks the resources or expertise to use a particular activity, there are a few options to consider. Of course, the practitioner can work to obtain the skills and resources needed. Depending on the activity, this could be a small investment of time (learning how to facilitate initiatives that require spotting techniques), or it could take years of practice experience to become proficient (leading sailing experiences). Another option is to contract a professional with technical expertise to lead the activity (sailing captain, high ropes facilitator, e.g.) while the practitioner provides the clinical expertise. Pursuing this option requires that the practitioner verify the expertise of the contracted provider and orient them to the clinical considerations involved. It is unethical to simply contract with someone to "do what they usually do" without consideration for the potential impacts for a clinical population or orientation of the contractor to fundamental rules, such as laws surrounding confidentiality and protected health information.

Activities That Are Aligned with Industry and Organizational Standards

Practitioners are responsible for developing and following policies and procedures, implementing risk management protocols, and providing equipment that is maintained and inspected in accordance with industry standards. This will include establishing activity guidelines, detailing qualifications for leading activities, having and practicing emergency action plans, documenting incidents and near misses, and inspecting equipment according to a regular schedule. Practitioners need to be aware of laws impacting service provision, to consider what levels of insurance are appropriate for their choice of activities, and to obtain the necessary permissions before operating on public lands. The Association for Experiential Education's *Manual of Accreditation Standards for Outdoor Behavioral Healthcare Programs* (Nordquist et al., 2023) is an excellent resource related to standards of practice for adventure therapy programming. Refer to Appendix 2 – "Standards of Practice" for more information.

Customizing Interventions

Customizing is the act of "fine-tuning" an activity after it has been selected so it fits the participant's unique needs. Activities do not need to be led in the same way each time. Rather, practitioners make numerous decisions related to the structure of the activity, how experiences are processed, and the way the session is facilitated.

Options for Changing the Structure of the Activity

One benefit of working with participants individually is the flexibility to adjust intervention activity structure to match participant's needs, both in treatment planning and during the session. These customizations are focused on facilitating experiences with the highest probability of achieving treatment goals. **Therefore, the practitioner's job is to consider what they know about the participant in designing, presenting, and facilitating interventions in session.**

When thinking about how to customize activities, remember that there are many different types of interventions used in adventure therapy, ranging from initiatives, climbing elements, paddling adventures, hiking, and many more. In all these applications, changes can be made to tailor the intervention in the following ways:

- **Rules**: Rules can be adjusted—added, removed, or modified—to highlight different elements of an activity and better align it with participants' needs, ensuring an appropriate level of complexity while allowing for stepwise increases as they progress.
- **Activity Objectives**: The objective of an activity can be adapted to match the appropriate intervention targets for a participant. Objectives may be clearly stated or more open-ended to evolve as the activity progresses. They may be task-focused (i.e. complete this task) or instead focus on clinical goals such as identifying and managing emotions or overcoming barriers.
- **Consequences**: Implementing consequences for rule infractions can increase challenge or work to build integrity. Take care that the consequences align with clinical goals – for example, although starting over after a mistake may be appropriate for building frustration tolerance, it could hinder relationship-building skills. Often, a negative consequence is not necessary to facilitate a useful experience and can distract from clinical goals or negatively impact the relationship between the practitioner and participant. In this case, implementing "positive consequences" for the demonstration of strengths that support goal attainment may be more effective. (i.e., after every mistake, the participant highlights one strength they are exhibiting in the process).
- **Limitations**: Limitations are commonly used in adventure therapy and should be carefully considered in relation to session goals and social justice concerns. While restrictions like silence, limited movement, or vision impairment can facilitate change, practitioners should account for participants' existing limitations, offer alternatives for those with trauma or anxiety, and reinforce that engaging with these constraints is always a choice. It is helpful to remind participants that it is okay for them to peek if they cannot safely keep their eyes shut. Choose limitations with specific clinical intention and be intentional.
- **Roles and Responsibilities**: Responsibilities in an intervention should be thoughtfully divided between the practitioner and participant, ensuring tasks support treatment goals. Whether in initiative activities or nature-based experiences, practitioners can set participants up for success in treatment by encouraging participants to take on appropriate roles,

such as sharing route-finding duties on a hike to foster accountability and executive functioning skills.

- **Props/supplies**: Props and supplies can make adventure therapy engaging and fun, but they may also be distracting or uncomfortable, so practitioners should choose them carefully to support clinical goals. Sensory-sensitive participants may struggle with a harness; young children might be too excited by pool noodles to focus; adjusting the size or weight of a prop can help tailor difficulty to the participant's skills.
- **Setting**: Practitioners often have the option to adjust the setting, deciding whether an activity is better suited for indoors or outdoors, in a larger or smaller space. Consider space constraints, such as whether there's a hallway in addition to a cramped office or if weather has limited the session to an outdoor pavilion with picnic tables, and use the setting creatively to adapt the activity structure and better engage the participant. Of course, sessions done virtually need additional considerations of how to use the space during the intervention.
- **Difficulty or level of challenge**: Adjusting the difficulty level of activities to accommodate age, ability, and participant functioning involves considering whether the participant needs small successes to build confidence, a challenge to reflect their strengths and consolidate treatment gains, or an experience that increases awareness of issues or conflicts and planning accordingly to match the desired level of challenge.

Options for Processing the Experience

How practitioners choose to help each individual participant reflect on the meaning of an experience is one of the primary considerations for customizing interventions. Depending on the participant, processing styles may vary to include nonverbal reflection, concrete review of what happened, or discussion of the activity's isomorphic alignment with the participant's life outside of the session. See Chapter 8 for more in depth discussions around processing the experience.

Options for Style of Facilitation

As the practitioner facilitates interventions, they are making a series of decisions to optimize the experience. These decisions relate to how the intervention gets presented to the participant, how the practitioner chooses to lead the intervention, and how the participant's responses are processed or reflected upon to achieve meaning and significance. This will also be covered in Chapter 8. Practitioners also decide what style they will use in facilitation. The following are some examples:

- **Use of Self**: How one chooses to use themselves in each session is a part of customizing interventions. The practitioner can change the tone of the activity, making it light-hearted, serious, focused, or exploratory. These decisions are made depending on the needs of the participant and which approach will be best suited to support progress.
- **Nondeliberative or Structured**: Being nondeliberative allows participants to determine the direction of the session through their responses. Alternatively, a more structured approach uses clear instruction and guidance. Which to use depends on how the practitioner understands the participant's clinical needs. A practitioner may choose to facilitate in a more deliberative or directive manner based on Point A factors such as the participant's age, level of impulsivity and emotional dysregulation, or the presence of a developmental delay, such as cognitive impairment or autism spectrum disorder.

- **Practitioner Participation**: Deciding whether to actively participate in the intervention or remain outside of the activity to facilitate the experience without direct involvement is an important decision. In individual adventure psychotherapy, it is common for the practitioner and participant to engage in activities together. Practitioners may engage directly to enhance safety, demonstrate desired behavior, and strengthen relationships or step back to encourage the participant's independence.

Box 6.6 Brian's Case Example: Selecting and Customizing Interventions

This session focused on Brian's treatment goal of improving his ability to express emotions in the moment in a regulated way, which would increase the likelihood he will feel heard. He and the practitioner collaboratively updated this goal as he improved his ability to regulate his trauma responses and express himself in an effective manner.

Selecting the Intervention

The practitioner concluded that Brian was in the middle phase of treatment and that interventions could move from developing aspects of the treatment environment to more squarely focus on addressing his treatment goals. It was decided that problem-solving activities that required collaborative efforts with the practitioner would mirror the need to balance his strength in taking initiative with the need to consider other people's thoughts and desires.

Within this category of problem-solving interventions, the practitioner chose to introduce **The Dump** (see Appendix 1). The practitioner thought this activity would engage Brian's interest in figuring things out, that it fell well within his skills, and required collaborative effort with the practitioner. The challenge is to transfer water from one cup to another without directly touching either cup. Two circles, each with a two-foot diameter, are drawn around the cups using string, webbing, or rope. One cup is filled with water, and participants must pour its contents into the empty cup.

Customizing the Intervention

Brian had recently started to share small samples of his private inner processes and was clearly working on being able to verbalize the connection between thoughts, behaviors, and emotions. The practitioner focused on customizing this activity in a manner that built on gains made and encouraged forward progress toward his goal. Below describe the many ways the practitioner customized this activity.

Rules: The rules the practitioner decided to establish for the intervention included the following:

- Participants could not reach across either of the two-foot barriers around each cup and had to always stay at least 12 inches away. This rule encouraged Brian to seek assistance and practice collaborative engagement in his interactions with others.

- When water spilled to the floor, the activity continued. This rule allowed for a parallel process to his relationships, which can be messy without needing to start over, emphasizing that there is no perfect way to engage collaboratively with another person.
- If a hand ever came closer than 12 inches from one of the cups, the activity would restart from the beginning. This rule was intended to ensure that Brian could not easily complete the activity without asking for help.

Activity Objectives: Rather than focus on the problem-solving skills (at which Brian excelled), the decision was made to *attend* primarily to managing the issue of asking for help from another person effectively, *dealing* successfully with any trauma responses or anxiety that may emerge and communicating his thoughts and feelings with the practitioner.

Consequences: In this case example, the consequences were that if water spilled, the activity would continue. If the participant's hands came closer than 12 inches to the cup, the activity would start over. The consequences were explained as being true to life: Relationships can be messy (spilled water), and one strives to work through conflict with no need to start over. If someone breaks an agreement, however, the consequences are often that the parties in the relationship need to acknowledge what happened and start over.

Limitations: The practitioner decided not to participate in the activity until asked or invited by Brian. Once invited to participate, the practitioner would wait for Brian's instructions. This limitation was intended to increase the need for Brian to communicate with another person while solving the problem. The limitation of not getting closer to either cup than 12 inches was upheld to increase the need for Brian to ask for help.

Roles and Responsibilities: Brian was given the role of making a plan to complete the task and the responsibility to communicate the details of the plan to the practitioner. This role made it possible for the practitioner to observe Brian's interpersonal interaction in the midst of a problem and for Brian to practice effective communication strategies.

Props/Supplies: Two plastic cups, webbing or rope to create two circles approximately two feet in diameter, and a rubber band with six 18-inch strings attached were all given to Brian. The rope circles were placed approximately 10 feet apart. One cup was filled with water and placed in one circle. The empty cup was placed in the other circle.

Setting: This activity took place in a clinical office because it was raining with high winds the day of Brian's appointment.

Level of Challenge: Since the objective was not to develop problem-solving skills (Brian was already skillful at solving problems), the rubber band with strings attached was presented to Brian already assembled. In this way, the challenge level was moderate with the hope that work on problem-solving would not distract Brian from the goals related to *how* he approached the problem.

Processing Style: The practitioner decided to frame the activity by stating that the water in the cup was a metaphor for Brian's hopes and dreams (Point B) for therapy. Successfully dumping the water into the second cup would represent achieving his goals of expressing emotion appropriately, managing his anxiety well, and improving his relationships. The intention was to engage with Brian in verbal reflection of whether the things he did during the intervention would be a resource or an obstacle for attaining his goal.

Facilitation Style: Based on the participant's strengths in problem-solving, the decision was to take a nondeliberative approach to create the opportunity to observe how he handles problem-solving situations. In terms of the practitioner's case conceptualization, The Dump activity fit well with Brian's personal strengths in problem-solving, as well as with his primary clinical needs of learning to interact with other people effectively, solve daily life problems, and manage interpersonal conflict. And, finally, the practitioner was open to helping Brian with the activity but chose to remain a non-participating observer unless specifically asked for help. The intent was to require Brian to acknowledge his need for help and communicate that need effectively.

Conclusion

Matching interventions to fit participant needs involves knowing the participant's Point A and Point B and selecting and customizing interventions that are sequenced appropriately and thoughtfully scaffolded. The scope of what practitioners are required to match to participant needs does not end with activity selection. How one chooses to facilitate an intervention is also matched to fit the individual participant. Matching interventions in a way that supports development of an effective treatment environment is explored in the next chapter.

Reflections

- Think of a treatment plan for a specific participant. What aspects of that plan can help you make decisions about matching interventions?
- After deciding that the optimal sequence of interventions for a participant is to offer problem-solving activities, how would you scaffold the skills needed to complete activities from easy to more complex?
- What is one change you could make to each of the following components of an intervention:
  - How you present the activity
  - How you lead, or facilitate, the activity
  - How you engage the participant in reflection on what happened in the activity

Now What?

- Create time in your schedule to thoughtfully match interventions with participant's needs.
- Look over the options discussed for how to help participants process their experiences. Consider what might influence your decision about what style to utilize with different participants. You may also look ahead to the chapter *Facilitating the Experience* for additional information.
- Consider what aspects of activities you can change to customize them to the needs of a specific participant.

Matching in Action

The authors are delighted to share with the readers a remarkable example of how adventure activities were matched to fit the needs of a nonverbal adolescent. It was given to us by Patrick McMillion. Pay attention to what Patrick does to match an intervention to fit this participant's needs prior to the session, as well as during the session.

Practitioner Information

Patrick McMillion, PhD, LCMHC, CCAT. At the time of work for this case study, I was at Adventure Works of DeKalb County in DeKalb, Illinois, and had a master's degree. Now I work as an assistant professor and adventure therapy certificate program coordinator at Westminster University in Salt Lake City, Utah. I am a counselor who has been practicing adventure therapy since 2012 and have been a CCAT since 2020. There are two primary things that are appealing to me about adventure therapy: (1) I really believe in the importance of combining the body and mind in the healing process. I think AT is the most natural way of building that connection through movement and challenge. (2) It is where I can be my most authentic self as a counselor. This is important to me, especially through my existential lens. I feel more engaged in the counseling process. My brain operates through finding meaning and engaging in challenging and bold exploration, and I find that AT offers the best opportunity for those to happen.

Participant Description

The participant was a sixteen-year-old male diagnosed with selective mutism co-occurring with social anxiety disorder. He was referred to Adventure Works from an individual outpatient practitioner primarily due to his selective mutism in the hopes that more experiential approaches would offer more opportunities for change. His parents indicated they were most concerned about his selective mutism. For the last three months, he had only spoken to his mother sporadically and a single friend at church sporadically. Prior to the occurrence of selective mutism, there were no speech-language difficulties, and the participant had developed normatively. I will use the pseudonym of Thomas for the participant moving forward.

Treatment Context

Thomas was in his fourth week of treatment at Adventure Works, which included weekly 1-hour one-on-one sessions, along with two 3-hour groups per week. Although Thomas attended groups, he had not yet directly interacted with any other participants and would stand or sit off to the side. The only communication in any engagement was a physical response to yes-or-no questions from me. He would put one finger up below his waist for "yes" and two fingers up below his waist for "no".

He had participated in several activities, but had shown the most engagement in archery, so at this point in treatment, I had decided to utilize that activity primarily.

For this session, we were at a local indoor archery range. The goal for this session was to continue to increase the number of responses to engagement from me and depth of engagement in the activity. This could be any new physical engagement or, especially, any new vocal sound. The hope was not to pressure Thomas into speaking, so any engagement was fine because his response patterns at this point were so limited. I had not heard a word, grunt, sigh, or laugh from him. He also declined to write anything as part of communication.

Session Description

To promote greater engagement and responses, we were shooting from the 25-foot line at a variety of sizes of inflated balloons on the target wall. I had switched to inflated balloons rather than paper targets in the hopes of increasing his engagement and reaction because hitting the balloons adds a greater sensory experience with the sound of the pop and the deflating of the balloons. With prior participants, I had noticed it encouraged them to take the process of shooting the arrow more seriously because the reward for a successful hit seemed higher. I also hoped this would elicit the increased likelihood of any sound from Thomas.

As part of this process, I explained to Thomas that I would share aloud an inner running monologue of my own thoughts that he could respond to if he chose. This would look like me saying things like, "I'm checking to make sure my feet and body are aligned right. Oops, my shoulders aren't straight. I always do that. I need to make sure I check that every time". If Thomas or I shot and hit a balloon, I would say things like, "Yes!" or "Nice!" or "Oh yeah!" I would also provide feedback on Thomas's shot process. He was responding accordingly with his body positioning but not offering any other direct interaction. Around 30 minutes into the session, his success rate with hitting balloons was increasing, so I increased the challenge by reducing the size of inflation of the balloons and continued aloud my inner monologue.

Thomas made a truly incredible shot on a small balloon and continuing with my monologue I said, "Holy cow, I should hire you as an assassin!"[1]

Thomas let out a blurted and blunted laugh.

The first vocal sound I had heard from Thomas in 1 month and a total of 28 hours with him. To not overplay the moment and accidentally reduce his likelihood of responding more, I just turned and smiled at him and said, "let's see if you can do that again". We continued that way for the rest of the session, although Thomas did not make any more sounds.

At the end of the session, his mother came to pick him up. As he was walking to the car, I said my normal, "See you next week, Thomas". With his back turned to me Thomas said, "See you next week, Patrick", and quickly entered the car.

It was truly wonderful to hear his voice.

Practitioner Comments Regarding Session

From that session on, Thomas continued to engage verbally with me more when others were not around. It took another two months, but then he started to verbally engage with group members as well.

In retrospect, I think archery worked so well for Thomas because it is a fun and exciting activity, but it also requires a great deal of success with experiencing control to effectively make shots. Selective mutism in and of itself is another practice of control. I think with Thomas having another outlet for control in archery in conjunction with a supportive and engaging person, he was able to feel comfortable speaking again.

There was certainly a lot of trial and error on my part as a counselor because all my training was primarily oriented to talk therapy. This was an instance where processing through talk was not much of an option. Through my existential lens, I was focused on reducing his feelings of isolation and whatever anxiety was contributing to that isolation. Selective mutism almost acts as a self-fulfilling isolation machine. My intent behind providing my inner monologue along with the activity was to disrupt that machine – to connect Thomas with the goings-on of something other than himself. Even if those goings-on were from a dorky dad-joke machine of a counselor.

When starting in adventure therapy, or clinical work in general, I had not conceived of working with a participant with selective mutism. Now I cannot think of any better way other than adventure therapy. What an amazing modality for people who struggle with this. An outlet for processing without words that also naturally challenges them to express themselves.

Note

1 This clinician is aware that it may sound counter-therapeutic to jokingly talk about assassins or assassination in treatment, but please consider the context with a 16-year-old male who plays video games. During this time period, the game series Assassin's Creed was one of the most popular games there was.

Submitted by Patrick McMillion, PhD, LCMHC, CCAT

Adventure Works (at the time of this adventure therapy session)

DeKalb, Illinois

References

Alvarez, T. G., Stauffer, G., Lung, D. M., Sacksteder, K., Beale, B., & Tucker, A. R. (2021). *Adventure group psychotherapy: An experiential approach to treatment*. Routledge.

Bettmann, J. E., Speelman, E., Blumenthal, E., Couch, S., & Schmalz, D. L. (2024). Nature exposure, even as little as 10 minutes, is likely to yield short-term benefits for adults with mental illness. A meta-analysis. *Ecopsychology*, *16*(3), 174–190. https://doi.org/10.1089/eco.2023.0063

Cozolino, L. (2010). *The neuroscience of psychotherapy: Healing the social brain* (2nd ed.). W. W. Norton & Co.

Frank, L. S. (2013). *Journey toward the caring classroom: Using adventure to create community* (2nd ed.). Wood 'N' Barnes Publishing.

Gass, M. A. (2025). *Delivering effective adventure therapy: A therapist's guide to producing transformative change for clients*. Routledge.

Gass, M. A., Gillis, H. L., & Russell, K. C., (2020) *Adventure therapy: Theory, research, and practice* (2nd ed.). Routledge.

Itin, C. M. (1995). Utilizing hypnotic language in adventure therapy. *The Journal of Experiential Education, 18*(2), 70–75. https://doi.org/10.1177/105382599501800203

Itin, C. M. (2003). The double diamond model of experiential education as a framework for adventure therapy. In K. Richards & B. Smith (Eds.), *The therapy within adventure: Proceedings of the Second International Adventure Therapy Conference* (pp. 111–125). Zeil Verlag.

Lung, M. D., Stauffer, G., & Alvarez, T. G. (2008). *Power of one: Using adventure and experiential activities within one-on-one counseling sessions*. Wood 'N' Barnes Publishing.

Mitten, D. (2021) Critical perspectives on outdoor therapy practices. In N. J. Harper & W. W. Dobud (eds.). *Outdoor therapies: An introduction to practices, possibilities, and critical perspectives* (pp. 175–187). Routledge.

Nordquist, J. et al. (2023). *Manual of Accreditation Standards for Outdoor Behavioral Healthcare* (3rd ed.). The Association for Experiential Education.

Schoel, J., Prouty, D., & Radcliffe, P. (1988). *Islands of healing: A guide to adventure based counseling*. Project Adventure.

Song, C., Ikei, H., Kobayashi, M., Miura, T., Taue, M., Kagawa, T., Li, Q., Kumeda, S., Imai, M., & Miyazaki, Y. (2015). Effect of forest walking on autonomic nervous system activity in middle-aged hypertensive individuals: A pilot study. *International Journal of Environmental Research and Public Health, 12*(3), 2687–2699. https://doi.org/10.3390/ijerph120302687

Sudimac, S., Sale, V. & Kühn, S. (2022). How nature nurtures: Amygdala activity decreases as the result of a one-hour walk in nature. *Molecular Psychiatry*, 27, 4446–4452. https://doi.org/10.1038/s41380-022-01720-6

Tucker, A. R., & Norton, C. L. (2013). The use of adventure therapy techniques by clinical social workers: Implications for practice and training. *Clinical Social Work Journal, 41*(4), 333–343. https://doi.org/10.1007/s10615-012-0411-4

Vygotsky, L. S. (1978). *Mind in society: The development of higher psychological processes*. Harvard University Press.

Wood, D., Bruner, J. S., & Ross, G. (1976). The role of tutoring in problem solving. *Journal of Child Psychology, Psychiatry, & Applied Disciplines, 17*, 89–100.

Chapter 7

Shaping the Treatment Environment

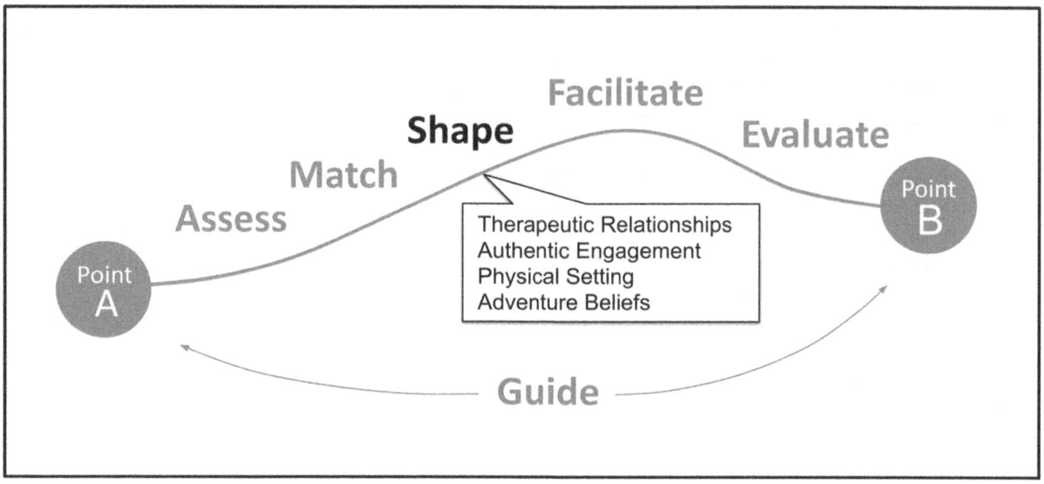

A belief in the transformative power of experience and a unique understanding of how to shape and manage the influence of the therapeutic environment are central elements in the practice of individual adventure therapy. This chapter will focus on what the practitioner does to shape a therapeutic environment that gives the participant the best chance for achieving their treatment goals.

One of the authors recalls working with a 13-year-old participant who was a ward of the court due to delinquency in the community. The therapeutic relationship was developing nicely, and he was engaged in the sessions despite a marked refusal to talk about his emotional or somatic responses. The first six sessions were conducted inside a typical therapy office, but the seventh session took place in a wooded area just three blocks from the office. It was planned to last three hours as opposed to the typical 50-minute session.

As they walked toward the woods, they both shared a **Weather Report** describing how the "weather" was inside their bodies (see Appendix 1). When they reached the desired location, the practitioner continued to talk about making the "weather" inside this session the best it could be, which included both taking actions to ensure the session remained safe and private.

DOI: 10.4324/9781003457893-7

Figure 7.1 Building the treatment relationship through action.

The primary activity was then presented in a non-directive manner. The participant and practitioner engaged in building a **Nature Sculpture**, using only nonliving objects, with the caveat that it needed to mirror similar sculptures that appear naturally (like Stonehenge) by having at least one portal or opening. From that starting point, the participant could do whatever they chose to do (see Appendix 1) (Figure 7.1).

The outcome was remarkable! The participant chose a fallen, 30-foot-long oak tree for his sculpture. He did a timeline of his life along this tree that included a chaotic "mess of branches" to depict when he was 8 years old, and his mother was murdered. There were several strong straight branches to indicate his move from Florida to live with his grandparents, whom he loved. A pile of mud was used to depict his first arrest when he was "almost 12", as well as three additional mud piles to represent time spent in the county detention center for subsequent offenses. He shared emotions and details about his body getting tight and ready to fight as he talked about his creation.

There is no question in the practitioner's mind that this extraordinary level of self-disclosure was made possible because of the treatment environment that existed in the woods. The natural setting, the presence of conditions of safety and trust, the positive rapport that was developed in the treatment environment, and the participant's genuine desire to work on achieving treatment goals all worked together to make self-disclosure possible.

What is Shaping the Treatment Environment?

Most people understand that one's actions and interactions are heavily dependent on what they believe their environment will allow. For example, someone who is comfortable leaving dirty dishes in their own home is likely to feel differently when they are in the home of their best friend. In the same way, the environment that exists in the therapy setting has a powerful impact on what participants do.

It is important to distinguish between the broad environmental context a person lives in and the specific environment that is shaped in the therapeutic setting. Many environmental factors impact the participant in their daily lives, including family, friends, work or school, social and economic status, legal issues, community engagement, political and economic policy, race, gender, and equity issues. All these factors, and more, influence who shows up and what shows up with them to every therapy session.

The broad environmental context that one lives in and the specific environment shaped in individual therapy both consist of things that are external to the participant's Point A. Both environments are important for the practitioner to assess, acknowledge, and value; however, it is primarily the environment within the treatment setting that the practitioner can shape.

When participants come into the physical space used for their treatment, whether that is a clinical office, a hiking trail, a park, or a climbing venue, something transformative needs to happen. **It is essential that the treatment space becomes a place where all the conditions necessary for growth and change come together to give the participant the best opportunity to achieve their treatment goals.** The practitioner's role is to anticipate what those conditions are and work to successfully shape them into the container needed for each participant.

In the Facilitated Wave model, the place where all the conditions necessary for growth and change come together is referred to as the treatment environment. This environment is shaped by focusing on these four core elements:

1 **Treatment Relationship**
2 **Authentic Engagement**
3 **Physical Setting**
4 **Adventure Beliefs**

The Practitioner's Mindset for Shaping the Treatment Environment

There is no one perfect set of conditions for all participants when preparing to shape an effective treatment environment. It is the job of the practitioner to assess what type of environment is needed for each individual participant. For some, being indoors for a session is more desired than a walk in the park. For others, a room cluttered with toys, books, and building block pieces is desired over a sterile, "doctor's office" look.

Furthermore, shaping the environment is a dynamic and ongoing process that practitioners influence, not one thing they do. This overarching process, that continues throughout the entire course of treatment, requires two things of the practitioner:

- that they cast a vision of what the desired environment will look like and engage the participant in the quest to shape that vision.
- that they thoughtfully match specific interventions to shape the desired environment.

Three clinical mindsets are critical to the task of shaping the four core elements of the treatment environment.

Valuing the Person Over the Problem

Valuing the person over the problem is an important perspective that individual practitioners need to incorporate into their practice. The idea, supported by experts promoting neurological strategies such as connection before correction (Siegel & Bryson, 2011) and the general movement from behaviorism to relational strategies, is NOT to think of engaging with a depressed person, for example, but to embrace the perspective that this person with depression is asking for help. This person-first perspective has its roots in the American with Disabilities Act of 1960 (Turnage & Radecki, 2024). **The bottom line is to avoid defining the person as the problem, acknowledging that problems arise from complex systems interactions, including oppression** (Asnaani & Hofmann, 2012). Engaging with the person first and pledging allegiance to helping them achieve their treatment goals is a powerful force in shaping an effective treatment environment. **Simply put, work on the identified problems comes *after* knowing and interacting with the individual.**

Engaging in Shared Experience

Engaging in shared experience is one of the adventure practitioner's superpowers. It is primarily during shared experiences that practitioners demonstrate the importance of the norms they are attempting to develop. **A treatment environment shaped through collaborative experiences can be a dominant force moving away from the oppressive practices that have been commonplace in many participants lives.**

One example of how shared experiences influence shaping the treatment environment can be seen in the use of the plate activity described at the end of Chapter 3. As the practitioner is setting up, framing, and facilitating this activity, norms for how communication will flow and the desire to work collaboratively with the participant are developed. These same norms will guide discussions needed about cancellation policies, payment, and what the participant can expect from the experiential nature of individual adventure therapy.

Providing Trauma-Informed Care and Anti-Oppressive Practices

Shaping an environment that incorporates the principles of trauma-informed care and anti-oppressive practice is an ongoing endeavor. Below are some practical suggestions for how practitioners can prepare themselves for this work:

- Make certain that the **treatment environment** will accommodate all participants. For example, furnish your office space with chairs that are big enough for all participants to sit comfortably (Mullans, 2023). Ensure that safety devices and equipment needed for adventure interventions meet industry standards and are the proper size for your participant. For example, do you have smaller and larger harnesses for participants and helmets that can be worn with a headdress or braids? If you cannot ensure these basic needs for your participant, then don't present that intervention in the first place.
- Consider whether your **external messaging and marketing** is consistent with the clinical focus and ethical values of your practice. Does your website and other marketing tools show diverse individuals doing adventure activities and/or enjoying the outdoors so that potential participants can imagine themselves doing the same? How can your practice communicate about inclusivity and justice for all participants in a way that is safe for your position in the

community (Mullans, 2023)? For example, there are some communities where displaying a pride flag on the exterior of the office may result in harassment or displays of hatred that are toxic for the practitioner and the participants who use that space. While this public display may help participants feel welcomed, it may ultimately result in a more unsafe space. Understanding your community is important in making these decisions.

- How can the **props bag and decorations** in your office space reflect the values of anti-oppression? For example, putting up a rainbow poster, Black Lives Matter poster, or other diverse decorations might have great significance. If you use card decks with pictures of people on them, do the images include diverse representations of people of varying abilities, racial and ethnic identities, and gender expression?
- Consider the **accessibility of the location** where you meet participants, whether that is in an office space or other type of meeting spaces (park, recreation area, climbing gym, etc.). Think about parking spots, bus routes, lighting, typical socio-economic status of residents in the area, physical abilities needed to access the meeting space, and whether all participants will feel comfortable simply arriving in that location. Not all outdoor spaces feel safe to participants, for example. Where you connect with them and how you orient them to the space has an impact.
- If meeting inside, consider what the **waiting area** communicates and offers to the diversity of participants you will be serving.
- Integrate an exploration of the impact of extended **family and ancestral history** into your assessment practices and ongoing therapeutic work with participants. For example, explore a participant's personal and cultural experience with the outdoors and nature if you aim to bring participants outdoors. The collaborative exploration as well as prior practitioner education is key in culturally responsive treatment (Asnaani & Hofmann, 2012).
- Be conscious of **cultural appropriation** of Indigenous and cultural practices and rituals. The fact that a certain practice has been used in wilderness and adventure therapy approaches previously is not an accurate way to measure whether it is appropriate for use in your individual practice. Being willing to explore the origins of these practices can demonstrate active anti-oppressive strategies - including the participant in the exploration can model authentic curiosity and cultural respect. **However, it is also important to consider the inclusion of culturally specific modifications and cultural strengths into treatment to match participant's needs and responses** (Asnaani & Hofmann, 2012).
- Engage in **ongoing/constant consent** with participants so they are aware of what is being asked of them and can make choices about their participation. This caution is especially relevant in adventure therapy activities that require physical engagement, produce somatic responses, and include participant and practitioner involvement that is outside of the norm for individual psychotherapy.

Four Core Elements of the Treatment Environment

Now that aspects of the practitioner's mindset have been discussed, the focus of this chapter will move to exploring the four core elements of the treatment environment.

The Treatment Relationship

The treatment relationship is the most significant common factor when measuring the positive impact of treatment (Gelso et al., 2018; Wampold & Flückiger, 2023). The literature is also clear in noting that some general practices, including using empathy, valuing the participant's story, and fostering collaboration rather than using a more directive or authoritarian approach can be important to nurturing the treatment relationship regardless of one's approach to one's practice (Wampold & Flückiger, 2023).

Right next to the treatment relationship, the idea of successfully ascribing meaning to one's treatment approach is a vital component of successful treatment. This objective is especially relevant in individual adventure psychotherapy because experiential interventions may be different from what participants are expecting when they engage in therapy. Practitioners need to find their own way of communicating the following things to their participants during the beginning stage of treatment:

- The participant and the practitioner will be actively involved in clinical interventions.
- The experiences that the practitioner and participant engage in will be a primary agent of change.
- Attending to safety will be a joint responsibility of the participant and practitioner.
- A clear description of what physical setting the practitioner intends to use for the treatment sessions will be discussed with the participant.

Two important aspects of the relationship between the practitioner and participant which impact outcomes are: 1) the sense of **positive regard** for one another (Farber et al., 2018) and 2) the **alliance** between them to center their work on achieving the treatment goals (Wampold & Flückiger, 2023). While they generally develop together, it is quite possible for them to have positive regard for each other without achieving a treatment alliance to focus their work together on achieving specific goals. For this reason, it is necessary for the individual adventure practitioner to keep their eye on both aspects.

Beginning Phase of Treatment

Activities in the beginning phase of treatment aimed at developing a positive rapport and alliance with the participant usually involve opportunities for the participant to share about themselves while the practitioner listens intently, uses empathy, and seeks opportunities to foster collaboration in the session. For example, **Continuum** activities create an ideal opportunity for participants to move physically and share about themselves (see Appendix 1). Imagine both the practitioner and the participant are asked to stand on a spot along a continuum that represents their answer to questions that vary depending on the practitioner's ongoing assessment. Sample questions could include, "How much energy do you have?", "How satisfied are you with your closest relationships?" Nonthreatening prompts, such as, "Stand on one side of the rope if you like vanilla ice cream or the other side if you prefer chocolate ice cream", are useful in developing therapeutic rapport and engagement in experiential activities.

Other activities aimed at building positive regard during the beginning stage of treatment include:

- Choosing an object they can hold in their hand or point to that tells a story about some aspect of their lives (**Personal Object Check-In**, see Appendix 1).
- Building a structure (from nonliving objects found in nature, clay provided by the practitioner, newspaper and tape, etc.) that can be joined with one built simultaneously by the practitioner (**Tower Building**, see Appendix 1). This task will involve collaboration and agreed upon (mutual) actions.

- Completing a "**Me... By a Thread**" placard (see Appendix 1). This activity invites participants to put their name in the middle of an 8 x 11 inch piece of cardstock and write their answer to four questions placed in each of the corners. The questions vary depending on the participant's Point A. The participant and the practitioner are invited to decorate their placard any way they wish.
- **The Four Corners** activity, described fully in Chapter 5, is also valuable for building positive rapport (see Appendix 1).

The treatment alliance, or commitment by the participant and practitioner to work collaboratively toward mutually agreed upon treatment goals, grows along with positive rapport in the activities listed earlier. Activities that target treatment goal setting are useful in developing the treatment alliance.

- In the **Rubber-Band Goal Setting** activity, participants are invited to choose one rubber band from an assortment of them (see Appendix 1). The task presented is to choose an object somewhere in the physical setting and predict how many flicks of the rubber band will be necessary to hit the target. Processing what the participant did (made an easy, non-challenging goal or started acting silly and missed their prediction badly, e.g.) can be generalized to the process of setting treatment goals. The fun and engaging nature of this activity is great for use in the beginning stage of treatment to assist in the process of goal setting.
- There are several balloon activities that are useful to build the treatment alliance. **Balloon Rocket Release** involves releasing a fully inflated balloon and predicting its flight path and final destination is one way to prime the discussion of setting goals for treatment (see Appendix 1). It can also work to write the goals on a sheet of paper that is folded as small as possible and inserted in a deflated balloon. Once the balloon is loaded with the participant's treatment goals, it is fully inflated. The participant and practitioner work together to write words on the balloon with a marker describing the things that will be required to reach the goals (safety, trust, confidentiality, and so on). If desired, the practitioner and participant can decide to do something with the balloon, such as keep it afloat for as many hits as possible. This action is a metaphor for what actions, guided by the items written on the balloon, will be needed to bring the goals in the balloon to the finish line (**Balloon Contract**, see Appendix 1).
- Approaching experiences with an eye toward collaboration and setting a standard for mutuality in making choices will pay dividends in terms of establishing positive regard. One's mantra can be "more 'we' and less 'you'". For example, after agreeing to a hike along the river, the practitioner might invite the participant's voice in determining whether 'we' should cross to the other side using the regular bridge or whether 'we' might want to partake in a more unique and challenging way to get across.

Middle Phase of Treatment

Once the treatment relationship is "good enough" for the participant to begin taking the risk involved in working more directly on the treatment goals, the middle stage of treatment begins. The general goals for this stage of treatment are as follows:

- Work on goals
- Ongoing assessment
- Update goals
- Transition from working "on" to working "with"

While the practitioner is always keeping an eye on the rapport with participants, **the primary focus in the middle stage of treatment regarding the treatment relationship shifts to strengthening the therapeutic alliance**. Relationship ruptures, which happen most often in this phase of treatment, can be about the challenges, disappointments, and frustrations inherent in the treatment process, or tests of the practitioner's sincerity. Attending to how these squigglies impact the here and now functioning of the participant can provide the opportunity for rich therapeutic work.

For example, during several failed attempts at creating an **Inukshuk** (see Appendix 1), the participant's frustration boiled over onto the practitioner and their inability "to be clear about the rules" or "to provide the appropriate tools for successful attainment of the task". Rather than get enmeshed in an oppositional battle of wills, the practitioner attended to the participant's current experiential functioning by acknowledging the frustration and expressing appreciation for the persistence and perseverance they demonstrated. The focus on what was happening in the moment helped the participant share a specific frustration with how the practitioner seemed to trivialize their complaints regarding other people they loved. Working through this rupture allowed the participant to move from a place of frustration and failure to a place of appreciating their demonstrated skills AND appreciating the practitioner for pointing them out.

The adventure therapy practice model provides an experiential venue for the expression and resolution of conflict, disagreement, and negative feelings in a manner that paves the way for effective work on the participant's treatment goals. The active engagement with the practitioner provides rich opportunities to bring these issues into the treatment session.

To highlight this, one of the authors remembers doing a **Tower Building Activity** with PVC parts with a participant in the middle stage of treatment (see Appendix 1). Very early in the activity, the practitioner had the sense that a participant cut them off abruptly and wasn't interested in hearing what they had to offer. When this observation was presented to the participant, they were genuinely surprised by the comment and reported having a long-standing argument with their spouse who tells them the same thing. Within the safety of the treatment environment, issues related to effective communication (eye contact, body language, facial expressions, as well as other nonverbal and paraverbal actions) were practiced and subsequently applied to this participant's relationships outside of the therapy. The practitioner's intervention enhanced the participant's genuine engagement in the therapy, as well as provided the context for deepening the treatment alliance.

End Phase of Treatment

When thinking about the treatment relationship in the **end stage of treatment**, practitioners pay close attention to fostering independence and to building the participant's "trust in self". Reflecting on the positive choices made throughout the treatment process will accomplish both objectives, reinforcing their own self-wisdom.

One objective in the end phase of treatment is to reduce dependency on the practitioner and highlight the participant's ability to be their own guide now. Activities that involve remembering things the participant has done and physically going to the site where significant therapeutic work happened, all assist the participant in reflecting on and evaluating the efforts they made during treatment. Developing a treasure hunt in which the participant finds cards with one of their strengths written on it is one example of helping the participant reenvision their Point A.

It is critical that practitioners help participants leave this treatment relationship knowing, trusting and having confidence in their hard-earned skills and increased knowledge level. This confidence will impact positively on their capacity to make the right decisions for themselves in life situations and around the need for further guidance.

An Authentic Engagement

When the participant is genuinely engaged in the quest to achieve treatment goals, the following behaviors will be noticeable:

- What the participant *says* they want to do matches what they actually *do*.
- A natural flow occurs to apply what happened during the experiential intervention to treatment goals.
- The participant will willingly explore the content of their experiential functioning.

The participant's engagement begins with understanding how the experiential approach to clinical practice works and what will be expected from them in working toward their goals. The attribution of meaning to the action taken during interventions is critical to developing a meaningful treatment alliance. In addition, the practitioner needs to send the message that their primary motivation is to see the participant achieve their goals.

As the treatment progresses, so does the level of expectation for the participant to align what they do with what they are saying about their goals for treatment. **Confronting and dealing with potential misalignment (a facilitation skill) of these two aspects of the participant's current experiential functioning presents a great opportunity for therapeutic progress**. On the other hand, ignoring the contradiction between what the participant does and what they say they want to accomplish can result in decreasing the sense of trust, minimizing the treatment alliance with the practitioner, and decreasing the authenticity of what happens throughout the treatment process.

Presenting activities with the task of moving from one point to another is a common way adventure practitioners set the stage for discussion of what is needed to move toward goal achievement. These activities can be a metaphor for the journey toward treatment goals. Classic adventure activities such as **River Crossings/Stepping Stones** (use of boards/mats to travel from one spot to another) will yield details that illuminate the search for next steps, what barriers may be encountered, and what sources of strength and resilience the participant can draw to progress toward achieving their treatment goals (see Appendix 1).

When all is said and done, the practitioner's words about the importance of the treatment environment need to be consistent with the actions they take during sessions. One of the authors recalls working with an eighth-grade student in a school setting. Soon after the participant had come in for their second session, there was a knock on the door, and the Assistant Principal came in asking for time with the practitioner. Their choice to ask whether it was an emergency that could not wait or something they could attend to later, led to a message being sent that the appointment time was valuable and not easily tossed aside. The principal's decision to wait affirmed the importance of the participant's work.

Practitioners should aim to launch the participant into life with a growth mindset by the end of treatment. Throughout treatment, the participant is learning about how to set and work toward goals, which has relevance to their life after therapy. Reflecting on and celebrating how the participant engaged fully and authentically in the treatment process is an important way for the participant to accomplish this objective. This growth perspective on life can result in the participant continuing to work on goals for themselves even after the therapy ends.

Physical Setting

Effective adventure practitioners adapt the physical settings to match the needs of the participants. Several of the authors recall hearing from other practitioners that "*my agency gave me this small room behind the conference room, full of old books and file cabinets! No way can I do adventure therapy there!*" Such a narrow view has no place in this work! Although most practitioners don't always have access to the Colorado Rockies or the Utah high desert, **offices can be transformed IF practitioners see the value in that transformation!** Alternatively, similar stories are heard from providers practicing in wilderness spaces who do not incorporate aspects of the natural setting into their one-on-one sessions. In both examples, it is the mindset of the practitioner that puts a limitation on the potential positive effect of an intentional, desired physical setting on treatment.

In the beginning stage of treatment, it is important to attend to some things that seem to be mundane or insignificant aspects of the physical setting. How will the waiting area be defined and decorated? Will I leave my adventure bag open and in view of the participant? Do I need tissues nearby? How can the participant's needs for privacy be met? How can the setting be enhanced to promote physical and emotional safety for the participant? What aspects of the physical setting will enhance the process, and what can be adapted to shape an environment that will help the participant move toward their Point B?

As already addressed in this chapter, **some issues in the physical setting have major social justice implications** (see the "Providing Trauma-Informed Care and Anti-Oppressive Practice" section). Be aware and explore any culturally significant issues that can be attended to even before the participant enters the space. For example, the woods have historically been unsafe spaces for African Americans (Finney, 2014). Practitioners should explore the implications of different spaces with participants prior to relying on those spaces.

An important consideration in individual adventure psychotherapy is the ramification of providing therapy in public spaces. Mental health practitioners have been grappling with these issues for decades, so this is not necessarily a new or unique issue (Cooley et al., 2020). Engaging in activities in public spaces can draw unwanted attention or contribute to a participant feeling self-conscious. It is important for practitioners to discuss these dynamics with their participants and make the necessary accommodations to protect participant confidentiality and comfort level.

It is also incumbent on the practitioner to assess the physical setting to ensure they have the necessary supplies to accommodate potential needs, such as a first aid kit, extra clothes should they be needed, towels, food, and water. If one chooses to engage with participants in a natural setting, it is certainly the practitioner's responsibility to do what they can to prepare for the unexpected.

One of the practitioner's tasks is sharing their vision for where the therapy can be conducted and engaging the participant in collaboration about the preferred location. Some thoughts about performing that task include the following:

- Be prepared for the possibility that many participants will have expectations for therapy taking place in a clinical office.
- Consider resetting those expectations by scheduling the very first session at a park for an initial information-gathering hike.
- If logistics dictate that the first session, or maybe all sessions, take place in a clinical office, the practitioner can set a precedent for taking an experiential approach to the treatment by making a point to engage the participant in an experiential activity in the very first session. Turning the floor space in your clinical office into a medium for the **Four Corners** activity or introducing the **Bridge Drawing** activity are just two examples of how one might operationalize this suggestion (see Appendix 1).

The physical setting can also be re-designed to invite curiosity and newness in the process. For example, a practitioner met a participant in the parking lot, walked up to the office door, and opened it. The entrance had duct tape zigzagging over the opening. In the center of the door opening was a sign saying: Do not get stuck in the opening when there is so much more to discover inside! After appreciating the humor, they worked together to get inside the office without "getting stuck!"

As the treatment progresses into the **middle phase of treatment**, the practitioner will provide more opportunities to match the setting with the participant's needs by:

1 Allowing time at the end of a session to offer the option of having a conversation about where to meet in future sessions, which is one way to include the participant's voice.
2 Inviting more participation in the physical tasks involved in this approach, like grabbing paddles and life jackets from storage, inspecting the perimeter of a climbing site, or unknotting webbing and ropes to get them ready for new use.

Having demonstrated the impact that the physical setting has had on the participant's successful goal attainment throughout the treatment process, **it behooves the practitioner to engage the participant in reflection on how current physical settings in their life might be adjusted, adapted, or changed to enhance their functioning as they approach the end stages of treatment**. For example, it may be important to intentionally allow participants the space to go for a walk in a natural setting when they find themselves having difficulty managing their emotions. To this end, it is wise for practitioners to engage the participant in critical observation of how the physical setting influenced their clinical work and to consider how they could mimic those conditions in their life moving forward.

The Adventure Beliefs

Cocreating a vision for what the treatment environment can become is very significant for successful treatment (Amorim & Ventura, 2023; Wampold & Flückiger, 2023). This process begins with the practitioner casting their vision for how the adventure beliefs can make the treatment environment unique and different from other settings. **The authors believe there are**

seven adventure beliefs or conditions that need to be established in the treatment environment, for optimal growth and learning to occur:

- **Safety**: the physical well-being along with the emotional and psychological protection of the individual.
- **Challenge**: how difficult and/or novel interventions and physical space are for the participant.
- **Belonging**: a sense of being in the right place and fitting into the treatment space, as well as accepted and valued by the practitioner.
- **Freedom**: the sense of being without coercion or constraint to make independent choices, as well as the resilience to deal with the consequences of those choices.
- **Enjoyment**: play and fun are introduced into the adventure therapy practice model to increase the participant's sense of pleasure and promote emotional, psychological, and physical well-being.
- **Trust**: reliance on the character, ability, strength, or truth of someone or something.
- **Effective Communication**: the verbal, nonverbal, and paraverbal methods of sending a message to another person in a clear manner, including developing clear definitions of the beliefs that are being developed in the treatment environment. Effective communication includes the ability to have difficult conversations as well as consideration of the needs of those involved in the communication (i.e. matching messages to recipients).

As practitioners cannot create these conditions on their own, they work to cultivate them through collaboration and co-creation with participants. It is useful to point to a wall hanging or props that list these beliefs and create a vision that sees the practitioner and the participant working together in a way that honors all seven of the beliefs. Communicating that these conditions will create a treatment environment that gives the participant the best chance of achieving what they came into treatment for is essential.

One of the primary outcomes of the beliefs operating effectively in the therapeutic setting is the participant's clear *focus* on what is happening in the here and now. Conversely, **when a squiggly appears in the environment that robs the participant of this focus, it often boils down to the fact that one of the beliefs has been compromised**. Knowing this, practitioners can use the adventure beliefs as a foundation to explore issues emerging in the environment when these squigglies are encountered.

The list of activities to address development or renewal of the beliefs is almost limitless. Putting a thumb up or down and anywhere in between to physically express a participant's assessment of how the beliefs are showing up or what they are feeling inside can be easily used (**Thumb-o-Meter**, see Appendix 1). The classic activity of keeping a beach ball in the air for as many hits as possible (**Moonball**) can also work as an experiential intervention aimed at developing the beliefs and how they define the treatment relationship (see Appendix 1).

Practitioners also invite the participant's voice in defining the beliefs. Having a set of floor spots with the beliefs printed on them is very useful. One can start by spreading the spots on the ground and asking the participant to arrange them around themselves according to how important they think each one will be for them in this treatment experience (see Figure 7.2). It can then be effective to use the spots throughout the duration of the therapy as prompts for the participant to reflect on after activities or to evaluate what beliefs are strong and which ones need more focus.

Figure 7.2 Reflecting on the adventure beliefs is a valuable intervention

Practitioners will discover that the beliefs work in tandem with each other as sometimes enhancing Safety, for example, allows Belonging to flourish. Almost always, one needs Safety in the environment to achieve an appropriate level of Challenge for a participant. When participants feel safe, along with having a positive connection with the practitioner, they often find more courage inside themselves to face whatever issues or problems that brought them into therapy, and the appropriate level of challenge can be accomplished.

Developing a Common Language around the Adventure Beliefs

Developing a common language around what the beliefs mean is central to attempts to shape an effective treatment environment. This process begins during the very first contact with the individual participant. Using words like safety, belonging, and trust, for example, in the practitioner's description of the adventure therapy practice approach is valuable for the eventual development of the beliefs as defining features of the treatment environment. **Even more impactful is identifying how one of the beliefs was demonstrated during a session and highlighting the importance of that belief in shaping the necessary treatment environment**.

The authors are reminded of an initial session with an adult participant who stopped a game of **Moonball** (hitting a beach ball in the air) to move a lamp that was in danger of getting damaged (see Appendix 1). The practitioner responded by saying, "I really appreciate your attention to safety here. We will be doing a lot of things to ensure we remain physically and emotionally and safe during every activity". Simply using the name of the belief (in this case, safety) goes a long way toward cocreating an understanding of what that belief means in the environment.

Safety

Safety is central to adventure therapy. It refers to the physical well-being, as well as the emotional and psychological protection of the individual. When humans don't feel safe, they engage in fight, flight, and freeze responses to make up for their vulnerability. **The goal in every adventure therapy session is to provide conditions that allow individuals to share fully about who they are without the need to use defenses or other protective measures while present in the treatment environment.**

Effective practitioners attend to safety well before the first session with participants. Statements on the practitioner's website, decorations in the clinical space, and intake forms that take care to include everyone (i.e., use of more than male/female pronouns) are important. Initial phone calls that include an explanation of how the experiential approach to practice includes the use of activities that will be mutually agreed upon and clarified fully before engagement contribute to establishing safety as the norm. How one's clinical office is set up, including things like whether the chairs are too close or too distant, whether the chairs available are large enough for all participants, and what hangs on the office walls all contribute to managing safety. Similarly, the details of an outdoor space matter and call on practitioners to recognize the potential impact on safety and to engage the participant in reflection on those issues, especially if participants may have reasons to feel unsafe outdoors.

Practitioners need to be aware that safety is easily compromised during individual therapy. Sometimes, just meeting the practitioner, or the participant, during the first session can be triggering. Factors like gender identity, race or ethnicity, accent, cologne or perfume, and clothes can sometimes create a connection or a barrier. Communicating these nuances from the very beginning of treatment can result in the development of felt safety for both the practitioner and participant. It can also establish an accepted practice of addressing needs and wants quickly and directly. The accumulation of shared knowledge from experiences brings more clarity about what each person needs around safety in the treatment environment.

Owning the reality that unexpected "things happen", that there are things unknown about each other, and that the possibility of making mistakes is always present can be important messages that increase the potential to learn and/or benefit from experiences. When squigglies or other events arise that threaten the sense of safety, it's important to acknowledge them. What the practitioner is likely to notice is an escalation in emotionally dysregulated responses. It requires the practitioner to seek clarification and set the necessary limits to assist the participant in regaining a more optimal level of arousal that will allow for learning and change. The sooner it is noticed and attended to, the less negative impact that squiggle can impose. Hence, discussing this squiggly, clarifying the participant's response to it, and developing norms within the treatment environment to manage these issues is an important part of shaping the environment.

There are many manifestations of the need for physically safe practices in adventure therapy. Water activities, climbing, hiking, high adventure, and a walk in the park all have differing safety protocols that the adventure practitioner is required to manage (Nordquist et al., 2023). Likewise, emotional safety will take on different perspectives depending on the participant's Point A and the nature of the activity. It is the responsibility of the practitioner to explore and deal with each of these issues as well as be competently trained in the risk management and facilitation techniques for the activities they choose to use with participants. Just because a practitioner loves to rock climb does not mean they are ready to facilitate climbing interventions. Practitioners still need the proper training, certifications, and supervision to offer these interventions to participants safely and within their scope of practice.

Beliefs around "safety" are also central to anti-oppressive and trauma-informed practice. For example, when the practitioner makes a statement like, "It is important to me that this space becomes a place to talk about and express every part of yourself, especially the things that may be hard to talk about like race, beliefs, sexuality, ancestry or family history", the importance of safety is prioritized and the door to anti-oppressive practices is opened. The practitioner's initiative in naming these issues and the permission given to have these conversations are important first steps, without which that door often remains closed. It is a practitioner's main responsibility to avoid re-traumatizing and/or harming participants.

For some participants, shaping a "brave" versus a "safe" environment is preferred (Arao & Clemens, 2013). In brave spaces varying opinions/disagreements are ok, participants agree not to respect each other, own when their responses negatively impact others and participants have choice around engaging in challenging conversations (Arao & Clemens, 2013). Due to histories of trauma and/or oppression, some participants may never truly feel safe but trust the practitioner enough to show up. Developing a treatment environment that allows the participant to work through these uncomfortable situations is what the "brave" environment is attempting to accomplish with the aim to create opportunities for growth and learning.

Challenge

As described in Chapter 1, challenge refers to how difficult an activity is for the participant. Since practitioners are not omniscient, the primary way to accurately understand how challenging an activity is for the participant in your individual practice is to collaborate with them and honor their voice in the treatment decisions. **Boredom or lackadaisical engagement are often expressions of the need for increased challenge. Withdrawal, visible anxiety, frustration, distractibility, and dysregulated behavior in general often indicates that the challenge level is too high**.

For many, engaging in individual therapy is a bold enough challenge. What is, after all, more challenging and scarier than looking at yourself, your choices and your current life situation. Introspection is challenging and risky and healthy. When this process is undertaken intentionally, it must be done in a manner that keeps the participant engaged in the process and able to explore any "fight or flight practices" or other issues that disconnect them from the process of knowing and change.

There are two nuances to the use of this belief that will be applied throughout this text. **First is that considerations about how much challenge is needed will be about the appropriate level of arousal (or dosage) for the specific participant**. Based on neuroscience already discussed, practitioners should strive for the level of arousal in which the participant is involved, not bored or disengaged, as well as not overly aroused to the point of becoming impulsive or dysregulated.

Second, the authors do not believe challenge, or being out of one's comfort level for that matter, is necessary to produce change. They think most humans do well when appropriately aroused within their comfort level and that change may be enhanced by these conditions. Fredrickson (2001) established that when humans are experiencing positive emotions, they can think more broadly and build upon that foundation to address change.

Here is the crux of the issue: practitioners use challenge in the treatment environment to produce the conditions that give the participant the best chance of reaching their treatment goals. In the effort to provide the optimal level of arousal, it is often necessary to increase or decrease the level of challenge in an activity. Rules, consequences, and limits on physical abilities can be adjusted to alter the level of challenge. Consider a classic **River Crossing** activity which involves the participant moving from one area to another without touching the ground (see Appendix 1). The participant is given several resources they can stand on during their journey. To increase the level of challenge, a rule can be added stating that any resource that loses contact with a human is lost for the duration of the journey, the participant could lose a physical ability, or the number of resources reduced. To reduce the challenge, additional resources could be provided or the distance the participant is required to travel can be reduced.

Throughout the practitioner's efforts to successfully manage the level of challenge, honoring the voice of the participant reaps a windfall of benefits in building the treatment relationship and strengthening the beliefs of safety and trust.

Challenge squigglies often show up as a response to a poor match between where the participant is and the activity the practitioner has chosen, hence why collaboration with the participant is essential. The poor match could be about any of these issues:

- The assessment of Point A is not accurate (i.e., poor sleep the night before left soreness in the participant's back, making the bouldering experience doubly difficult).
- The environment isn't what is currently desired (i.e., asking a participant to continue to construct an earth sculpture while the rain has intensified).
- The participant's engagement to the work, their Point B, is changing (i.e. a participant recently deciding their investment in mindful eating is not important, so doing this "online shopping for really good ingredients is boring").
- The choice of intervention tool does not match with participant needs. Most examples of this mismatch happen when practitioners neglect to fully check in with the participant or fail to collaborate about structuring the activity. Think about structuring a very challenging intervention, aimed at passing through a swampy area, based on your assessment at the end of the previous session that a higher level of challenge would aid in developing trust in the treatment relationship. The person who showed up for the next session, however, was dejected and angry about what they perceived as several personal failures during the past week. A check-in at the beginning of the session may result in reducing the level of challenge to recognize strengths and offer greater opportunity for success. If there is no check-in, the activity is likely to be a poor match with participant needs.
- The practitioner has not provided adequate information about the nature of the intervention (e.g., the participant shares, "I just don't get why anyone would use mouse traps!").

Hence, it is important to be curious with participants in exploring their responses to understand where the mismatch occurred, so the practitioner and participant can address it and change direction if needed.

Belonging

Every individual therapy participant needs to experience a sense of being accepted and valued by the practitioner. The benefits that come with the participant's sense of belonging in the treatment environment are immeasurable as belonging in treatment profoundly affects a person's cognitions, behaviors, and emotions (Gere & MacDonald, 2010). In fact, belonging is a protective factor (Masten, 2014).

Hence it is the practitioner's responsibility to attend to a participant's sense of belonging. The following are some ways of doing this by

- seeking the participant's voice during sessions,
- acknowledging and appreciating the participant's efforts and their strengths,
- avoiding judgment of the participant or their efforts,
- seeking mutuality in the relationship and avoiding condescending responses, and
- paying attention to and valuing what the participant shares during sessions.

When a sense of belonging is established, participants will demonstrate involvement in what happens in the session and responsibility to make the session productive. This level of engagement is a manifestation of knowing their contributions will be heard and valued.

Squigglies related to "belonging" often surface as "fight or flight" responses. Arguing and disagreeing about insignificant things might be explained by the participant thinking, "I am not valued here so I will fight to be seen!" Or a "why bother?" attitude may result from the participant not feeling a sense of belonging and thinking, "It doesn't matter what I say here!" Missing appointments, avoiding expression of any feelings, or reluctance to fully engage in interventions can often be traced back to a failure in establishing a sense of belonging. Hence, squigglies related to belonging usually show up as some form of disengagement from the work necessary for therapy that needs to be acknowledged and explored collaboratively.

Freedom

The belief that participants have the freedom and power to make independent choices, as well as the resilience to deal with the consequences of those choices is an integral part of the adventure therapy practice model. Chapter 2 explores the fact that valuing the participant's voice and choice (aka, their freedom) is an integral part of anti-oppressive, trauma-informed care, as well as integral to ethical and effective practice of adventure therapy. For this standard of practice (where the participant embraces their freedom) to be fully operationalized, practitioners need to be fully aware of the power that comes with their role and make intentional efforts to relinquish it in a way that equalizes the position of the participant (Todić & Christensen, 2022).

A practitioner's choice to facilitate in a non-deliberative manner highlights this focus on choice. The act of allowing the participant to make their own choices about how to respond during experiential interventions, even if a particular choice is problematic, underscores the participant's personal freedom and provides an opportunity for the consequences of their choices to become relevant to the treatment process (Tucker et al., 2016).

One author recalls doing **The Dump** activity with an individual participant (see Appendix 1). The activity tasks the participant with lifting a cup of water without touching it and dumping the contents into an empty cup. The only tool they can use is a rubber band with six strings attached. This task is nearly impossible to accomplish without help. The activity was presented to the participant in a non-deliberative manner followed by the practitioner engaging with the participant but not offering suggestions for how to pick up the water. The participant struggled to do the activity independently. They focused on the details of the set up and attempted multiple solutions but were never able to lift the cup of water. The processing that was ongoing throughout the activity was about the multiple strengths this participant used to stay focused, think outside the box, and validate their own efforts rather than becoming self-deprecating. In this example, the practitioner validated the participant's freedom to make choices and to accept the consequences of each decision made, as well as their power to do things their way. The debrief reviewed all these strengths used by the participant, as well as initiated reflection on their decision to not ask for help. The practitioner made a conscious choice to validate the multiple strengths on display throughout the intervention. How these strengths interacted with the participant's tendency to not rely on other people for help made for a dynamic reflection.

Most of the squigglies related to freedom come from the things the participant has internalized about themselves. The participant's self-limitations, their inhibitions and attempts to meet socially prescribed roles and/or expectations, and their beliefs about their own abilities are the most common things to interfere with freely using their freedom to make independent decisions and to assert the appropriate level of personal power in social settings. These squigglies show up when participants

- stop themselves from expressing dissent or other things they don't think will be accepted in the therapy session,
- struggle to solve a problem but never think to ask the practitioner for help, or
- give up on a task because they assume they are incapable of the solution.

Guiding the participant in a process of understanding more about their choices is at the heart of the adventure therapy practice model. By not judging or arguing with the participant about their choice, the door is open to learn more about what motivated their thought process. The exploration may reveal a parallel process with other decisions the participant has made outside the therapy setting that can be explored collaboratively together.

Enjoyment

Enjoyment may be the most undervalued of the adventure beliefs. Having fun should never be underestimated. There is enjoyment in learning new things about one's self and working hard to achieve a task, even when those things are difficult. Being on a path toward healing and growth can bring enjoyment. Enjoyment leads to the experience of many other positive emotions that are wrapped up in the work of adventure therapy. The joy of making it to the top of a climb or the satisfaction of learning something significant about your oppositional behavior in response to repeatedly failing to reach the goal that was targeted, are examples of this. **When participants experience any type of enjoyment, they become more engaged and connected to the therapy experience.**

Enjoyment and fun should not be limited to children and youth, as research shows that participants, regardless of age, respond to the experience of positive emotions by broadening their thinking and being able to build new ideas for how to manage situations. (Fredrickson, 2001). To promote enjoyment, various forms of play and fun are introduced into the adventure therapy practice model to promote emotional, psychological, and physical well-being. Here are some key ways in which fun and play can be beneficial:

- *Stress Reduction:* Playful interactions release endorphins, which are natural mood lifters, and can help individuals reduce stress and anxiety (Siviy, 2016).
- *Emotional Expression:* Play provides a nonthreatening environment for individuals, particularly children, to act out their feelings, which can facilitate communication and understanding (Garaigordobil et al., 2022).

- *Building Trust and Rapport:* Play creates a positive and accepting atmosphere, making participants more comfortable sharing their thoughts and feelings (Goodacre et al., 2023).
- *Cognitive Development:* Play encourages problem-solving, creativity, and cognitive development, which improves a participant's ability to think critically, make decisions, and develop coping strategies (Haoyou and Oyam, 2024).
- *Social Skills:* Play often involves interaction with others, which helps improve social skills (Yogman et al., 2018).
- *Emotional Regulation:* Fun and playfulness offer participants opportunities to learn and practice regulating emotions, including learning how to explore various emotions, to identify the continuum and complexity of emotional response, and to develop healthier ways to navigate and express their emotions (Elias & Berk, 2002).
- *Physical Health:* Interventions that incorporate physical activity also promote physical health and the somatic embodiment of mental health. This is especially beneficial when addressing clinical issues such as ADHD or trauma (Yogman et al., 2018).
- *Creativity and Self-Expression:* Play encourages participants to explore their thoughts and feelings in unique ways (Domini, 2021).
- *Learning and Skill Development:* Play can be used to teach specific skills or behaviors, such as communication skills or problem-solving skills, in an engaging way (Wenner, 2009).

Practitioners can enhance enjoyment by acknowledging when it shows up. For example, "I am noticing the joy that is showing in your face as you sit up on that ledge. Can you talk more about that?" Lowering the challenge level of an activity that is bringing about frustration in a way that allows the participant to see "the light at the end of the tunnel" also increases enjoyment and may be appropriate for a particular participant. **In addition, being playful as a practitioner provides role modeling for participants, especially adults, that it is not only acceptable to be playful, but it can be a central part of the therapy process**.

Squigglies to the experience of enjoyment begin with the fact that therapy is work. It takes work to unburden oneself from long carried secrets, for example. When enjoyment is missing, other positive emotions diminish, and the participant narrows their perspective to things they perceive as safe. Hence, participants are more likely to give up and eventually stop coming to therapy. When that work is associated with enjoyment, additional positive emotions emerge that encourage the work to continue and expand. **Educating the participant about the importance of play and enjoyment and providing opportunities for them to experience these emotions are central in attending to the treatment environment**.

Effective Communication

All aspects of how the practitioner and participant send messages to each other, including the verbal, nonverbal, and paraverbal methods of sending a message require attention to ensure effective communication. Nonverbal communication includes gestures, facial expressions, and bodily movements. Paraverbal methods are things that come along with what is said verbally, including tone, volume, and cadence of what is said. Somatic and emotional responses of the participant are often seen through awareness of their nonverbal and paraverbal responses.

Pretty much every aspect of individual adventure therapy requires the practitioner and participant to establish norms around effective communication. Active, intentional listening is an essential part of effective communication. The practitioner can model these norms in early discussion about payment, cancellations, scheduling, and confidentiality. When the practitioner uses I-messages, makes eye contact with the participant when talking, listens to the participant's feedback, and/or demonstrates that they value the participant's input, this helps shape the communication patterns needed in the treatment context. The fact that the practitioner is modeling these skills while engaging in shared experiences such as listening intently, asking for clarification, and letting the participant know what your actions mean lends a great deal of significance. Nothing is more important in the process of shaping these norms for practice than the practitioner's ability to listen to the participant.

Shaping guidelines and expectations for effective communication is also central to anti-oppressive practice. Putting difficult issues about diversity, equity, inclusion, and belonging on the table for open exploration requires the development of a shared language that operationalizes the beliefs and gives assurance that the participant's story will be valued. In this way, the practitioner models the ability to tolerate and accept differences by communicating about these issues openly.

There are numerous squigglies to effective communication. Suffice it to say that anything that disrupts the clear expression of that experience is a squiggly. Emotional dysregulation can make it more difficult to access verbal processing capacities in the brain (Cozolino, 2010), and deficits in verbal communication skill sets contribute to squigglies in communication. Unfortunately, those squigglies can come from the practitioner, as well as the participant. One primary strategy for addressing squigglies related to effective communication is to regularly check in with the participant and remain curious about their experience rather than assuming that what was expressed was truly understood.

Trust

Merriam Webster defines trust as "reliance on the character, ability, strength, or truth of someone or something" (2025). That definition applies well to individual adventure therapy in that both the practitioner and the participant are on a journey of developing a belief in the other person's ability and strength to achieve the goals of treatment. They will work together to solve problems, generate ideas, affirm positive movement toward goals, and have many other interpersonal interactions that unfold during their shared experiences that build mutual trust.

When the practitioner follows through on the things they say they are going to do and does things that are consistent with the discussed beliefs, a sense of trust can evolve in the therapeutic relationship. **In fact, it is typical for trust to develop by giving attention to and developing the other beliefs**. When the practitioner attends to safety, for example, benefits are also paid to the development of trust. When the participant's voice about how they want to proceed in an intervention is listened to, valued, and acted upon, trust is developed. One ironic aspect of developing trust is that adventure practitioners frequently present activities requiring trust BEFORE trust has developed. The intent is to provide an experience requiring trust as the tool to develop that belief.

Squigglies related to trust often show up as issues of engagement. **Participants who engage minimally or express negative thoughts about the adventure therapy practice approach are often experiencing a lack of trust**. Resistance is often a legitimate expression of the lack of trust. In the adventure therapy approach to practice, these squigglies are dealt with as normal and expected responses from the participant that have great value to the treatment when resolved collaboratively.

Systemic oppression and ecological factors often present as squigglies to developing trust. Generations of marginalization and oppression may result in deeply ingrained suspicion of mental health services, for example. Other logistical problems, such as lack of reliable transportation and inflexible work schedules, may lead to missed appointments and present obstacles to development of an effective treatment environment. It is important that practitioners don't continue the cycle of oppression by treating these issues as resistance from the participant. Identifying the difficulty involved and joining in a collaborative problem-solving effort demonstrates respect for the participant and understanding of the systemic nature of the squigglies. It is one way to break through the cycle of oppression.

Choosing Activities That Develop Adventure Beliefs

Activities are always selected intentionally. Whether the beliefs are just being developed, often in the beginning stage of treatment, or being refreshed during the middle stage, activities can be chosen with an eye toward highlighting a specific belief or beliefs. As treatment progresses, a collaborative approach, between practitioner and participant, is used more with the intent of cocreating what each of the beliefs means in the here and now. It's important to understand that making decisions about what belief is needed in the environment is not left up to the practitioner's wisdom or intuition. **Developing the practice of working collaboratively with participants to gather the information necessary for matching clinical needs with interventions is central to efforts aimed at shaping the treatment environment**.

For example, if the participant has expressed a need to trust other people in their life, the practitioner may introduce the idea of doing an **Unsighted Walk**, along with the expectation that they engage in a collaborative process to determine how to scaffold trust-related interventions (see Appendix 1). Would it be valuable to engage in **Mirror Spotting** or a **Trust Lean** before initiating the **Unsighted Walk** (see Appendix 1). Considerations that can be addressed collaboratively include whether the **Trust Lean** starts with the practitioner's fingers resting softly on the faller's back, or if leaning back into thin air toward the practitioner would be most useful (see Appendix 1). This opportunity to cocreate the next experience allows for empowerment and participant voice to enter the environment.

In the previous scenario, a practitioner may choose a trust activity that does not thrust the participant too deeply into a position of vulnerability. A **Trust Lean**, for example, with both people facing one another, palms of the hand touching above both of their heads may be a helpful way to introduce the importance of mutual trust in the therapeutic relationship (see Appendix 1). As both people step away from the other person, keeping their bodies stiff, there is an increased need to rely on each other. Their movement requires trust, and if they do not feel ready to take the next step, there is the opportunity to practice how to communicate that and place a limit on how far each person is willing to step out or lean into each other. Attention to the participant's whole-body responses to this activity will be rewarded with the opportunity to explore any issues related to not feeling safe and strategies for communicating when this occurs.

When treatment is not going well, or when it seems like something is not right, the search for a solution often ends up at the feet of one of the beliefs. Often the practitioner needs to attend to one of the adventure beliefs to rectify an issue. For example, if a participant seems disengaged in activities or is distracted from tasks quickly, there may not be enough challenge (or too much risk) in the environment. Adding some challenge or reducing difficulty, based on the assessed need of the participant, may address the lack of engagement. Attempts to engage the participant will be successful only if conditions of challenge are dealt with openly, therefore discussion about the dynamics of challenge are likely to be useful to the process. This is the same process for any of the beliefs, which includes noticing what is happening, collaboratively assessing which belief needs attention then working toward attending to that belief with the participant.

Conclusion

As part of the mindset of individual adventure practitioners, the focus on shaping the treatment environment is ever present. It is a major factor in what is attended to by practitioners. In addition, the practitioner's efforts to attend to the environment throughout the entire process of treatment makes it less likely that issues related to the environment will interfere with the clinical work being done. In short, shaping a treatment environment that gives the participant the best chance of achieving their treatment goals is an important part of how adventure practitioners think about their work. In the next chapter, the process of facilitating experiences is explored in-depth, highlighting the many in-the-moment decisions that exemplify experiential practice.

Reflections

- What will potential participants see and feel about the treatment environment as they talk to you over the phone and preview your website and intake materials?
- What aspects of the treatment environment would you value the most if you were searching to find an individual practitioner for your own individual therapy? What aspects of the treatment environment would be the most important to you as you enter the middle stage of treatment?
- What would you say to new participants to cast the vision of how the treatment environment can be different from other social settings?
- What would it look like if you responded to problems in the treatment by attempting to build up one of the core elements of the environment rather than focusing directly on the problem that is occurring?

Now What?

- Take a fresh look at how you attend to the environment in your practice.
  - Identify any obstacles that may interfere with shaping an effective treatment environment.
  - Identify the resources or strengths in your practice that enhance the treatment environment.
- Consider how you will communicate these aspects of the adventure therapy approach to participants:
  - Describe how the participant will be invited to engage in action with the practitioner as the primary type of intervention.
  - Explain that consent to engage in the interventions will be sought by the practitioner and mutual decision-making will be the norm.

- Consider that the participant's responses during experiential interventions will be like how they respond to life circumstances. How will you help the participant understand this as the primary agent of change?
- Imagine a treatment environment that nurtures growth and change. How will it be co-created or shaped by the practitioner and the participant?

Shaping in Action

The case example used to illustrate how one goes about shaping the environment was a gift to the authors by Lynette Spencer, one of the pioneers in the practice of individual adventure therapy. Her individual participant is joined by their younger sibling in this example. The involvement of family members in the individual treatment of children is a common practice, and what she presents in this sibling session applies equally to individual work.

Practitioner Information

I am well into my third decade of clinical social work practice, which has included in- and outpatient mental health, home health, and community-based outpatient outdoor behavioral health. I was certified and began practicing equine assisted psychotherapy in 2004, which eventually led me to learn about adventure therapy in 2009. At that time, I was teaching a MSW course on expressive and experiential therapies, using some of the more mainstream experiential therapies, such as music, art, dance and movement, and play therapy, as well as animal assisted therapies. Through an equine assisted psychotherapy seminar I taught, I met some participants who worked with Chicago Adventure Therapy, who soon introduced me to the founder, Andrea Knepper, who then agreed to speak in my class and introduce adventure therapy to my students (and me) through an on-campus orienteering experience. This relationship led me to John Conway, then clinical director for OMNI Youth Services and he introduced me to the Therapeutic Adventure Professionals Group. After attending my first conference in 2010, I was hooked! The class, my new colleagues, a desperate community need for a new answer for accessible youth mental health, and my ingenuity led me to found Adventure Works of DeKalb County, Inc. in 2010, which became the first community-based nonprofit outdoor behavioral healthcare organization to ever become accredited with the Association for Experiential Education.

Participant Description

Now in solo private practice, with little infrastructure to support a full outdoor behavioral health practice, I have made the indoor office setting as adventurous as possible. I have a number of grade school aged children in my practice, and this case study will focus on a set of two siblings, a boy I will refer to as Benjamin, Black male age 5, and his half-sister I will refer to as Nema, Biracial (Black/Latina) female, age 8. Nema's mother was Black and her father Latino. The children's mom died a premature death due to medical complications in June of 2023. Each of the children's fathers is uninvolved in their lives. Grandma reports that she and Grandpa have been the primary caregivers for all of the children's lives due to substance use, domestic abuse, and employment/financial hardship. The children knew and loved their mom, and each child has little regard for their biological father.

I see each child individually, together in sibling sessions, with and without their legal guardians, who are their maternal grandparents. Grandma is a Black 68-year-old woman, and Grandpa is a Black 79-year-old man. Grandpa is retired, and Grandma works full time. Grandma contacted me through her insurance provider directory and identified the need for family and individual help.

Treatment Context

The session in this case example was a planned sibling session, focused on grief and loss of their mother in addition to processing traumatic experiences caused by Benjamin's father and the parents' substance use. In a previous sibling session, the children acted out the story of how Benjamin's father pushed their grandmother, hit their mother, and ended up in jail in a very animated and emotional way. Within the course of that session, the children expressed feelings of anger, sadness, shock, and feelings of inappropriately feeling responsible for their mother's death.

The goal of this session was to use a strengths-based approach to identifying positive attachment to their mother, even in her absence. A secondary goal was to normalize discussion about their mom in her death. Grandma shared with me that Benjamin talks about death "all the time", and Nema keeps it all inside. She further shared that she is uncomfortable in her own grief and doesn't like to talk about her daughter's passing.

Session Description

The children agreed to act out a scene in which they felt as close to their mother as possible. Both reported that they dream about her and believe she is a protective angel. Benjamin has both positive dreams and nightmares about his mom, so we had to sort through the nightmares before he was able to think about his mom in a positive way. Because the children identified they wanted to use their dreams about their mom in the session, it was agreed that we would have a "slumber party". The children proceed to convert my office into a party room, turning on my twinkle lights and turning off all the other lights in the office. There are no windows in the office, so it was very dimly lit. They moved the pillows off the couch and under my desk to create a dark, safe, den-like space to pretend they were sleeping (Figure 7.3).

During their "sleep", they dreamed out loud. Nema leading the dreaming narrative and Benjamin following his big sister's lead, replicating his version of her dreams. This led to them cocreating a vivid description of their "mommy-angel-unicorn" who had beautiful colors and floated around them while they were sleeping.

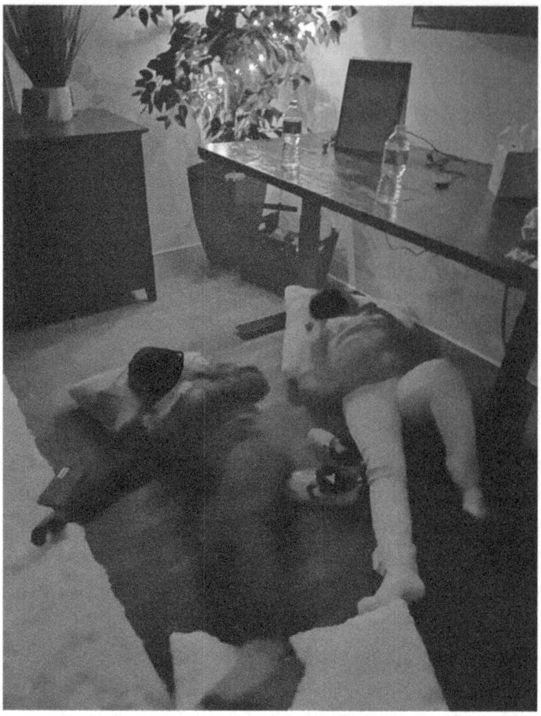

Figure 7.3 Shaping the physical environment in an office setting.
Photo from Lynette Spencer

As is usually the case in adventure sessions, the time constraint cut the process short but gave me enough information to springboard future sessions to guide a positive connection to discuss and expand on in future work with them. In a post-session grandparenting brief, the process I described here was shared. Grandma was surprised to know that the children conceptualize their mother in this protective angel-form, mainly because she'd only heard of the nightmares, and the children hadn't shared this with her.

Practitioner Comments Regarding Session

It's important to me that I allow participants, especially children, to have as much control of the process (environment, content, and how that content is delivered, etc.) as possible. In this session, the participants took full control of the setting and what they shared. If a child feels a sense of safety in the process, their creativity will increase and defenses will decrease, which is exactly what happened here.

Submitted by Lynette Spencer, LCSW, CCAT
Blue Dot Psychotherapy PLLC
St. Charles, Illinois

References

Amorim, J., & Ventura, A. C. (2023). Co-created decision-making: From co-production to value co-creation in health care. *The Journal of Medicine Access*, *7*, 27550834231177503. https://doi.org/10.1177/27550834231177503

Arao, B., & Clemens, K. (2013). From safe spaces to brave spaces: A new way to frame dialogue around diversity and social justice. In L. Landreman (ed.), *The art of effective facilitation: Reflections from social justice educators* (pp. 135–150). Stylus.

Asnaani, A., & Hofmann, S. G. (2012). Collaboration in multicultural therapy: Establishing a strong therapeutic alliance across cultural lines. *Journal of Clinical Psychology*, *68*(2), 187–197. https://doi.org/10.1002/jclp.21829

Cooley, S. J., Jones, R. J., Kurtz, A., Robertson, N. (2020). 'Into the wild': A meta-synthesis of talking therapy in natural outdoor spaces. *Clinical Psychology Review*, *77*, 101841. https://doi.org/10.1016/j.cpr.2020.101841

Cozolino, L. (2010). *The neuroscience of psychotherapy: Healing the social brain* (2nd ed.). W. W. Norton & Co.

Domini, H. (2021). Evoking never never land: The importance of imaginative play and creativity. *LEARNing Landscapes*, *14*(1), 45–66. https://doi.org/10.36510/learnland.v14i1.1043

Elias, C. L., & Berk, L. E. (2002). Self-regulation in young children: Is there a role for sociodramatic play? *Early Childhood Research Quarterly*, *17*(2), 216–238. https://doi.org/10.1016/S0885-2006(02)00146-1

Farber, B. A., Suzuki, J. Y., & Lynch, D. A. (2018). Positive regard and psychotherapy outcome: A meta-analytic review. *Psychotherapy*, *55*(4), 411–423. https://doi.org/10.1037/pst0000171

Finney, C. (2014). *Black faces, white spaces: Reimagining the relationship of African Americans to the great outdoors*. University of North Carolina Press.

Fredrickson, B. L. (2001). The role of positive emotions in positive psychology: The broaden-and-build theory of positive emotions. *American Psychologist*, *56*(3), 218–226. https://doi.org/10.1037/0003-066X.56.3.218

Garaigordobil, M., Berrueco, L., Celume, M. P. (2022). Developing children's creativity and social-emotional competencies through play: Summary of twenty years of findings of the evidence-based interventions "game program". *Journal of Intelligence*, *10*(4), 77. https://doi.org/10.3390/jintelligence10040077

Gelso, C. J., Kivlighan, D. M., Jr., & Markin, R. D. (2018). The real relationship and its role in psychotherapy outcome: A meta-analysis. *Psychotherapy*, *55*(4), 434–444. https://doi.org/10.1037/pst0000183

Gere, J., & MacDonald, G. (2010). An update of the empirical case for the need to belong. *Journal of Individual Psychology*, *66*(1), 93–115.

Goodacre, E. J., Fink, E., Ramchandani, P., & Gibson, J. L. (2023). Building connections through play: Influences on children's connected talk with peers. *British Journal of Developmental Psychology*, *41*(3), 203–226. https://doi.org/10.1111/bjdp.12443

Haoyou, W. & Oyam, D. M. A. (2024). The role of play-based learning in early childhood cognitive development. *International Journal of Social Science and Humanities*, *12*(3), 139–144. https://doi.org/10.5281/zenodo.13143653

Masten, A. S. (2014). *Ordinary magic: Resilience in development*. Guilford publications.

Merriam-Webster Dictionary. (2025). *Trust* https://www.merriam-webster.com/dictionary/trust

Mullans, J. (2023). *Decolonizing therapy: Oppression, historical trauma, and politicizing your practice*. W. W. Norton & Company

Nordquist, J., BeVard, K., Funnell, A., Pace, S., Sacksteder, K., & Wolf, P. (2023). *Manual of accreditation standards for outdoor behavioral healthcare* (3rd ed.). The Association for Experiential Education.

Siegel, D. J., & Bryson, T. P. (2011). *The whole-brain child: 12 revolutionary strategies to nurture your child's developing mind*. Bantam Books.

Siviy, S. M. (2016). A brain motivated to play: Insights into the neurobiology of playfulness. *Behaviour*, *153*(6–7), 819–844. https://doi.org/10.1163/1568539X-00003349

Todić, J., & Christensen, M. C. (2022). Integrating critical, engaged, and abolitionist pedagogies to advance antiracist social work education. *Advances in Social Work*, *22*(2), 389–415. https://doi.org/10.18060/24972

Tucker, A. R., Norton, C., Itin, C., Hobson, J., & Alvarez, M. A. (2016). Adventure therapy: Non-deliberative group therapy in action. *Social Work with Groups*, *39*(2–3), 194–207. https://doi.org/10.1080/01609513.2015.1048416

Turnage, D. M., & Radecki, M. (2024). Person-centered language: Respecting language preferences in health care. *Journal of Psychosocial Nursing and Mental Health Services*, *62*(6), 3–4. https://doi.org/10.3928/02793695-20240506-01

Wampold, B. E., & Flückiger, C. (2023). The alliance in mental health care: Conceptualization, evidence and clinical applications. *World Psychiatry: Official Journal of the World Psychiatric Association*, *22*(1), 25–41. https://doi.org/10.1002/wps.21035

Wenner, M. (2009). The serious need for play. *Scientific American Mind*, *20*(1), 22–29.

Yogman, M., Garner, A., Hutchinson, J., Hirsh-Pasek, K., Golinkoff, R. M. (2018). The power of play: A pediatric role in enhancing development in young children. *Pediatrics*, *142*(3), e20182058. https://doi.org/10.1542/peds.2018-2058

Chapter 8

Facilitating the Experience

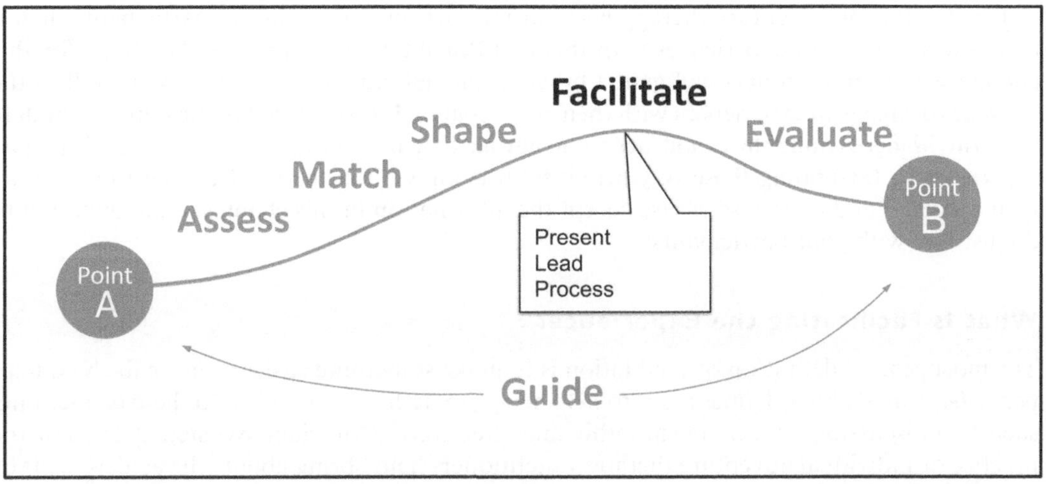

Sharice sought treatment for difficulties she was having in social situations. She identified as a Black, gay, female in a long-term relationship with her wife, whom she described as a source of encouragement and support. The primary presenting problem for Sharice was the limitations she placed on herself due to fear of negative comments and actions from her peers. She described a traumatic history of being bullied and ostracized in social groups, as well as feeling "betrayed" by the people she trusted. These life experiences resulted in issues related to negative body image, self-doubt, avoidance of social situations, and mistrust when dealing with current coworkers and friends who she says "have not done anything to hurt me".

During the initial phone call, the practitioner explained the experiential approach to treatment. Sharice expressed a guarded sense of agreement by stating she was willing to "give it a try". However, just the thought of engaging in adventure therapy and experiential interventions made her nervous. With that Point A in mind, the practitioner made their first facilitation decision: rather than scheduling the initial session in the office, they invited Sharice to meet at a park nearby. This decision changed Sharice's expectations. She shifted from expecting the familiar talk-oriented therapy of a clinical office to preparing for an unfamiliar experience in the outdoors. There, she would be asked not only to talk about what mattered most to her but also to take meaningful action.

DOI: 10.4324/9781003457893-8

The plan for the first session was to begin with a check-in activity to figure out Sharice's comfort level with meeting in an outdoor public setting. The activity required that Sharice and the practitioner stand somewhere between two points to express how comfortable they felt having a session outdoors, demonstrating their feelings on a visual **Continuum** (see Appendix 1). The practitioner's choice to participate in the activity with Sharice created the opportunity for role modeling and supporting her to engage in similar actions required in this intervention. In addition, it presented a perfect opportunity for the practitioner to share their vision for a safe treatment environment where Sharice could work effectively toward her goals. The practitioner also discussed how their ability to work together effectively would be affected by various elements of the treatment environment, including the treatment relationship, the seven adventure beliefs, Sharice's authentic engagement in the work, and being in a physical space that supported and enhanced the process.

The practice of adventure therapy gets put into action with a clinical participant when it comes to engaging in experiences with them and facilitating the process. The hope for this chapter is that practitioners will gain a broader understanding of facilitation, as well as the courage to engage in experiences with their participants. **It is somewhat ironic that the antidote to a practitioner lacking the confidence to engage participants in experiential activities is to gain experience by facilitating those very activities**. It is known that people learn best by calming their anxieties and acting, so please accept the information in this chapter as an invitation to do just that with your participants!

What Is Facilitating the Experience?

The most general definition of facilitation is to make something easier or more likely to happen. *Merriam-Webster* defines it as "to help bring (something) about" or "to help (something, such as a discussion) run more smoothly and effectively" (Merriam-Webster, 2025). For the practice of individual adventure therapy, practitioners help "bring about" the achievement of the participant's treatment goals.

Understanding how these skills relate to the adventure therapy approach is imperative. **A core belief is that the experience itself is the overarching change agent**. The experience includes the activity, the environment in which it occurs, and the processing that occurs throughout.

Processing refers to how one makes meaning of the experiences in one's life. In therapy, in one way or another, a participant is always making meaning of what they discuss, practice, and do with the practitioner. The processing of an activity facilitates the incorporation of the experience and enhances the impact of the intervention. Processing supports participants in connecting information learned through experiences with their clinical goals; for the practitioner, the overarching Point B always guides processing choices. **Much of the skill of processing is the ability to interpret what is happening in the session and respond in a way that connects to the overall treatment plan**.

To effectively facilitate individual adventure therapy, the practitioner must enter sessions and the environment fully prepared to guide. Think for a moment about taking a walk with a participant. This simple activity becomes an intervention when the practitioner approaches it with the necessary clinical mindset, such as fully believing in the transformative power of an experience. The prepared practitioner will attend to and explore what the participant says, how they behave, what emotions they express, and how they interact with the practitioner and the natural setting, as well as what somatic body expressions are demonstrated. **All the skills**

used by practitioners are based on the belief that each moment they share with the participant has the power to produce change.

Guiding a participant toward Point B involves carefully considering how the adventure therapy process is explained, how interventions are presented, how the practitioner intervenes during the activity, and how experiences are processed to support meaningful connections.

Initial Engagement in Adventure Interventions

A common question about facilitation, especially in an individual setting, is about how to engage the participants in activity. Practitioners often fear that their participant won't feel comfortable getting up and doing things during the therapy session. In a group setting, there is the advantage (and sometimes distracting disadvantage) of having peers to help with the social modeling of participation, clearly influential in human behavior. **However, in individual therapy, there may be more hesitation, because there is not a social norm of participation. This factor, along with the power dynamic between practitioner and participant, can often be resolved by joining in on the activity together**, like wading in the water together versus giving instructions from the shore. Another strategy is selecting an environment that provides a social norm of participating, like paddle boarding in a public area where other folks are doing the same thing. The following are a few general practices that may influence a participant's willingness to engage in the experiential process.

Helping participants understand the experiential approach to adventure therapy is an important practitioner task. Participants may be reluctant to do an activity in a session intended to address their personal struggles, especially if they do not see how those activities will be relevant to addressing their reasons for seeking treatment. Often, participants have preexisting ideas about how therapy "works" and benefit from a clear explanation of what to expect with this approach to practice. Simply put, the activities will elicit responses that mirror how they behave in daily life. By reflecting on these real-life patterns, the adventure therapy process provides opportunities to uncover both the challenges and strengths needed to get to their Point B.

It is equally important that the practitioner dedicate time in the initial sessions explaining the importance of the treatment environment. This includes emphasizing that the therapeutic relationship is best when defined by collaboration and mutual positive regard between the practitioner and participant. Additionally, the participant must be assured that the practitioner will make every reasonable effort to establish a treatment environment founded on the adventure beliefs (safety, trust, belonging, challenge, freedom, effective communication, and enjoyment). These conditions are essential for fostering a treatment environment that promotes the self-disclosure and personal risk-taking essential to clinical progress.

A common reason for a participant's reluctance to engage is the lack of peer role models in the session. Their position as the only clinical participant heightens their sense of visibility and self-consciousness. **One thing that can ease this discomfort is the practitioner's active involvement throughout the session**. Initiating the required action by gathering props and moving around in space makes it easier for the participant to follow suit and engage.

How the practitioner scaffolds their presentation of activities can influence engagement in activity. Some participants will eagerly engage in challenges from the start, and others will require a more gradual progression.

When met with reluctance, the practitioner may invite the participant to begin with small activities to increase engagement with the experiential practice. For example, a simple check-in activity, such as using a **Thumb-o-Meter** to indicate how they are doing that day, requires both words and physical actions in a manner that may engage them experientially without being too intimidating (see Appendix 1). Another check-in could involve physically positioning themselves along a **Continuum** from feeling great to feeling awful, helping them become more comfortable using their bodies to communicate their emotional states (see Appendix 1). Once this participant buys into simple check-ins, they may accept the invitation to walk in a park or sit on a bench swing as they talk about their struggles. **Attention to individual differences and accepting the participant exactly as they are is central to trauma-informed care. Starting at a participant's level of comfort and taking small steps from there honors participant choice and celebrates their diversity, including neurodiversity**. There are numerous ways to scaffold or adjust sessions to meet these participants' comfort levels with experiential therapy.

Finally, do not underestimate the power of confidence and preparation from the practitioner! A tentative or insecure invitation to take an experiential approach to treatment communicates to participants that self-disclosure and vulnerability is risky. The antidote to this self-defeating cycle is to fully embrace the clinical mindset of the adventure practitioner (see Chapter 4). **A practitioner who conveys confidence in the transformative power of experience and is enthusiastic about curating a safe treatment environment is more likely to work through the participant's reluctance.**

Session Structure

The transition a participant makes from the outside world into the clinical space and focus is of as much, if not more, importance as the actual therapeutic intervention. A thoughtful shift out of the clinical focus developed during a session is important too. This process is typically achieved with a session structure, simply thought of as the beginning, middle, and end phase of each session. Quality facilitation adapts strategies for different phases and nurtures the transitions throughout the session.

Beginning Phase of a Session

The beginning of the session is focused on this transition from the headspace of a participant's day-to-day life into the treatment environment. Many aspects of curating the treatment environment attended to in the beginning of sessions are discussed in Chapter 7. For example, the practitioner may renew the expectations and attend to the conditions necessary for the participant to feel safe at the beginning of each session.

Adventure facilitators often begin sessions with a check-in, not only to determine the current state of the participant and what issues may be bubbling up but also to connect within the safety of the treatment relationship by demonstrating genuine interest in the participant. A check-in may be informal as they enter the session, gently exploring and assessing their verbal, behavioral, somatic, or emotional cues. Statements such as, "I noticed you were sitting with your eyes closed while waiting for the session", or "I see that you are gripping your hands tightly" can be sufficient to launch a check-in. Alternatively, practitioners may opt for a more structured, experiential check-in, such as

- selecting picture cards to represent how the participant is doing in the moment (**Processing Tools**, see Appendix 1; Figure 8.1),
- facilitating a **Mindfulness** activity to ritualistically open each session (see Appendix 1), or

Figure 8.1 Check-ins provide opportunity for participants to share their current experiential functioning.

Photo of Anamalgam Cards from Adventure Therapist, LLC

- picking up or standing near an object in the immediate physical space to represent their daily coping since the last session or how they are feeling in the moment **(Personal Object Check-In**, see Appendix 1).

Additionally, checking in each session is an opportunity for both assessment and refreshing focus on clinical goals. Check-ins can illuminate changes since the previous session and a participant's current experiential functioning. They also provide valuable information about what the practitioner may need to do to shape that day's treatment environment. The beginning phase of each session is also a good time to work on establishing and/or reemphasizing the adventure beliefs and how they impact the treatment environment.

Check-ins to start a therapy session set the tone and influence the facilitation choices that will be made in the middle phase of the session. For example, if the participant describes struggling with apathy and depression since the previous session, the practitioner may change the framing of the intervention to match this level of experiential functioning. The invitation to begin the session from a state of depression and apathy both validates their experience and empowers them to begin where they are and take a step closer to their Point B.

The whole process of therapy can be described as developing through a beginning, middle, and end phase – similar to how each individual session is structured. The primary tasks during the beginning phase of the treatment are as follows:

- **Developing a positive regard** (treatment rapport) between the practitioner and participant
- **Establishing a working contract** (treatment alliance) for what the participant will work on in the therapy
- Initiating the work of **establishing the adventure beliefs** as the culture within the treatment environment and norms for behavior

Middle Phase of a Session

The practitioner's efforts during the middle phase of each session turn toward responding to what comes up during initial activities, facilitating the primary experiential activity, and guiding the reflection on what happened. The participant's primary work is reflecting on what happens and applying it to the clinical goals. The single issue that defines the middle phase of each therapy session is working collaboratively with the participant toward their clinical goals.

The middle phase of the treatment begins once a therapeutic rapport and treatment alliance have been established and the adventure beliefs have been accepted as norms for the treatment environment. This foundation sets the participant up for success, supporting them as they prepare to do the work necessary to achieve their treatment goals. Think of an adolescent participant that was unusually distant as they entered the treatment session and offered several flippant comments toward the practitioner during the check-in. Exploring these responses revealed that they feel betrayed by the practitioner for sharing too much with the participant's mother. Even though there was a breach in rapport, the opportunity to listen, demonstrate accountability, and model relationship repair opened the door to discuss similar experiences in which the participant felt betrayed by the people they trusted the most in their life.

The middle phase of a therapy session starts with the practitioner and participant collaboratively reaching agreement about how to move forward in the session. Then, the practitioner's task is to match the intervention to what the participant has presented so far in the session. For example, after hearing an elderly participant's check-in about finding themselves lost in their own neighborhood, the practitioner changed the way they introduced an **Orienteering** activity (see Appendix 1). Rather than framing it with a story about being lost in the wilderness – which might reinforce the participant's concerns – the practitioner framed the compass as a tool for orienting oneself and gaining a sense of direction. The activity was an opportunity for them to work together at developing a new skill and helping the participant build adaptive skills, resiliency, and the confidence to seek out assistance related to memory loss.

As the elderly participant traveled through the orienteering course with the practitioner as their guide, opportunities emerged to identify patterns in the participant's responses and aspects of their current experiential functioning that were relevant to their treatment goals. **Shouldering up with the participant to address these clinical challenges, using strengths, and applying the skills necessary for their journey toward better health is what makes up most of the work in the middle phase of a session**.

End Phase of a Session

The ending phase of individual sessions, like the ending phase of treatment, provides an opportunity for reflection, closure, and evaluation. This may include reflection on successes, assessment of what to do next, evaluation of progress, identifying things to be accomplished between sessions, or naming the next steps toward reaching treatment goals. This process is linked to the experiential learning cycle discussed in Chapter 2 by supporting the participant in moving from their in-the-moment experiences into active experimentation with new behaviors and applying the content from sessions to the participant's life outside of sessions (Kolb, 1984).

Experiential ways of closing a session include the following examples:

- Inviting the participant to stand in the spot that they think was most important or most valuable to them during the session
- Asking the participant to choose one prop used during the activity to tell the story of their experience
- Asking the participant to build a sculpture from a group of objects provided by the practitioner (stuffed animals, items from nature, a pile of leaves, a collection of random shaped blocks, e.g.) to express what they will be taking home with them from the intervention (**Tower Building**, see Appendix 1)

Discussing a participant's next steps in treatment is a process that can be enhanced with experiential interventions. Activities that incorporate specific pathways and steps, such as a circle of numbers on the ground from one to ten, used as a rating system, provide an excellent framework for discussing where the participant has been, where the participant is now, and where the participant wants to go. Similarly, asking the participant to stand on the floor spot with the adventure belief word printed on it that they think is the most important thing for them to work on can effectively generate thoughts about the next steps in the treatment process.

The following example illustrates how a practitioner can manage ending a session when time has elapsed or many treatment issues appear to be unfinished:

The participant demonstrated many strengths and skills as they engaged in building the tallest **Spaghetti-Marshmallow Tower** they could (see Appendix 1). After some reflection on the meaning of those strengths from the participant, the practitioner proceeded to describe the next phase of the exercise: "Without destroying the structure, connect it to the structure built by the practitioner on a different tabletop nearby". In this phase, the participant struggled. They sought no help from the practitioner. They asked to use cardboard and other materials around the office; but they were not successful in moving their tower to make a connection with the practitioner's tower. As the session wrapped up, the few minutes remaining went to considering the many skills and personal strengths the participant took advantage of, as well as reflecting on what made the transfer so difficult. The practitioner's effort to transition out of the therapy session went like this: "Creating this great tower in my office worked really well for you. As you leave here, think about what made it difficult for you to connect with my tower and whether the same things make it difficult for you to make connections with colleagues as you shared with me previously".

In this session ending, a seed was planted for the participant to continue the work until the next session while also quickly summarizing the practitioner's observations of strengths demonstrated in that session.

Facilitation of the Experience

Facilitation involves maintaining a constant balance between allowing the experience to do much of the work and guiding the participant in reflection that links their responses during the

experience to their broader clinical goals. It becomes possible to identify patterns and clarify a parallel process between these responses and the participant's life.

Deeply valuing the participant's responses is critical to the practice of individual adventure therapy. This mindset allows the practitioner to engage flexibly with whatever the participant brings into the session. Careful attention to the participant's responses keeps a focus on the here and now of what is important to the participant, and therefore positions the practitioner to always be in tune with the participant. **Valuing the participant's responses is one of the primary drivers of the belief that sitting and talking about an issue is not as productive as seeing that issue acted out in a therapy session**. The whole-person responses that occur in the moment set the stage for making meaning of the experience.

The practitioner's mindset of valuing the participant's responses guides what is chosen to attend to during sessions. Practitioners develop ideas of how best to respond to participants during the assessment and matching phases. The words participants choose to express themselves are one important response. The actions, thoughts, emotions, and somatic responses that the participant experiences are equally important. What is attended to varies from a tone of voice or the facial expression that accompanies the words, to physical behaviors or any of several somatic responses (heavy breathing, sweating, lightheadedness, and so on) the participant elicits during an intervention. All these actions by the participant are the relevant nuggets of adventure therapy.

Adventure therapy incorporates diverse types of activities, each having some unique guidelines for facilitation. Introducing a hiking experience will look different than introducing an initiative activity. or online experiential session. Engaging participants in a paddling experience may include some instruction about basic paddle strokes in addition to the clinical components of the presentation. At a minimum, activity presentations need to include safety instructions (if applicable) and an overview of the potential risks and how to manage them (if applicable). Optimally, practitioners also invite participant understanding and agreement in the clinical purpose of the experience. **The practitioner's understanding of the participant's needs will inform how they choose to present activities, lead activities, and respond to participants during the session, as well as process activities to encourage reflection and develop meaning from the experience**.

Presenting the Experience

The way interventions are introduced to participants impacts their effectiveness. A straightforward, direct presentation of an experience may simply let the participant know what to expect from the experience and what will be expected from them, but even this simple and direct presentation sets the stage for meaning making, as it shapes how the participant will engage with the experience.

For example, early in the treatment process when clinical dynamics are being assessed, explanations of activities may be more ambiguous to allow patterns to emerge in the activity and then be identified during reflection. **As treatment progresses, introductions may be more directly targeted to specific change processes as the use of specific skills or the interruption of unproductive patterns is encouraged**. This flow may be entirely reversed depending on the participant's needs. For example, a participant's need for structure to assist in emotional and behavioral regulation may well dictate the need for interventions in the early stages of the treatment process to be more structured and directive in nature.

Clarity about the basic objectives and rules for an activity matters. Informed consent requires the participant to fully understand what is being asked of them. In fact, **continual informed consent is central to effective practice. Although prior generations of adventure therapy may have intentionally provided confusing instructions or withheld information, resulting in increased stress for participants, those approaches are no longer considered best practice.** Rather, practitioners are encouraged to let participants know what to expect in the intervention, what is expected of them, and what can be expected of the practitioner. To achieve this level of clarity, practitioners often cover the following topics when introducing an activity:

- **Confirm consent** – Once the activity has been presented to the participant, ask if they are ready to start before the action begins.
- **Objective** – What is the outcome of the activity that the participant is working toward? What is the goal? When is it complete? How is success measured?
- **Rules** – What are the rules of this activity? What can the participant do and not do? Most often, practitioners focus on what the participant can NOT do with an eye toward leaving the possibilities for what they CAN do wide open to the participant.
- **Safety** – What information does the participant need to stay safe? Consider the timing of this discussion for optimizing attention and understanding of the safety guidelines. Typical practice is for practitioners to give the general or basic safety guidelines initially and clarify the more nuanced details if there is a need as the intervention unfolds.
- **Boundaries** – Where can the participant go within the physical space? What boundaries (or markers) exist to remind them where to be? What objects can and cannot be touched? One consideration especially relevant to individual treatment is to account for the practitioner's line of sight as one boundary since there are no other eyes on the participant.
- **Limitations** – What limitations are there? What ways might you limit speech, movement, participation, etc.
- **Consequences** – What happens if the participant makes a mistake or tests the boundaries previously set? How strict will the practitioner be with the rules and consequences? Who acknowledges failures and sets and/or enforces consequences? The implications that enforcing consequences can have on the treatment relationship are very significant in individual treatment. For example, one can easily get caught in the "parent role" with participants. Understanding this dynamic and dealing with it effectively is essential to effective facilitation.
- **Framing/Story** – What frame or story can be used to enhance meaning making? (Framing is discussed in the next section in more detail.)
- **Time for Questions** – Allow time for questions. Consider what types of questions you will address, and which questions you will encourage the participant to work out for themselves. Participant questions are common throughout the entire intervention process since there are no other participants present to engage with about what to do.

Many adaptations can be made to meet the individual needs of participants when presenting activities. **It is important to be mindful of the cognitive and developmental needs of participants when giving instruction.** Practitioners will generally need to provide simpler steps for younger participants. Consider writing the rules on a poster for participants to reference, especially if they are complicated. Some participants may struggle with abstract concepts and metaphors, so be mindful of language choices to ensure they meet your participant's needs. If a participant struggles with perfectionism, for example, you might encourage them to "try again with new knowledge" instead of saying "start over" to emphasize how they can learn and grow through failures. A simple practice to accommodate participants with difficulty seeing color differences is to use stripes of tape to identify objects. Lastly, the practitioner should listen closely to the language participants use during sessions and seek opportunities to incorporate this language, framing activities in a way that feels meaningful to them.

Framing

Framing refers to the way in which an experience is introduced to the participant. Framing theory, promoted by Bateson (1972), explains that the way information is presented to people influences how they process that information. To that end, it is important for adventure practitioners to be mindful of how activities are framed for participants.

In the frames described next, the *rules* of the activity do not change, but the framing method does, influencing the way the participant engages in the activity (Priest & Gass, 2017).

- **Reality framing** describes the objectives, rules, and expectations of an activity in a matter-of-fact manner (Priest & Gass, 2017). For example, one might say the following to introduce an activity in which the task is to retrieve a bucket from the center of a circle: "*Using the resources available, you need to retrieve this bucket from the circle without touching it or having it tip over*" (see Appendix 1, **The Dump**). A tendency toward distractibility, dysregulation, or a need for concrete direction are all indicators that a literal and straightforward description of the intervention may be preferred. These participants will find engagement in the intervention easier when a clear focus is presented to them, which makes reflection on what happened in a meaningful way more likely.
- **Fantasy framing** uses an imaginative story to frame the activity (Priest & Gass, 2017). This framing is aimed at increasing interest and motivation for participants and may activate deeper cognitive schemas, such as that of a rescuer or hero (Činčera et al., 2020). For example, in presenting the same activity described earlier, the facilitator may say, "*You are the only one who can save the people in the bucket. They need your help! You're their only hope*". The authors have found fantasy frames to be contraindicated for participants who struggle with reality testing themselves, are easily dysregulated, or generally in need of external structure to enhance their personal functioning. The choice to use a fantasy or imaginary frame is often influenced by a desire to connect with a special interest of the participant. For example, choosing to frame an activity in the style of a video game going from room to room with different challenges is likely to increase the engagement of a participant who enjoys the use of video games in their free time.
- **Isomorphic framing** involves presenting the activity with a frame that metaphorically matches the clinical dynamics and is structured so that what is required from the participant to complete the task is the very same as what is required to achieve the clinical goals (Priest & Gass, 2017). Isomorphic framing is a good opportunity for participants to make stronger connections between experiential interventions and their clinical content. With **the Dump** activity, the structure requires using resources to retrieve something important. If the participant is struggling with depression and has expressed they have "lost hope", the bucket could reflect their hopes (perhaps even filled with objects representing those hopes). Then, to achieve success, the participant will need to use resources, including asking for the support of the practitioner, which is the same "action" they will need to reach their treatment goal of regaining hope and reducing the depression. This presentation

often results in the participant being able to integrate clinical material into how they understand their daily functioning.

Frontloading

Frontloading involves directly addressing the clinical focus of the activity before the experience to help the participant attend to that issue (Priest & Gass, 2017). For example, the practitioner may frontload an activity by saying, "In this activity, listening and effectively communicating are necessary for success". Frontloading highlights the clinical focus on communication during the intervention and increases the likelihood of the participant practicing needed skills or making meaning from the experience that leads to progress toward achieving the clinical goal. **Participants who are ready to focus on a specific goal or who are ready to practice skills are a good fit for frontloading. However, this technique can elicit resistance in participants who have not committed to a change process related to the identified focus of the frontload.**

Priming

Practitioners can prime or prompt participants to be aware of a specific focus. Priming an intervention activates neural pathways that bring subconscious areas of the mind closer to conscious awareness, increasing their availability during the therapeutic session (Lindsey et al., 2020). For example, a practitioner may ask a participant to recall a time when they were successful in pushing through their anxiety to reach a goal and identify what strengths they saw in themselves that allowed this to happen. This primes the participant to current awareness of their strengths before they work on an activity in which they will be addressing an issue using those same strengths. **Priming is different from frontloading and framing in that it involves subtly presenting a suggestion to the participant, activating neural pathways that can be drawn on in the experience rather than directly naming a specific focus (frontloading) or adapting the way the activity is presented (framing).**

Leading the Intervention

Once the activity has been presented, the practitioner observes the participant closely for reactions and responses, looking for patterns and parallels to clinical issues. The practitioner considers the physical, emotional, social, and cognitive impact the activity has on the participant while also discerning to see if the optimal amount of nervous system arousal is being maintained. Is the participant bored and disengaged? Is the participant actively working? Is the participant becoming overly stressed or activated?

A challenge for all practitioners is managing their own discomfort when a participant is struggling. It can be tempting to provide aid or answers too soon, preventing the participant from working through the struggle to find their own solution. These issues are magnified in individual adventure therapy where the practitioner is the only person the participant has to strategize with and observe the process that is ongoing. It can be a challenge to know the "right time" to intervene or interrupt the activity and when to let the participant struggle to find their own solutions.

The answer to these facilitation dilemmas, such as, "What do you do when (insert behavior here)", is that **it depends**. The clinical lens (i.e., theoretical understanding), case conceptualization, and Point B for each intervention guide the decision about (how to lead the intervention?) whether and when to interrupt or intervene.

Adventure practitioners often facilitate interventions in a "nondeliberate" manner (Tucker et al., 2016). The practitioner does not direct the participant in what to do during the intervention. Rather, the participant has the freedom to respond in any manner they choose, even if their approach differs from what the practitioner expected. These responses are often the crux of the processing and reflection that leads to therapeutic growth.

While leading the experience, practitioners are simultaneously assessing, shaping the environment, matching, facilitating, and evaluating what is happening. The various roles that practitioners can take include being an active observer, a cheerleader, a boundary enforcer, a comforter, a narrator, or a co-participant, just to name a few. The nature of individual treatment requires the practitioner to be actively involved during interventions that require collaboration, as well as those where shared experiences are integral to the overall treatment process.

Staying grounded in the case conceptualization, the practitioner facilitates interventions based on how the participant responds. **Aligned with the nondeliberative approach, the experiential nature of this work often requires practitioners to wait and observe what emerges**. However, a more direct or coaching response is sometimes needed. Finding the correct balance between monitoring and intervening is both an important facilitation skill and somewhat of an art.

Mitten (2023) has suggested that one overarching consideration for how adventure therapy interventions are facilitated is related to choosing an appropriate **pace. Pace allows time** for the

> the facilitator to demonstrate care, and for the participant to receive it, for the participants to continually process, internalize, and embody their experience, skill development and sense of competency [to be realized by the participant], for exploring choice and healthy engagement in activities [by the participant] and engagement in healthy and reciprocal relationships with the natural environment and other people. All which are crucial for reaching certain goals, including inclusivity.
>
> (p. 1)

The reader is encouraged to think about adopting a pace in their leadership efforts that allows the core elements of the environment to be established and allows the participant to proceed at their own rate to make sense or meaning from the experience. **In individual treatment, this suggestion usually means that the practitioner needs to slow down and allow time for the participant to engage fully in what is happening**.

Why and How to Respond or Intervene During Activities

Since there are several reasons **why** one might intervene in the activity or interrupt the flow, it helps to start with some ideas about **how** a practitioner might do this. A practitioner's choice is influenced by the theories they have learned and align with. For example, a cognitive behavioral approach may include identifying thinking errors (Ruffalo et al., 2016), whereas a solution-focused approach will likely explore exceptions to problematic responses (Neipp et al., 2021). **Table 8.1** offers a range of options for intervening, depending on the goals of the session and the needs of the participant:

As you read through the options for *how* to intervene, consider the significant difference between telling and asking. **Telling provides direction and guidance, while asking invites reflection and discovery**. Knowing when to use each approach is key. For example, if the participant is working to "stop and think" instead of rushing to action, the practitioner may intervene by asking the participant a question rather than giving a specific direction. Asking a question encourages the participant to practice thinking before acting. Even if the reason for this

Table 8.1 Intervening During Sessions

How to Intervene	*Why to Intervene*
• Remind	• Refine goals
• Ask a question	• Manage safety
• Give a direction	• Provide encouragement or support
• Share an observation	• Identify clinically relevant patterns
• Invite reflection	• Explore clinical content
• Praise or affirm	• Address clinically relevant behavior
• Encourage/support	• Highlight opportunities for learning or practicing skills
• Coach	• Reinforce strengths
• Adapt something	• Create optimal level of challenge, neuro-arousal, or engagement
• Stop the action	• Address emotions
	• Attend to other pertinent responses that arise

interruption is about reinforcing a safety guideline, choosing to ask a question may be a better way to set the guideline. Depending on the participant's Point B, asking a participant, "What are you doing right now to stay safe?" might be more effective than "slow down" or "be careful." This example highlights the interaction between **how** to intervene, **why** the intervention is needed, and the participant's unique Point A and Point B.

Intervening during activities is driven by intention (the **why**) and includes deciding **how** to go about facilitating that intervention. For example, practitioners may decide to refine a goal by asking a question or to reinforce strengths by offering praise. Either way, intervening during an activity is an intentional decision made by the practitioner in the moment guided by their observations of current participant responses.

Facilitation During Activities: Putting the "How" and the "Why" Together

Responding to what shows up during activities is at the very heart of facilitation skills in the adventure therapy practice model. What the practitioner does to respond during activities is heavily influenced by their clinical lens and their understanding of the participant's case. The following are brief descriptions of how some common facilitation skills are used in practice.

MATCHING IN THE MOMENT

Practitioners should adapt how they intervene according to how the participant is presenting in the moment. To successfully match an intervention, the practitioner needs to engage in an ongoing process of clinical assessment. The practitioner assesses how the participant shows up that day, what they bring with them, how they respond to the initial activities of the session, and which issues seem most relevant. This information helps guide the practitioner's decision on which type of activity is most appropriate for that moment.

In some cases, successful matching can require abandoning the planned activity and choosing a completely different one, if the participant arrives in an unexpected state. More often, however, the planned activity can be modified in a variety of more subtle ways. The practitioner can change the rules or the consequences for violations of the rules, for example. Practitioners could also manipulate resources by adjusting the type and/or number of props provided. In addition, they could identify a new or different goal, shifting the outcome or Point B for the intervention. **Modifications can be used as a tool to align the intervention with the participant's current state and clinical goals**.

One of the authors recalls planning an activity for a 10-year-old participant, where the goal was for the participant to use ten 3-foot-long pool noodles to construct a cube. However, when the participant arrived that day, they were extremely agitated and hyperactive. Since these behaviors were part of the presenting problem, the practitioner was glad for the opportunity to observe them firsthand. Instead of tempting the participant with the potential of ten pool noodles, the practitioner chose an exchange-places intervention using only two noodles (**Round and Round**, see Appendix 1). The practitioner and participant stood about 10 feet apart, each holding a swim noodle upright (one end on the ground, the other held by a finger to keep it steady). They were allowed a brief time for collaboration about strategy, then the practitioner and participant attempted to exchange places **without either noodle hitting the ground**. Before beginning the activity, the practitioner facilitated deep breathing to enhance mindfulness. This was an opportunity to practice mindfulness and proceed in a controlled, thoughtful manner when the participant was agitated. Reducing the number of props from 10 to 2 made the activity manageable. Even though the original plan turned out to need a replacement, it provided the foundation – an activity using pool noodles – for a new activity better suited to the participant's needs.

CONNECT TO THE PARTICIPANT'S ACTIONS

Possibly the most universal of all facilitation techniques within adventure therapy is observing, out loud, or physically imitating what the participant is doing. One of the authors recalls work with a young adult participant who was nonverbal throughout his first session. When he entered the therapy space for the second session, he picked up a tennis ball and began bouncing it on the floor. Rather than ask him how he was doing, the practitioner picked up another tennis ball and began bouncing it in a similar manner. Soon, they were bouncing both balls back and forth in a fun game of catch. Talking about this shared experience provided a spark to developing a positive rapport and engaging in the treatment. Similarly, if a participant heaves a heavy sigh and slumps down in their chair, the practitioner can ask how things went this past week or join with the participant by also heaving a heavy sigh and asking, "what was that sigh about?" The practitioner's intent in both cases is to connect with the participant's current experiential functioning and invite them to share more about themselves.

SHARING OBSERVATIONS

An observation focuses solely on what the practitioner sees the participant doing – without interpretation, judgment, or additional commentary. Using a tone of curiosity, the practitioner might share an observation, such as "your whole body got tight when you started talking about work". This invites the participant to reflect more about their experience and behavior, without the practitioner placing a value judgment on it.

Observations can draw attention to positive behaviors, leveraging the principle that the more often a behavior is noticed, the more it will occur (Grusec, 1992). One of the authors recalls working with a participant named Nicole, a ninth-grade student with cerebral palsy. She was nonverbal, used a wheelchair for mobility and a computer program to communicate. The presenting problem was her frustration over trying to communicate with teachers and the related vocal disruptions in the classroom. The individual therapy took place in her school setting, which afforded the practitioner easy access to the teaching staff involved.

The practitioner made the clinical assessment that Nicole often did not clearly communicate her needs. It was also clear that the teaching staff was consistently missing her nonverbal cues and then responding punitively to her resulting frustration. The treatment plan included work with the other adults in the equation, as well as the individual sessions with Nicole.

One of the first interventions was designed to address the co-created goal of Nicole learning to communicate more effectively in her classroom. The objective of the activity was for both the practitioner and Nicole to move across a gymnasium without touching the floor (**River Crossing**, see Appendix 1). They had three 3-foot square pieces of a tarp as their only tools. The rule that neither of them could initiate movement without first collaborating with the other was sufficient to establish a parallel process between the communication that was taking place during the activity and what needed to happen in the classroom.

Nicole and the practitioner refreshed their collaborative agreement to work toward developing communication skills that would be effective in a classroom setting and set out on their journey. She sometimes wrote a message on her screen and looked at the practitioner expectantly (like her ineffective attempts to communicate in the classroom), only to get no feedback. When she raised her arm and motioned with her head that something was written, the practitioner shared an observation about what she did to communicate and looked to see what she wanted to convey. She also attempted to communicate during the activity in the same manner that was causing the most classroom difficulties (but generally worked well in one-to-one situations) by making vocalizations to get the practitioner's attention but not communicating in any other way. On these occasions, the practitioner did not offer any feedback, replicating a pattern that occurred in her classrooms daily, and that Nicole acknowledged was causing her difficulty. She found these instances very frustrating and began to act out angrily just as she did in the classroom. When she communicated clearly through her gestures and text on the screen, the practitioner would comment on the message she sent and move forward in the activity as she was asking. The observation comments that recognized her efforts to communicate in a manner that would be effective in a classroom resulted in increasing her use of those skills and improving her classroom experiences. This process also informed the practitioner of the specific communication efforts that classroom teachers needed to be aware of and to respond to reasonably.

NARRATING ABOUT THE PRACTITIONER'S PERSPECTIVE

Sometimes it can be helpful for the practitioner to give their subjective account of what is happening during the session. This may include their assessments, opinions, and affirmations. Comments like, "I really appreciate the way you asked me for help" or "I can see that you are taking deep breaths to help you calm down and stick with this activity", are examples of the practitioner letting the participant know how they view what is happening in the session. Unlike group and family treatment, the practitioner is the only human available to provide this outside information for the participant. **Narrating in this way has many uses**, including the following:

- Assisting a participant in self-regulation
- Reinforcing a skill the practitioner feels is important to goal achievement
- Pointing out to a participant what the practitioner sees as a problem area or obstacle to goal achievement
- Highlighting strengths that will help the participant achieve their goals

POINT OF PERFORMANCE COACHING

This intervention skill involves being present at the point where participants take action and telling the participant what would be useful in that moment. The opportunity to respond immediately when a pattern emerges or to offer affirmation when the participant uses a coping skill is a powerful thing. This point of performance coaching (Barkley, 2021) is typically more valuable to a participant than talking about their report of an experience of panic, for example, that happened many days ago. It can be far more meaningful to the participant to practice managing the anxiety being felt in the moment by the practitioner guiding them to use a resilience skill, such as "now would be a good time to take a deep breath".

Another example of the beauty of coaching at the point of performance comes from work with participants who experience depression. Lack of interest, difficulty initiating action, extreme tiredness, and irritability often show up during an intervention and are gateways to engaging with the participant about their depressed affect. These moments allow practitioners to observe how depressive symptoms affect a participant's experiential functioning and explore how the participant can use personal strengths to overcome barriers and reach clinical goals.

CLINICAL CLARIFICATIONS

The practitioner will have many opportunities to clarify facts or intent for the participant. Clinical clarifications are less frequent but play a more significant role in the therapeutic process. **A clinical clarification seeks to connect a participant's behavior to their inner thoughts, emotions, and somatic responses**. For example, if the participant gives up on attempting a challenging aspect of an intervention and expresses feeling anxious about making a mistake, a clinical clarification might be, "When you get anxious about making a mistake (inner process), you tend to give up on the task at hand (behavior)".

An accurate clinical clarification demonstrates an understanding of the participant, deepening the practitioner's attunement and strengthening the therapeutic relationship. In addition, an inaccurate clinical clarification often prompts the participant to share additional information about their experience, which can lead to an expanded awareness of how their behaviors reflect their internal states.

CONFRONTING INCONGRUENT BEHAVIORS

Sometimes a participant's behavior does not align with their stated intentions or goals. An observation statement noting this incongruence can result in the participant's increased awareness and action to resolve the inconsistency. The adventure practitioner's unique position to observe the participant responding in real time enhances the opportunity for this intervention. In turn, participants can actively adjust their responses to better align with their treatment goals. For example, a practitioner may use this intervention by saying, "When the activity started, you said you were going to focus on communicating more with me, but then I noticed you didn't say anything to me. What do you make of that?" The exploration of this issue will naturally lead to generalizing where there are similar inconsistencies in the participant's functioning.

Imagine walking with a participant who was talking about wanting to be less anxious in their personal relationships when they became visibly stressed about the practitioner stepping into some mud to stay side by side on the walk. They apologized profusely for the mess on the practitioner's shoes. The desire of the participant to be less anxious in their personal relationships and their behavior in the moment were incongruent. The practitioner's task was merely to point out the contradiction that was demonstrated in the session. For example, "Wow, you were just talking about wanting to be less anxious in your relationships and then your body tensed up and you became apologetic about my choice to step into the mud". This in-the-moment intervention invites the participant to explore the issue in more detail.

Practitioners need to also be alert to the possibility that their participant's actions may not be incongruent at all. It is possible that the practitioner's perspective needs to change or that the treatment goals need further clarification to accurately reflect the participant's Point Bs.

SUPPORT RESPONSES

Offering support to a participant is an important role of the practitioner. **Verbal and nonverbal encouragement communicates the practitioner's investment in the participant's work and can offer needed validation and motivation. Support can also be used to acknowledge or validate a participant's struggle and let them know the practitioner sees their difficulty**.

There are many circumstances when it is clinically appropriate for the practitioner to take on a full-blown cheerleader role for a participant, encouraging them to push through an obstacle to reach a goal. However, giving encouragement or supporting a participant in their efforts is not as simple as it sounds. There are also situations when doing so is clinically contraindicated and a better practice would be to allow the participant to quit working on the activity, set a limit for themselves, or hold a boundary. As usual, the determination depends on the clinical goals and the case conceptualization one has developed with the participant. These interventions also require the practitioner to consciously proceed at a pace that allows the participant to take charge of the decisions that are made.

INVITING THE PARTICIPANT TO STEP BACK AND NOTICE

One of the Universal Point Bs for participants is to develop a meta perspective that allows them to see their current presenting problems from a broader point of view. This intervention is often initiated by engagement in a mindfulness exercise that removes the problem from its emotional baggage. It is also possible to use an activity like **The Plate** with the specific intention of looking at the problem from as many perspectives as possible (see Appendix 1 and the case example in Chapter 3).

The same thing is true for the practitioners. Rather than getting caught up in the participant's immediate struggle to complete a task, it is helpful to take a step back and view the problem through a lens that includes the participant's entire environmental context. **A simplistic application of this skill is the practice of always taking the time to clearly define the problem before attempting to provide solutions.**

A vivid example comes from a day-long outdoor climbing experience. While climbing, the participant was quite distressed and kept shouting that they were falling and needed the rope to be tightened. As requested, the practitioner provided a tad more tension on the rope. After two rounds of this process, the participant's agitation was growing; but they remained determined to finish the climb. When the participant was asked to explain more clearly what the problem was, they shouted that the "damn rope is pulling me off the rocks!" When a bit of slack was provided in the rope, an audible sigh of relief was followed by the participant continuing their climb.

Processing what happened during that climb culminated in the participant being asked to step back and notice how the conflict over tension in the rope was like their life outside of therapy. Their response was immediate: "My mom is like the belayer. I yell at her for not letting me do what I want. She reacts to me being mad by tightening her hold on me, which makes me scream at her more".

There is often a force during experiential interventions that draws practitioners into the intensity of how the participant deals with their life circumstances, essentially recreating the emotional scene that brought them into treatment. **The ability to step back and provide an alternate perspective on how to address these situations is central to effective facilitation**. This ability is also essential to the practitioner's identification of a parallel process, work with metaphor, and match an intervention in the moment.

STOPPING THE ACTION

It may be useful to pause the action if the participant is not following safety guidelines, is not making progress despite repeated efforts, or is experiencing emotional flooding. Stopping the action allows participants the opportunity to process what is happening or to engage in grounding and emotional regulation. In addition, if the practitioner notices a strength that can support therapeutic progress or a squiggly that interferes with it, it can be effective to stop the action and take the time (slow the pace) to focus on recognizing and understanding more about what is happening.

MANAGING SQUIGGLIES

As described in Chapter 3, squigglies are anything that shifts the focus of the participant away from the intended clinical goal. The issue can be something they view as positive and welcome in their current functioning (a resource) or something they identify as a negative factor (an obstacle). Both factors arise in the participants' daily lives as well. **If either one is empowered to become more important than work toward their goals or their focus on the task at hand, the resource or obstacle is seen as a squiggly**.

The irony is that although squigglies shift focus away from work toward clinical goals, addressing them is one of the most useful things that can be done in the quest to assist participants in the process of change. Yalom (2002) identifies his most important work as identifying and removing the obstacles that block the path to goal achievement. Often, the clinical work in individual psychotherapy centers around addressing these very things in sessions.

Squigglies can often be related to one of the environmental components, such as the treatment relationship, one of the adventure beliefs, the physical setting, or how engaged the participant is in working toward their goals. For example, a middle-aged woman of Hawaiian descent sought treatment for a chronic sense of disillusionment and failure to pursue the aspirations she held for her life as an adult. The practitioner engaged her in an intervention that required each of them to exchange objects by throwing random things to the other person in increasingly difficult circumstances, such as different throwing motions and increased distances (a variation of **Catch**, see Appendix 1). A squiggly showed up and the practitioner noticed that she was distracted and appeared to be troubled as she engaged in the intervention. By stopping the activity and sharing this observation with the participant, a great deal of clinical material emerged. She shared that, in her culture, throwing something at an elder is considered very disrespectful, and she couldn't find a way to participate without damaging the important relationship with the practitioner. Further exploration illuminated that her ancestral history included a great deal of loss and defeat, mirroring the internal sense that nothing she did would ever matter. Exploring that squiggly led to an increased understanding of how her ancestral history and the impact of colonization related to her reasons for seeking treatment.

Decision-Making in the Moment: It Depends

Practitioners make many facilitation decisions in the moment. New practitioners often desire clear cut answers about "what-to-do-when". Unfortunately, those decisions often depend on many factors, each unique to the participant's specific situation. The scenario presented in Table 8.2 attempts to demonstrate how these decisions are made using a process-recording

Table 8.2 Scenario Reflecting Decision-Making and Use of Interventions in the Moment

Session Content	*Thought Process of Practitioner*
Rosa: "I don't think it's quite right. I'm sure I've messed something up. Can we start from the beginning? I know we've checked a couple times but I just want to be sure".	*This could be part of Rosa's pattern of doubting herself and needing everything to be perfect. We've reviewed the structure twice already as we've been going through. Should I review it again as requested, encourage her to move ahead and see what happens, or explore more about this content right now?*
Practitioner: "I'm curious about what is going on for you. Can you tell me more about your concerns? What are some of the thoughts and feelings you're experiencing?"	*[Exploring Content] I want to know more about what is going on for Rosa before I decide what to do next.*
Rosa: "Well, I just think I messed something up, and I'm feeling a lot of worry about it being wrong. Like, am I too stupid to listen to a simple instruction? Ugh".	*I hear Rosa name self-doubt in a way that puts all the responsibility on her. As this is a pattern we've talked about before, I'm considering asking her to confront this issue and practice a different response. I also want to challenge the thinking that she is solely responsible for mistakes in this situation.*
Practitioner: "It sounds like you are thinking that, if a mistake were made, it would be your fault. Doesn't our success really depend on communication as a team? What happens when you feel this way?"	*[Sharing Observation]* *[Sharing Practitioner Perspective/Narrating]* *[Clinical Clarification]*
Rosa: "I totally get stuck. I just can't move forward because I'm afraid it will just confirm what I'm thinking. This happens all the time".	*Rosa has named a behavioral response to this feeling that impacts her life outside of session. This is an important awareness. We should focus on identifying when she gets stuck and practice how to get unstuck when it happens.*
Practitioner: "Ah, that sounds really important, that you get 'stuck' when feeling anxious about making a mistake".	*[Clinical Clarification] Getting stuck is the behavior and the anxiety is the internal process.*
Rosa: "Yeah, that happens to me all the time".	
Practitioner: "Let's explore some things you can try to help get unstuck. One thing can be challenging those negative thoughts with more useful thoughts. Making a mistake here does not mean you are stupid. Human communication is messy, and things are rarely perfect. It might be helpful to practice telling yourself that it's okay to make a mistake. We can also try taking a few breaths and getting grounded before we unveil our results. Which one will help you the most to get going again on completing this structure?"	*[Point of Performance Coaching]* *[CBT-challenging thinking errors]* *[Point of Performance Coaching]*

style presentation of a clinical session. The first column presents content from the session, and the second reflects the thought process of the practitioner throughout the intervention. The purpose of this scenario is to highlight how the techniques described earlier may be implemented in the session.

The practitioner presents a block building challenge to Rosa in which she has her back turned or eyes closed, and the practitioner describes a structure they are building with the intent of her reproducing the exact structure (**Tower Building**, see Appendix 1). Generally, Rosa is working on addressing anxiety and perfectionism. During the activity, she struggles to move ahead due to her anxiety about making a mistake.

Processing the Experience: Techniques for Guided Reflection

Processing involves a variety of strategies to assist participants in making sense of their experiences during an intervention and connecting those insights to their broader life contexts. Examples of these processing tools include facilitated self-reflection, verbal processing, the use of metaphors, exploring the impact of the experience, and presenting activities that allow participants to process what happened nonverbally. Verbal reflection stimulates neural pathways that support healthy brain development. However, the neurons activated during the experience become more strongly connected in both verbal and nonverbal processing, indicating that practicing skills improves brain functioning whether or not verbal processing occurs (Cozolino, 2010).

Ultimately, the clinical work must be connected to the overarching treatment goals and yield the desired life changes. Initially, processing often focuses on assessment and relationship building. As treatment progresses, the focus tends to shift toward learning coping skills, adjusting dysfunctional belief structures, or increasing feelings of self-worth. **Whatever the primary focus, the practitioner must continually explore the connection between what comes up in the session and how the participant experiences these themes in their life.**

A distinctive aspect of adventure therapy is that it invites participants to engage in activities as their authentic selves. As a result, their responses during sessions often mirror how they respond to similar situations in everyday life. Somatic responses, like quickened breathing or jaw clenching, frequently reflect the underlying issues that led them to seek therapy. **Highlighting this parallel process and guiding participants to explore the meaning behind their reactions can lead to deep and meaningful therapeutic insight.**

For example, in response to a **Thumb-o-Meter** check-in activity, an adolescent participant held their thumb completely down and attempted to hide it from the practitioner's vision (see Appendix 1). When asked to explain, the participant launched into a tirade about how their math teacher singled them out for talking in class when "everybody in the room was doing the same thing". The participant was sent out of the classroom for speaking disrespectfully to the teacher about the unfairness of what happened. After validating, providing empathy, and connecting with this participant during the check-in, the practitioner pointed out the similarity between this situation and their primary clinical goal of "not making situations worse by arguing and acting out aggressively over discipline at home". The processing that followed was the first time this participant was able to accept that they contributed to the problem, and therefore, that they had some power in making it stop.

What? So What? Now What?

The "What? So What? Now What?" Model (Borton, 1970) is a verbal processing tool rooted in the experiential learning cycle, which provides a way of thinking about how one learns from experience. In the experiential learning cycle, the learner has a concrete experience, engages in reflective observation about that experience, develops some abstract conceptualizations about the meaning of that experience in their lives, and then explores incorporating their new learning into their lives through active experimentation with new ways of being (Borton, 1970; Kolb, 1984). The "What? So What? Now What?" processing model, described next, provides a structure for engaging the learner in the experiential learning cycle directly (Figure 8.2).

- **What? = Observation**
  In the "What?" stage of this processing model, **the facilitator or the participant shares observations of what actually happened in the moment**. The focus is directly on the experience itself, including exploring behaviors, feelings, thoughts, and somatic responses. When reflection explores the "here and now", participants are supported in gaining greater awareness of their cognitive, emotional, somatic or behavioral patterns and responses to various situations. For example, if a participant tends to respond to barriers by giving up quickly, discussing this observation can be invaluable for the participant to be more aware of how their behavioral response impacts them in completing the task at hand. The facilitator might ask what thoughts or feelings were going on when a certain behavior occurred.
- **So What? = Application**
  The discussion of what happened during the experience evolves to include what it means for the participant. **This focus addresses what was important about the experience for them, including what was significant about the feelings, thoughts, attitudes, behaviors, and somatic responses that participants acknowledged as their personal response to the circumstances.** Parallel processes between what happened in the intervention and what happens in the participant's lived experience outside of the session are identified. "Reflective observation" leads to "abstract generalization" as participants explore the meaningful takeaways from the experience. The "so what" phase of processing includes exploring what patterns they identified that may parallel those in life outside of sessions, what skills they learned or

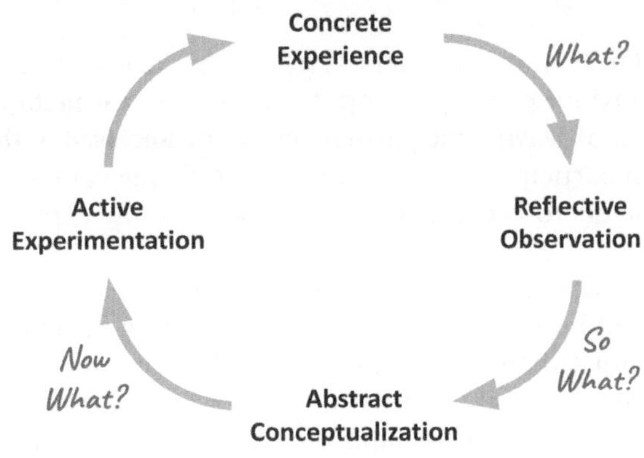

Figure 8.2 Combining two familiar concepts.

rehearsed, what treatment progress was made, and how the experience connects to their personal relationships. The facilitator often asks questions such as, "Does the same thing happen in your life outside of this session?"

- **Now What? = Transfer of Learning**
  In the "Now What?" stage of this processing model, **participants consider how this new knowledge will be incorporated into their lives**. The "active experimentation" stage of the experiential learning cycle may include using new skills, approaching life circumstances with healthier attitudes and beliefs, or navigating life's challenges with more stable emotional responses. **The primary consideration in this phase of processing is what the participant will do next because of this awareness.** If the participant doesn't initiate this discussion, the facilitator can invite them to consider their next steps by asking a question like, "What can you do between sessions to keep moving in this direction?"

Use of Metaphor to Enhance Processing

In the world of mental health treatment, metaphor is thought of as a way to link what happens in the therapy session to some aspect of the participant's daily functioning (Törneke, 2017). It is useful for identifying those dynamics of parallel processes that inform understanding of the problems the participant is experiencing, as well as how they might be addressed (Gass, 2025). **Adventure therapy provides the practitioner with rich snippets of the participant's current experiential functioning and lends itself to the use of metaphor as a way of enhancing what the participant takes from the therapy sessions into their real-life functioning.**

In Chapter 6, a process for selecting and customizing activities that have a metaphoric match to the clinical dynamics impacting participants was discussed. The importance of being attentive and intentional were highlighted as central features of good matching by the practitioner. **This section expands on these concepts to explore four types of metaphors practitioners can use to enhance meaning making and processing with participants**:

- Practitioner-Developed Metaphors
- Structural Metaphors
- Isomorphic framing
- Metaphors that Arise from the Experience

Practitioners also need to be wary of potential pitfalls in the use of metaphors. First, effective use of metaphor must involve participant input and buy-in. **Any metaphor that is driven by the practitioner runs the risk of leaving the participant disenfranchised in the process**. If the metaphor is not aligned with participant needs or not culturally relevant to their life circumstances, for example, they are likely to become disengaged because the experience no longer belongs to them.

It is also important to note that participants are capable of recognizing and learning from a parallel process without necessarily naming and developing the connection metaphorically. Adventure therapy sessions allow for learning from behavioral rehearsal, interpersonal learning, problem-solving, decision-making, frustration tolerance, communication, and skill building, for example, without the use of metaphoric transfer of learning. **In addition, metaphors require a level of abstract thinking that not all participants may have; hence, when used, participants can become confused and/or disengaged as well.**

PRACTITIONER-DEVELOPED METAPHORS

Practitioners formulate case conceptualizations and engage in assessment that informs their understanding of the case. **They observe current experiential functioning and note parallels between the participant's life and their responses in sessions**. During this process, the practitioner develops their own cognitive schemas about the metaphoric potential for varying activities to bring clinical dynamics to life in the session.

For example, when working with a participant who has expressed a goal of needing to trust other people in their life, the practitioner may plan to facilitate an activity in which the participant is unsighted and dependent on the facilitator to guide them through an obstacle course (**Unsighted Walk**, see Appendix 1). If they make attempts to find their own way without direction, a parallel process between behavior in the session and the treatment goal is straightforward. This metaphorical structure also places the participant in an experience that provides the opportunity to practice goal-related responses.

With practitioner-developed metaphors, practitioners engage with participants prior to the activity to design interventions with a metaphor in mind. **The practitioner's task becomes to pay attention to how the participant responds, encouraging them to reflect on or make connections related to these metaphors**.

STRUCTURAL MATCHING

As discussed in Chapter 6, the practitioner often chooses an activity that will place the participant in an experience that elicits dynamics that are like those impacting their life outside of therapy (an isomorphic metaphor; Gass, 2025). This may provide an opportunity to increase a participant's awareness of their responses to these dynamics or to practice responses that are required for successful completion of their treatment goals. **The structure of the activity is adapted before the session starts in a manner that makes the actions necessary for success in the activity isomorphic (the same as) with the actions necessary for the participant to reach their treatment goals**. Consequently, the activity as a whole is a metaphor for treatment success. When facilitating this form of metaphorical activity, the practitioner simply presents the activity and allows the isomorphic elements to emerge spontaneously from the experience.

ISOMORPHIC FRAMING

Metaphors can also be introduced by a practitioner with isomorphic framing, as discussed earlier (Gass, 2025). **The intervention plan is developed during the matching phase of the facilitated wave, but what the practitioner does in presenting the metaphor with an isomorphic frame happens during the session**.

The following example gives a quick overview of two sessions with an individual participant. In the first session, this participant was on the verge of successfully completing a difficult task when they started to act impulsively and ended up falling short of the goal that was well within their reach. During the reflection time, they acknowledged that the pattern they demonstrated during this activity is commonly repeated in their life. They indicated that they often "ignore potential consequences" and just "go for it without thinking first". They closed the session by stating, "I just threw everything away", referring to the impulsive actions that they engaged in without thinking. During the matching phase for the next session, the practitioner chose an activity that would require the participant to gather throwable objects (approximately 30 items) from inside a large rope circle without ever crossing the rope barrier (**Basket Toss**, see Appendix 1). Once all the objects were collected, they could earn 5 points for throwing an object into a crate located near to them or 50 points for getting the object in a crate placed a far distance away.

The practitioner decided to use an isomorphic frame for this intervention that included language that would apply equally to actions in the session and the prescribed out-of-session actions needed to reach the participant's treatment goals. The first choice was to change the name of the activity to "Think First". The practitioner's instructions were, "After doing all the work to gather the objects, you will have the choice of shooting for the basket far away and earning 50 points for each object that goes in or shooting for the basket very close and earning 5 points. You can risk 'throwing it all away' by choosing the basket far away for a lot of points or making slow, steady progress by shooting at the basket close to you". This way of framing the activity in isomorphic language and creating the metaphor of 'Think First' makes a direct connection between what the participant does during the intervention and what they need to consider in reaching their treatment goals. Either choice made by the participant would be isomorphic with what is needed to reach the treatment goals as long as they remembered to "think first" and act in a thoughtful manner.

METAPHORS THAT ARISE FROM THE EXPERIENCE

Another common way metaphor is used in adventure practice is what Hovelynk (1998) referred to as generative metaphor development. **In this use of metaphor, the experience is offered first and a novel or unique metaphor is developed from what happens during the intervention. The metaphor arises from the collaborative experience with the participant during the intervention rather than being derived before the activity by the practitioner**.

There are three things the practitioner can watch for in order to begin the process of generative metaphor development: (1) the moments a participant appears to be in a flow or deeply immersed in finding solutions to some aspect of an activity (Itin, 1998), (2) when they are stuck on some aspect of the intervention, and (3) when they use humor to comment on their situation in an experience (Hovelynk, 1998). These moments offer the practitioner the opportunity to engage the participant in exploring what is happening in more detail. **By fully exploring the content surrounding an experience, the participant can name and own what happened. That process results in a metaphor generated by the participant that becomes a vivid shorthand for their understanding of either a challenge they need to overcome or a strength they need to bring to bear on the problem**.

One of the authors remembers a participant who was unable to focus on the task. As the participant was vacillating about how to begin a **Tennis Ball Pyramid** (see Appendix 1), they chuckled as they made a joke about a time they ended up wandering around in the frozen food section of a grocery store unable to make a decision. The participant described finding themself moving up and down the frozen food aisle of the grocery store aimlessly, the same way they were now looking up and down the problem at hand with no idea where to start. "Being in the frozen food section" became the metaphor for working through their dissociative responses stemming from complex childhood trauma.

Experiential Processing Techniques

Experiential processing techniques are aimed at engaging a participant in exploring meaning and activating human expression. Metaphoric tools such as picture cards, containers of toys, and various objects can be used to evoke connections between experiences and a participant's life outside of sessions. Ultimately, the practitioner's aim is to help make something that is hard to describe (like feelings or thoughts), more accessible to the participant through the use of metaphors and objects.

As discussed in *Adventure Group Psychotherapy* (Alvarez et al., 2021, p. 148), some examples of nonverbal and/or metaphoric processing techniques include the following:

- Selecting objects or cards with pictures on them to represent their experience during the session (**Processing Tools**, see Appendix 1) (Figure 8.3).
- Using items numbered from 1 to 10 and asking participants to stand by the number that indicates how helpful the session or activity was for them (scaling or **Continuums**, see Appendix 1).
- Asking participants to stand along a continuum from "very negative" to "very positive" on the place that best represents their experience (**Continuums**, see Appendix 1).
- Sculpting with clay or natural items to represent how they see themselves (**Tower Building**, see Appendix 1).

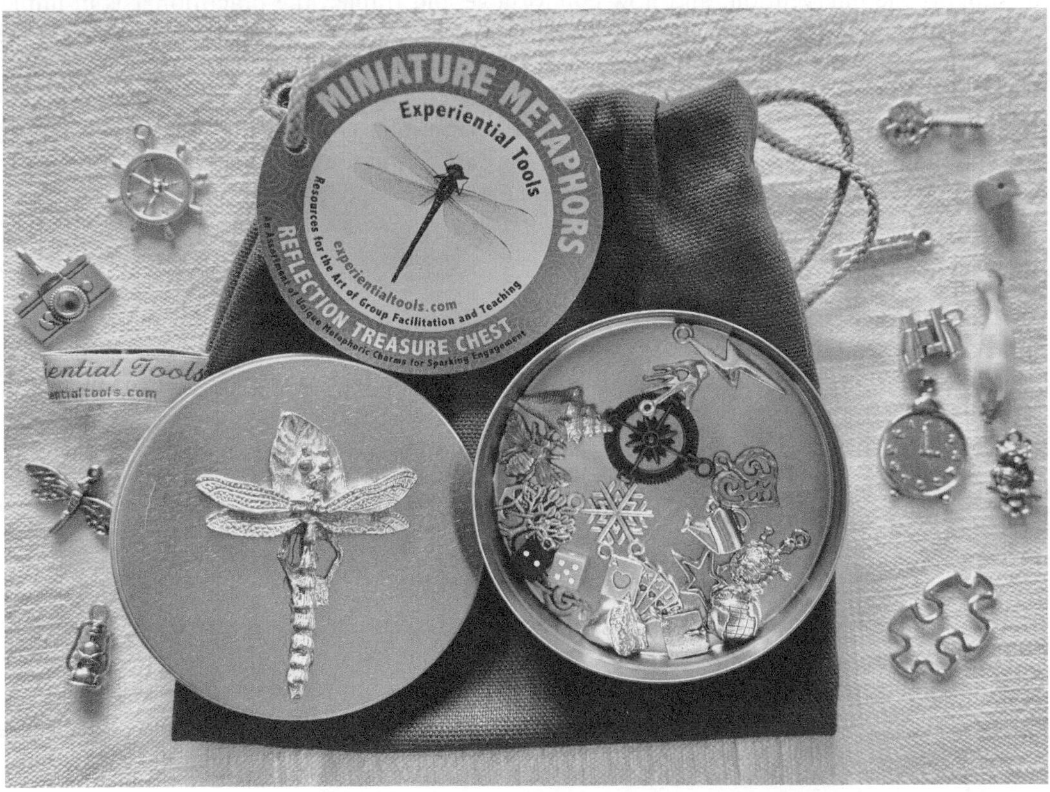

Figure 8.3 Allowing participants the freedom to choose enhances treatment.

Photo of Miniature Metaphors from Jen Stanchfield/Experiential Tools/LLC

- Standing in a part of the environment that best represents their role during the session (under the table, at the door, etc.).
- Find something in nature that represents a relationship that is important to them.
- Using an annotate tool or similar functionality in a virtual session to draw on a picture or whiteboard.
- Using art supplies to draw or create representations of thoughts, feelings, behaviors.

The aforementioned processing techniques can be used to reflect on the specific intervention just presented, the overall progress of therapy, one of the core elements of the environment, the effectiveness of the practitioner, or the progress being made toward the participant's clinical goals.

Due to the importance of making meaning from the experiences presented during individual psychotherapy sessions, the practitioner is encouraged to work diligently to reserve time in the session to process each experience throughout the session and reflect on the overall experience before the session ends.

Conclusion

Many of the questions that are asked about facilitation cannot be satisfied with a definitive, easy answer. It always depends on what assessment has been made, what environment exists to support the intervention, and how comfortable and trained the practitioner is in implementing the intervention. The many in-the-moment decisions made while facilitating are guided by a clinical mindset that values experience and attends to participant's responses.

Being anti-oppressive and trauma informed in practice is a consistent theme in how practitioners choose to facilitate adventure therapy interventions. One's facilitation can take many forms, but in the end the intention is to guide the participant toward achieving their treatment goals. In the next chapter, the process of evaluating this progress is explored in depth.

Reflections

- Can you describe the difference between these three methods of presenting an intervention to a participant: framing, frontloading, isomorphic framing?
- What does it mean to facilitate in a nondeliberative manner? When might you decide to be deliberative?
- What are some ways that you can help participants make meaning from their experience in the therapeutic intervention?

Now What?

- Looking back over the chapter, you will see 11 interventions a practitioner can use when facilitating. Identify the ones you are familiar with and already use in your practice. Now identify the ones that represent skills you hope to master or refine in your practice.
- Take the opportunity to write a process recording of one or more critical moments during an intervention you led and review it with a colleague or supervisor.
    - An example of a process recording can be found in Table 8.2.

- If you don't currently have participants in a clinical setting, practice with a friend or family member who is willing to identify something they are working on and willing to engage in an intervention with you.

Facilitation in Action

In addition to being an engaging and fun read, the case example given to the authors by Phillip Stallard illustrates many aspects of how to facilitate adventure interventions. First, Phillip is aware of the environmental conditions, physically, as well as socially and emotionally. He is also clear about the Point B of the session and tailors the interventions to present the opportunity for his participant to work toward that objective. One can see how Point B guided Phillip throughout this four-hour experience.

It is delightful to read about how Phillip can verbalize the parallel process that is occurring during the challenging portions of the session and how he created an environment around the campfire and hammocks to continue processing of those experiences.

Practitioner Information

My initial interest piqued when I was involved in the outdoor scene as an instructor. I studied at Ireland's first BA program in adventure tourism management and moved on to an MA through research in adventure tourism networking and collaboration. Through a workplace opportunity during this time, I found myself in a social care role. This role was a huge shift for me, as it was in a Special Care unit where young people in Ireland are placed by the High Court when they are deemed to be a significant risk to themselves or others. Being launched into this role with an unconventional skillset really showed me the potential power of experiential approaches, as most therapeutic offerings to these young people were traditional clinical therapy, which they were not very open to.

I began to research the area of adventure therapy and learned about the AEE, OBH, and training pathways. Realizing the potential for exploring therapeutic intentionality by harnessing outdoor experiences and adventures, I decided to become a social worker to begin my adventure therapy career. I established New Wave Adventure Therapy in June 2017 as soon as I had completed my MSW. Reflecting on some of the more complex presentations of some of my participants over several years, I wanted to increase my scope of practice and move into a more clinically therapeutic space, so I retrained as an integrative psychotherapist and added some key skills such as REBT (CBT).

In 2021 I became a clinically certified adventure therapist (CCAT), which has been a personal and professional milestone. The journey to becoming an adventure therapist for me has spanned over 15 years since my initial outdoor training, and I continue to add new skills and build awareness each year. The vast range of training and expertise I have worked on over the years has come together into a framework of practice that funnels these major professional disciplines and supplementary skills and competencies, combined with the benefits of nature and direct and indirect experiential approaches into a comprehensive framework of adventure therapy that is intentional, responsive, and purposeful.

Participant Description

"Adam" is a 16-year-old self-identified male who lives in long-term foster care. He was referred for adventure therapy by his social worker who hoped the intervention would help to stabilize the foster placement, which was at risk of breakdown. The social worker described Adam's evidence of self-harm and reports of aggressive behavior at school and toward foster carers and property. Adam had disengaged from school and peers, and there were concerns of an imminent placement breakdown. There were other children in the home and Adam's behaviors were of concern. Adam has significant experiences of early life trauma relating to parental substance misuse and domestic violence. Adam said he has been "restless" all his life and has a recent diagnosis of ADHD, for which he is trialing a new medication. In Adam's initial sessions, using experiential assessment tools and a feedback informed treatment (FIT) model, I worked with Adam to capture a clear picture of his experience and views, and he identified having difficulty with self-regulation, effective communication, and low mood.

Adam is a sincere and honest young man. He is fond of his foster family and values their efforts to support him. He recognizes that his behaviors have become problematic, and he feels remorseful over outbursts; describing an overwhelming anger. Adam is very active and was a keen soccer player in the past. He enjoyed training and matches and derived confidence from the sport and his team. Adam began to respond with aggression to authoritarian coaching styles and subsequently withdrew from sport. He is motivated to reengage with sports in an alternative setting.

Treatment Context

This was session 5 of Adam's first 12-session block of one-to-one adventure therapy. Sessions were 4 hours in duration and the location of this session was a beach in County Kerry linked to hiking trails and a river mouth. It was mid-autumn, and the conditions were challenging with 12k knot, southwest winds.

In the previous sessions we worked on building up engagement, identifying therapy goals, establishing the safe space, and working on the alliance. I noted that Adam was less inclined to assimilate information from discussion; rather, he responded well to the physical exertion of a task which embodies the therapeutic goal. I had gently introduced aspects of REBT into previous sessions when Adam spoke about recent turbulent events, asking about what he was thinking in the moment and afterward, and some initial work on identifying feelings.

Having spoken about feeling distressed about the emotional aftermath arising from his aggressive behaviors at home, Adam described feeling guilty and sensed a residual uneasiness around him. He described feeling very sensitive to this and wanted to help resolve things with others. The treatment goal for this session centered around managing low frustration tolerance and initiating a repair after a challenging event: "building a bridge".

Session Description

This session was over four hours and broken up into three phases. The first part was building the bridge to get to the beach. The second part was making our way, wild walking through the sea to the sheltered bay area. The third part was setting a reflection space around the firepit and hammocks.

The session began with a welcome and review of how things had been for Adam since the last session. We talked about the events of the week so far and I checked in with him about how he was doing. I tasked him to gather some stones from the beach to create three separate stacks, each representing him in terms of how he is feeling: physically, mentally, and emotionally.

We donned wetsuits, packed drybags with supplies, and grabbed fins, masks, and snorkels and set off. It is important for me to use the same gear as my participant. We have the same type of wetsuit and pack an almost equal share of the food into our bags, while I take the added necessary safety equipment. This helps me to accurately gauge his comfort level and removes any sense of hierarchy. These subtle pieces of communication are ones that I refer to during sessions and speak to participant about in terms of communicating values and nonverbal messaging.

I tasked Adam with building a bridge to cross the river. I suggested to him that he could use any materials from the surrounding area, and he could direct me to help with any aspect. The physical task involved sourcing materials, finding the best crossing point, and setting the stones and logs optimally to support us to cross the river.

Next, we waded into the sea to lower chest height and set off wild walking along the coast and in the waves, heading toward a nearby sheltered bay. We carried fins & snorkels, navigating the waves as they moved over us. The weather was wet and windy, and the conditions provided an element of challenge without feeling too risky. Adam moved along steadily, watching the waves along the horizon and anchoring himself appropriately while taking direction from me as we walked. Between waves, we talked about the different challenges that we were managing in this space and what we were doing to minimize the impact, such as consistently observing, using verbal and visual communication between us, keeping a close distance, and using physical stance and techniques to navigate waves more easily. I reassured Adam that he can stop, slow, and ask for support throughout the activity, ensuring that he felt comfortable and maintained autonomy. The task was not about throwing him into the deep end; it was about navigating through challenges. Physical exertion is one part of the process, but the objective of Adam's program is to build frustration tolerance and to create a personal strategy to manage difficult feelings and to communicate better with others.

We reflected on the journey once we reached the bay. We decided that we had to keep moving forward to the sheltered bay. The route was challenging and necessitated using the right strategy and equipment. More importantly, Adam had support available to him throughout the activity. He had to do the work to get from A to B but maintained autonomy and the option to ask for help. We spoke about how it can feel a bit hard managing unexpected challenges but having the right gear and support makes it possible, even enjoyable and satisfying.

Reinforcing CBT work, we spoke about moments of feeling less control in the water, and about how thoughts affect feelings. We connected this short-lived feeling to the much bigger ones related to trauma experiences in childhood. We discussed how losing a sense of control can feel frustrating, and a low tolerance for frustration can build and explode out of us through aggressive behaviors, as Adam had described having difficulty with. The session created a controlled situation that emulated the feeling of being challenged. Adam had to focus and progress to the next point.

In the water, Adam spoke about the sense of joy he got from exploring the bay. He said he felt his head was clearer and he could take in more of the surroundings when he was in the calm in the sheltered bay. We explored the entire bay, tracing the seaweed shrouded rocks beneath the surface and seeking out undersea life. This, combined with the accomplishment of completing the journey to the bay well within the time planned brought him pride and satisfaction. Although he said it was challenging in parts, he admitted that it was worth the effort. I spoke with him about the simple therapeutic effect of play.

On the shore, we built a fire, which provides a psychological safe point in the session, anchored to the firepit. While cooking and eating at the firepit, the space opened up for more direct discussion about the preceding activities and related ideas. We pitched hammocks and took some time for mindful reflection, followed by some feedback about the session through the session rating scale.

Practitioner Comments Regarding Session

The session followed a Wave Model that I most often employ, which follows a pattern of activity (beginning with high energy/effort), then calming, and finally reflection.

The bridge and coasteering brought an initial exertion, followed by gentler snorkeling, and then the calm and reflective space of cooking and hammocks. I tend to follow this structure in all sessions, which participants enjoy the reliability of.

Integrating the REBT (CBT) structure into direct therapeutic work in the sessions also provided some predictability and relevance to previous sessions' discussions about thoughts, feelings, and behaviors. Using a simple model that is easily mapped to physical activities helps to communicate the message and keep Adam on track with his therapeutic objectives.

Behavioral therapy, cognitive therapy, FIT and person-centered therapy are all incorporated into this therapeutic framework.

Drawing on kinesthetic metaphor in these sessions can be a hugely powerful piece. I find it most relevant to refer to these either initially or as a review in the calming/reflecting phase while cooking or in hammocks. The use of metaphor can really help because it tends to be visual or kinesthetic, combined with the use of specific language. This facilitates recall and appeals to a variety of learning styles. Metaphors can be selected and interpreted according to the flow of the session and direction of discussion and understanding.

Submitted by Phillip Stallard, MSW, CCAT

New Wave Adventure Therapy

Ireland

References

Alvarez, T. G., Stauffer, G., Lung, D. M., Sacksteder, K., Beale, B., & Tucker, A. R. (2021). *Adventure group psychotherapy: An experiential approach to treatment*. Routledge.

Barkley, R. A. (2021). *Taking charge of adult ADHD* (2nd ed.). Guilford Publications.

Bateson, G. (1972). *Steps to an ecology of mind: Collected essays in anthropology, psychiatry, evolution, and epistemology*. Chandler Publishing.

Borton, T. (1970). *Reach, touch, and teach: Student concerns and process education*. McGraw-Hill.

Činčera, J., Johnson, B., Kroufek, R., Kolenatý, M., & Šimonová, P. (2020). Frames in outdoor environmental education programs: What we communicate and why we think it matters. *Sustainability, 12*(11), 4451. https://doi.org/10.3390/su12114451

Cozolino, L. (2010). *The neuroscience of psychotherapy: Healing the social brain* (2nd ed.). W W Norton & Co.

Gass, M. A. (2025). *Delivering effective adventure therapy: A therapist's guide to producing transformative change for clients*. Routledge.

Grusec, J. E. (1992). Social learning theory and developmental psychology: The legacies of Robert Sears and Albert Bandura. *Developmental Psychology, 28*(5), 776–786. https://doi.org/10.1037/0012-1649.28.5.776

Hovelynk, J. (1998). Facilitating experiential learning as a process of metaphor development. *Journal of Experiential Education, 21*(1), 6–13. https://doi.org/10.1177/105382599802100103

Itin, C. M. (1998). The seventh generation in adventure therapy. In C. Itin (Ed.), *Exploring the boundaries of adventure therapy: International perspectives. Proceedings of the International Adventure Therapy Conference* (pp. 120–130). Association for Experiential Education. https://files.eric.ed.gov/fulltext/ED424056.pdf

Kolb, D. A. (1984). *Experiential Learning: Experience as the source of learning and development*. Prentice Hall.

Lindsey, A., Bunker, L., Mozeiko, J., & Coelho, C. (2020). Primed to cue. *Journal of Communication Disorders, 86*, 105998. https://doi.org/10.1016/j.jcomdis.2020.105998

Merriam-Webster Dictionary. (2025). *Facilitate*. https://www.merriam-webster.com/dictionary/facilitate

Mitten, D. (2023). Pace, care, and competency to support healing. *International Journal of Adventure Therapy, 4*, 1–13. https://journal-adventure-therapy.com/product/pace-care-and-competency-to-support-healing/

Neipp, M.-C., Beyebach, M., Sanchez-Prada, A., & Alvarez, M. del C. D. (2021). Solution-focused versus problem-focused questions: Differential effects of miracles, exceptionns and scales. *Journal of Family Therapy, 43*(4), 728–747. https://doi.org/10.1111/1467-6427.12345

Priest, S. & Gass, M. (2017). *Effective leadership in adventure programming* (3rd ed.). Human Kinetics.

Ruffalo, M. C., Perron, B. E., & Harbeck Vashal, E. (2016). *Direct social work practice: Theories and skills for becoming an evidence based practitioner*. Sage Publications.

Törneke, N. (2017) *Metaphor in practice. A professional's guide to using the science of language in psychotherapy*. New Harbinger Publications.

Tucker, A. R., Norton, C. L., Itin, C., Hobson, J., & Alvarez, M. A. (2016). Adventure therapy: Nondeliberative group work in action. *Social Work with Groups, 39*(2–3), 194–207. https://doi.org/10.1080/01609513.2015.1048416

Yalom, I. D. (2002) *The gift of therapy*. HarperCollins Publishers.

Chapter 9

Evaluating the Process

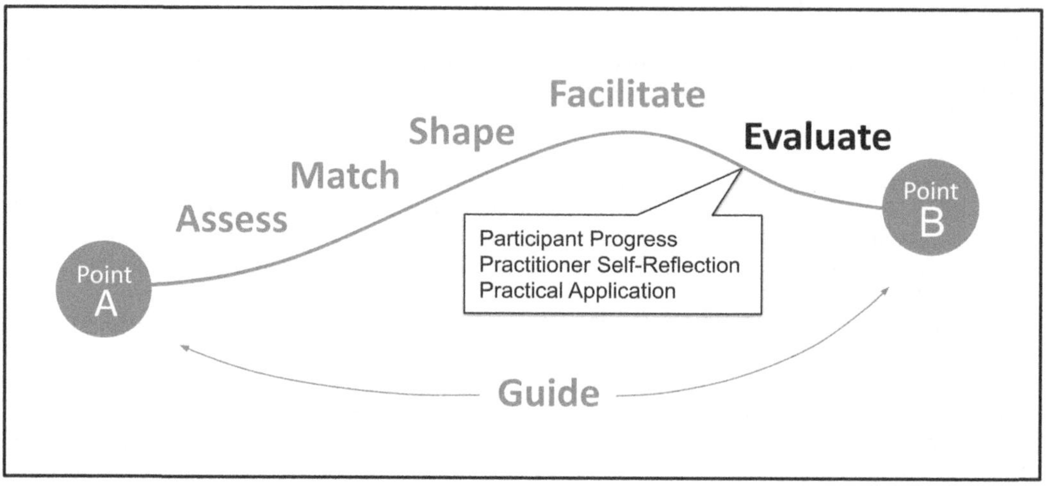

What Is Evaluation?

Don't let the word "evaluation" put you off or intimidate you. Individual adventure practitioners are very seasoned in making initial and ongoing assessments. This same skill is directly linked to evaluation. However, **rather than trying to understand the current level of functioning before any intervention (e.g., assessment), evaluation is an attempt to understand the impact for the participant after engaging in treatment**. Furthermore, it is essential to the success of the adventure therapy interventions to explore what worked, or didn't work, as well as understanding how and why interventions were and were not successful.

Hence, part of this process is ongoing participant-informed feedback of the intervention, which in and of itself is related to improved outcomes (Jensen-Doss et al., 2018). Operationally, evaluation is the intentional act of understanding, measuring, and documenting the impact of the treatment interventions. Additionally, it is looking critically at the treatment environment and the facilitation by the practitioner. The information gathered through evaluation has several benefits, including

- documenting or improving treatment efficacy,
- understanding clinical utility,

DOI: 10.4324/9781003457893-9

- informing practitioners of their professional development needs, and
- potentially contributing to the growing evidence that supports the legitimacy of the adventure therapy field.

Through evaluation the practitioner should be looking to understand how the participant has progressed. **This could include participants gaining an awareness of issues, responsibility for self, awareness of self in relation to others, experimenting with new ways of being, and integration of new behaviors into environments outside of the session.**

This chapter does not attempt to describe the broad spectrum of evaluation or even program evaluation. Rather, discussion will focus more narrowly on the practitioner's actions to gather data about the participant's experience and the practitioner's facilitation of the experience, which can be helpful for both the practitioner and the participant.

Anti-Oppressive Focus of Evaluation

Like the discussion in Chapter 5, the ongoing marginalization and oppression present in the lives of many participants impacts how practitioners engage in evaluation as well. Practitioners need to continue to be aware of the depth and potential impacts of this dynamic on participants. As discussed in Chapter 2, trauma and ongoing oppression can impact the participants' ways of thinking and behaving, as well as their affective and somatic responses. In taking an anti-oppressive practice approach in evaluation, especially as the practitioner is making meaning of progress or the participant's Point B, practitioners should remain actively engaging in critical consciousness and awareness of the systems of oppression that exist in the environment, as well as with participant's family and ancestral history. Similarly to assessment, in evaluation the practitioner may focus solely on the changes that occurred related to the reason the participant sought (or was brought) to treatment. **This "identified problem" and its related "problematic behaviors" can be limited by focusing only on the individual's responsibility for change and possibly ignoring the systems and institutions which are inherently racist, sexist and oppressive.** Hence evaluation should include an understanding of the context of the participant and a realistic acknowledgment of things within the control of the participant and practitioner. **It is also important to recognize that the evaluation may show the need for practitioners to engage in more macro practices that fight to help mitigate systems of oppression that impact participants.** So, the work moves beyond the clinical setting and into the larger system of care in the forms of advocacy and policy work to increase awareness and consciousness of these issues (Mallinckrodt et al., 2014).

Furthermore, as mentioned previously, trauma-informed practices are closely aligned with anti-oppressive practice, hence practitioner evaluation should also include gathering information about the participant's felt sense of safety, trusted and transparent relationships in their lives, the choice and voice in their current situation, as well as how cultural, historical and gender issues impact them. **Engaging in ongoing critical reflection helps practitioners minimize biases and conclusions and decisions made about participants and their progress** (Ortega & Garvin, 2019).

Evaluating the Participant's Progress

It is exciting and rewarding for both the participant and the practitioner to observe change that is occurring in treatment and how well the interventions work toward the progress of the participant's Point B: their identified treatment goals.

When working with individuals, a key part of evaluation is to provide opportunities for participants to evaluate themselves. This process also provides opportunity for skill development; thus, the practitioner may often start by providing a reflection in a way that can be heard by the participant or by reinforcing accuracy of a participant's self-reflection. **To truly engage the participant in this process, the practitioner must also consider what skills, knowledge, or resources the participant needs in order to effectively evaluate themselves.** Do they have the ability (1) to share how their behavior influenced the experience, (2) to communicate needs for self or from others that support the desired change, and (3) to identify how change shows up (e.g., what would they see or hear if changes were actually happening). It is also imperative to address power dynamics when evaluating individual therapy, as there are often fewer voices in the room (as opposed to group therapy). Similarly, a practitioner should address any previous negative experiences and the potential stress or shame when receiving feedback, especially about sensitive topics. However, if the practitioner and participant have created a collaborative and authentic relationship, feedback and reflection have been actively used to check in with each other about the treatment process. So, when evaluation occurs, the stage has been set for this process already.

In addition to the participant, it can be greatly beneficial to gather information from external sources when possible, such as established evaluation instruments, conversations with the participant's supporting or significant individuals (e.g., family members, teachers, probation officers, medical professionals), and observations of how the participants shows up (what do you see and hear) during each session. **This triangulation of information helps to increase confidence in the evaluation of progress of the participant** (Carter et al., 2014).

When to Evaluate?

Although often only thought about intentionally at the closing process (e.g., termination), intentional evaluation is helpful during a session, after a session, and after a series of sessions, as well as when ending treatment. **During a session, when the practitioner is evaluating in the moment, and using the data immediately after gathering it, it can appear quite similar or parallel to assessment.** This type of evaluation data is typically used to make decisions about interventions, including activity adaptations or sequencing. **It is more common to take time at the end of a session to evaluate the process and participant's progress. This is particularly helpful to gather information about what worked, or didn't work, as it relates specifically to the participants Point B and allows for changes if needed.**

When evaluating over time (or comparing data over time), the practitioner will also likely review and update the treatment plan. Additionally, the practitioner may evaluate for organizational performance goals or funding sources. If there was a formal assessment of participant functioning prior to beginning treatment or during the first few sessions, it can be useful to complete the same instrument at the end of services (i.e., pre-post testing) to show a change in that specific level of functioning, or an instrument that was developed to measure a specific level of achievement (i.e., post-test only).

Despite its importance, evaluation is often overlooked due to time restrictions, practitioner or participant discomfort, or lack of preparation or money. Regardless, **it is the ethical responsibility of practitioners to engage in evaluation of the impact of their work. Hence, it should become an integral part of their planning process.**

Active Evaluation and Observation in Adventure Treatment

Like assessment, adventure practitioners will also utilize the power of observation and exploration to gather information about change when evaluating the process. The participant offers their evaluative perspective through self-reflection, especially their observations of the experience, their relationships to the environment in relation to the experience, and their connection with the practitioner. Observationally, the practitioner will begin to notice the experience of the participant from a slightly distant and comparative view over time. **Practically, a participant's progress should be formally documented with progress notes after each session. Documenting the amount of contact as well as progress toward goals is needed not only for record keeping, but often also for insurance and supervision.**

Observational assessment and evaluation are integrated. When practitioners are assessing, they are refining their understanding of the participant based on evolving evidence. That evolving evidence is the evaluation part! It remains imperative to be aware of personal biases during this process. **Key aspects of observation in active evaluation in adventure therapy include the following**:

- **Real-Time Insights**: Observation of a participant in a natural environment provides immediate and direct information that can be compared to information gathered from the participant directly or ancillary sources.
- **Nonverbal Cues**: Nonverbal behavior, such as body language, facial expressions, and tone of voice, provides opportunities to evaluate the participant's emotional state, engagement level, and social interactions.
- **Contextual Understanding**: Observation of a participant in their actual environment or during regular tasks provides opportunities to evaluate the influence of external factors, such as the environment, social dynamics, and available resources.
- **Holistic Evaluation**: Practitioners can capture the complexity of human behavior, including somatic, cognitive, emotional, social, and physical aspects, offering a more comprehensive evaluation than one-dimensional testing methods.

Gather Information about Participant's Point B

Although goals and expectations evolve over the course of treatment, it is important to engage in regular evaluation of change toward the desired Point B of treatment. All along, the practitioner has been gathering information to inform treatment intervention decisions. Likely, these have included evaluative processes, such as providing reflection time at the end of each session, which offers opportunities to evaluate strengths, skills, preferences, progress, or limitations demonstrated in that session.

Regardless of a practitioner's treatment modality or theoretical lens, evaluation gathers information about a participant's emotional, psychological, and behavioral health to capture changes that occur for the participant. As a practitioner, one of the goals is to choose the most effective ways to begin the reflection so that the method helps the participant think and talk about their experience. The evaluation tools a practitioner chooses depends on the type of information needed to be gathered as well as unique participant considerations, hence no one tool fits all situations. The primary information gathered for evaluation is typically related to the specific treatment goal; however, the following are common general areas often collected during the evaluation process:

- **Psychological Well-Being:** reduction of symptoms of distress, improvements in self-esteem and self-concept, and changes in coping strategies, thought patterns, daily functioning, risk behaviors, and habits.
- **Social, Cultural, and Environmental:** improvements or changes in interpersonal dynamics, support systems, social identities, navigating the impact of culture, community, society, or environmental stressors, and relationship with nature.
- **Cognitive Functioning:** improvements or changes in memory and attention, problem-solving and decision-making, learning assets, and challenges.
- **Developmental and Medical:** improvements or changes in developmental markers, trauma responses, and medical conditions.
- **Intrapersonal:** clarification of, or changes in, identity formation, roles, sense of purpose, skills, talents, knowledge, abilities, habits, integration of past experiences, and decreases in risk of suicide, self-harm, and harm to others.
- **Clinical Treatment Goals:** improvements toward or changes to the participant's (and often ancillary sources) ideas about their desired outcomes and clinical goals.
- **Impact of the Experiential/Adventure Experience:** level of (and influence of) risk (physical, emotional, social, etc.), influence of props, influence of the environment (i.e., external people or nature), participant actions required to successfully complete the activity.

To help gather this information, practitioners can engage in the following actions:

- Facilitate any activity that includes opportunities to review treatment goals and discuss perceived changes.
- Use a self-report instrument, such as a standardized questionnaire, or a mood/symptom tracking app.
- Use a practitioner-administered instrument, such as a structured interview or a cognitive or functional measure that tracks progress over time.
- Gather formal or informal feedback from ancillary sources (i.e., caregivers, teachers, employers, or other professionals involved in care).
- Use journaling, goal reflection worksheets, or experiential activities, such as **Change Three Things** (see Appendix 1) to observe changes in knowledge, skills or behaviors, or attitudes.
- Facilitate an activity that provides an opportunity to observe the participant's body language, eye contact, and engagement during sessions as an opportunity to reflect on progress.
- Evaluate the flow of conversation, interruptions, and responsiveness and share/reflect on these observations with the participant.
- Invite the participant to provide direct feedback on techniques or interventions and their impact on their progress and treatment.

During this process, practitioners should notice participant's willingness to reflect on their actions and connect them to what they have achieved by being in treatment.

Evaluating the Treatment Environment

Evaluation also includes gathering information about the environment of the treatment process, such as the physical space, the nurtured norms and beliefs, the therapeutic relationship between participant and practitioner, and the authentic engagement to the work. The following are some questions practitioners can consider about the environment during the evaluation process:

- **Physical Space**: Did the practitioner and participant safely manage to be outside (i.e., bees, allergies, animals, etc.)? Did the setting provide enough emotional safety for the participant to experience fully? Did the gear help the participant feel comfortable? Was the gear appropriately functional? How did the selected location influence distractibility, confidentiality, and focus?
- **Nurtured Norms and Beliefs**: Were any of the seven adventure beliefs missing or not operating optimally? What norms or beliefs are being integrated successfully?
- **Therapeutic Relationship**: What was the collaboration process like? What was the participant's level of vulnerability? Was a warm, trusting relationship with the practitioner evident? What fears or concerns needed to be addressed?

To help address these questions, practitioners can engage in the following actions:

- Engage the participant in planning for the session – e.g., have them make a list of the appropriate clothing or gear for the outdoors or the activity.
- Invite the participant to scale their level of comfort (i.e., on a scale of 1–10, where 1 is terrible and 10 is perfect) in the equipment or in the activity (see **Continuums**, Appendix 1).
- Select or adapt the activity to highlight the adventure belief or norm desired to be evaluated – e.g., using a playground setting for an initiative activity without being distracted by the playground equipment.
- Narrate (i.e., verbally observe) or invite the participant to reflect on the norms/beliefs that support the desired changes. This can also be done when looking for evidence of applying insights or skills learned in treatment.
- Use journaling or art activities to provide opportunities for self-reflection about participant changes in thinking or behavior inside and/or outside or sessions.

Progress Monitoring

Progress monitoring involves systematically tracking and assessing changes in the participant's symptoms, behaviors, and overall well-being over time, usually weekly. Progress monitoring is considered an evidence-based practice and aligns with best practices in mental health care, ensuring treatment is effective and tailored to the participant's needs. Lambert & Shimokawa (2011) found that participants whose practitioner implemented progress monitoring were 2.6 times more likely to experience reliable improvement versus those who did not. Due to the interactive and flexible nature of adventure interventions and processing methods, this practice approach is conducive to gathering feedback and implementing changes. It is like evaluation (and often used to gather information for evaluation) in the following ways:

- **Objective Measurement**: Progress monitoring provides structured tools, such as standardized assessments, self-report scales, and practitioner observations, to measure changes in mental health conditions. This is important as research suggests that practitioners do not always recognize risk of treatment failure in participants (Hatfield et al., 2010).

- **Informed Decision-Making**: Practitioners use progress monitoring to make data-driven decisions about treatment plans, including whether to continue, modify, or intensify interventions (Jensen-Doss et al., 2018).
- **Participant Engagement and Motivation**: Progress monitoring when done regularly, can help participants see tangible improvements, reinforcing their motivation to continue treatment (de Jong et al., 2021).
- **Early Identification of Challenges**: Progress monitoring provides opportunities to identify barriers, setbacks, or stagnation early, enabling timely intervention and adjustment of therapeutic approaches (Hatfield et al., 2010; Lambert & Shimokawa, 2011) .
- **Communication and Collaboration**: Progress monitoring facilitates better communication between the practitioner and the participant, as well as with other healthcare providers when interdisciplinary care is needed (de Jong et al., 2015).

Effective progress monitoring requires high-quality data, in a time-efficient manner (as well as timely), for the practitioner to make feedback-informed treatment decisions. **Additionally, practitioners must be able to interpret the data and support the participant to draw conclusions about treatment effectiveness, which could require seeking consultation and support if it does not currently exist in a practitioner's practice setting.** Russell et al. (2018), who studied the integration of progress monitoring into adventure therapy programming, stress that "implementation needs to involve staff, be flexible, empower participants, and be integrated into the culture of programs" (p. 403). They even go so far as to suggest that waiting until termination of treatment to gather evaluation data is unethical, as it deprives the participant and practitioner the opportunity to change the course of treatment.

Practitioner Self-Reflection and Evaluation

Treatment efficacy is also used in evaluation to consider the practitioner's ability to clinically utilize the interventions. In other words, how well does the practitioner match the intervention, facilitate the interventions, assess the participant's response to the interventions, and use this information to make decisions for future interventions.

In adventure therapy, practitioner self-evaluation includes a post-session task evaluation, which is used to help a practitioner determine the interventions for the next session. **This might include self-reflection about what the practitioner did (or did not do) that influenced the participant's outcomes**. This often includes documenting participant responses to address in future sessions or with other secondary actions (i.e., supervision, formal reports, or collaboration with other providers).

Performance evaluations can help hone strengths and identify gaps in the skills or knowledge of the practitioner and assist with training needs and decisions. Performance evaluation may also be as simple as a discussion with the supervisor regarding the practitioner's self-reflection, or it may include a more formal evaluation instrument. More formal performance evaluation approaches include supervisor observation, participant feedback surveys, or an organization specific performance evaluation tool (typically completed annually).

Gather Information about Practitioner Performance

Like participant evaluation, practitioner evaluation requires the practitioner to have the knowledge and skills to self-evaluate as a whole practitioner (not just their facilitation actions). Likely a mentor, supervisor, or continuing education will be needed to acquire the knowledge, hone self-evaluation skills, or access the resources needed to effectively self-evaluate. Checklists or rating scales can be a simple first step. For example, the Four Buckets Assessment Tool (see Chapter 5) can also be used as a self-reflective evaluation tool. In addition, there are specific adventure therapy competency skills recommended for practitioners engaging in adventure therapy (Gass et al., 2020; TAPG, 2025) that can be used to guide a practitioner's evaluation. Finally, Appendix 10.1 in *Adventure Group Psychotherapy* provides a thorough formal evaluation tool, which can be used for any type of adventure therapy practice (Alvarez et al., 2021, pp. 207–217). The following are some questions practitioners can consider during self-evaluation, supervision, or organizational performance evaluation processes:

Assessment Skills

- How well was the assessment of the participant's current functioning understood prior to the session?
- How did the participant's commitment to goals evolve?
- How was the activity adapted to compensate for what the practitioner saw in the participant related to physical safety, emotional risk, and how the participant showed up to the session?

Shaping the Environment Skills

- How did understanding the physical setting influence responses to the physical setting?
- How well did the establishment of a set of beliefs become norms for behavior?
- What does the therapeutic alliance look like (e.g., the relationship with the practitioner)?
- How were props/facilitation tools presented and used to enhance the experience?
- How did the practitioner attend to squigglies that showed up in the session(s)?

Matching Skills

- What is the practitioner's skill at creating a thoughtful individual session plan?
- How well did the selected activity guide the participant to address particular issues related to their desired outcomes?
- How effective was the practitioner at matching individual participant needs in the moment?
- How did the practitioner use the participant's words and actions to adapt interventions to match their experiential functioning at that moment in the session?

Facilitation Skills

- How did the practitioner match in the moment the actions, movements, or energy level of the participant with the actions in an activity?
- How well is the practitioner able to read the room and adapt to who shows up (contextual awareness)?
- How did the practitioner show up for the session or was engaged in the session?
- How did the practitioner's engagement influence the participant's experience?

- How did the structure of the facilitation influence the participant's experience?
- How were the rules, guidelines, safety considerations, space, and time considerations presented in ways that enhanced the experience?

Guiding the Learning

- How did the practitioner make use of direct observation to gather information about the participant response and use it to guide the participant toward their Point B?
- Were metaphors (or analogies) established or affirmed that were related to the direct experience and/or the desired outcomes?
- Was the participant current experiential functioning within the session connected to functioning in other settings?
- Were participant thoughts, behaviors, emotional, and/or somatic responses identified in order to enhance progress toward Point B as well as ones that may interfere with achieving the participant's desired results?

Evaluation Skills

- Are the evaluation tools appropriate to the participant and to the data desired to be gathered?
- Does the participant feel comfortable giving both positive and constructive feedback?
- Does the practitioner have the skills to successfully select and administer the evaluation instrument?
- Can the practitioner accurately, and meaningfully, analyze the data collected?

Technical Skills

- What is the practitioner's subject knowledge related to the participant treatment needed? (aka, what is in their toolbox)
- What is their knowledge and ability to comply with procedures?

Competency Skills

- What is the practitioner's ability to organize, promote, plan, coordinate, instruct, negotiate, teach, write, present, etc.?

Personal Growth Skills

- What are traits or personal characteristics that contribute to work performance, such as the ability to be efficient, flexible, resourceful, or diplomatic?

Leadership Skills

- What are the practitioner's abilities to take charge of tasks, responsibilities, projects, processes, workflow, goal setting, decision-making, and personal and career development?

To help address these questions, practitioners can engage in the following actions:

- Use journaling to reflect on the facets of facilitation in the session that drew out specific learning for the participant. For example, if the participant loves making videos to post online, and the practitioner framed the story of the challenge as a viral video, how well did the participant connect with this story? Similarly, if a participant is constantly moving and climbing on things both in session and outside of session, requesting a climbing wall experience for session, how did this influence their behavioral expression or need for redirection during a session on the climbing wall?

- Use a t-chart to consider what was required of the participant to complete the activity successfully and compare it to the things that will be required to achieve the treatment goals. They should be aligned to move the participant toward Point B.
- Utilize process recordings to reflect on the interactions with the participant and choices made by the practitioner within the session. Explore in supervision or peer consultation sessions.
- Use an ongoing activity, such as **The Stick** (see Appendix 1), to practice self-evaluative skills.
- Use storytelling methods to share information from personal experience or from other relatable folks of the activity to evaluate the integration of learning.

Conclusion

Like assessment, evaluation is ongoing. The practitioner engages with the participant to identify the desired outcomes (Point B), define what success looks like and sounds like, and create opportunities for this information to be reflected upon. So, not only does the practitioner notice the changes that are occurring for the participant, but the practitioner also then needs to explore with the participant the meaning and source of those responses. This information will help the participant to integrate changes and transition out of treatment. Good evaluation is offered in every session, not only to meet the changing needs of the participant but also to support the participant's voice and choice throughout treatment. In addition, ongoing evaluation of the practitioner's skills, tools, and functioning is essential to be an effective and authentic guide for participants. The importance of ongoing training, professional development, and supervision that include self-reflection are key to meeting this goal.

Reflections

- How might ongoing active evaluation change the way you work with participants? How might including the participant actively in this process influence their experience?
- Consider your own personal experience engaging in evaluation (maybe a survey at a restaurant or a formal evaluation with a medical provider). How could you gather this same information in a more interactive way?
- Have you ever assumed to know the right "outcome" or "success" for a participant, only to learn your assumption was wrong? How might you have been curious in that situation to better evaluate it?

Now What?

- Think about some of your favorite activities and select two or three activities that you can use or learn to use as an evaluation of a participant's Point B (desired results) based on the environment in which you are working.

- Go back to an assessment activity, such as the four corners, and add/change information based on what is happening now for your participant, thus implementing it as an evaluation tool. What do you notice is different? What was unexpected? How did the assessment influence the facilitation or activity selection for the session?

Evaluation in Action

The authors were given this case example by Christina Blanchard. This example shows how assessment and evaluation are parallel processes, as well as how to invite the client to participate in the reflection of those processes. This is a great example of how an evaluation of the session led directly to the evolution of the participant's goals in real time.

Practitioner Information

I am a Licensed mental health counselor with Life Adventures Counseling and a clinical supervisor with Family Resources Inc. located in the greater St. Petersburg, Florida, area. My work is client centered, with a theoretical orientation of solution-focused and narrative. I integrate the modality of adventure and nature whenever possible. My primarily clientele are marginalized youth and their families. What's most appealing to me about the practice of adventure therapy is the freedom for clients and practitioners to be able to choose to navigate the learning and growth process in a way that is meaningful, engaging, and impactful, especially in working with youth who don't like the idea of (talk therapy) counseling on principle. It's exciting to have such a dynamic way of being able to facilitate the growth process.

Participant Description

(Identifying details have been excluded or changed to protect anonymity)

Demographics: 15-year-old, self-identified male, non-White, lives with grandmother

Diagnoses: ADHD (history of diagnosis), adjustment disorder

Strengths: Excellent problem-solver, independently explores and learns about things that interest him (taught himself to build computers), strong communicator, empathetic toward peers, takes initiative to help others in and out of the classroom

Referral Reason: Participant was referred to services due to struggling academically and reported an increase in behavioral concerns since starting high school. Participant struggled with motivation to follow through on goals set for himself across different areas of his life. He was also increasingly engaging in risk-taking behaviors like skipping classes, failing to complete assignments, substance use, and increased peer associations that he acknowledged negatively influenced choices and behaviors. Participant was in an appropriate developmental stage of establishing identity but struggled due to feeling unheard, unsupported, and secondary to his brother, who's schedule/concerns/comforts were always prioritized due to his chronic health issues since birth. Participant had been living with his grandmother for most of his life and had little to no contact with most of his family. Mother was incarcerated most of his life and struggled heavily with substance use. Father lived in another state with another nuclear family, visiting once a year.

Treatment Context

This session was during the beginning stage of treatment and held at an indoor rock climbing gym frequently used for meeting with participants. There is an agreement with the gym about access and privacy. Sessions occur during low-use times. I am trained with the gym to facilitate and provide oversight of the session, so no gym staff are needed for facilitation. The gym offers self-belay options as well. Our session was focused on goal setting, reflecting on the process for setting goals, how to strategize and "tackle" goals, how perceived barriers to accomplishing goals impact motivation levels, assessing capacity to pivot and adjust goals, and then evaluating that through the activity of climbing.

Session Description

After completing the facility orientation and safety training to be able to properly navigate the facility (it was his first time), I initially discussed with the participant what they learned and noticed from that experience. This helps me to assess some of the skills needed for both assessment and evaluation. I then asked the youth to identify one thing he wanted to accomplish that day at the gym. He explained feeling most excited to try rock climbing and what made him feel most comfortable starting there. He identified his goal as "getting to the top". I engaged the participant in defining the goal a bit more (getting up and down, touching the last piece of the trail with one hand or above it, getting to the top of a particular difficulty level, etc.). He wanted to rush through this part and felt confident in "keeping things simple".

I let him know that wherever he started, I would climb the trail right next to him and try to stay level with him. He immediately climbed a path at one of the highest difficulty levels and did not make it very far off the ground. After several attempts at restarting, we paused to reflect on the process so far, and he decided to switch to start at a beginner level path (with a frustrated huff). He found this path much easier and, in his excitement, rushed straight to the top. He whooped and gushed his excitement then announced that he would be starting his descent down. But, instead of descending, he stayed unmoving right where he was. I checked in on him, and he shared that it was easier to get down from lower heights, but he was having a hard time letting go and trusting the belay would support him to descend the way he had learned. We revisited the skills learned during our orientation and practiced some new skills to respond to his dysregulated nervous system. The story that ultimately emerged was his history of feeling unable to trust his support system to show up for him when he needed them.

After some additional co-regulation (deep belly breathing and grounding activity), we were slowly able to make our way down side by side. We took a water break and during that time, processed more regarding his experience of having to place his trust in the belay, and whether or not he felt he accomplished his goal for the day, comparing it to what he had identified earlier as success. He reflected on how feeling like he could not trust his support system has contributed to the narrative that "no one will make the time or want to help me anyway" and has negatively impacted his motivation to make an effort toward goals or ask for help. He also reflected on not feeling conflicted about whether or not he accomplished his goal because, despite getting to the top, he didn't feel successful the way he imagined he would. We talked about what he initially imagined and how that information, in the frame of SMART goals, could be used to redefine his initial goal. With that in mind, the youth wanted to try climbing again and decided to set a different goal for himself. Toward the end of the session, we reflected on the difference between the way he engaged in goal setting, how that impacted his ability to accomplish that goal or feel a sense of accomplishment, and how that experience could be useful for approaching other goals he currently has.

Submitted by Christina Blanchard

Life Adventures Counseling and Family Resources

St. Petersburg, Florida

References

Alvarez, T. G., Stauffer, G., Lung, D. M., Sacksteder, K., Beale, B., & Tucker, A. R. (2021). *Adventure group psychotherapy: An experiential approach to treatment*. Routledge.

Carter, N., Bryant-Lukosius, D., DiCenso, A., Blythe, J., & Neville, A. J. (2014). The use of triangulation in qualitative research. *Oncology Nursing Forum*, *41*(5), 545–547. https://doi.org/10.1188/14.ONF.545-547

de Jong, K., Conijn, J. M., Gallagher, R. A. V., Reshetnikova, A. S., Heij, M., & Lutz, M. C. (2021). Using progress feedback to improve outcomes and reduce drop-out, treatment duration, and deterioration: A multilevel meta-analysis. *Clinical Psychology Review*, *85*, 102002. https://doi.org/10.1016/j.cpr.2021.102002.

de Jong, K., Douglas, S., Wolpert, M. et al. (2015). Using progress feedback to enhance treatment outcomes: A narrative review. *Administration and Policy in Mental Health and Mental Health Services*, 52, 210–222. https://doi.org/10.1007/s10488-024-01381-3

Gass, M. A., Gillis, H. L., & Russell, K. C., (2020) *Adventure therapy: Theory, research, and practice* (2nd ed.). Routledge.

Hatfield, D., McCullough, L., Plucinski, A., & Krieger, K. (2010). Do we know when our clients get worse? An investigation of therapists' ability to detect negative client change. *Clinical Psychology & Psychotherapy*, *17*, 25–32. https://doi.org/10.1002/cpp.656

Jensen-Doss, A., Haimes, E. M. B., Smith, A. M., Lyon, A. R., Lewis, C. C., Stanick, C. F., & Hawley, K. M. (2018). Monitoring treatment progress and providing feedback is viewed favorably but rarely used in practice. *Administration and Policy in Mental Health*, *45*(1), 48–61. https://doi.org/10.1007/s10488-016-0763-0

Lambert, M. J., & Shimokawa, K. (2011). Collecting client feedback. *Psychotherapy*, *48*(1), 72–79. https://doi.org/10.1037/a0022238

Mallinckrodt, B., Miles, J. R., & Levy, J. J. (2014). The scientist-practitioner-advocate model: Addressing contemporary training needs for social justice advocacy. *Training and Education in Professional Psychology*, *8*(4), 303–311. https://doi.org/10.1037/tep0000045

Ortega, R. M., & Garvin, C. D. (2019). *Socially just practice in groups: A social work perspective*. Oxford University Press.

Russell, K. C., Gillis, H. L., Law, L., & Couillard, J. (2018). A pilot study examining outcomes associated with the implementation of progress monitoring at a substance use disorder treatment program for adolescents. *Child & Youth Care Forum*, *47*(3), 403–419. https://doi.org/10.1007/s10566-018-9437-2

Appendices

Appendix 1

Activities

This appendix lists common activities used by individual adventure therapists, along with very brief descriptions. Where possible, we give a reference where the reader can pursue additional information.

The activities that were used as examples in the book include the general reference of where it can be found in the book and how it was applied in the clinical session. Several other activities that are not used in the book are included in this listing because they are especially useful in individual therapy. References are provided, but please note, in the field of adventure therapy, games and initiatives have been evolved and changed so many times that their original sources sometimes are hard to know and/or they are listed in multiple books with different names. Hence, the references provided may be just one of many places that the activities can be found.

Alphabetized Activity List

Name	**Possible Use**	**Source** *(See References for Full Citation)*
Back-to-Back Drawings (aka Engineer)	Communication	Lung et al. (2008)
Balloon Contract	Collaboration Goal Setting Establishing Beliefs	Lung et al. (2015)
Balloon Rocket Release	Communication Decision-Making	Lung et al. (2008)
Basket Toss	Decision-Making	Unknown
Bridge Drawing	Assessment Goal Setting Virtual	Lung et al. (2008)
Burden Bearing	Coping Strategies Goal Setting Engagement	Unknown
Catch/Ultimate Juggle	Communication Engagement Fun Regulation	Fraser et al. (2009)

(Continued)

(Continued)

Alphabetized Activity List

Name	**Possible Use**	**Source** *(See References for Full Citation)*
Change Three Things	Assessment Coping Strategies Evaluation Frustration Tolerance	Lung et al. (2008)
Continuums	Assessment Check-In Evaluation Virtual	Universal
Cultural DNA	Assessment	Alvarez/Authors
Don't Pick the Card	Communication Fun Regulation	Cummings (2007)
The Dump	Engagement Problem-Solving Virtual	Lung et al. (2008)
Egg Drop Challenge (aka Values Protector)	Problem-Solving Safety	Lung et al. (2008)
Fists	Engagement Relationship Development	Alvarez (2022)
Four Corners	Assessment Engagement Evaluation Virtual	Alvarez et al. (2021)
Help Me Please	Communication Relationship Development	MacPhee-Bower (2013)
Infinite Circle (aka Handcuffs)	Problem-Solving	Lung et al. (2008)
Human Camera	Communication Relationship Development Trust	Lung et al. (2008)
Inukshuk	Assessment Decision-Making Evaluation Virtual	Alvarez (2022)
Junk in the Middle (also "Quail Shooter's Delight")	Coping Strategies Regulation	Rohnke (1989)
Key Position	Problem-Solving Relationship Development	Lung et al. (2008)
Maze Journey (also "Game of Life")	Communication Frustration Tolerance Goal Setting Resilience	Lung et al. (2008)
Me....by a Thread	Assessment Belonging Engagement Virtual	Lung et al. (2015)

(Continued)

(Continued)

Alphabetized Activity List

Name	**Possible Use**	**Source** *(See References for Full Citation)*
Mindfulness: e.g., Gong	Emotional Regulation, Engagement Virtual	Universal
Moonball	Fun Engagement Goal Setting	Rohnke and Butler (1995)
Mousetrap Challenges (aka Mousetrap Bounce)	Coping Strategies Impulse Control Safety Trust	Lung et al. (2015)
Nature Sculptures	Communication Relationship Building Virtual	Lung et al. (2008)
Orienteering	Problem-Solving Skill Development	Universal
Personal Object Check-In	Assessment Check-In Evaluation Virtual	Universal
Plate Activity	Assessment Goal Setting	Alvarez/Authors
Polygon Press (aka Swim Noodle Cube, Blind Polygon)	Engagement Problem-Solving	Lung et al. (2008)
Pressure Points (aka Hamburger Press)	Decision-Making Problem-Solving Trust	Lung et al. (2008)
Processing Tools	Unlimited Uses Virtual	For examples of various props/processing tools, see trainingwheels.com experientialtools.com climercards.com
River Crossing/Stepping Stones	Engagement Communication Problem-Solving	Rohnke and Butler (1995)
Rope Swing/Nitro Crossing	Problem-Solving	Rohnke (1984)
Round and Round	Communication Problem-Solving	Lung et al. (2008)
Rubber-Band Goal Setting	Assessment Engagement Goal Setting Virtual	Alvarez (2021)
Stick Activity	Assessment Engagement Relationship Development Virtual	Alvarez/Authors

(Continued)

(Continued)

Alphabetized Activity List

Name	**Possible Use**	**Source** *(See References for Full Citation)*
Spaghetti and Meatballs (aka "Foam Foiling")	Engagement Fun Relationship Development	Lung et al. (2008)
Squiggle Drawing	Assessment Communication Engagement Relationship Development	Lung et al. (2008)
Tennis Ball Pyramid (aka "Stacking Up")	Asking for Help Problem-Solving Resilience	Lung et al. (2008)
Thumbs Up/Thumbs Down (Thumb-o-Meter)	Assessment Check-In Evaluation Virtual	Universal
TOWER BUILDING 1 Newspaper 2 Block/Lego Structure 3 Spaghetti and Marshmallows 4 PVC Pipes	Engagement Communication Problem-Solving Skill Development Virtual	Lung et al. (2008)
Trust Leans	Communication Relationship Development Skill Development Trust	Lung et al. (2008)
Unsighted Walk	Relationship Development Resilience Trust	Cavert (1999)
Vision Path	Communication Decision-Making Goal Setting	Lung et al. (2015)
Weather Report	Assessment Check-In Communication Relationship Development	Lung et al. (2008)

Back-to-Back Drawing (aka "Engineer")

DESCRIPTION: Begin by sitting back-to-back with the participant or facing one another with a barrier shielding the view of what each other is doing. Each person is given a bag with identical supplies for building a structure. One builds a structure of some sort and takes on the task of describing it to the other, who attempts to build an exact replica.

LOCATION: Chapter 6 Matching

CONSIDERATIONS: This activity requires the practitioner to provide identical building materials (Legos, random objects, or other small items that can be handled easily).

Balloon Contract

DESCRIPTION: This activity involves writing the goals or strengths (depending on what the participant is working on) on small pieces of paper and stuffing them into a deflated balloon. The balloon is then fully inflated and tied off. An option is to write words on the balloon that each of you agrees will be needed to achieve the treatment goals, such as safety, belonging, etc. The next option is to do something with the balloon that will demonstrate the things you wrote: reaching a goal for number of hits in Moonball, traveling a distance with the balloon without touching it with hands or arms, etc.

LOCATION: Chapter 7 Shaping

CONSIDERATIONS: Permanent felt tip markers are the best for writing on the balloon.

Balloon Rocket Release

DESCRIPTION: The participant is invited to inflate a balloon and NOT tie it off. The rocket is now in their hands. The task of the activity is to predict how far the balloon will travel, when released, before landing.

LOCATION: Chapter 6 Matching; Chapter 7 Shaping

CONSIDERATIONS: Using a different color balloon or marking each one will ensure you do not exchange germs when repeatedly blowing up the balloons.

Basket Toss

DESCRIPTION: This activity requires a large space with a rope circle on the ground/floor approximately 30 feet in diameter. Twenty or more soft, throwable objects are scattered inside the circle. The participant is tasked with gathering all the objects **to one place** outside of the designated area while being prohibited from stepping inside the boundary line. Once all the objects have been "earned" and concentrated in the designated area outside of the circle, the practitioner places two equal sized baskets (milk crates work well): one inside the circle close to the participant and one outside the circle a long distance away. While remaining in the designated area, the participant is invited to engage in an activity of tossing the objects into the containers: 5 points is awarded for every object they get into the close basket and 50 points for every object they get into the far away basket.

LOCATION: Chapter 7 Facilitating

CONSIDERATIONS: Collecting the objects, as described earlier, can be omitted or adjusted to the level of challenge needed for the participant. The participant's engagement may be higher if they had to work hard to "earn" the throwable objects; but, many issues, such as time available for the activity or the participant's Point A, may indicate granting the objects at the beginning of the activity or making them easier to earn.

The Bridge Drawing

DESCRIPTION: Begin by describing the basic components of every bridge: (1) a beginning where they start, (2) a definite ending point, (3) a pathway between Point A and Point B, and (4) a foundation(s) that serves as a support and prevents collapse. Then, provide drawing materials and invite the participant to draw any sort of bridge that contains these four components. After the bridge is drawn, invite the participant to draw themselves where they fit in the picture.

LOCATION: Chapter 3 Overview, Chapter 7 Shaping

CONSIDERATIONS: This activity is generally very accessible. However, some participants may be intimidated by the task of drawing. The practitioner can model the risk-taking required by drawing a rudimentary bridge and allowing the participant to see their work. Another option is to switch to a different art medium, such as clay or popsicle sticks.

Burden Bearing

DESCRIPTION: Begin by designating a starting and ending point, usually 75–90 feet apart. The participant is asked to survey the space provided and choose one object they will carry with them. Once chosen, the participant cannot lay the burden down until they reach the finish line. Progress toward the finish line is made by answering the practitioner's questions and moving in the prescribed manner for every acceptable answer. Note: what is an "acceptable answer" is determined collaboratively by the participant and the practitioner.

1 Take **two giant steps** toward the finish line for naming one of your goals.
2 **Two scissor steps** for naming a weight or burden you carry
3 **Three hops** forward for describing how long you have been carrying it.
4 Three **baby steps for** sharing whether anyone else knows about this burden.
5 **Two giant steps** for naming one thing that would ease the weight of this burden.
6 And so on, according to the participant's specific needs.

LOCATION: Chapter 5 Assessment

CONSIDERATIONS: A physical setting that offers multiple options for choice of the burden object, from heavy to light, is ideal.

Catch/Ultimate Juggle

DESCRIPTION: This is a straightforward activity intended to engage the participant in a repetitive pattern of throwing and catching an object. The repetitive action can be helpful to the participant's efforts to regulate their body, relax, and enjoy the connection with the practitioner. It can also be adapted with different ways to throw. Some suggestions are listed next:

- Throw object up into air, clap hands under elevated leg, catch.
- Throw object to your partner, do a 360, catch the object coming at you.
- Bounce your object off of any part of your body, then catch it.
- Throw object to your partner, clap three times, catch the object coming at you, and so on.
- Use your imagination and invite the participant to add steps.

LOCATION: Chapter 4 Preparing, Chapter 7 Facilitating, Chapter 8 Facilitating

CONSIDERATIONS: There are multiple ways to adapt this activity to fit participant's needs. The size, density, and type of tossable object can be significant. Bouncing the ball to the other person can add interest. If there is no need for emotional regulation, throwing it off of one of the office walls to reach the other person, adding to the number of balls that are moving to create a shared juggling experience, or attempting to achieve as many throws back and forth as possible in one minute are other ways of engaging the participant.

Change Three Things

DESCRIPTION: Stand back-to-back with the participant and invite them to change three things about their appearance. When they are ready, face each other and guess those three things. Once guessed (or shown), turn around, KEEPING those three things, add five more changes. Again, turn around and guess (or eventually show) the changes. Do this one more time, keeping those eight changes now (three from the first round and five from the second), and add ten more changes. Again, turn around and guess (or eventually show) the changes.

LOCATION: Chapter 9 Evaluating

CONSIDERATIONS: This can be used to highlight the change process, strategies under stress (adding time limits, not providing the answer of the changes until the end), noting how the participant used additional resources. (Did they pick up ten crayons on the last round? Did they use a change that the practitioner used previously?)

Continuums

DESCRIPTION: There are countless ways to use a physical continuum by inviting a participant to stand from one extreme of a topic to the opposite extreme. For example, inviting the participant to stand where they see themselves on a line from being totally full of energy on one extreme to totally empty on the other end.

LOCATION: Chapters 3–9

CONSIDERATIONS: The Point B for using cards with images or words is extremely diverse. They can be used for assessing Point A or gathering information about any other aspect of the Facilitated Wave process. Such as, how does the participant feel at that moment [e.g., from being on top of the world (one end of the continuum) to being on rock bottom of human existence (other end of the continuum)].

Cultural DNA

DESCRIPTION: First, on a sheet of paper, create a circle in the middle with about six circles around the center circle. One of six surrounding circles is larger than the other five. The participant is invited to answer a variety of questions for each circle: the middle circle is the participant's name and a few personal facts. The surrounding circles are the names of all the cultural groups to which the participant connects. The largest circle is used to write down the *primary* cultural affiliation. From this list, the practitioner can process any somatic responses noted during the creation of the cultural DNA or pose a number of questions, such as something they are proud of, a ritual or habit associated with an affiliation, a negative stigma or stereotype, any other implications of having this DNA.

LOCATION: Chapter 5 Assessment

CONSIDERATIONS: It may be useful for the practitioner to be directive, as well as observing and listening compassionately, while completing the Cultural DNA sheet to help participants probe these issues more deeply.

Don't Pick the Card

DESCRIPTION: One person starts by holding a full deck of cards. They guess a card number before flipping the top card on the playing surface. If they guess correctly, the game is over. If they guess incorrectly, the game continues, and the deck passes to the other person. The goal is to go through the entire deck without predicting one correctly.
LOCATION: Chapter 4 Preparing
CONSIDERATIONS: This activity is a lighthearted, fun way to address perfectionism and performance anxiety.

The Dump

DESCRIPTION: Invite the participant to pick up a plastic cup filled with water (or small objects such as pebbles or paper clips) and dump the contents into a receptacle – without directly touching the cup. Their only assist is a rubber band with six 18-inch strings attached. Although extremely difficult for one person to accomplish this task alone, it is very possible when the participant and practitioner hold the strings together, stretch the rubber band to fit over the cup, lift carefully, and move it to the receptacle where it must be cooperatively tipped and dumped out.
LOCATION: Chapter 6 Matching, Chapter 7 Shaping, Chapter 8 Facilitating
CONSIDERATIONS: This activity can be adapted to meet the needs of most participants. For example, add challenge by adjusting the materials (i.e., longer strings or different lengths of string) to build the rubber-band tool. Those needing an assurance of success can be allowed to move hands closer to the cup and transport solid materials, such as paper clips, instead of water.

Egg Drop Challenge

DESCRIPTION: The basic idea is to create a safety system that protects a raw egg when dropped from height. There are numerous ways to frame this activity. The reader is referred to Lung et al. (2008, p. 125) and to Cavert (1999, p. 63), for two very different ways to present this activity.
LOCATION: Chapter 6 Matching
CONSIDERATIONS: Plan ahead for clean-up.... the safety systems don't always work!

Four Corners

DESCRIPTION: This activity is usually done with pencil and paper but can also be done in a more physically active manner. The basic version uses a piece of paper divided into four equal quadrants. Each quadrant represents one of the following components: family, friends, school/work, or community. The very middle of the diagram is a space for placing one's 'self', that is, the things that are true about them no matter where they are.

Invite the participant to list things that are true in each quadrant, along with an assessment of whether those things cause stress or provide support.

To transform the activity into something more physically active, the practitioner uses rope, webbing, or similar material to make a large square on the floor or ground of the session space. Then, two ropes are used to mark off four equal quadrants within the square. From here, the participant physically moves into each quadrant and talks about things that come to mind while the practitioner takes notes. (There can also be representative pictures or items to place in the quadrants.) The participant can adjust the diagram by adjusting the size of the quadrants by their importance (or influence) to the participant.

LOCATION: Chapter 5 Assessment, Chapter 7 Shaping

CONSIDERATIONS: It is useful to keep a copy of the written document and update it regularly with the participant.

Help Me Please

DESCRIPTION: Select which role the participant and the practitioner will play: the shooter attempts to throw objects into a container; the gatherer gets objects in the shooter's vicinity so they can do their job. Gatherers cannot touch any objects with their body (using a short rope or webbing as their only tool) and can only do what shooters ask them to do. The shooter must stay in a designated space and use the phrase "help me please" when asking the gatherer to help.

LOCATION: Chapter 4 Preparing

CONSIDERATIONS: Practitioners need to enforce the rules related to how communication travels and how the objects can be handled. Setting a time limit or suggesting "how many objects need to be contained for success" is often needed to end the activity.

Human Camera

DESCRIPTION: Invite the participant to choose to be a "camera" or a "photographer". The camera has their eyes closed and bumpers up for safety as they are guided by the photographer to a location to "take a picture" of an object chosen by the photographer. The photographer guides the camera and positions it (focusing the lens) to take the desired photograph. The photographer can either stand behind the camera with their hands gently resting on the shoulders of the camera or not touching and relying only on verbal directions to guide the camera, depending on the needs and abilities of the participant.

Once at the site to take the picture, the photographer gently positions the camera's head so that the "camera's" eyes (lenses) are directed toward the item to be photographed. When the photographer taps the camera on the shoulder, the camera quickly blinks their eyes to take the picture. The photographer guides the camera back to the starting point where the camera describes the picture that was taken and their experience of being unsighted. This activity is best when each person gets to do both roles.

LOCATION: Chapter 5 Assessment, Chapter 6 Matching

CONSIDERATIONS: There are always safety issues when someone cannot see. Spending time to be aware of safety issues and responsibilities of each of the roles is important.

Infinite Circle

DESCRIPTION: The participant is invited to put their hands through loops tied on each end of a rope or webbing (approximately five feet long). The practitioner literally connects with the participant by crossing a similar rope under the participant's rope and then putting their own hands in the loops of their own rope. (Two ropes, four loops, each hand is in a loop at the end of their own ropes.) From this position of being linked together, the challenge is to get free without taking the ends of the rope off any wrists.

LOCATION: Chapter 6 Matching

CONSIDERATIONS: This activity can be extremely frustrating. It almost invariably ends with no solution or the practitioner demonstrating how it can be accomplished. Either outcome can be useful to the process of treatment. It may not be an appropriate intervention for participants who have a tentative relationship with the practitioner or who struggle with frustration tolerance.

Inukshuk

DESCRIPTION: Traditionally constructed by the Inuit people, an Inukshuk is a figure made of piled stones or rocks used to communicate (Hallendy, 2020). In this activity, the participant is asked to build a rock structure using seven rocks/stones with this additional caveat: "If one can remove a rock without causing the structure to fall apart, it is not an Inukshuk".

LOCATION: Chapter 7 Shaping

CONSIDERATIONS: If a facilitator chooses to use this activity, it is important to acknowledge its cultural meaning and provide background on the use of Inukshuks by indigenous groups. Using this activity without this larger context is considered an act of cultural appropriation. For more information visit: https://thecanadianencyclopedia.ca/en/article/inuksuk-inukshuk.

Junk in the Middle

DESCRIPTION: One person stands in the middle of an open space. Various soft throwable objects (20–30 total) are thrown up over the person's head all at the same time. The task for the person standing in the open space is to catch as many objects as possible before they hit the floor/ground.

LOCATION: Chapter 3 Overview

CONSIDERATIONS: This activity is adaptable to small indoor spaces, as well as the outdoors.

Maze Journey (aka, The Game of Life)

DESCRIPTION: Create a 4 x 4 or 4 x 5 grid of floor spots or squares drawn out on a tarp. A predetermined "secret pathway" to cross the area includes forward, backward, sideways and diagonal moves within the maze. No space can be used twice. There is a traffic cop who knows the route and a traveler who must guess the route as they step one square at a time through the maze. When the traveler steps onto a space, the traffic cop must indicate non-verbally whether the move was correct. A correct move allows the traveler to proceed forward. If the move does not match the predetermined route, the traveler must return to the beginning and start their journey over again.

LOCATION: Chapter 4 Preparing, Chapter 5 Assessment

CONSIDERATIONS: Requires ability to tolerate mistakes and to remember long sequences. Easily accessible, requiring minimal coordination or other physical ability. A blank map of the area to be crossed must be provided for the participant to create their own pathway and experience the "traffic cop" role.

Me... By a Thread

DESCRIPTION: Invite participants to create a poster that highlights who they are (use a piece of cardstock or a larger poster board). The participant places their answers to four questions in each corner and their name (decorated as they wish) in the middle. Sample questions include the following:

- What is one of your prized possessions?
- What strengths do you bring into the classroom/office? On the playground/recreationally?
- What are some of your special family activities?
- What quotes or sayings impress you or guide you?
- What would you like to change about yourself?

LOCATION: Chapter 7 Shaping

CONSIDERATIONS: Have a variety of supplies, such as markers or crayons or magazines for cutting out pictures. Additionally, supplies to display the finished product is a nice added touch.

Mindfulness

DESCRIPTION: Many activities are available to assist participants to release tension in their bodies and come to a relaxed presence in the here and now. The participant is often invited to sit comfortably with both feet on the ground and aware of their breathing, as well as any areas of tension in their body. When fully prepared, the specific activity is introduced, such as a gong being struck, progressive tensing and releasing of the tension from feet to head, or a breathing exercise.

LOCATION: Chapter 3 Overview, Chapter 8 Facilitating

CONSIDERATIONS: While both participants and practitioners can both benefit from activities intended to increase mindfulness, try a variety to see what the participant engages with easily. This can also be used for skill development and used outside of treatment.

Moonball

DESCRIPTION: The classic version of Moonball is for the participant and the practitioner to work together to keep a beach ball in the air for as many hits as possible.

LOCATION: Chapter 4 Preparing, Chapter 7 Shaping

CONSIDERATIONS: There are many variations of Moonball, however, some versions may match the needs of a specific participant better than others. The type of ball (a balloon, a beach ball, etc.) as well as the rules, such as the number of consecutive hits, how many hands a player can use, and where each person can stand, will all change the activity.

Mousetrap Challenges

DESCRIPTION: There are several challenges using mousetraps. One is simply to set the trap and set it down without triggering the trap. A second is to set live traps around the space and dribble a ball between them. Another is to invite the participant to set the trap while in their hand and then cover it with their other hand, so it doesn't go off until the top hand is removed quickly.

LOCATION: Chapter 6 Matching

CONSIDERATIONS: These activities are especially useful with participants experiencing anxiety because of the parallel process and opportunity to observe anxious symptoms in the moment. The third option is not recommended for highly anxious participants. It is more useful for engaging adolescents who express boredom or disinterest in the therapy process.

Nature Sculptures

DESCRIPTION: This activity can be adapted in countless ways to fit the needs of the moment. Invite the participant to find non-living objects in nature and create some sort of sculpture, ranging from something large that represents an important part of their life (often called earth sculptures) or small, such as finding one to three objects that appeal to them and using them as the session check-in.

LOCATION: Chapter 5 Assessment, Chapter 7 Shaping

CONSIDERATIONS: This activity is an ideal opportunity to share the "leave no trace" and "do no harm" ethics that surround attention to and respect for the natural world. Instructions to participants always prescribe using "non-living" items from nature that would also not disturb a habitat. For more ideas about nature based activities see Cornell's book (2015), *Sharing nature: Nature awareness activities for all ages*.

Orienteering

DESCRIPTION: The practitioner works with the participant to find pre-assigned waypoints using a compass.

LOCATION: Chapter 8 Facilitating

CONSIDERATIONS: A compass and the skills to use one effectively are required. An adaptation can include a variety of points that also have "treasure", such as snacks or other small items.

Personal Object Check-In

DESCRIPTION: Both the participant and the practitioner choose one personal object to share that will describe something about themselves.

LOCATION: Chapter 3 Overview, Chapter 7 Shaping, Chapter 8 Facilitating

CONSIDERATIONS: This activity requires abstract thinking. If a participant does not have this ability, it may also be useful to simply ask the participant to choose a personal object and describe it with the intent of helping with any metaphor that may arise.

Plate Activity

DESCRIPTION: Invite the participant to write one of their presenting problems on a paper plate, designated as a *Cause* plate and place it on the ground/floor. Next, use as many paper plates as necessary to write down the *Effects* of that problem (called *Effect* plates) and place them on the floor surrounding the *Cause* plate. Using sticks with one end red (i.e., wooden shish kabob skewers painted), place the red tips on one of the *Effects* plates with the nonpainted end resting on the associated *Cause* plate. Once this sculpture is completed, the participant is asked to consider the full picture and remove the one plate that would have the largest positive impact if it ceased to exist. Removing plates stimulates a collaborative discussion of clinical goals, which becomes a prioritized list.

LOCATION: Chapter 3 Overview, Chapter 8 Facilitating

CONSIDERATIONS: This activity is intended to diagram cause and effects of the participant's presenting problems and develop a prioritized list of clinical goals. The process can be repeated for each presenting problem, if desired. Some preparation to create the necessary props is required. String can also be used instead of sticks, with different lengths or different types to represent the impact of the effects.

Polygon Press (aka Swim Noodle Cube, Blind Polygon)

DESCRIPTION: Participants are invited to use 12, three-foot long pool noodles to create a three-dimensional cube.

LOCATION: Chapter 8 Facilitating

CONSIDERATIONS: Using all 12 noodles to create a cube will require effective communication and a great deal of cooperation. It is difficult, and the ability to tolerate frustration is usually required. An inside version uses straws or toothpicks.

Pressure Points (aka Hamburger Press)

DESCRIPTION: Invite the participant to stack as many two-inch-thick pool noodle slices (think thick hamburger bun slices) as possible and transport them to another location. The participant will quickly notice that if pressed too hard, the pieces will explode out of their hand, and if held too softly, they will tumble to the floor.

LOCATION: Chapter 4 Preparing

CONSIDERATIONS: These pool noodle pieces, aka hamburgers, have many useful purposes, including as a soft throwable prop. They are also easy to make with a pool noodle and a serrated knife.

Processing Tools

DESCRIPTION: There are a wide range of different types and brands of image cards, word cards, trinkets, and objects available to help with things from checking in to processing session content. Practitioners use them to help participants share information about any aspect of the facilitated wave or their reflections on aspects of the session.

LOCATION: Chapter 4 Preparing, Chapter 6 Matching, Chapter 8 Facilitating

CONSIDERATIONS: Practitioners have many options to choose from in addition to commercially available cards and trinkets, including homemade versions or objects found in nature. It can also be helpful for the participants to make their own set of processing tools.

River Crossing/Stepping Stones

DESCRIPTION: There are many variations of this activity, however, all of them include inviting the participant to engage in a journey from one spot (Point A) to another spot (Point B) without touching the floor/ground. The participant is given a limited number of tools to assist their journey (e.g., boards, floor spots, old tires). The practitioner may join the journey or engage from the periphery depending on the participant's Point B. The difficulty level can be adjusted by changing the number of tools available to assist the participant or adapting the rules/guidelines for participation.

LOCATION: Chapter 7 Shaping; Chapter 8 Facilitating

CONSIDERATIONS: The physical ability of both the participant and practitioner plays a major role in how this activity is framed. For example, if the participant lacks the physical coordination or strength to bend over and pick objects up from the ground/floor, perhaps the practitioner also participates and plays this role. The guidelines, limitations, consequences for touching the floor/ground, and expectations of participants can all be adapted to accommodate various Point A's and Point B's.

Rope Swing/Nitro Crossing

DESCRIPTION: This activity requires a rope hanging from something high enough off the ground to allow for a swing that is long enough to meet the desired Point B. Generally, participants are limited to a space on one side of the swing and invited to use the rope to make it to another space on the other side of the swing without touching the ground/floor.

LOCATION: Chapter 4 Preparing

CONSIDERATIONS: Safety while the participant is swinging on the rope is a major issue. Generally, use of some standard commands to communicate when someone is going to start their swing and spotting the person during their swing are essential components when using this activity.

Round and Round

DESCRIPTION: Invite the participant to hold a noodle vertically with one end on the ground and the other being held with just one finger. From that starting point, any number of lighthearted challenges are possible. For example, try taking your finger off the noodle, running around it, and capturing it before it falls to the ground. The practitioner can also play and invite the participant to see how far apart they can each get and still exchange places without either noodle hitting the floor.

LOCATION: Chapter 8 Facilitating

CONSIDERATIONS: The participant needs to be regulated enough to follow the challenge directions.

Rubber-Band Goal Setting

DESCRIPTION: Both the practitioner and participant take one rubber band from a pile of assorted bands. Each person then chooses an object within the boundary limits set by the practitioner. The task is to predict how many flicks of the rubber band it will take to strike the selected object. After each person has hit their object, and discussed that experience, each person gets another opportunity to predict how many flicks it will take to strike their initial starting point with the rubber band.

LOCATION: Chapter 5 Assessment; Chapter 7 Shaping

CONSIDERATIONS: The practitioner does not have to do this activity along with the participant. This activity provides valuable information about the participant's typical approach to goal setting and how it changes with experience or new information.

Spaghetti and Meatballs (aka "Foam Foiling")

DESCRIPTION: Each person gets one, three-foot long pool noodle (the spaghetti) and a two-inch thick (think hamburger bun size) pool noodle piece (the meatball). Both parties put the meatball on the back of one hand and hold the long noodle in the other. When the competition begins, each person tries to simultaneously protect their meatball and force the other person's meatball to tumble to the ground.

LOCATION: Chapter 6 Preparing

CONSIDERATIONS: This is a great activity to use while creating conditions of safety in the therapy sessions. To increase the challenge, use the non-dominant hand for the "spaghetti" pool noodle. Note that if done outdoors, the wind may make it difficult to keep the "meatball" pool noodle slice on the back of the hand.

Squiggle Drawing

DESCRIPTION: Invite the participant to scribble on a piece of paper for a short time (20 seconds or less). Then, the scribbles are given to the other person who attempts to make a picture. The back and forth of this activity is parallel with the collaboration and mutuality that will be needed to achieve the participant's clinical goals.

LOCATION: Chapter 4 Preparing

CONSIDERATIONS: This "drawing" activity takes very little artistic talent and is very accessible to young participants or participants with art anxiety.

The Stick

DESCRIPTION: This project offers the participant an opportunity to partake in the transformation of a stick, which is often a parallel process to a participant's experience.

- **Choose a stick**: Be intentional. Consider how safe it will be when carried around – the more brittle, the more likely it could accidentally break.
- **Observe it** and observe others as they interact with it.
- **Spend purposeful time** with it. For example, go for a walk with the stick; introduce the stick to others, take it to dinner or to a basketball game, make a game using the stick as a central prop, invite others to meet the stick and to comment about this new relationship.

- **Physically transform it**. Consider and discuss plans to transform the stick and share any changes that occur to the stick over time with others. Feel free to take photos of this process.
- **Journal about it** throughout the time spent in therapy. This may include what the stick's life has been, what role it is playing in your life, how members of your community are accepting it into your life. Share the journal entries with the practitioner.
- **Present it** at the end of the treatment process (or a designated end of the experience).

LOCATION: Chapter 9 Evaluating

CONSIDERATIONS: A lot about this activity directly relates to the engagement and motivation of the participant toward treatment (or, metaphorically, the stick). Regular check-in's about "how is life with the stick?" will enhance the worth of the engagement. Typically, this experience is two to four weeks.

Tennis Ball Pyramid

DESCRIPTION: Invite the participant to create a pyramid three tennis balls high using **ALL** 14 balls provided. Once the pyramid is created, ask the participant to move the pyramid to another location without losing the pyramid shape.

LOCATION: Chapter 4 Preparing, Chapter 8 Facilitating

CONSIDERATIONS: Tennis balls are uniquely suited for this activity. Other options have proven to be too slippery or too easy to stack. Typically, the pyramid cannot be moved without asking for the practitioner to help (needs four hands), unless the practitioner has allowed for additional resources, i.e., something to move the pyramid with, such as a towel.

Thumbs Up/Down Check-In (Thumb-o-Meter)

DESCRIPTION: Invite the participant to rate something, such as how they are feeling in the moment, by placing one thumb along a continuum from 100% (thumb up) to zero (thumb down). If the question posed to the participant is how much energy they have, for example, they could place their up-raised thumb anywhere for straight up (lots of energy) to straight down (exhausted and without any energy currently) or any place in between.

LOCATION: Chapter 3 Overview; Chapter 7 Shaping; Chapter 8 Facilitating

CONSIDERATIONS: "Thumbs Up" is a common expression for agreement; however, some participants may not be familiar with the idiom, making careful explanation of the task necessary.

Tower Building

DESCRIPTION: This intervention takes many forms, including newspaper towers, PVC towers, marshmallow spaghetti towers, Lego structures, and towers made with items from nature or wooden blocks. Each form presents the same problem to the participant: using the supplies indicated, build the desired structure.

LOCATION: Chapter 6 Matching, Chapter 7 Shaping, Chapter 8 Facilitating

CONSIDERATIONS: Tower building activities can be adapted a great deal to meet the specific participant needs, not only by changing the supplies, but by changing the challenge, such as the height or free-standing (not propped or supported by other things in the room).

Trust Leans

DESCRIPTION: The classic version of this activity is that one of you is the person leaning back and the other is spotting and catching the person who leans back. Establishing conditions of safety, such as "leaning commands" and consent prior to leaning back is a required benefit of this activity. It can be minimally challenging by the spotter keeping their hands on the person's back and only allowing a small lean. It can also be a major challenge with the spotter down on one knee, allowing the person to lean straight back to just above the floor. The level of challenge depends on clinical needs. A second version is done with both parties facing one another and palms of their hands touching above their heads (aka Push Away). The challenge is to step backward, keeping your body stiff, as far as possible. This version allows for eye contact and easy assessment of risk as the activity progresses.

LOCATION: Chapter 5 Assessment, Chapter 6 Matching, Chapter 7 Shaping

Unsighted Walk

DESCRIPTION: There are many variations of the activity. The simplest version is for one person to close their eyes or put on an eye covering (i.e., bandanna or sleep mask) with the intent of the other person guiding them safely on a journey. The journey can be simple and straightforward or challenging with obstacles in the pathway, depending on the assessment of Point A and the Point B of the intervention.

LOCATION: Chapter 3 Overview, Chapter 7 Shaping, Chapter 8 Facilitating

CONSIDERATIONS: This activity has been referred to as "minefield" in some references. This name has been avoided for decades now due to the tragic consequences of real-life minefields in various regions of our world. Many veterans of armed services have also found that the use of that term activates trauma responses. Similarly, practitioners generally avoid referring to blindness in a manner that can be perceived as a pejorative or disrespectful manner.

Vision Path

DESCRIPTION: Invite the participant to draw two pictures (on two different pieces of paper): one depicting where they are right now and the other where they want to be in the future. The "present" picture is set down at the participant's feet. The "future" picture is placed at a distance that represents how far away the participant thinks they are from achieving the goal. Then, give the participant a stack of notecards and ask them to lay out a path they think is realistic for them to reach the future image. Finally, the participant is asked to talk about (or write on the cards about) something tangible that will help them reach the future image for each card on their path.

LOCATION: Chapter 5 Assessment

CONSIDERATIONS: This activity may work best in a session longer than the typical 50-minute hour. Priming the activity with plans for an extra-long session so there is time to consider how the participant is going to get to their goals is an exciting way to facilitate this activity. The index cards can become the treatment plan. One option is to keep them in an envelope or on a keychain and check in with progress or select one for the focus of the week.

Weather Report

DESCRIPTION: Invite the participant to talk about the weather conditions inside their body. The report can be a description of weather that passed through yesterday, the current conditions, or what they expect is coming in the forecast.

LOCATION: Chapter 4 Preparing, Chapter 6 Matching, Chapter 7 Shaping

CONSIDERATIONS: Care needs to be taken to not assume that the weather terms used by the participant mean the same as the practitioner expects. When working with inner city kids in Detroit, for example, a bright sunny day was not a good thing. The heat was described as suffocating and inescapable.

Walk-and-Talk Sessions

Walk-and-talk therapy, or hiking therapy, moves therapeutic sessions outside into nature. Sessions can be conducted in public parks or along local trails, incorporating fresh air and physical activity into the therapeutic process. Movement, whether a leisurely walk or a brisk hike, can better facilitate the discussion of feelings. Participants might like to walk or move around instead of sitting and talking to their practitioner in an office or looking at a computer screen. Some participants may feel more at ease in nature, which improves their ability to share.

The practitioner is cautioned that just being outside and doing something with a participant doesn't make it adventure therapy. The action the participant is engaging in also needs to be paired with the prerequisite clinical mindset. The adventure therapist's belief in the transformative power of experience, for example, will focus their attention on the participant's full body responses to the walk. How they interact with the practitioner, how they respond to the sudden appearance of an animal or other people along the way, how their breathing or their pace of walking is impacted by what is encountered are just a few examples of the myriad things that the adventure practitioner will notice and bring to the participant for reflection.

LOCATION: Chapter 6 Matching

CONSIDERATIONS: Practitioners considering integrating walk-and-talk therapy into their practice must consider therapeutic style, participant population, and the logistics of conducting sessions outside. Explore the local terrain (i.e., types of paths), accessibility to benches, bathrooms, and water. External factors, such as weather, noise, and seasonality can influence the success. Contingency plans are a must. Walk-and-talks may not be suitable due to limits of confidentiality. In office settings, therapy rooms provide a private space where participants can share their thoughts and feelings without fear of being overheard. In contrast, conducting sessions outdoors inherently risks breaches of confidentiality. Practitioners must carefully choose locations to minimize the risk of being overheard by passersby and discuss with participants the potential for unintended encounters. Finally, practitioners must also consider their own physical ability to walk for extended periods and the logistics of scheduling and conducting sessions outdoors.

References

Alvarez, T. (2021). *Experiential facilitation training manual*. Alvarez Consulting LLC.

Alvarez, T. (2022). *Adventure classroom activities manual*. Alvarez Consulting LLC.

Alvarez, T., Stauffer, G., Lung. D. M., Sacksteder, K., Beale, B., & Tucker, A. R. (2021). Appendix 6.1: The four corners assessment tool. *Adventure group psychotherapy: An experiential approach to treatment* (pp. 198–201). Routledge.

Cavert, C. (1999). *Affordable portables: A working book of initiative activities and problem-solving elements*. Wood 'N' Barnes Publishing.

Cornell, J. B. (2015). *Sharing nature: Nature awareness activities for all Ages*. Crystal Clarity Publishers.

Cummings, M. (2007) *Playing with a full deck: 52 team activities using a deck of Cards!* Kendall Hunt Publishing.

Fraser, K., Fraser, L., & Fraser, M. (2009) *175 best camp games: A handbook for leaders*. Boston Mills Press.

Hallendy, N. (2020). *Inuksuk (Inukshuk)*. https://thecanadianencyclopedia.ca/en/article/inuksuk-inukshuk

Lung, M. D., Stauffer, G., & Alvarez, T. G. (2008). *Power of one: Using adventure and experiential activities within one-on-one counseling sessions*. Wood 'N' Barnes.

Lung, D. M., Stauffer, G., Alvarez, T. G., Conway, J. (2015). *Power of family: An experiential approach to family treatment*. Wood 'N' Barnes.

MacPhee-Bower, N. (2013). *Adventure, play, peace: Insights and activities for social-emotional learning and community building with young children*. Wood 'N' Barnes.

Rohnke, K. (1984). *Silver bullets*. Project Adventure & Kendall/Hunt Publishing Co.

Rohnke, K. (1989). *Cowstails and cobras II*. Project Adventure & Kendall/Hunt Publishing Co.

Rohnke, K., & Butler, S. (1995). *Quicksilver: Adventure games, initiatives, problems, trust activities, and a guide to effective leadership*. Kendall/Hunt Publishing Co.

Appendix 2

Standards of Care

As with any practice approach to psychotherapy, integrating adventure therapy into your practice means being aware of and attending to standards of care. Practitioners are responsible for thinking practically about what structures and supports they will need to ethically incorporate interventions.

Intersecting standards in the mental health, outdoor, and adventure fields create complex dynamics for practice. It is not simply a matter of following established guidelines for each area. The guidelines need to be adjusted to address the added complexity. For example, facilitating activities indoors often means you are operating in a more controlled and predictable environment. As soon as activities are facilitated outdoors, the added complexity of weather and wildlife must be considered. Now, consider the unique needs of participants who are coping with mental health issues and another layer of complexity enters the equation.

The following content in this appendix is reprinted with permission from Adventure Therapist LLC (2025). This content integrates and applies the standards from AEE's *Manual of Accreditation Standards for Outdoor Behavioral Health Programs, 3rd edition* (Nordquist et al., 2023) to an individual adventure psychotherapy practice setting.

Professional Duty of Care

In addition to ethical standards guiding our professional work, practitioners are obligated to uphold a professional duty of care. This is a legal obligation to act within a reasonable standard of care that is generally recognized within the profession (Smith, 2021). When practitioners neglect this duty of care, they can be held liable. Adventure therapy practitioners' standard of care includes:

- Preparing by foreseeing issues, analyzing risks; providing a reasonably safe environment, including establishing policies and procedures and managing equipment; and adequately warning participants about risks, both through informed consent documents and safety briefings.
- During sessions being sure to provide proper instruction and supervision; enforcing policies, procedures, rules, and regulations; seeing, evaluating, and responding to injuries or issues, and acting within their training and scope of practice.
- Keeping appropriate records and documentation.

A key takeaway is that this is a legal responsibility that is carried not only by the organization, but also by individual practitioners within an organization. Organizations and practitioners should ensure that their work is appropriately covered by liability insurance for the activities they intend to use in practice.

Participant Care During Sessions

Attention to participant wellbeing needs to remain a constant focus of our work, and this is greatly impacted by the environment where the work is taking place. Consider the appropriateness of the spaces where sessions take place, including aspects of how participant identities are welcomed in that space. Below, key areas that support participant care during sessions are explored.

Informed Consent

Participants have the right to informed consent related to their treatment. In the adventure therapy context, there are additional considerations to share with participants to keep them informed. Providers are expected to honestly inform participants regarding the risks of activities prior to their participation in them, including both psychological and physical risks. Practitioners are advised not to make promises of safety and should share risks openly and discuss ways to manage risks in activities. Participants decide if they consent to participate or not, based on the information they are given. They are to be informed about specific safety risks before activities begin to allow them to have informed consent.

Physical Ability

Many activities in adventure therapy are not physically strenuous and are readily adapted to accommodate a variety of physical abilities. Even so, adventure therapy does often involve engaging in physical activities, and in ways that might be new and unusual for participants. Therefore, participants are informed about the level of activity and what to expect. They are encouraged to share information with practitioners about their physical abilities and limitations. Providers are expected to consider a participant's physical ability when planning sessions and work to accommodate a variety of abilities when planning. If there are any questions or concerns as to a participant's ability to safely participate, practitioners seek out guidance from the participant's medical provider.

Hydration and Nutrition

When engaging in activities, adequate hydration and nutrition are important considerations. Practitioners are expected to ensure that clean, drinkable water is available. When participants are in sessions for extended periods of time, such as for a camping overnight, it is also expected that their nutritional needs are met. Planned meals should account for increased activity and offer reasonable nutrition. Practitioners should know about safe food handling guidelines and participant food restrictions ahead of time and plan accordingly.

Hygiene

Hygiene can easily be forgotten amid activities but remains a critical area to focus on. Participants may not be aware of or implement appropriate hygiene; therefore, practitioners need to be mindful of this. For all sessions, ensure participants are washing their hands with soap and water before or after cooking, eating, toileting, or exploring the outdoors. Ensure that supplies such as soap and water are readily available. For overnight experiences, ensure that participants are trained on how to take care of hygiene needs in the environment you are in.

Equipment, Clothing, and Footwear

Practitioners are responsible for making sure participants have the equipment they need before engaging in activities, such as raingear, backpacks, hats, or water bottles. For example, participants may have limited access to adequate clothing for outdoor activities in colder temperatures.

Clearly establish with participants how to prepare for your planned activities. Typically, clothing that allows for freedom of movement and athletic footwear are expected. Participants should avoid wearing jewelry that may get snagged during activities (i.e. large hoop or dangling earrings or rings while climbing).

Footwear is an important consideration. Shoes that tie, buckle, or Velcro in place are preferred. Determine which activities require close-toed footwear. Running, hiking, and a variety of other adventure activities include a high risk of injury with inadequate footwear. Also, if operating any distance away from easy access to rescue vehicles, inappropriate footwear can significantly impede evacuation or rescue efforts.

Medical Management

In many practice settings, practitioners are not expected to manage or distribute medications to participants. However, they should know if a participant needs specialized medication, such as an inhaler or epinephrine, and to ensure that this medication is present during sessions. It is generally advised that practitioners avoid distributing over-the-counter medication, allergy medication, prescription medicine, or any item for medicinal purposes. Organizations that do engage in medication management should have well-developed protocols for managing medications.

If practitioners are responsible for handling and storing medications during sessions, medications should be safely stored in a secure location and always supervised. Emergency medications, such as inhalers or epinephrine, must remain accessible to participants.

Supervision and Ratios

When participants are trying a new activity, practitioners are expected to supervise, maintaining focus on ensuring participants understand and implement risk management practices correctly. Practitioners establish ratios for supervision that are appropriate to the activities facilitated and populations being served. For example, some practitioners will not operate in remote environments because a solo facilitator in a remote environment does not provide adequate emergency response. Others will utilize two instructors with one participant if they will be operating in a remote environment to address this concern. Consider which activities to offer and what appropriate ratios and supervision practices look like for each.

Facilitating solo requires careful consideration of risk, as the resources available to respond in an emergency are limited. The process of informed consent becomes even more critical in these circumstances. As risk factors become more complex, managing the risk also increases in complexity. Attention to scaffolding by building participant's experience levels slowly is a very helpful strategy for managing risk when practitioners are operating alone.

Participant Care Outdoors

When providing services outdoors, additional considerations for participant care are in effect. The outdoor environment presents different risks and conditions which are well-managed with a planful approach. This requires being aware of the weather forecast prior to any outdoor programming and preparing accordingly as well as knowing the nuances of the environment prior to conducting sessions there.

Sun

When providing services outdoors, the sun presents risks from sunburn. Practitioners should encourage participants to consider methods of protecting themselves from sun exposure through hats, sunglasses, protective clothing, or sunscreen and to facilitate in the shade when possible.

Heat

When outdoor temperatures are high, there are risks present related to heat exhaustion or heat stroke. Prevent these issues by ensuring the participants drink adequate water, get enough breaks from activities to avoid overheating, and monitoring for the symptoms of these issues throughout sessions.

Cold

When outdoor temperatures are low, there are risks present related to hypothermia and frostbite. It is important to prevent these issues by ensuring participants are appropriately equipped for the temperatures in warm, dry clothing and that they stay fed and hydrated, which contributes to our body's ability to keep itself warm.

Lightning

Lightning is a deadly risk that can be difficult to predict. Establish clear protocols for what to do when caught outdoors in lightning and consider pivoting to indoor programming when there is a risk of lightning and limited shelter is available. Typically, in outdoor programs, programming must be stopped and participants evacuated to the nearest shelter at the first sign of lightning or thunder. Determine when outdoor programming may be resumed, often 15 minutes after the last sign of lightning or thunder. If the session is in an area where there is no shelter, the most common practice is to use a lightning drill position. Individual practitioners should generally avoid being in this situation.

High Winds/Tornado

In tornado warnings, typically outdoor programming is stopped and participants evacuated to the nearest designated tornado shelter area if a tornado siren is activated. If weather forecasts call for tornados, pivoting to an indoor setting is advised. Avoid programming in wooded areas during high winds and if evacuating a wooded area during high winds, monitor for the risk of falling tree limbs.

Air Quality

Monitor air quality before sessions. Be aware if you have participants with air sensitivity concerns and attend to this when air quality ratings are "unhealthy for sensitive groups." When air quality is rated "unhealthy," consider canceling outdoor programming or moving indoors, especially if participants have air sensitivity issues (asthma, etc.). Outdoor programming should be canceled or moved indoors when air quality is at a "very unhealthy" rating.

Plants/Animals

Practitioners are to be aware of the risks present from plants and animals in the environment. They are expected to be able to identify plants that present risks, to know what to do to avoid these plants where possible and know how to clean skin once exposed. They need to know about poisonous or dangerous wildlife and the risks of disease transmission from them, as well as how to prevent exposure (i.e. avoidance of areas, use of protective clothing, insect repellants). For example, be sure to conduct tick checks after working in areas where participants may be exposed to ticks. Establish guidelines that participants are not to handle wild animals, which stresses the animal and may expose participants to bacteria or other risks.

Supervision

When working outdoors, separation of the practitioner and participant is generally avoided, as there are added risks of becoming lost or being unable to respond if the participant is injured. Practitioners attend to this by implementing strategies to prevent separation as well as instruction about what to do if the practitioner and participant become separated.

Risk Management

It is the practitioner's responsibility to assess risks, inform participants about risks, and manage those risks. The risks of the environment, activities, and people involved can never be completely removed, but practitioners can take action to prevent many issues from turning into negative incidents for our participants. Managing risk involves preventing incidents, informing our participants about risk, responding effectively to incidents when they do occur, and following up appropriately after incidents.

The first step in this process is knowing how to assess risk. Risk comes from the **activities** themselves, from the **people** involved, and from the **environment** sessions operate in. Take time to identify what risks are presented in each of these areas, as well as the interaction of these areas – for example, how might the weather impact the risks presented from the people involved? Do you have a participant with asthma that is triggered in cold weather?

Once risks are identified, the next step is to decide what to do with them. Some risks are accepted (bumps and bruises may happen when playing running games, for example) and some risks are avoided (do not climb over body height without a safety system in use). Other risks are transferred using informed consent documents (the participant or their guardian assumes the risk). It is important that facilitators do not make promises of safety, because these forms have already indicated there *is* risk involved, and that people can get hurt. Finally, risk may be managed through the use of safety equipment, policies and procedures, or other means.

A central concept to risk management is the idea of cost versus benefit. Once managed, the risks and costs involved should be well outweighed by the benefits to the participant. Does the cost of managing those risks mean that interventions are less accessible to participants?

Finally, risk management relies on the use of good data and an environment that encourages reporting of incidents and near misses. Data collected is used to inform practices in the future to ensure risks are managed adequately!

Components of Risk Management Plans

Several different strategies contribute to a good risk management plan. These strategies include well-developed policies and procedures, appropriate levels of training and certification, and systems that include incident and near miss reporting that inform future practices.

Before Sessions	*During Sessions*	*After Sessions*
• Hazard assessment • Risk analysis • Policy and procedure • Provider training • Accurate marketing • Participant screening • Informed consent • Liability releases • Liability insurance • Develop serious incident protocols	• Ongoing risk assessment • Safety briefing • Supervision • Instruction • Policy and procedure enforcement • Medical management • Emergency action plans • Follow serious incident protocols	• Incident and near miss reporting • Incident review and analysis • In the event of serious incidents, communications with participants, insurance companies, legal representation and the media

Preparing for Outdoor Sessions

When conducting outdoor sessions, there are several actions practitioners are expected to take and items they are expected to carry to ensure they can meet the standard of care. Creating a checklist supports systematizing the process, thus practitioners are encouraged to develop a preparation checklist that is customized for the areas in which they are operating. The following actions and items should be included in the checklist.

Item	*Details*
Weather Forecast	Knowing the forecast ahead of time is critical and having a device on hand that can access radar is very helpful.
Water	Clean, drinkable water should always be on hand, and available in adequate quantities for the environment and duration of the session.
Sun Protection	Sun protection may include sunscreen or protective clothing such as hats, sunglasses, or long sleeved or hooded shirts.
Insect Repellant or Protection	Insect repellant or clothing that protects from exposure to insect bites or stings should be considered as needed for the area.
Appropriate Clothing	Appropriate clothing will be region, season, and weather dependent. Include footwear requirements and do not engage in the session as planned if participants do not have adequate clothing.
Emergency Response Plan	An emergency response plan is in place that considers the necessary actions in the event of an emergency or the need to access outside assistance to respond. This will be location-specific and may include contact information for park rangers, evacuation routes, and considerations of what to do if the practitioner is injured.
Communication Device	The standard of care for professional outdoor programming is to have access to a reliable communication device in the event of a need to contact outside assistance in an emergency. If operating in areas outside of cell service, practitioners should have and know how to use devices such as satellite phones or personal locator beacons.
First Aid Kit	First aid kits should be appropriately stocked and inspected for completeness prior to sessions. Also, practitioners are expected to have the appropriate level of first aid training for the area they are operating. If practitioners are not within ready access of emergency medical services, they should seek training beyond community-level first aid and CPR such as Wilderness First Aid or Wilderness First Responder.
Participant Medical Information	Practitioners should have participant's basic medical information available during sessions, including their allergies, relevant medical conditions, and current medications. It is also prudent to have emergency contact information. If working with children, a medical consent to treat signed by a parent or guardian is required to be on hand to allow the practitioner to respond as well as emergency medical personnel.
Navigation Aids	Practitioners are expected to know the area they are working in. Additionally, carrying maps, compass, and/or other navigational aids such as GPS units is important.
Other Considerations	Practitioners may also consider carrying snacks, lighters or headlamps. Practitioners should also know and follow the regulations governing the area they are working in and obtain appropriate permits for the area.

References

Adventure Therapist, LLC. (2025). *Standards of care*. Unpublished document.

Nordquist, J., BeVard, K., Funnell, A., Pace, S., Sacksteder, K., & Wolf, P. (2023). *Manual of accreditation standards for outdoor behavioral healthcare* (3rd ed.). The Association for Experiential Education.

Smith, S. (Ed). (2021). *Beneficial risks: The evolution of risk management for outdoor and experiential education programs*. Sagamore-Venture Publishing.

Index

Pages in *italics* refer to figures and pages in **bold** refer to tables.

For Product Safety Concerns and Information please contact our EU representative GPSR@taylorandfrancis.com Taylor & Francis Verlag GmbH, Kaufingerstraße 24, 80331 München, Germany